Standard Distributions in Texture Analysis

Volume 2

by

Siegfried Matthies,
Galina W. Vinel
and Kurt Helming

Central Institute for Nuclear Research Rossendorf,
Academy of Sciences
of the German Democratic Republic

Standard Distributions in Texture Analysis

Maps for the Case of Cubic-Orthorhombic Symmetry

Akademie-Verlag Berlin 1988

Authors:

Prof. Dr. sc. nat. Siegfried Matthies
Dr. rer. nat. Galina W. Vinel
Dr. rer. nat. Kurt Helming
Zentralinstitut für Kernforschung
der Akademie der Wissenschaften der DDR, Rossendorf

Ges.-ISBN 3-05-500246-6
Vol. 2-ISBN 3-05-500248-2

Erschienen im Akademie-Verlag Berlin, DDR-1086 Berlin, Leipziger Straße 3—4

Lizenznummer: 202 · 100/425/88
Printed in the German Democratic Republic
Gesamtherstellung: VEB Druckerei „Thomas Müntzer", 5820 Bad Langensalza
Lektor: Dipl.-Phys. Ursula Heilmann
Schutzumschlag und Einband: Ingo Scheffler
LSV: 1175/1235/3305
Bestellnummer: 763 767 4 (9047/2 engl.)
05200

Preface

This volume of the edition is to be understood as a simple continuation of volume 1. The components considered in the maps and tables have already shortly been presented there in chapter 18. Additionally the maps and tables of the given volume are completed by an appendix. Its inclusion seemed to be useful by following considerations.

At present the harmonic method of ODF reproduction from pole figures is the most applied reproduction method in practice. In spite of complications appearing due to l-mixing by considerations of nonlinear problems the mathematical apparatus of this method is characterized by simplicity and elegance especially for linear problems and analytical investigations. Moreover, there are problems of quantitative texture analysis being in development yet, like the optimization of integration procedures for the F-coefficients or the ODF reproduction from incomplete pole figures and others.

Due to the stormy evolution of computer technics especially leading to a wide availability of powerful personal computers automatically the tendency appears to use the program systems of the harmonic method by such computers. On the other hand modern methodical investigations try to develop a truly quantitative texture analysis. In this connection it should not be forgotten that an insufficient precision of a computer, effects of series termination and others may considerably injure the value of the results of a calculation. For this reason and especially for tests of exactness the availibility of standard values is desirable concerning the most important quantities of the harmonic apparatus ($C_l^{\mu,\nu}$-coefficients, $F_l^{\nu}(\boldsymbol{h}_i)$-coefficients, $D_{\mu,\nu}^{l}(g)$-functions, $Y_{l,\mu}(\boldsymbol{r})$-functions, $A_l^{\mu,\bar{m}}$-coefficients).

Corresponding numbers (D-functions, Y-functions, A-coefficients) calculated with a precision of standard character have already been given in volume 1 for the special case of cubic crystal symmetry. Now with the help of the program CDFGL33 given in the appendix of this volume it is possible to calculate these quantities in analogy to the "universal" programs FFSGL33 and POLSGL33 of volume 1 with standard precision for the whole region of variation of parameters (e.g. crystal symmetry) being of interest in practice. The formula and reference numbers used in the text part of the appendix apply to those of volume 1.

Rossendorf, April 1987

S. Matthies, G. W. Vinel, K. Helming

Contents

Errata

Volume 1

p. 53,	(11.44):	for $C_l^{m,m}$	read $C_l^{m,n}$
	last line,	for $C_l^{o,o}$	read $C_o^{o,o}$
pp. 72, 73,	Table 14.1, first column:		
		for crystal class	read crystal system
p. 79	7-th line:	for $\geqq$	read $\leqq$
p. 81,	Fig. 14.3e, in the "exp" (100) pole figure:		
		for 3.05	read 3.95

p. 132: Unfortunately a line of the Subroutine PRCINT disappeared during the print process. After "60 CONTINUE" add "J = 4".

Volume 2

p. 168, Figure caption: for ⟨111⟩ read ⟨110⟩.

Standard Maps and Tables

List of the Arrangement of the Standard Maps

In the following like in volume 1 the arrangement of the standard maps is shortly described in order to simplify the work with them. For every component seven halfwidths b (7.5°, 10°, 12.5°, 15°, 20°, 25°, 30°) are considered. For the position of the component the g_0 is given within the "first" cubic-orthorhombic elementary region of the G-space only.

1) $\{101\}\ \langle 525\rangle$ — GAUSSIAN form, $M_{g_0} = 2$

$g_0: \alpha_0 = 15.793°$, $\beta_0 = 45°$, $\gamma_0 = 0°$ $\hat{=}$
$\varphi_1 = 74.207°$, $\Phi = 45°$, $\varphi_2 = 0°$

$f(g), \tilde{f}(g)$ (φ_2-section), $\tilde{R}_{y_j}(\boldsymbol{h})$, $\tilde{P}_{\boldsymbol{h}_i}(y)$ — page 4

2) $\{525\}\ \langle 151\rangle$ — GAUSSIAN form, $M_{g_0} = 2$

$g_0: \alpha_0 = 74.775°$, $\beta_0 = 47.124°$, $\gamma_0 = 21.801°$ $\hat{=}$
$\varphi_1 = 15.225°$, $\Phi = 47.124°$, $\varphi_2 = 68.199°$

$f(g), \tilde{f}(g)$ (φ_2-sections), $\tilde{R}_{y_j}(\boldsymbol{h})$, $\tilde{P}_{\boldsymbol{h}_i}(y)$ — page 32

3) $\{013\}\ \langle 100\rangle$ — GAUSSIAN form, $M_{g_0} = 2$

$g_0: \alpha_0 = 90°$, $\beta_0 = 18.435°$, $\gamma_0 = 0°$ $\hat{=}$
$\varphi_1 = 0°$, $\Phi = 18.435°$, $\varphi_2 = 0°$

$f(g), \tilde{f}(g)$ (φ_2-sections), $\tilde{R}_{y_j}(\boldsymbol{h})$, $\tilde{P}_{\boldsymbol{h}_i}(y)$ — page 60

4) $\{122\}\ \langle 221\rangle$ — GAUSSIAN form, $M_{g_0} = 1$

$g_0: \alpha_0 = 63.435°$, $\beta_0 = 48.190°$, $\gamma_0 = 63.435°$ $\hat{=}$
$\varphi_1 = 26.565°$, $\Phi = 48.190°$, $\varphi_2 = 26.565°$

$f(g), \tilde{f}(g)$ (φ_2-sections), $\tilde{R}_{y_j}(\boldsymbol{h})$, $\tilde{P}_{\boldsymbol{h}_i}(y)$ — page 88

5) $\{323\}\ \langle 131\rangle$ — GAUSSIAN form, $M_{g_0} = 2$

$g_0: \alpha_0 = 66.907°$, $\beta_0 = 50.238°$, $\gamma_0 = 33.690°$ $\hat{=}$
$\varphi_1 = 23.093°$, $\Phi = 50.238°$, $\varphi_2 = 56.310°$

$f(g), \tilde{f}(g)$ (φ_1-sections), $\tilde{R}_{y_j}(\boldsymbol{h})$, $\tilde{P}_{\boldsymbol{h}_i}(y)$ — page 116

6) $\{113\}\ \langle 110\rangle$ — GAUSSIAN form, $M_{g_0} = 2$

$g_0: \alpha_0 = 90°$, $\beta_0 = 25.239°$, $\gamma_0 = 45°$ $\hat{=}$
$\varphi_1 = 0°$, $\Phi = 25.239°$, $\varphi_2 = 45°$

$f(g), \tilde{f}(g)$ (φ_1-sections), $\tilde{R}_{y_j}(\boldsymbol{h})$, $\tilde{P}_{\boldsymbol{h}_i}(y)$ — page 144

7) $\{233\}\ \langle 011\rangle$ — GAUSSIAN form, $M_{g_0} = 2$

$g_0: \alpha_0 = 23.093°$, $\beta_0 = 50.238°$, $\gamma_0 = 56.310°$ $\hat{=}$
$\varphi_1 = 66.907°$, $\Phi = 50.238°$, $\varphi_2 = 33.690°$

$f(g), \tilde{f}(g)$ (φ_1-sections), $\tilde{R}_{y_j}(\boldsymbol{h})$, $\tilde{P}_{\boldsymbol{h}_i}(y)$ — page 172

8) $\{111\}\langle 011\rangle$ GAUSSIAN form, $M_{g_0} = 2$

$g_0: \alpha_0 = 30°$, $\beta_0 = 54.736°$, $\gamma_0 = 45°$ $\widehat{=}$

$\varphi_1 = 60°$, $\Phi = 54.736°$, $\varphi_2 = 45°$

$f(g), \tilde{f}(g)$ (φ_2-sections), $\tilde{R}_{\boldsymbol{y}_j}(\boldsymbol{h})$, $\tilde{P}_{\boldsymbol{h}_i}(\boldsymbol{y})$ page 200

Standard Maps

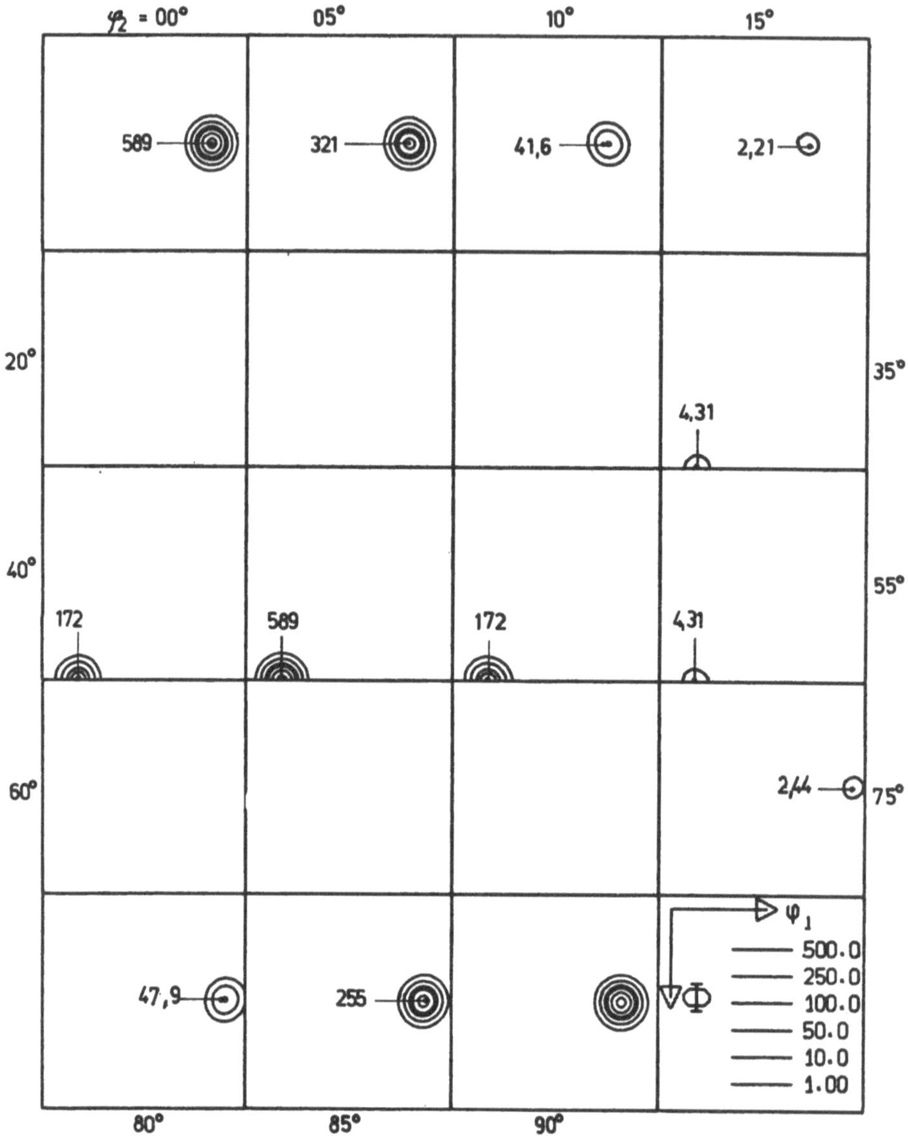

F, G, 7.50° , {101}<525>

F_{MAX} = 589.10 (00°, 45°, 90°)

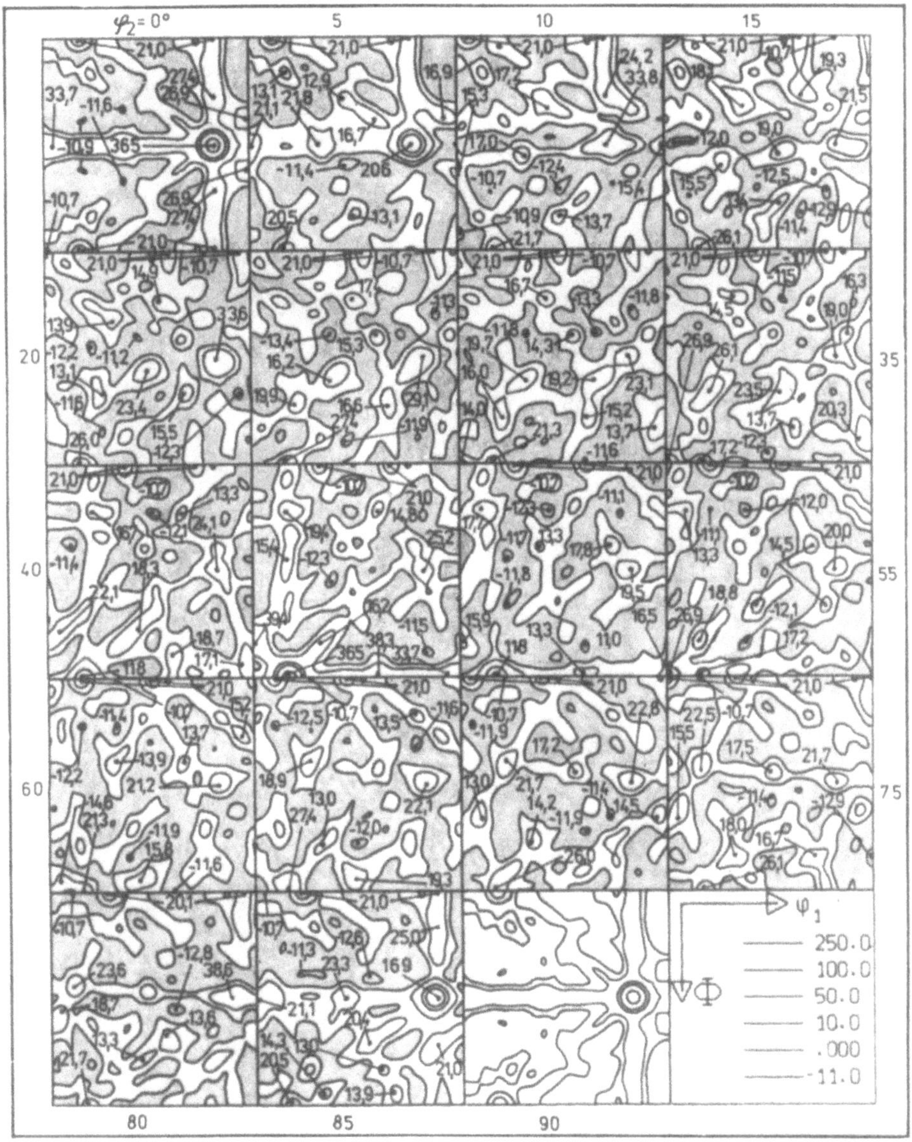

$\tilde{F}$, G, 7.50°, {101}<525>

$\tilde{\tilde{F}}_{MAX}$ = 365.17 (00°, 45°, 90°)

$\tilde{F}_{MIN}$ = −13.42 (25°)

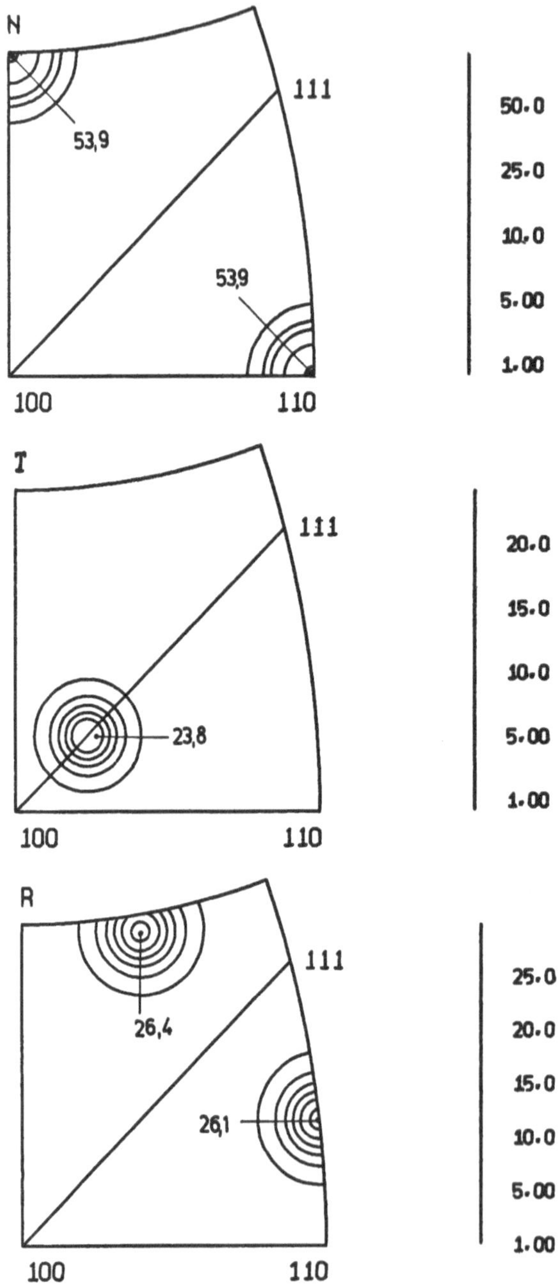

$\tilde{R}$, G, 7.50°, $\{101\}\langle 525\rangle$

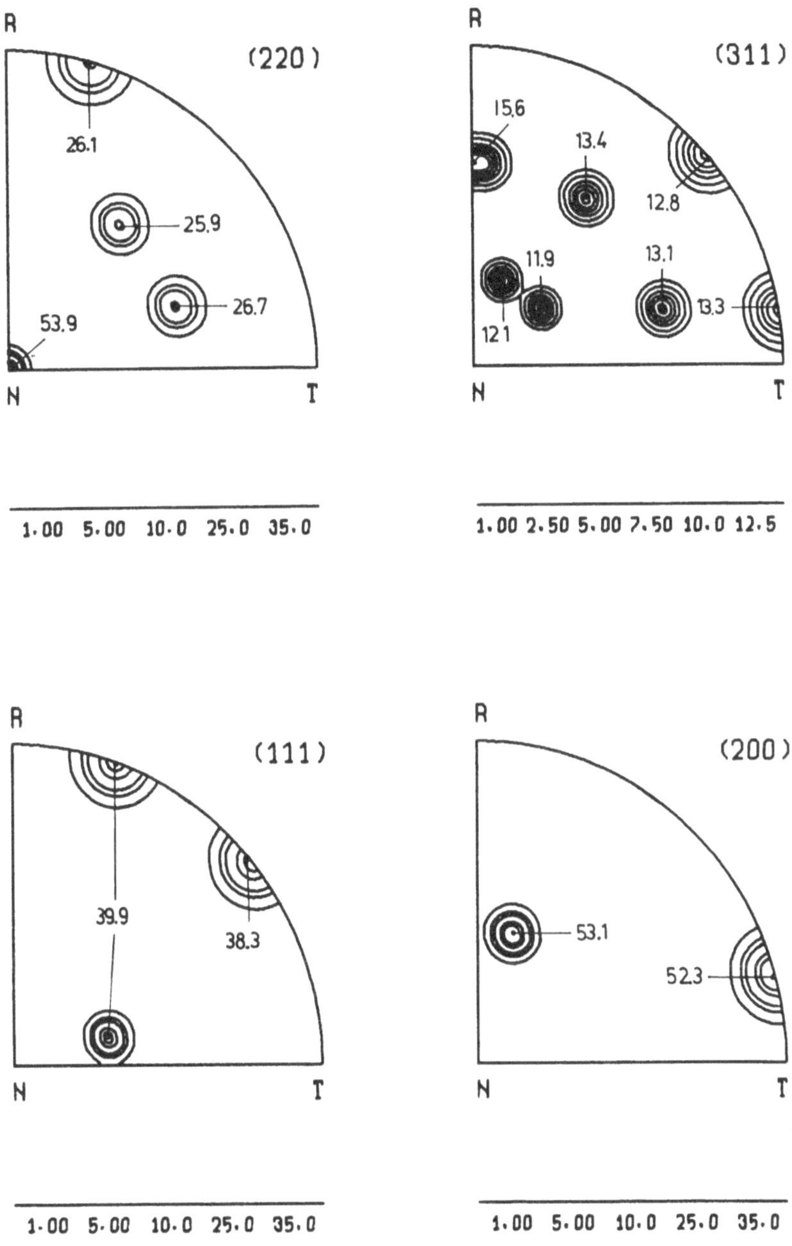

$\tilde{P}$, G, 7.50°, {101}⟨525⟩

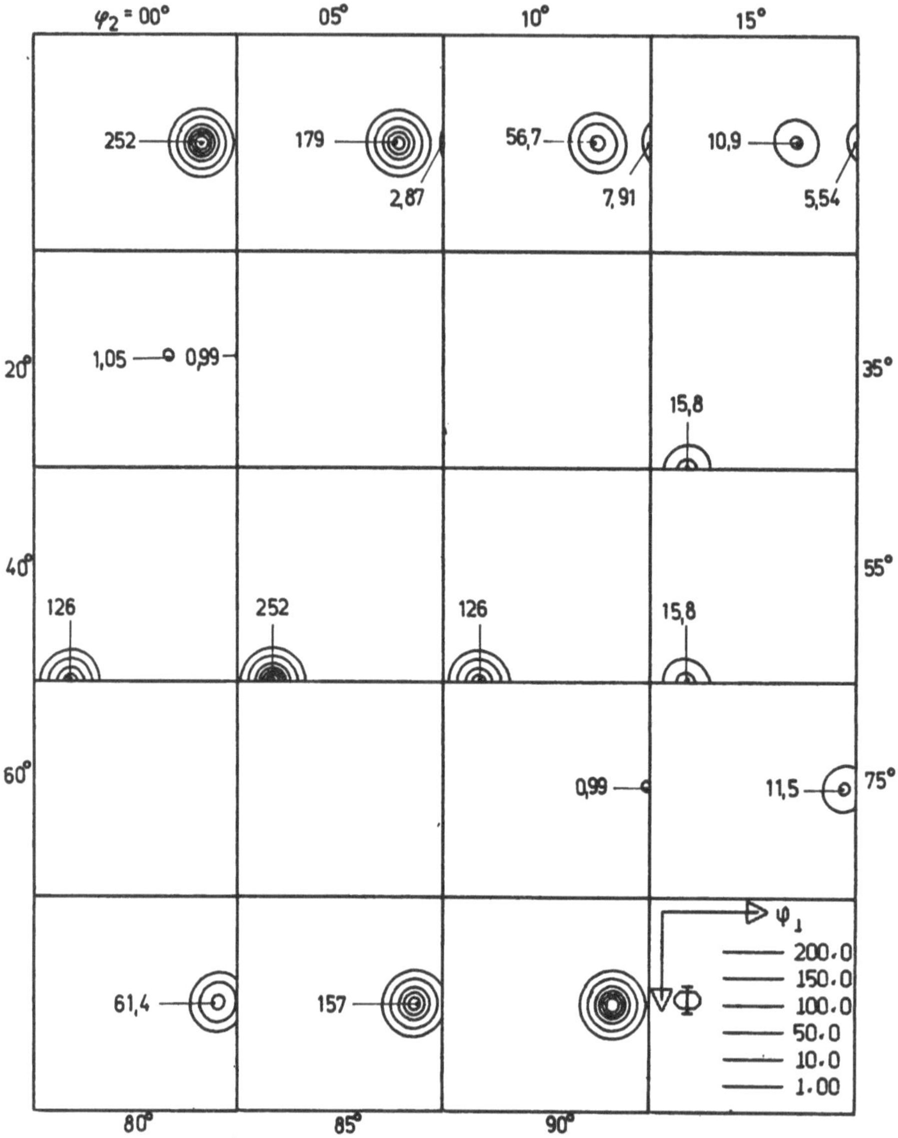

F, G, 10.0°, {101}<525>

F_{MAX} = 251.80 (00°, 45°, 90°)

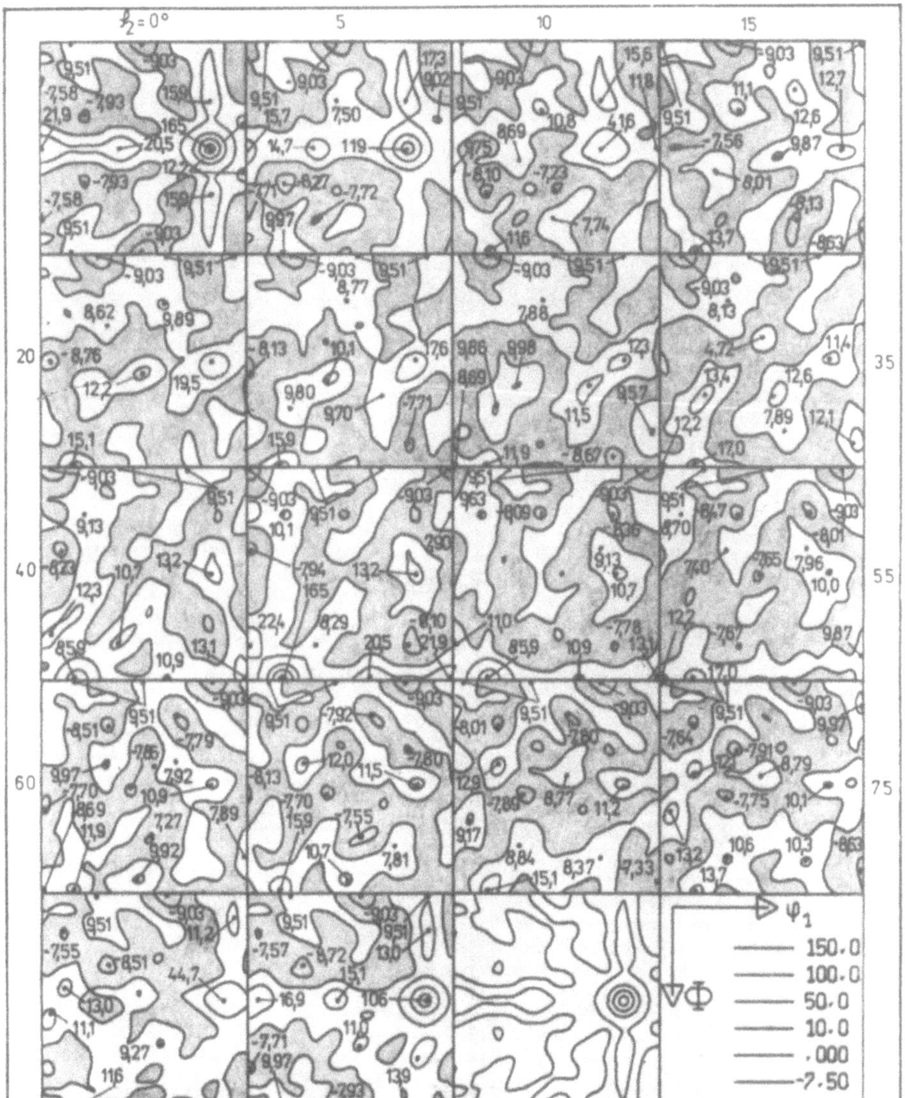

$\tilde{F}$, G, 10.0°, $\{101\}\langle 525\rangle$

$\tilde{F}_{MAX}$ = 164.54 (00°, 45°, 90°)

$\tilde{F}_{MIN}$ = −9.03 (00°, 05°, ... , 90°)

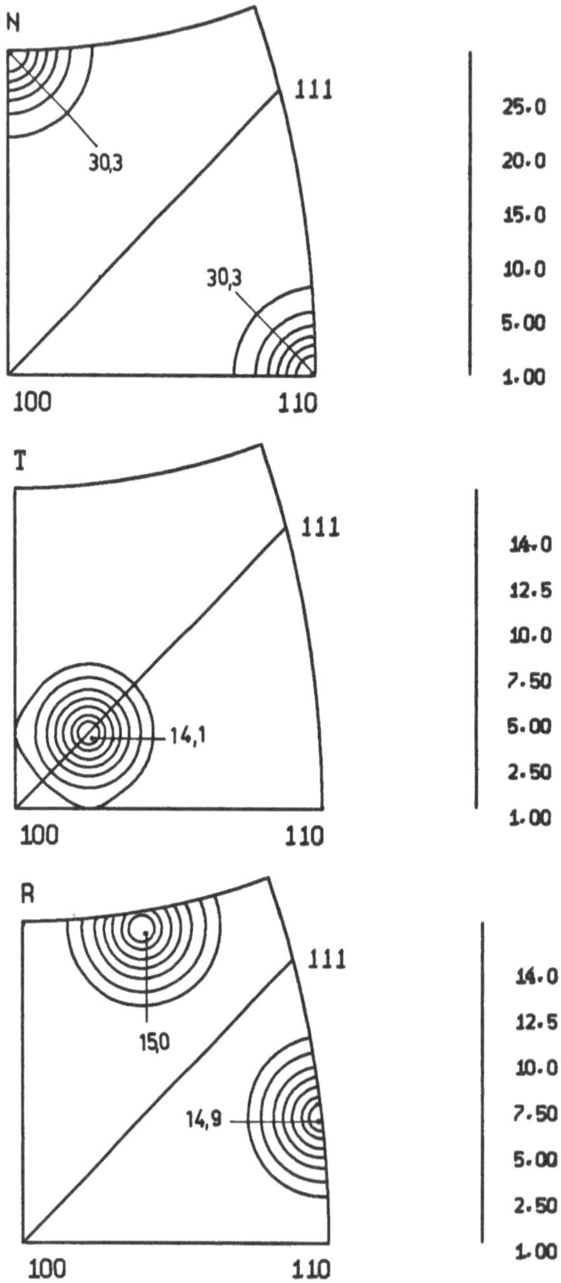

$\tilde{R}$, G, 10.0°, {101}⟨525⟩

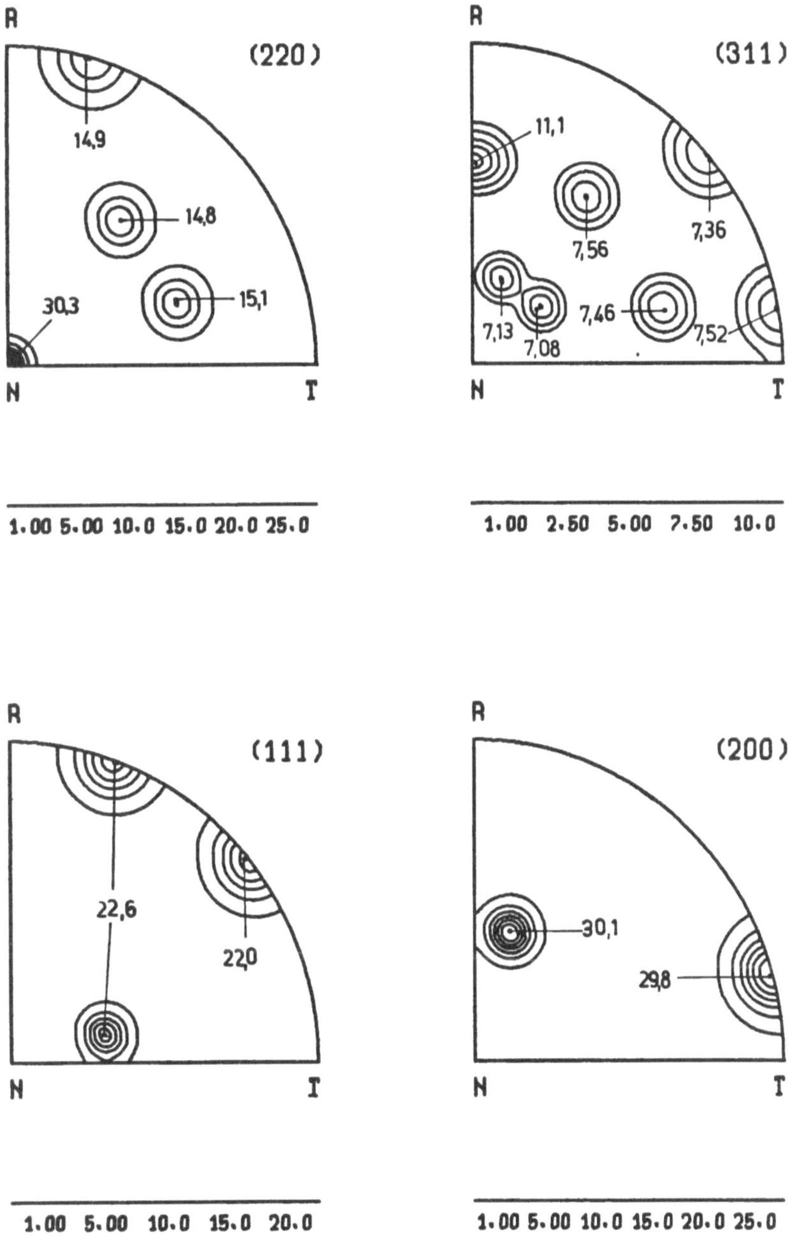

$\tilde{P}$, 6, 10.0°, $\{101\}\langle 525\rangle$

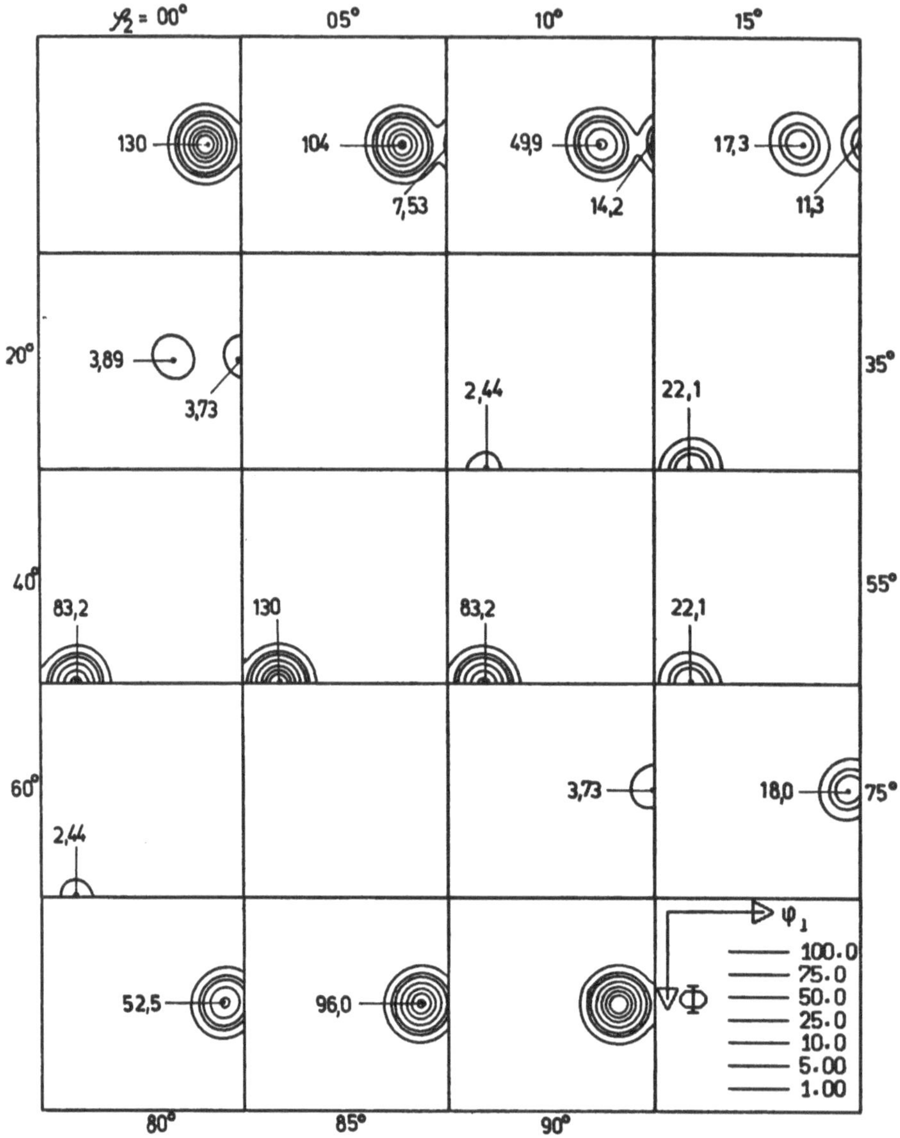

F, G, 12.5°, {101}<525>

F_{MAX} = 129.65 (00°, 45°, 90°)

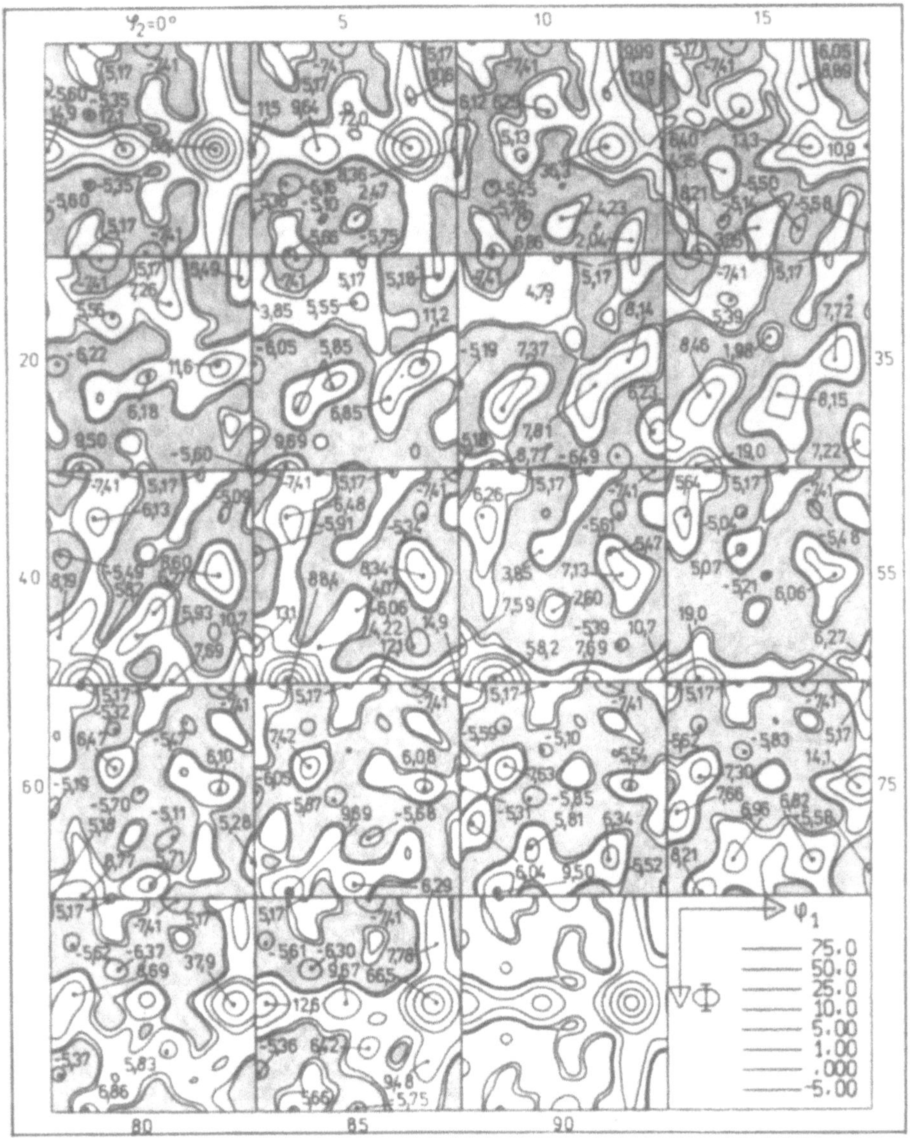

$\tilde{F}$, G, 12.5°, {101}<525>

$\tilde{F}_{MAX}$ = 88.37 (00°, 45°, 90°)

$\tilde{F}_{MIN}$ = -7.41 (00°, 05°, . . . , 90°)

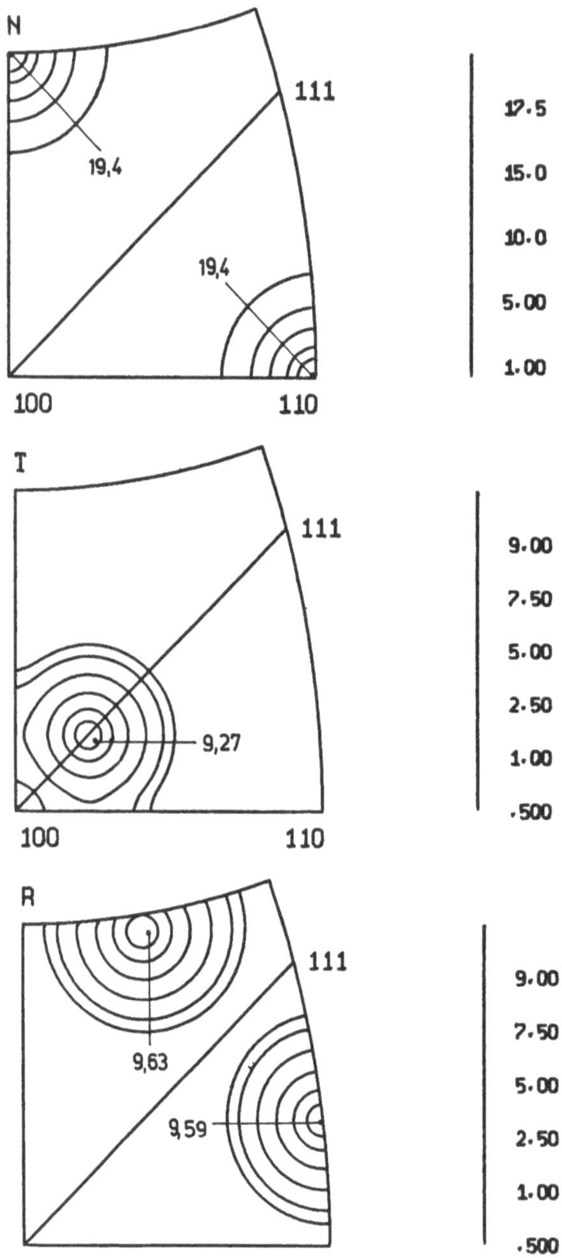

$\tilde{R}$, G, 12.5°, $\{101\}\langle 525\rangle$

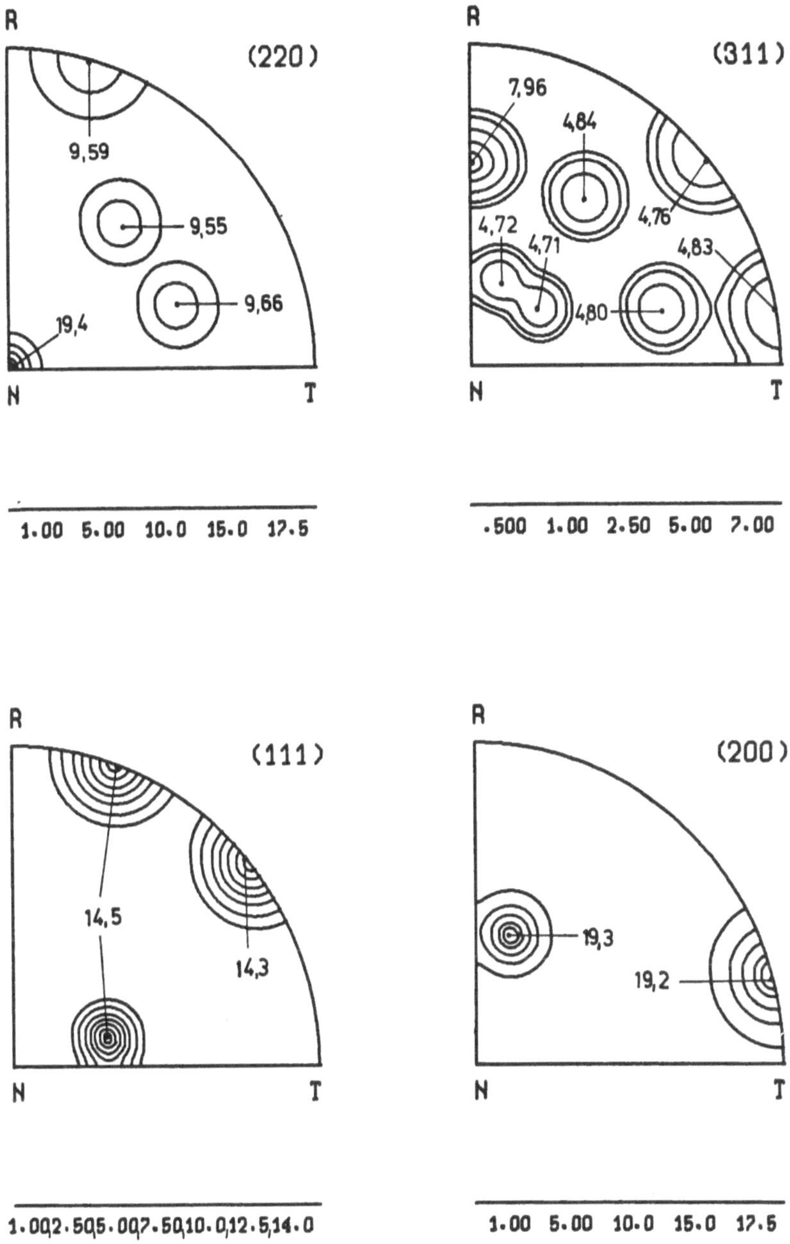

$\tilde{P}$, G, 12.5°, {101}⟨525⟩

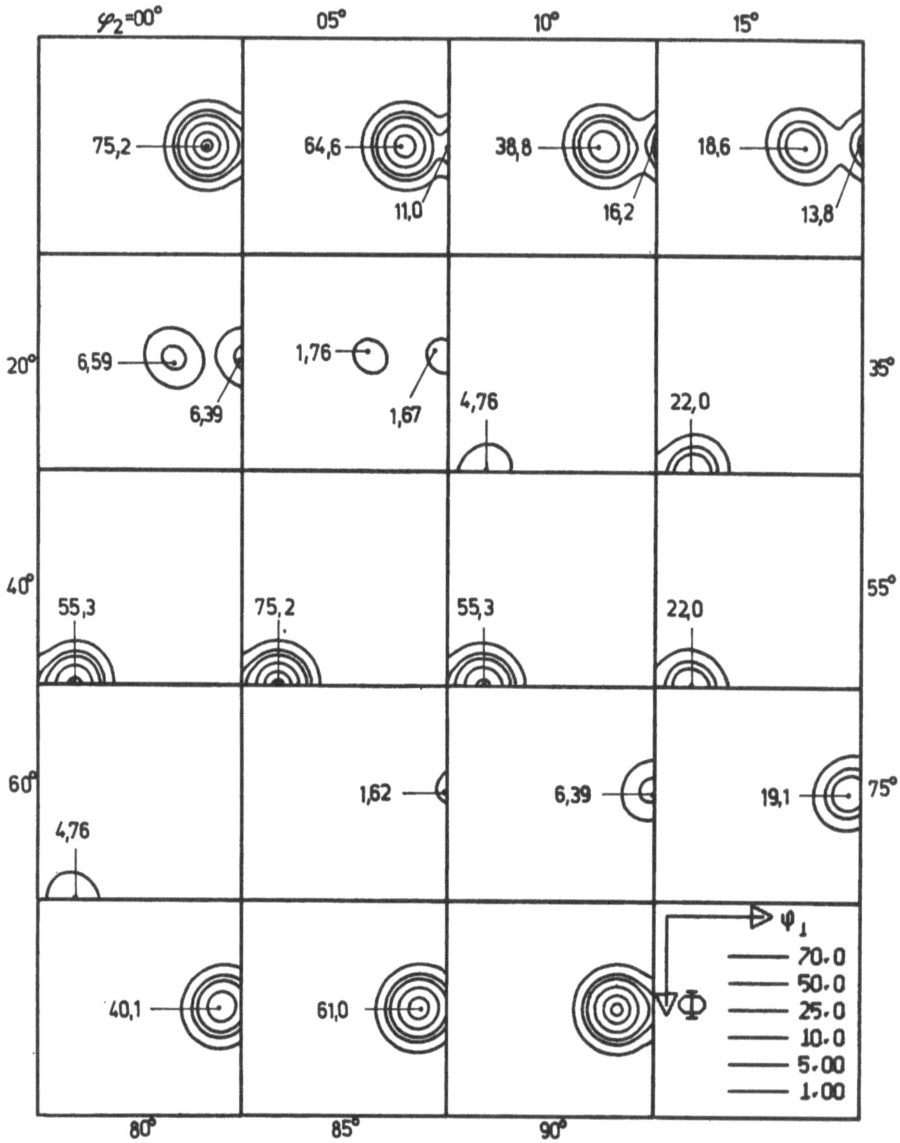

F, G, 15.0° , {101}<525>

F_{MAX} = 75.23 (00°, 45°, 90°)

$\tilde{F}$, G, 15.0°, $\{101\}\langle 525\rangle$

$\tilde{F}_{MAX}$ = 53.13 (00°, 45°, 90°)

$\tilde{F}_{MIN}$ = -5.18 (00°, 05°, . . . , 90°)

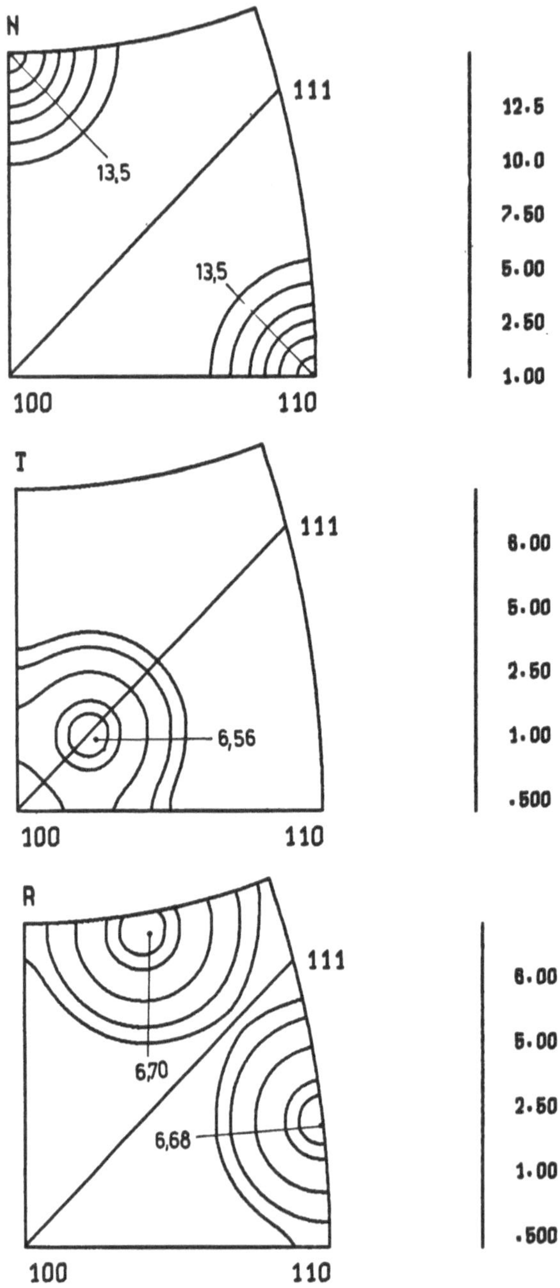

$\tilde{R}$, G, 15.0°, $\{101\}\langle 525\rangle$

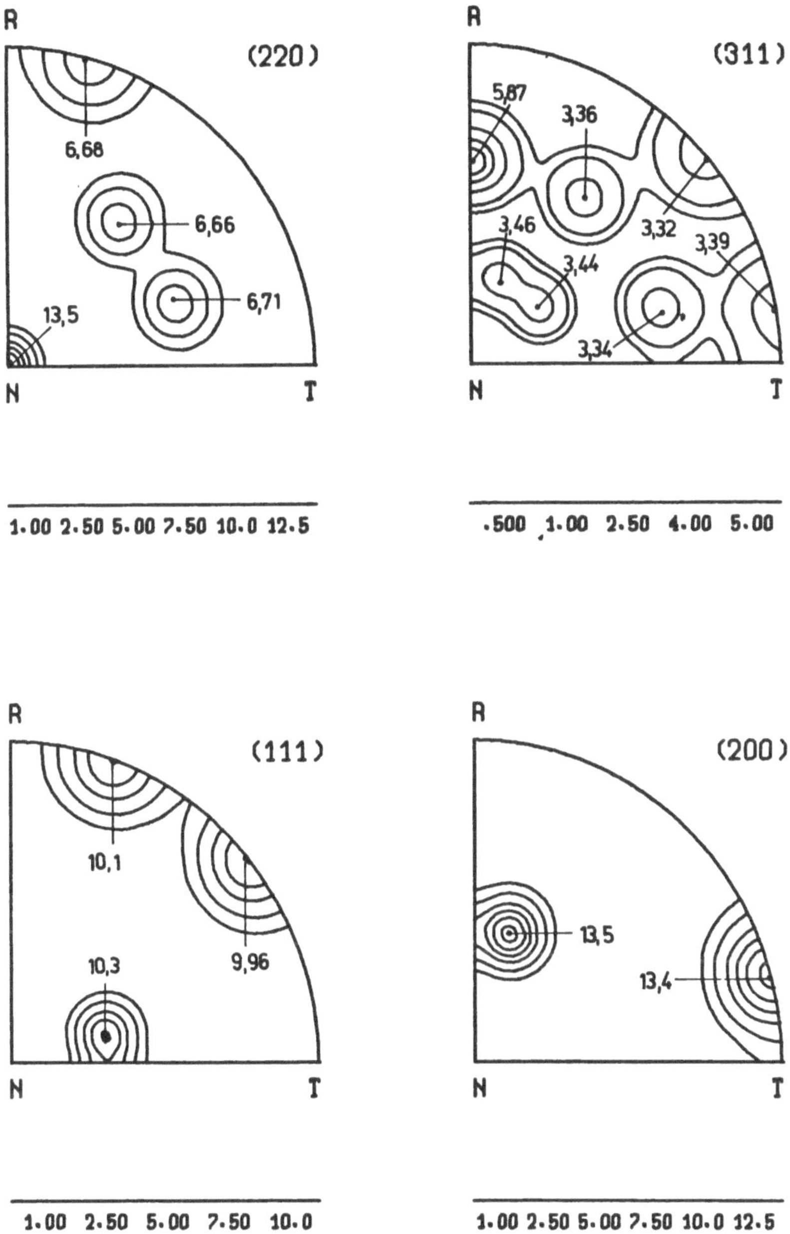

$\tilde{P}$, 6, 15.0°, $\{101\}\langle 525\rangle$

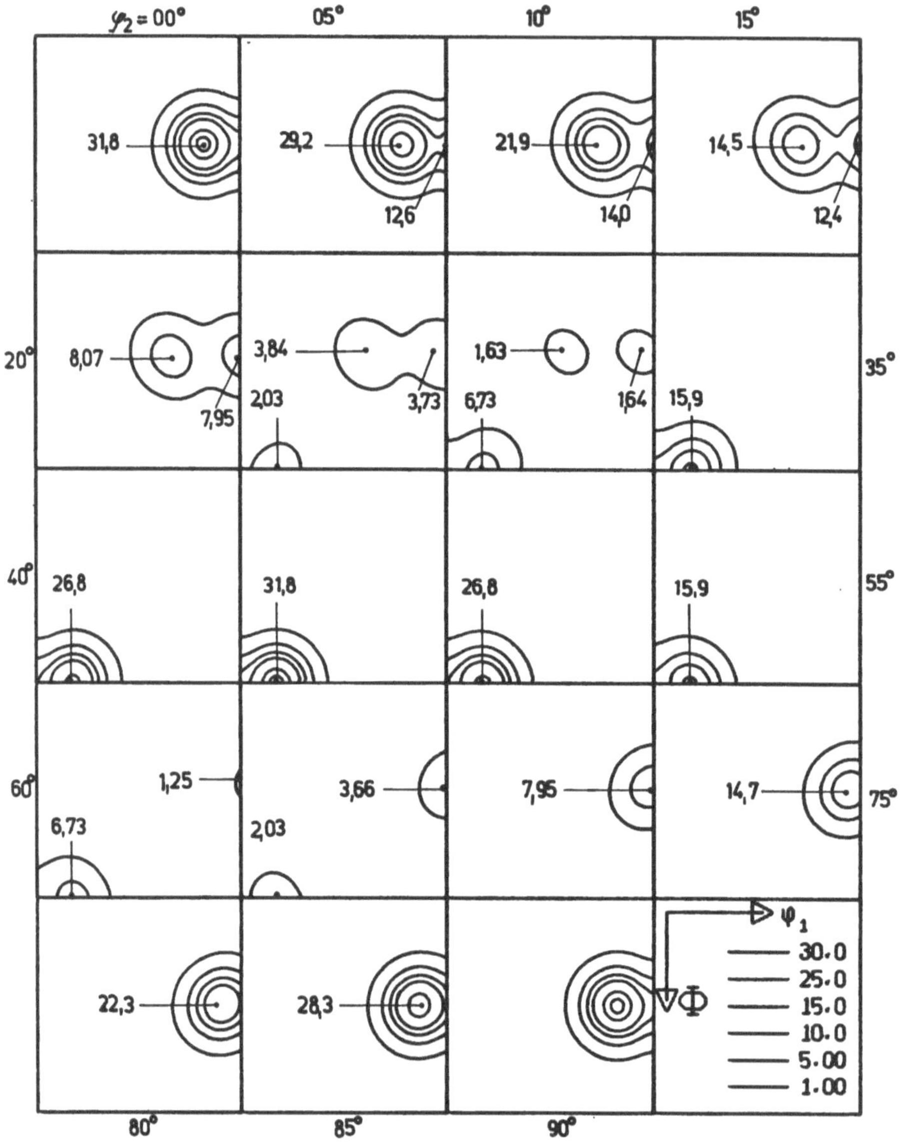

F, G, 20.0°, {101}<525>

F_{MAX} = 31.83 (00°, 45°, 90°)

$\tilde{F}$, G, 20.0°, {101}<525>

$\tilde{F}_{MAX}$ = 24.17 (00°, 45°, 90°)

$\tilde{F}_{MIN}$ = -2.51 (45°)

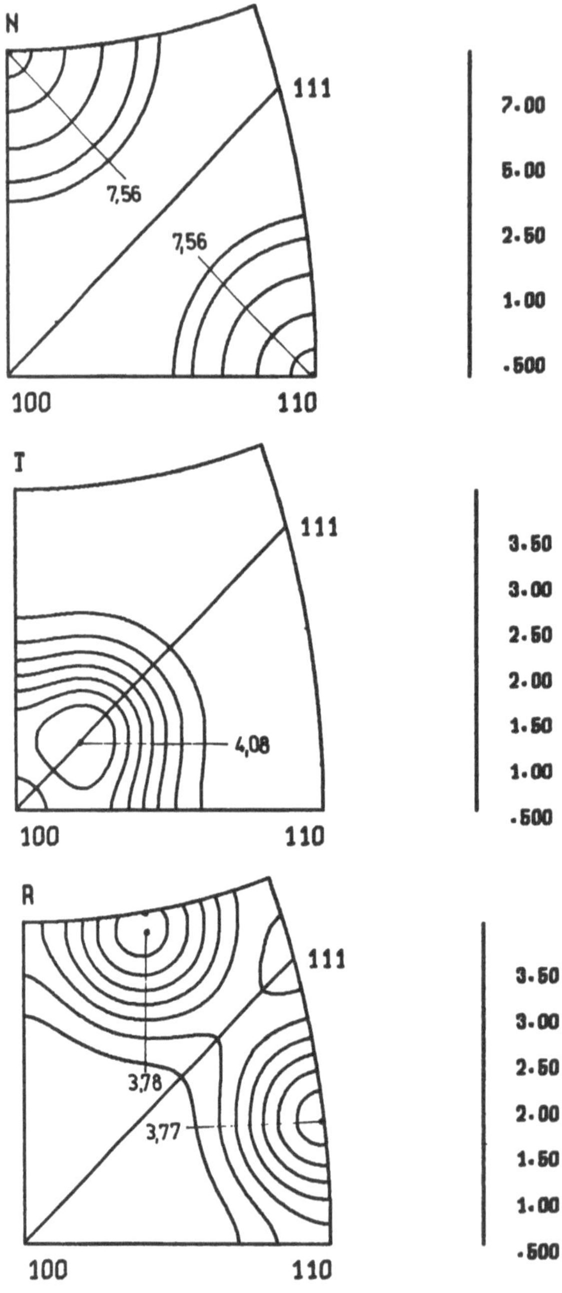

$\tilde{R}$, G, 20.0°, $\{101\}\langle 525\rangle$

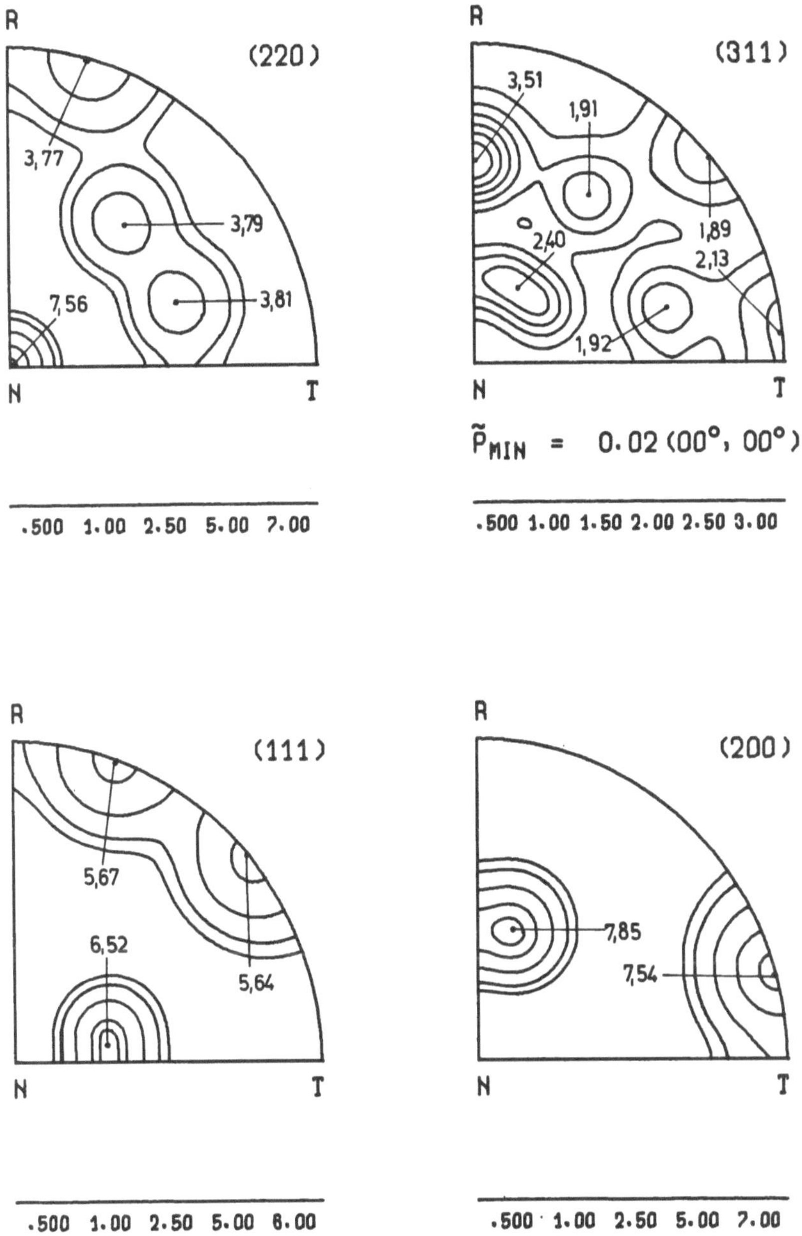

$\tilde{P}$, 6, 20.0°, {101}⟨525⟩

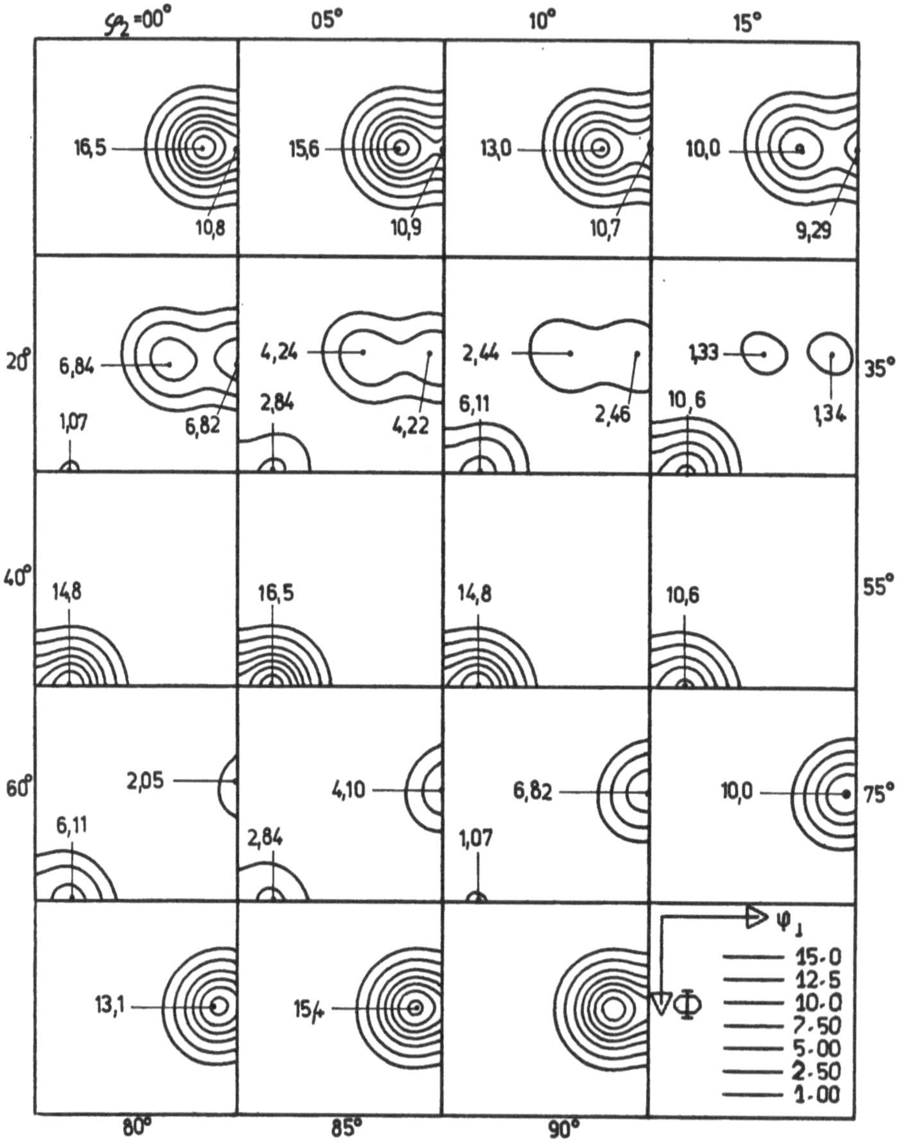

F, G, 25.0°, {101}<525>

F_{MAX} = 16.52 (00°, 45°, 90°)

$\tilde{F}$, G, 25.0°, {101}<525>

$\tilde{F}_{MAX}$ = 13.56 (00°, 45°, 90°)

$\tilde{F}_{MIN}$ = −1.35 (00°, 15°, 60°, 75°, 90°)

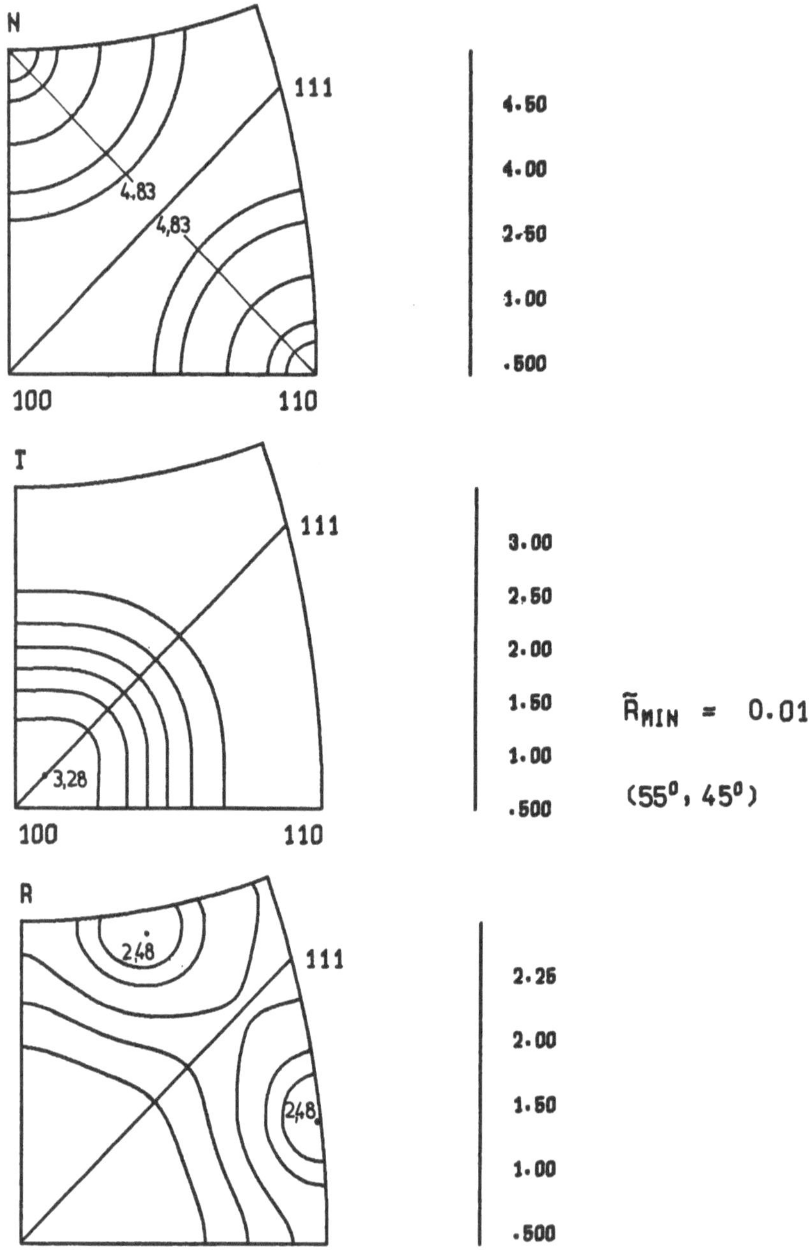

$\tilde{R}$, G, 25.0°, {101}⟨525⟩

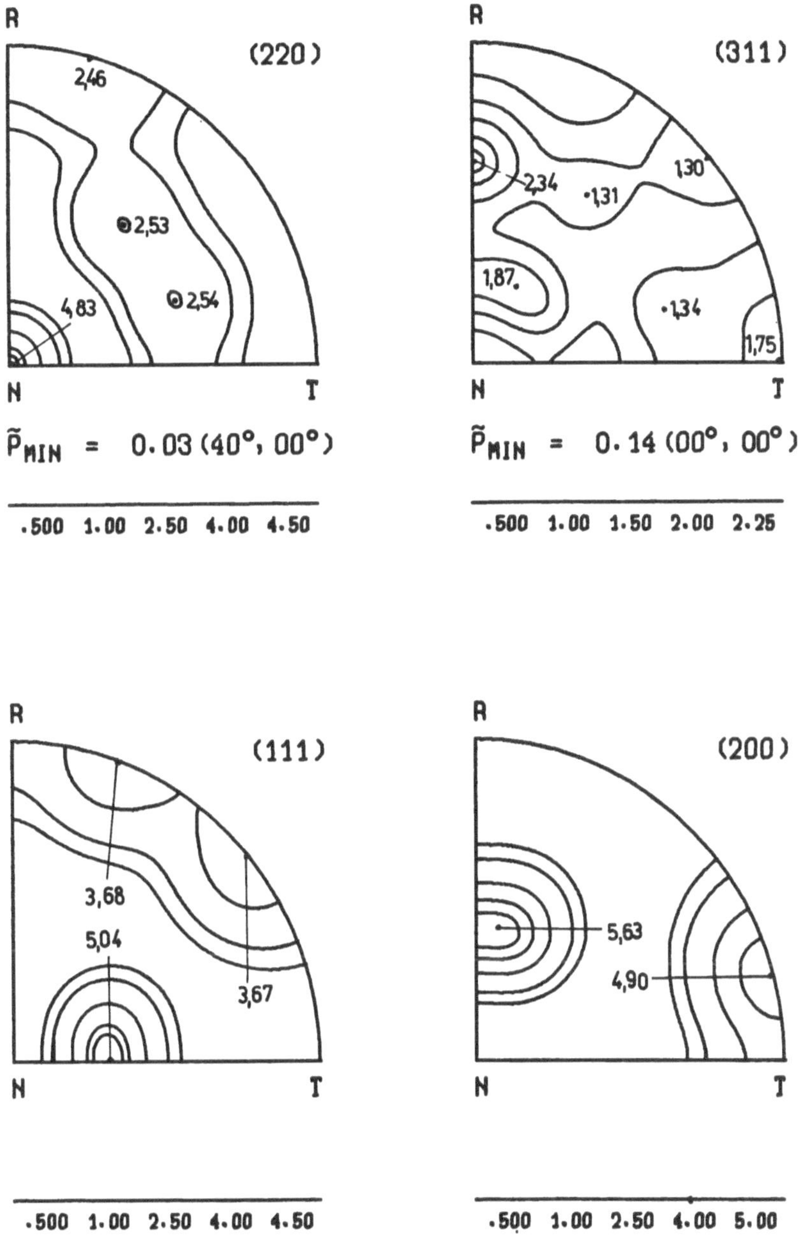

P̃, 6, 25.0°, {101}⟨525⟩

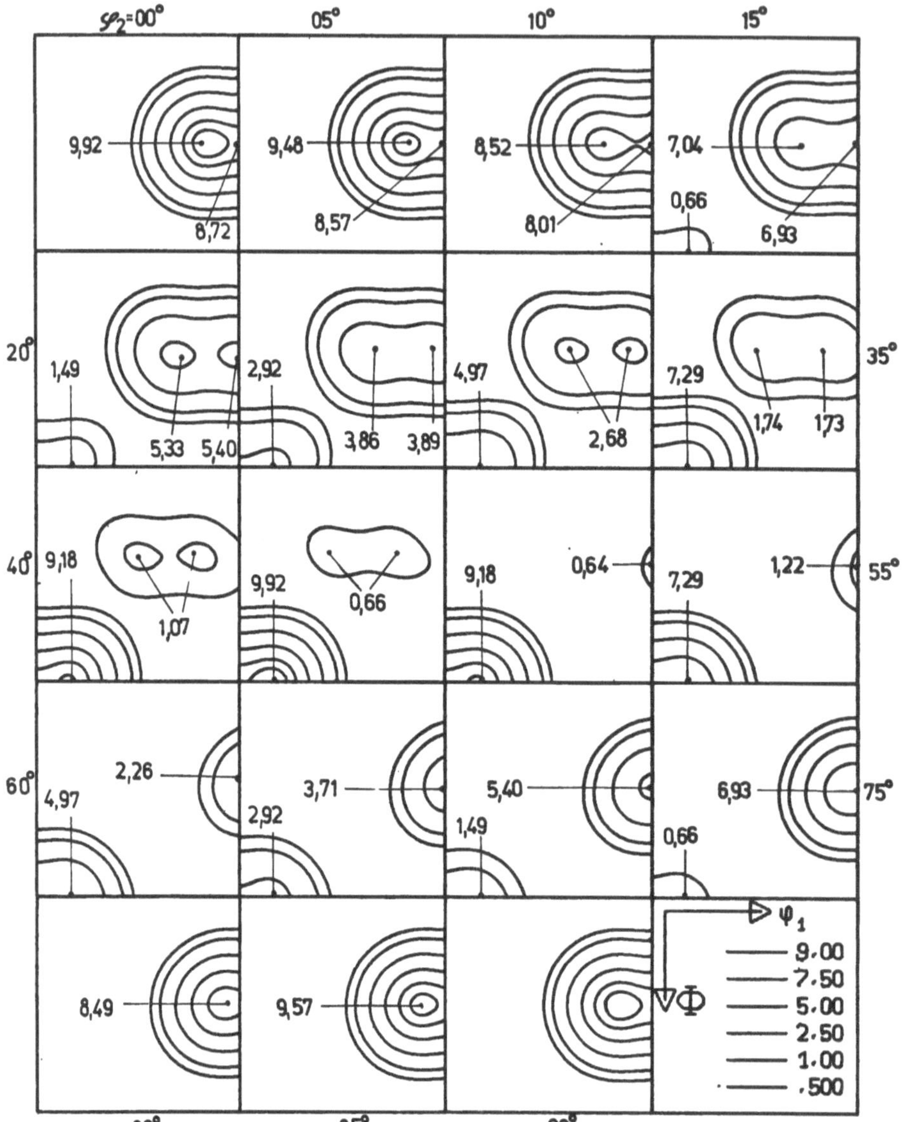

F, G, 30.0°, {101}<525>

F_{MAX} = 9.92 (00°, 45°, 90°)

$\tilde{F}$, G, 30.0°, {101}<525>

$\tilde{F}_{MAX}$ = 8.84 (00°, 45°, 90°)

$\tilde{F}_{MIN}$ = −.65 (60°)

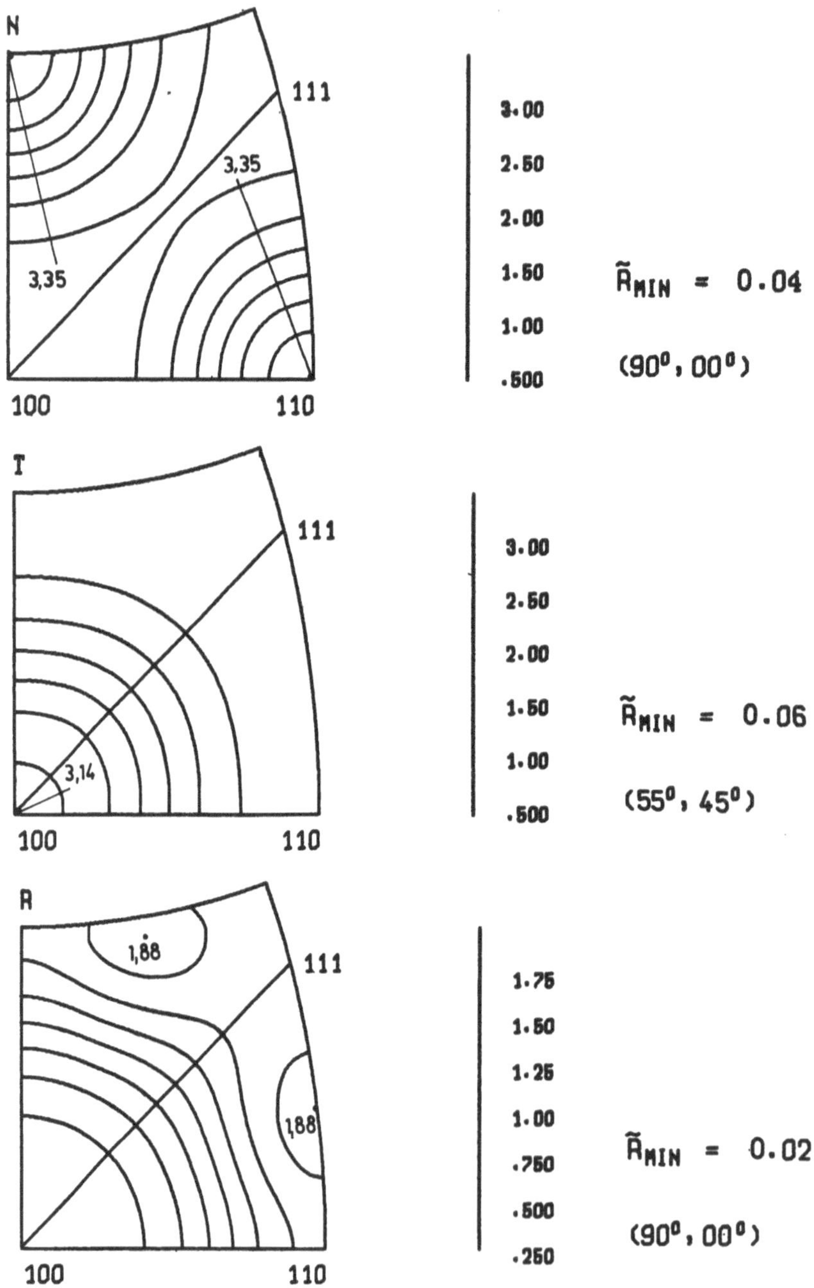

$\tilde{R}$, G, 30.0°, $\{101\}\langle 525\rangle$

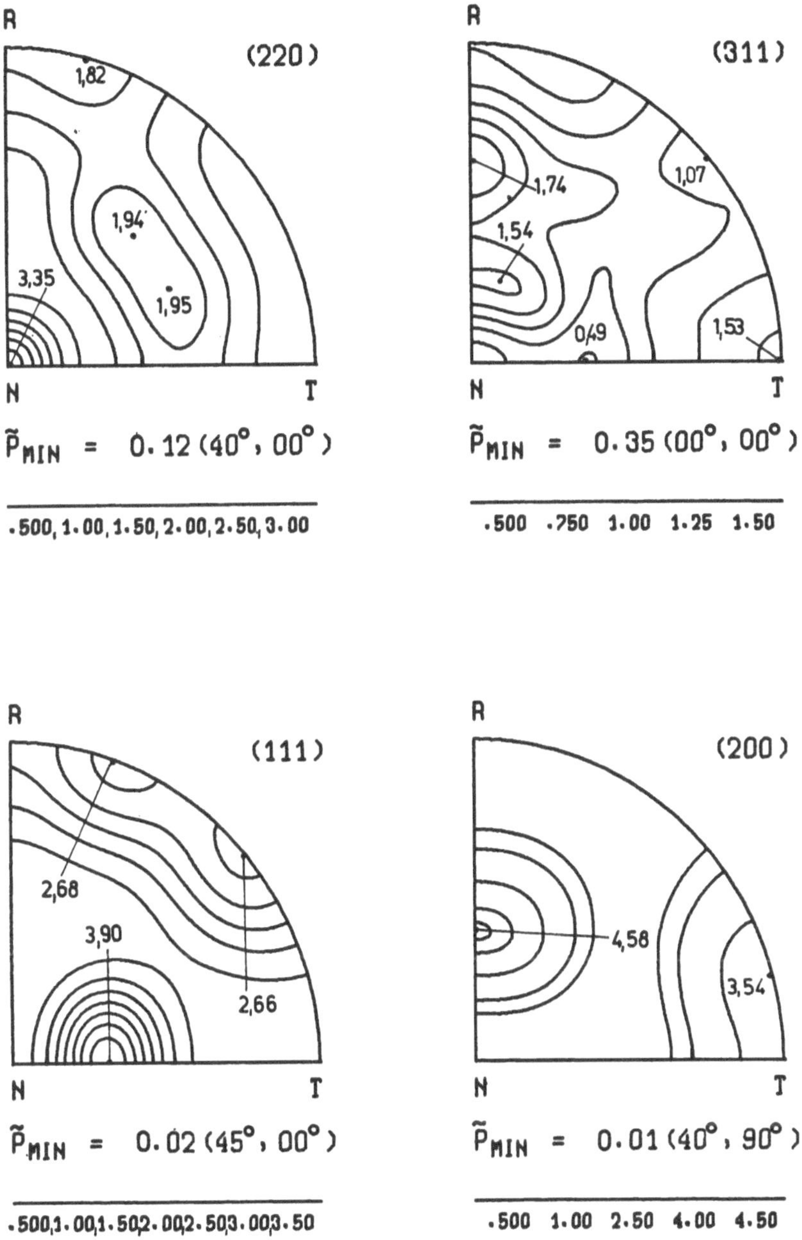

P̃, 6, 30.0°, {101}⟨525⟩

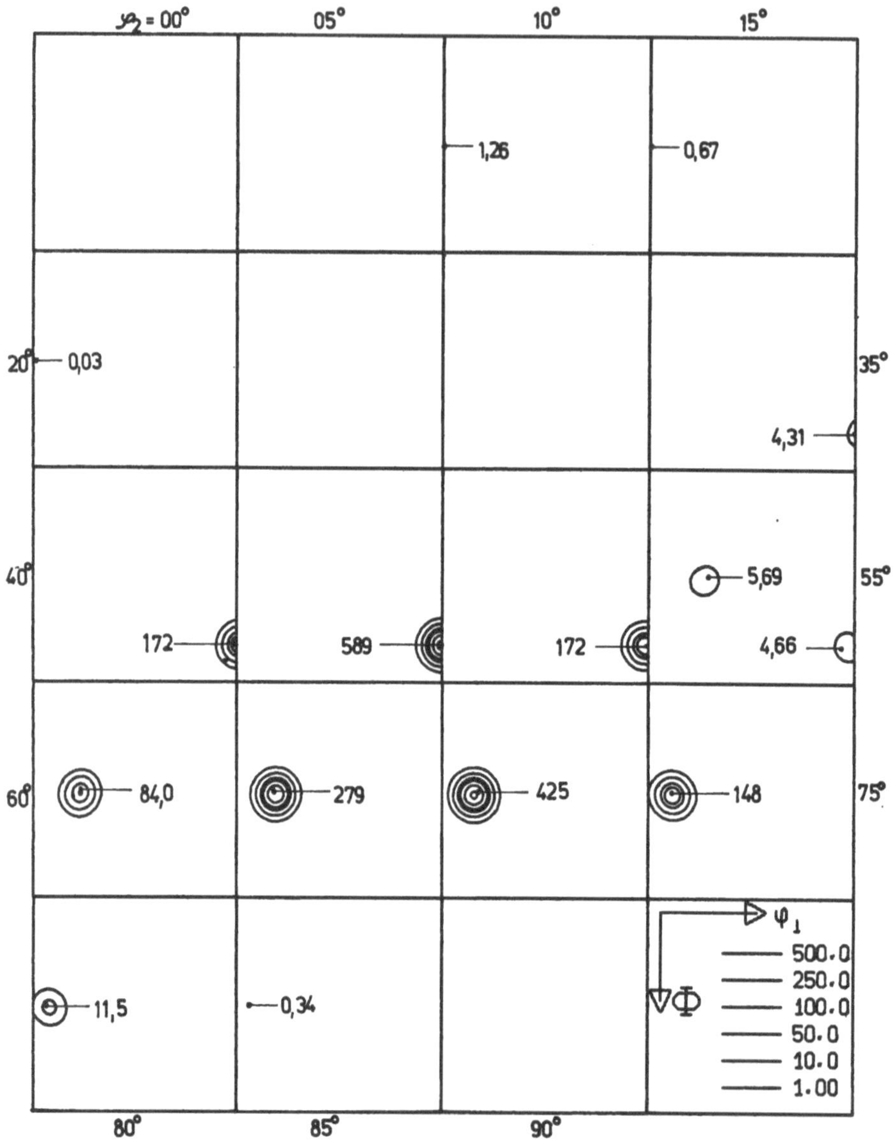

F, G, 7.50° , {525}<1̄51>

F_{MAX} = 589.10 (45°)

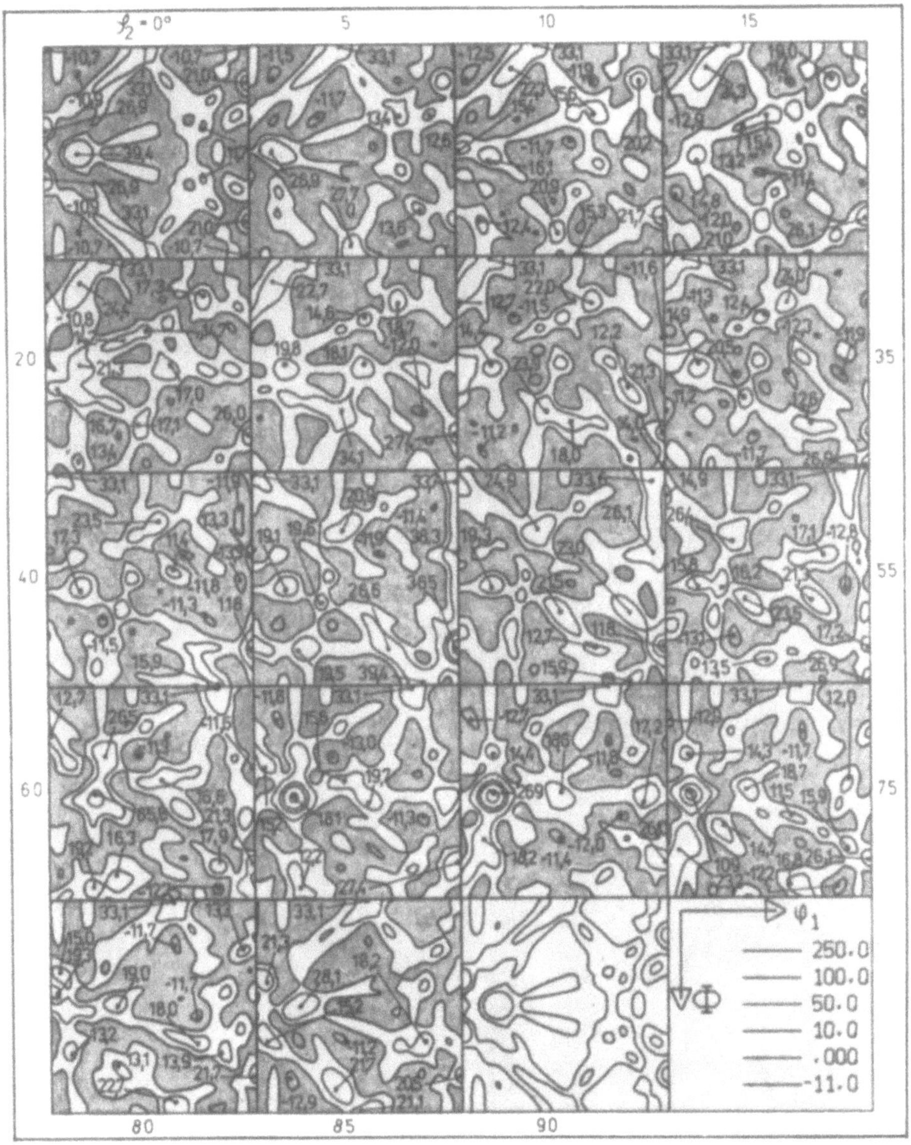

$\tilde{F}$, G, 7.50°, $\{525\}\langle 151\rangle$

$\tilde{F}_{MAX}$ = 365.17 (45°)

$\tilde{F}_{MIN}$ = -13.88 (40°)

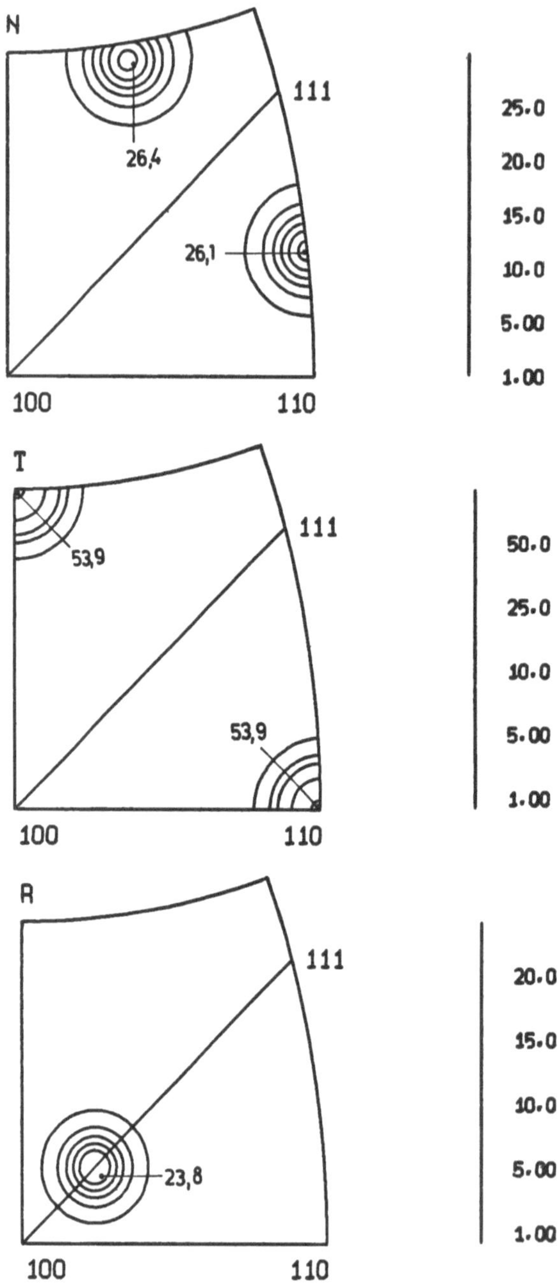

$\tilde{R}$, G, 7.50°, {525}⟨151⟩

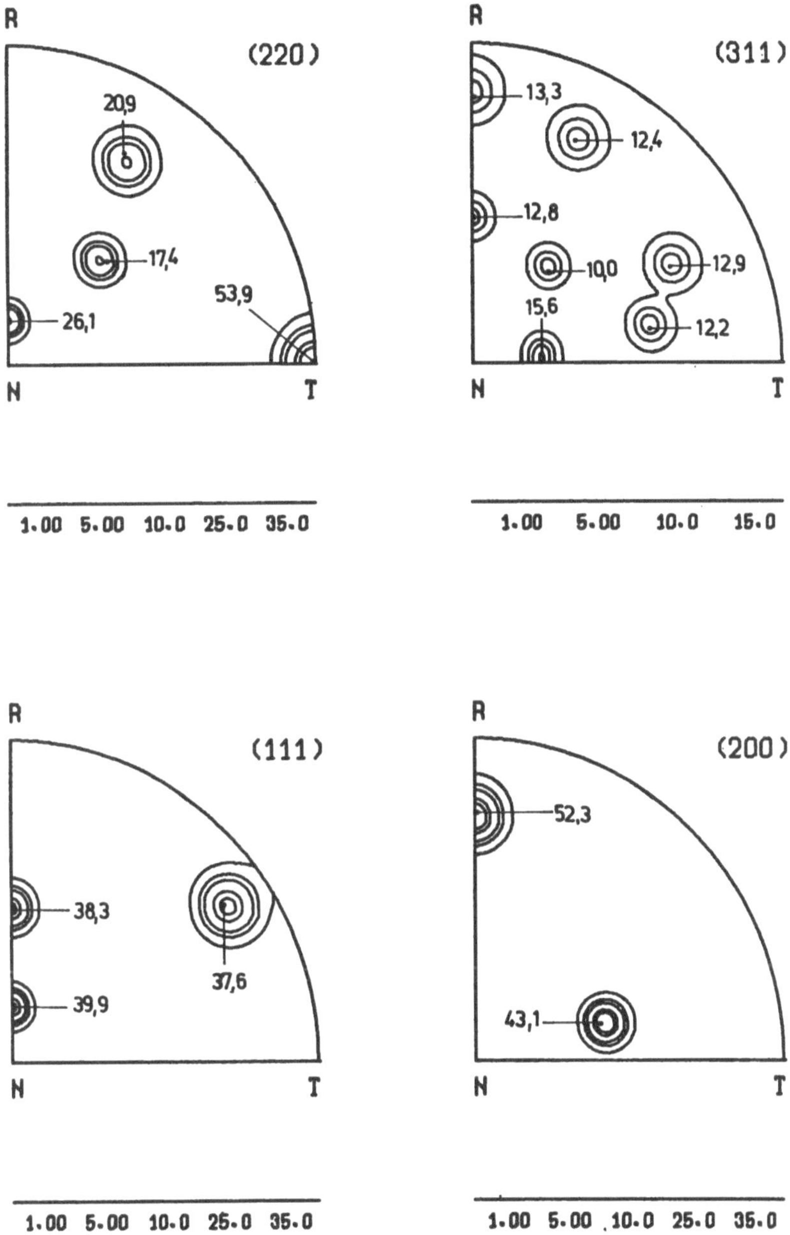

$\tilde{P}$, G, 7.50°, {525} ⟨151⟩

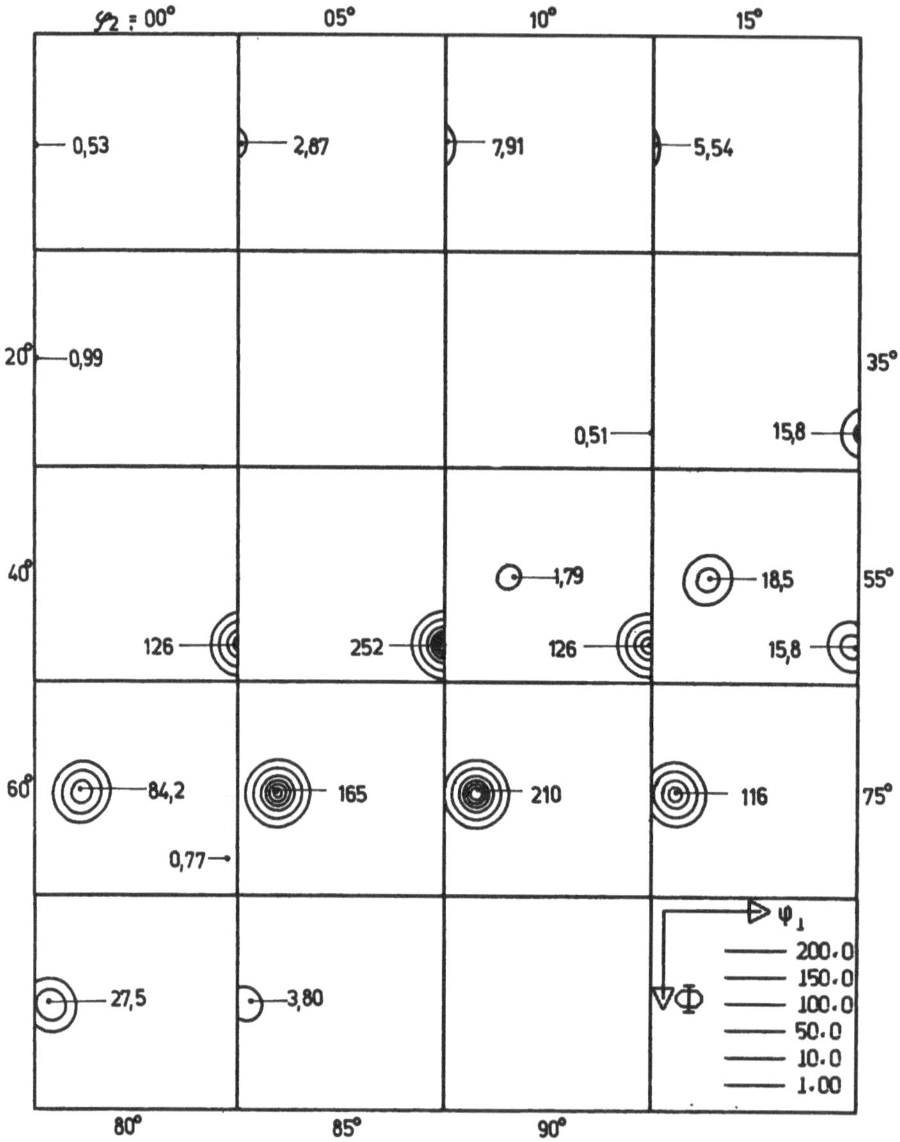

F, G, 10.0°, {525}<151>

F_{MAX} = 251.80 (45°)

$\tilde{F}$, G, 10.0°, {525}<151>

$\tilde{F}_{MAX}$ = 164.54 (45°)

$\tilde{F}_{MIN}$ = -9.03 (00°, 45°, 90°)

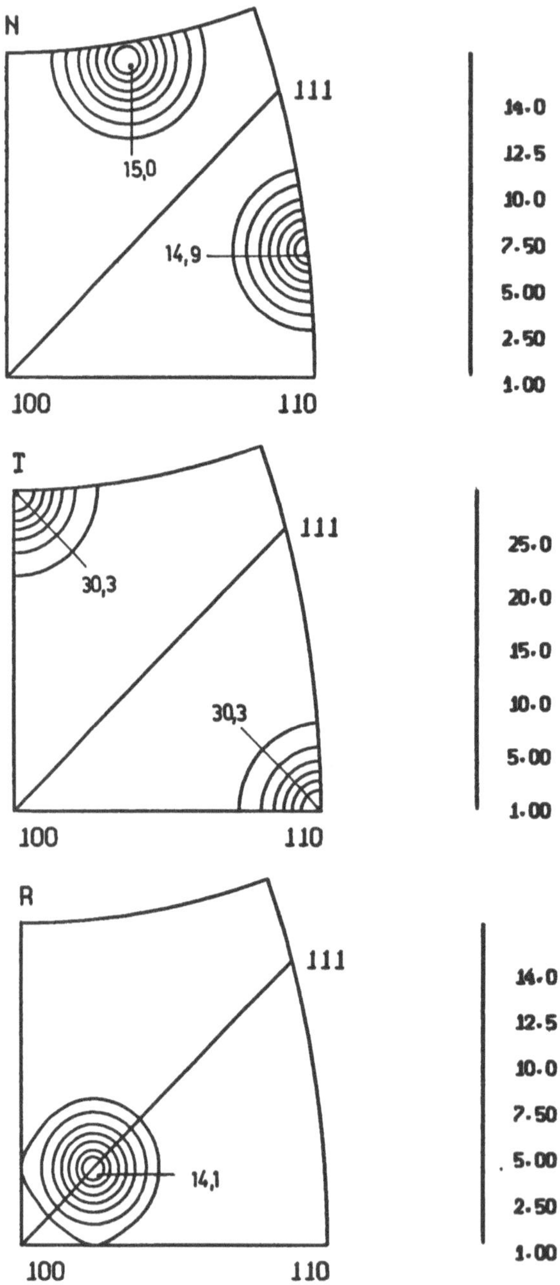

$\tilde{R}$, G, 10.0^{0} , $\{525\}\langle 151\rangle$

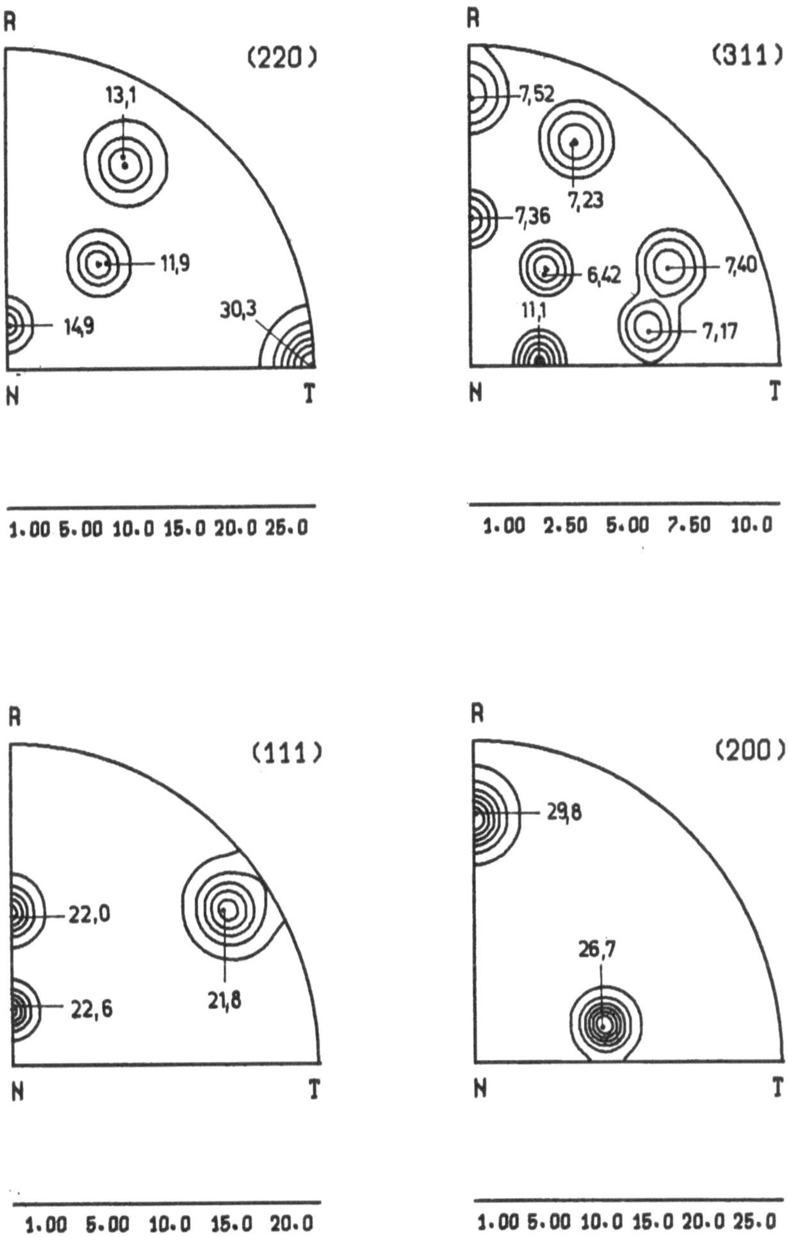

$\tilde{P}$, G, 10.0°, $\{525\}\langle 151\rangle$

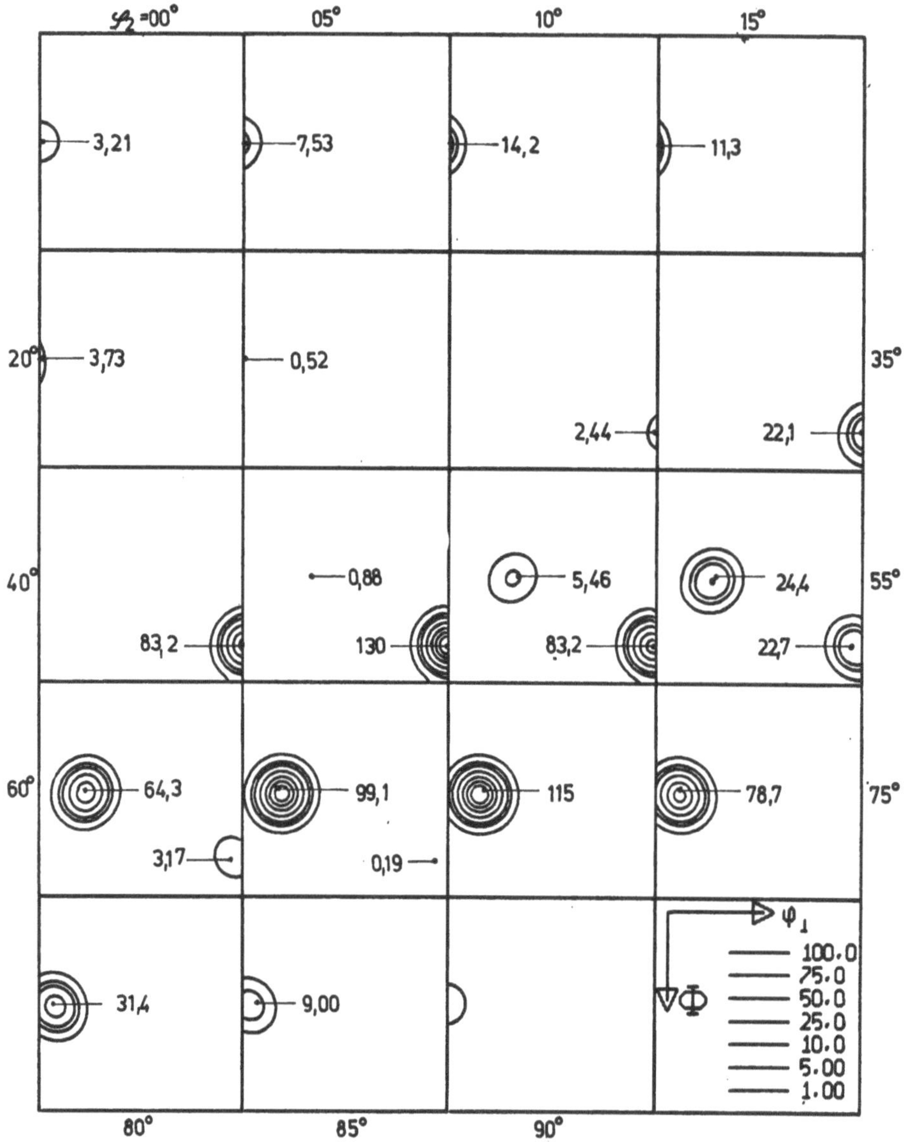

F, G, 12.5°, {525}<151>

F_{MAX} = 129.65 (45°)

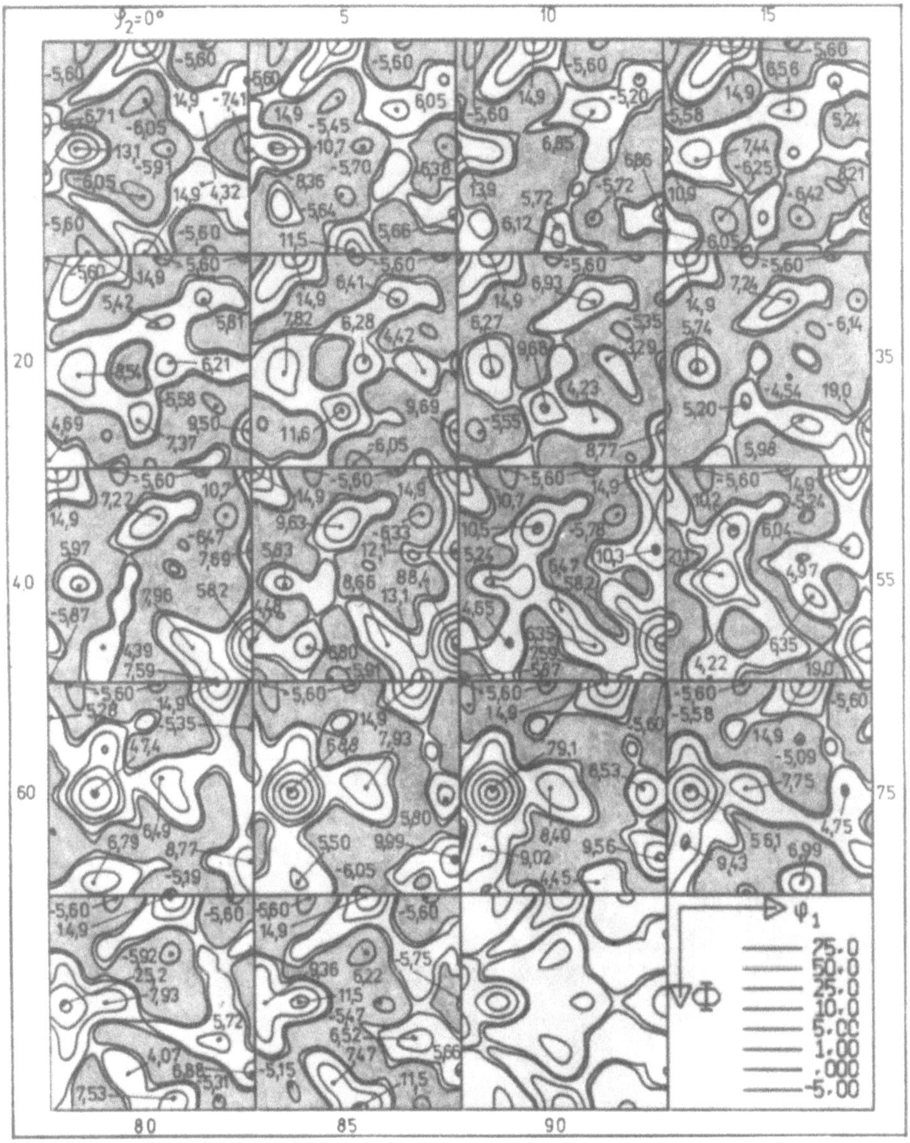

$\tilde{F}$, G, 12.5°, {525}<151>

$\tilde{F}_{MAX}$ = 88.37 (45°)

$\tilde{F}_{MIN}$ = -7.41 (00°, 45°, 90°)

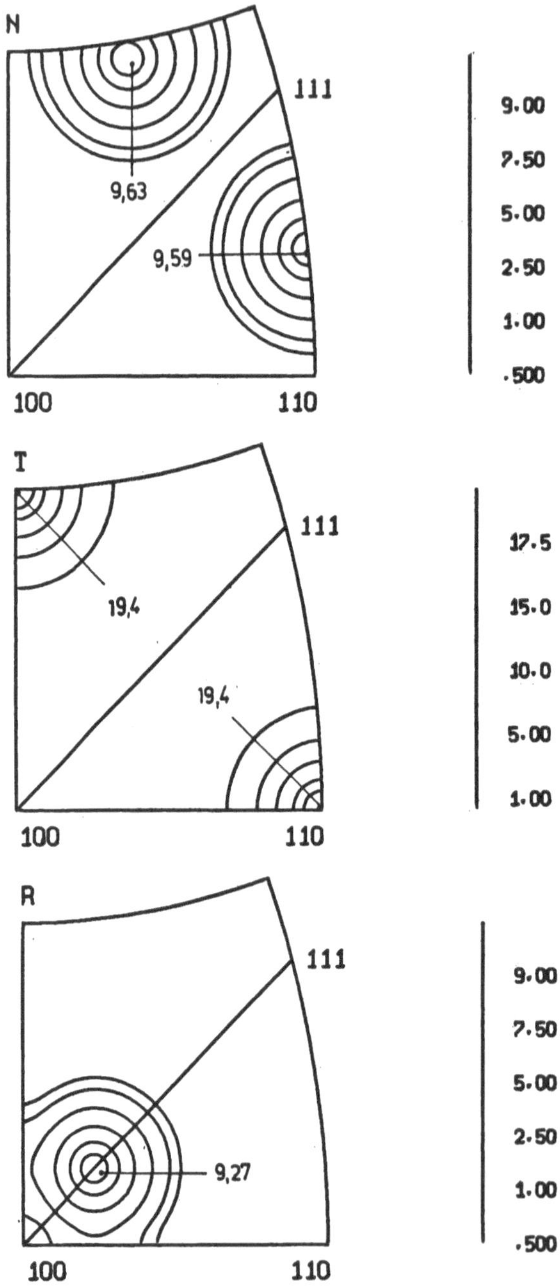

$\tilde{R}$, G, 12.5°, $\{525\}\langle 151\rangle$

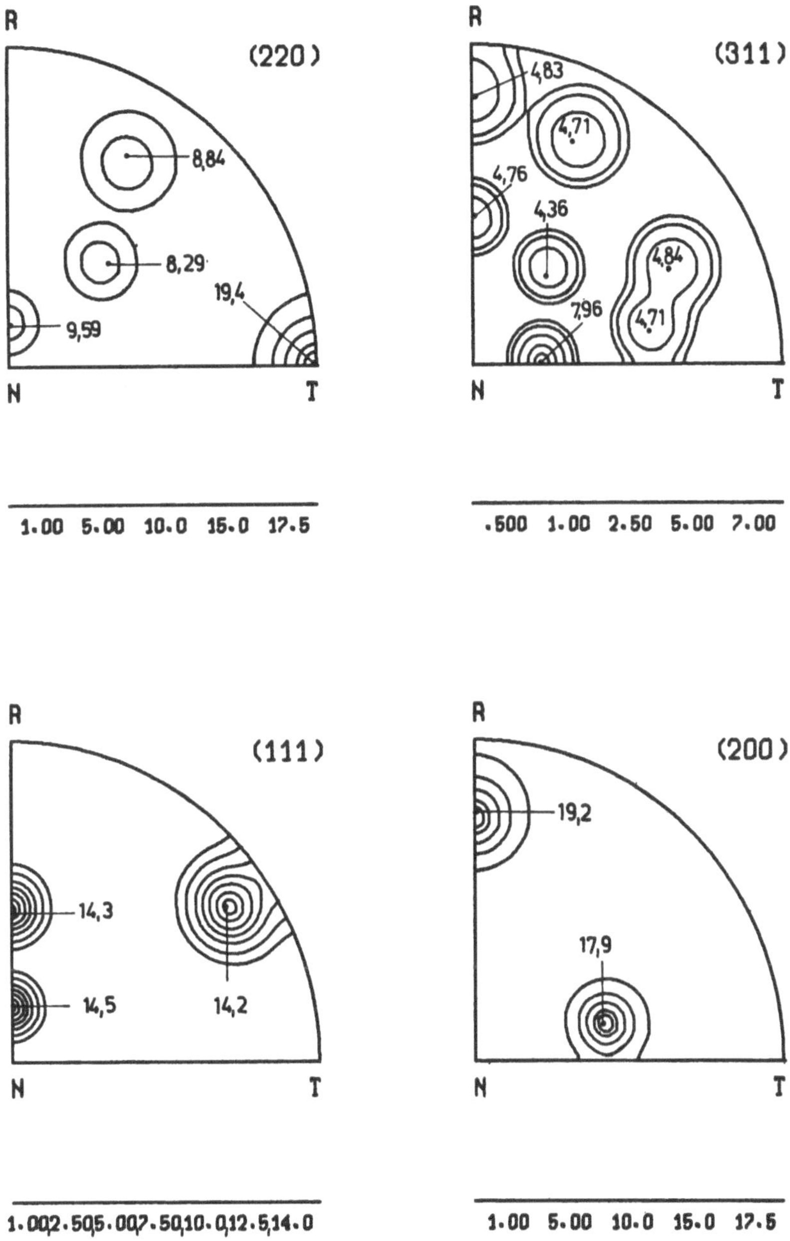

$\tilde{P}$, G, 12.5°, $\{525\}\langle 15\bar{1}\rangle$

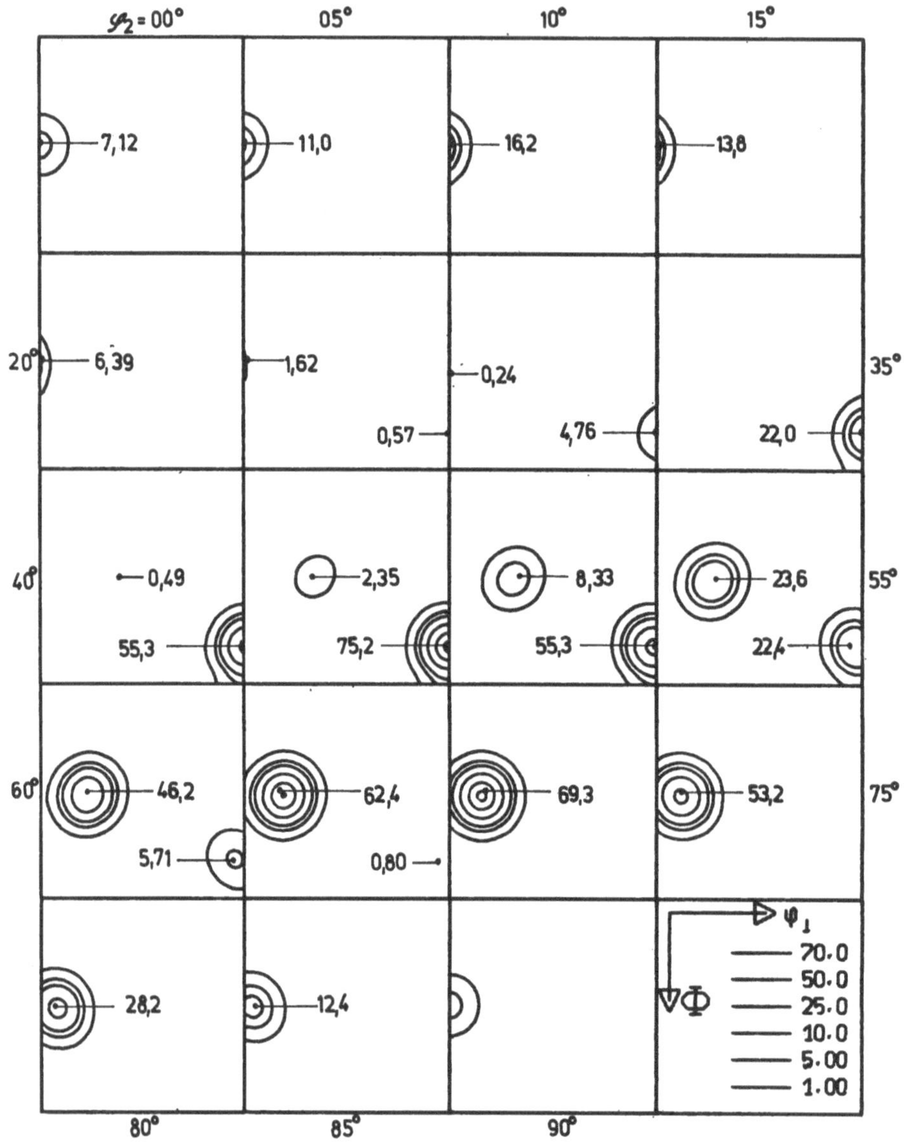

F, G, 15.0° , {525}<151>

F_{MAX} = 75.23 (45°)

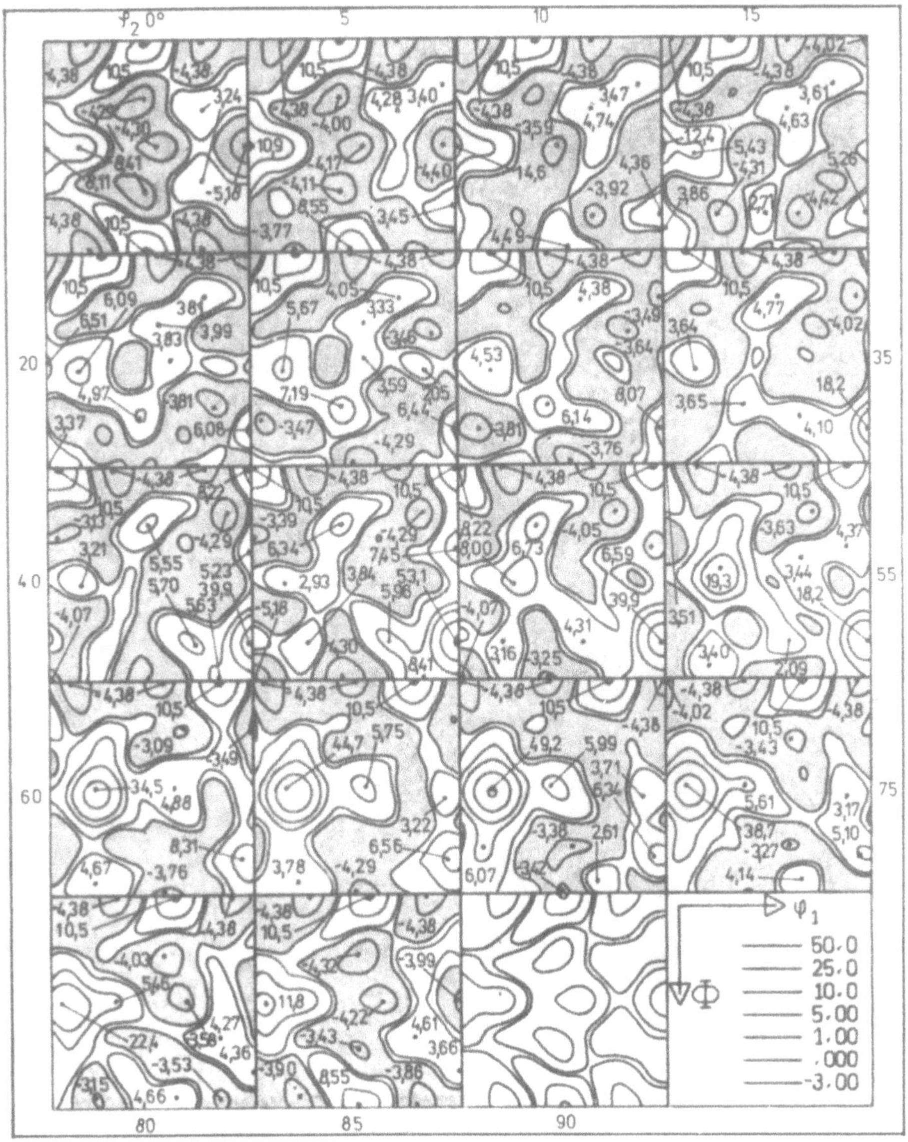

$\tilde{F}$, G, 15.0°, {525}<151>

$\tilde{F}_{MAX}$ = 53.13 (45°)

$\tilde{F}_{MIN}$ = -5.18 (00°, 45°, 90°)

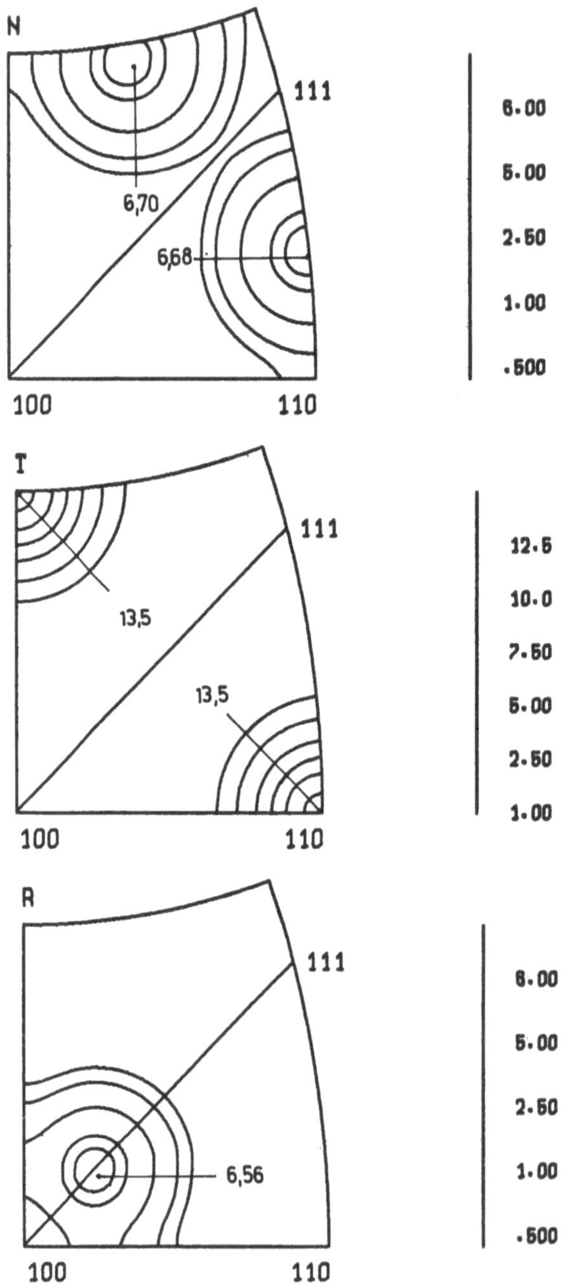

$\tilde{R}$, G, 15.0°, {525}⟨151⟩

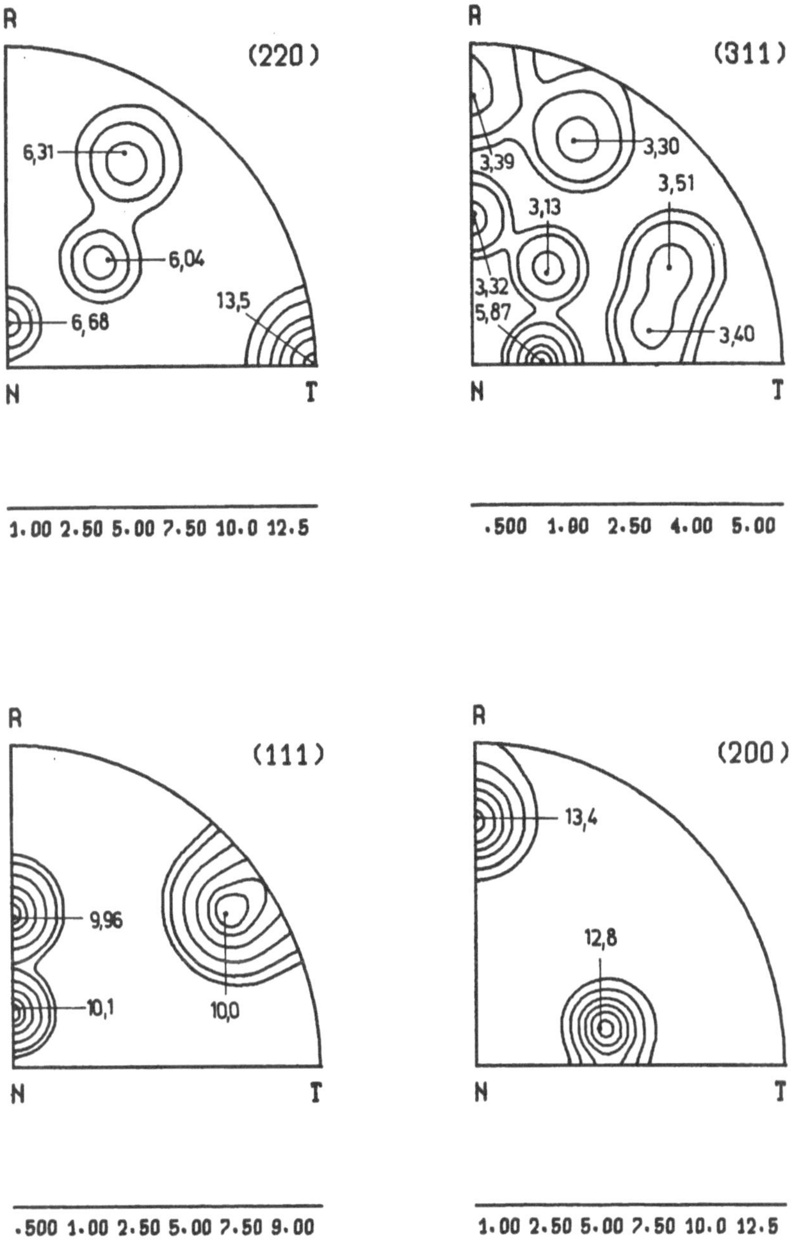

$\tilde{P}$, G, 15.0°, {525}⟨151⟩

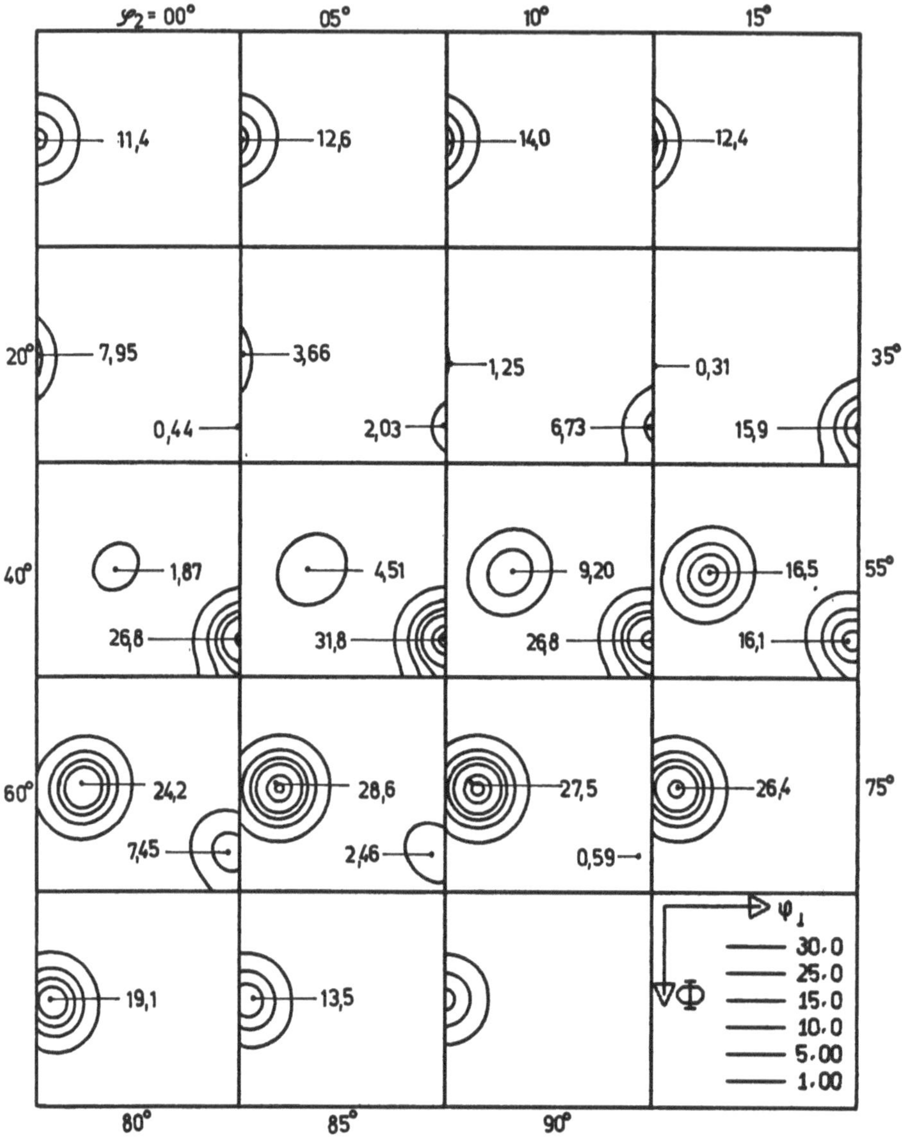

F, G, 20.0°, {525}<151>

F_{MAX} = 31.83 (45°)

$\tilde{F}$, G, 20.0°, $\{525\}\langle 151\rangle$

$\tilde{F}_{MAX}$ = 24.17 (45°)

$\tilde{F}_{MIN}$ = −2.51 (00°, 45°, 90°)

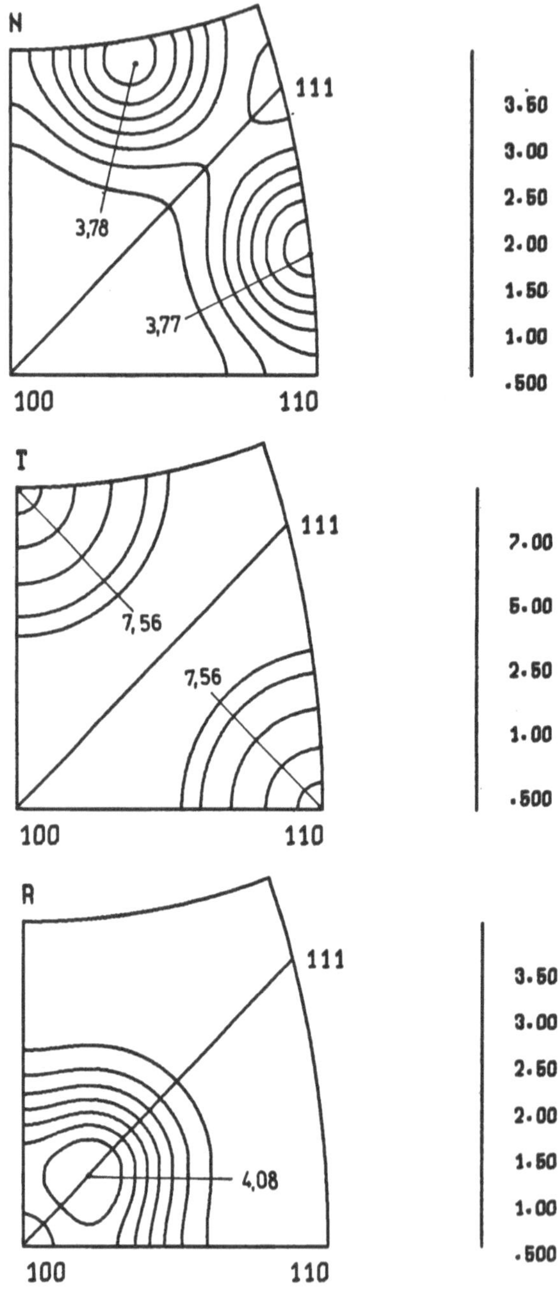

$\tilde{R}$, G, 20.0°, $\{525\}\langle 151\rangle$

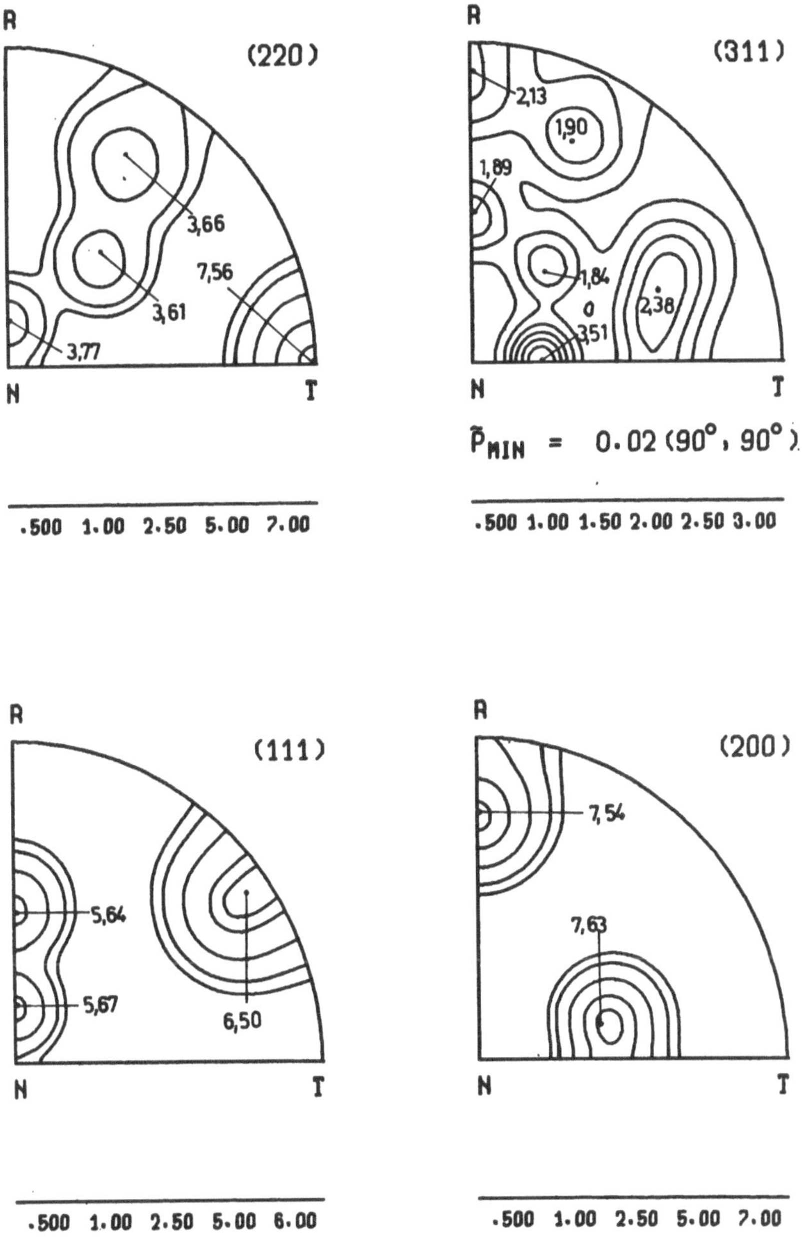

$\tilde{P}$, 6, 20.0°, {525}⟨151⟩

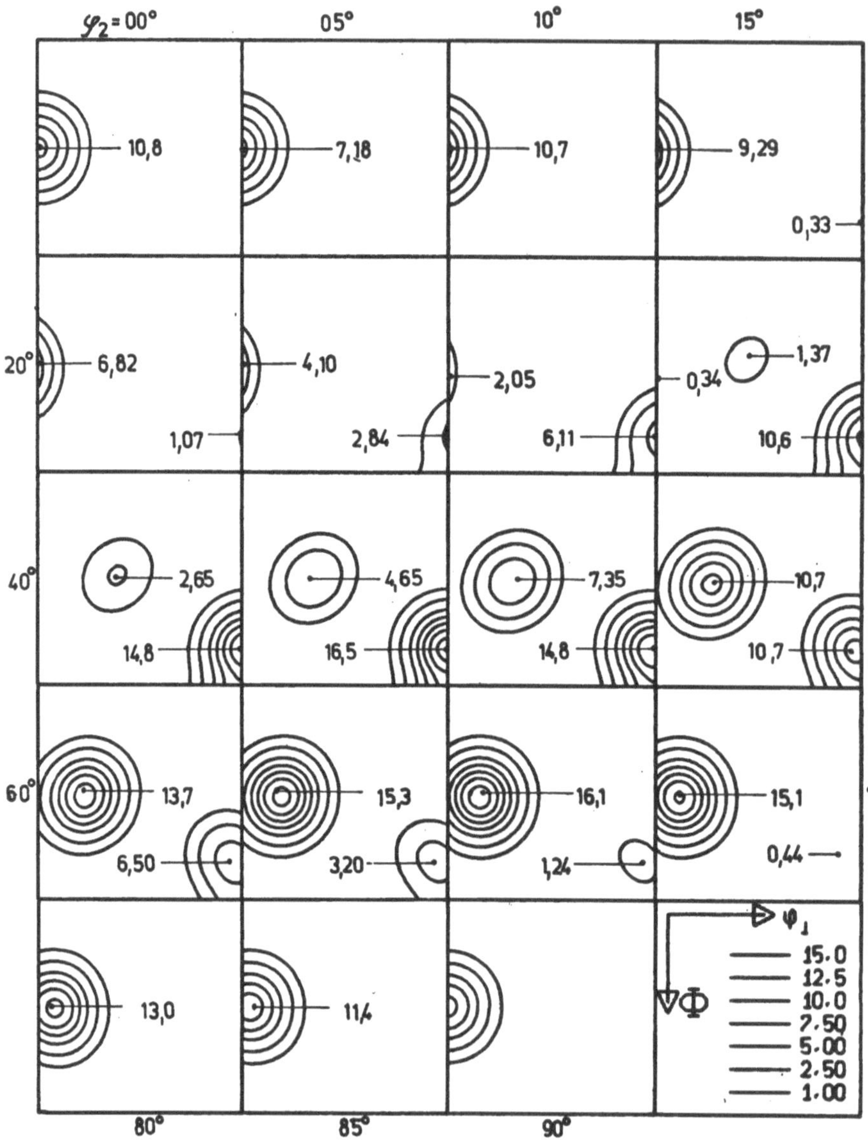

F, G, 25.0°, {525}<151>

F_{MAX} = 16.52 (45°)

$\tilde{F}$, G, 25.0°, {525}<151>

$\tilde{F}_{MAX}$ = 13.56 (45°)

$\tilde{F}_{MIN}$ = −1.35 (00°, 05°, ..., 90°)

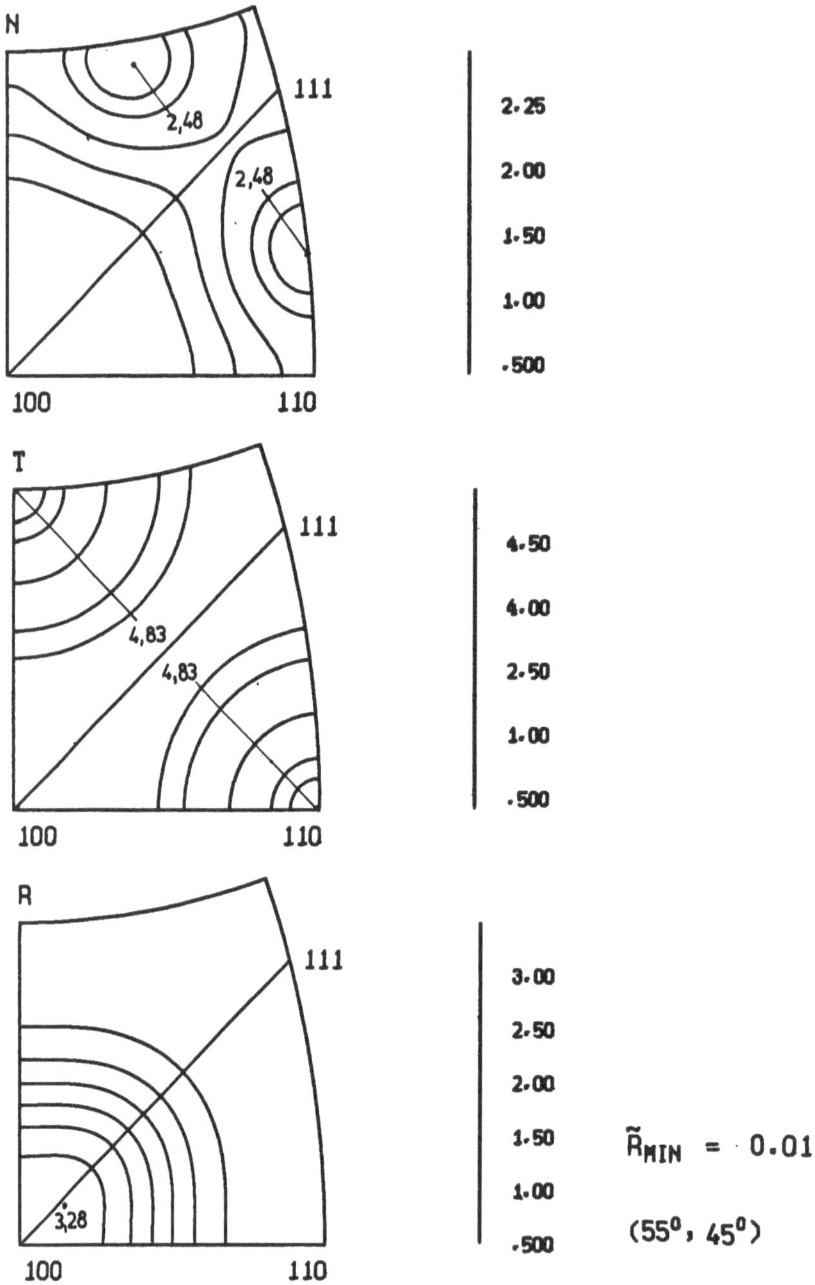

$\tilde{R}$, G, 25.0°, $\{525\}\langle 151\rangle$

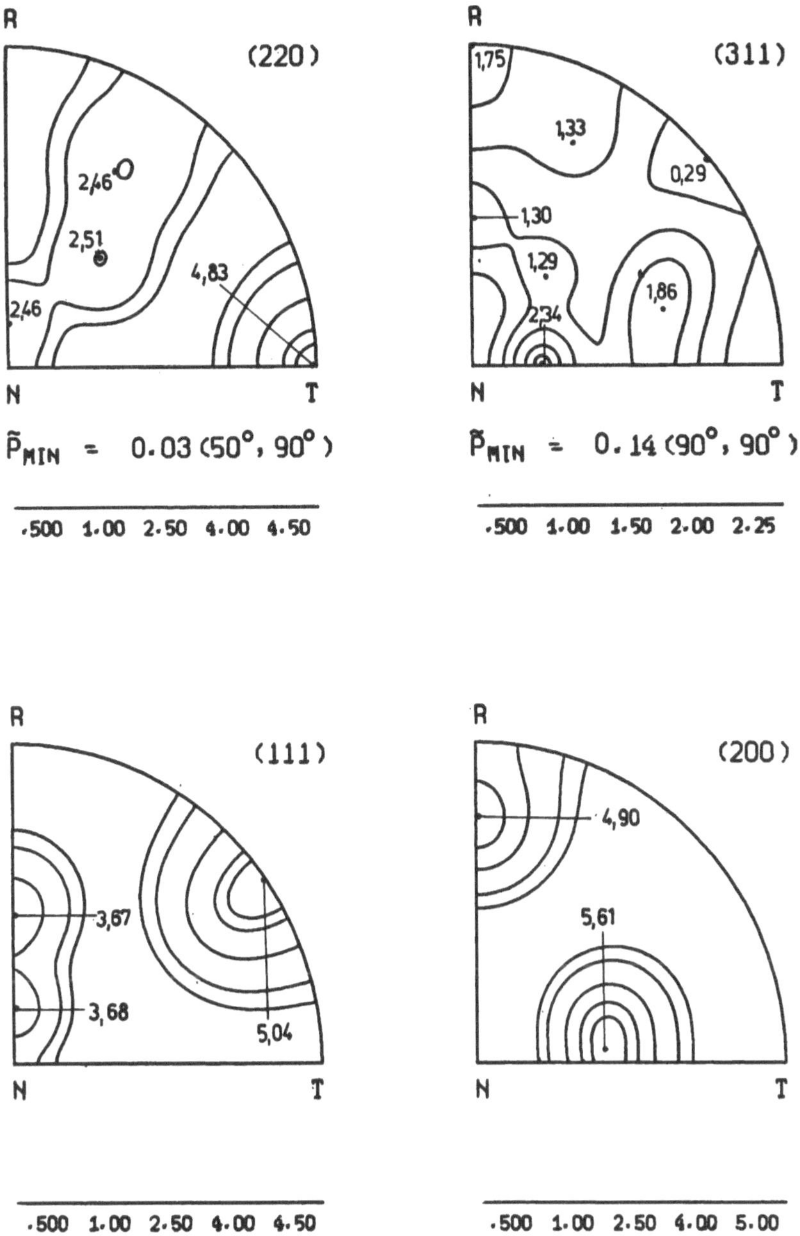

$\tilde{P}$, G, 25.0°, {525}⟨151⟩

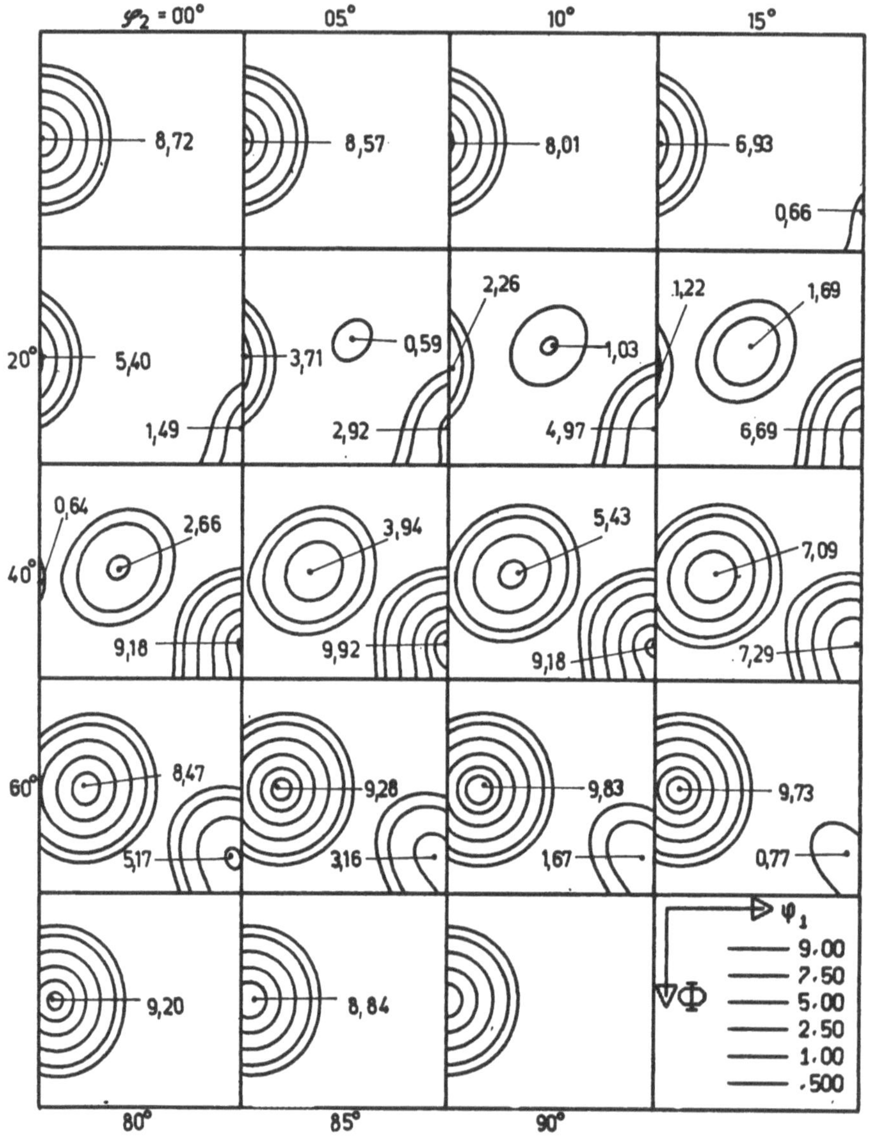

F, G, 30.0°, {525}<151>

F_{MAX} = 9.92 (45°)

$\tilde{F}$, G, 30.0° , {525}<151>

$\tilde{F}_{MAX}$ = 8.84 (45°)

$\tilde{F}_{MIN}$ = −.63 (00°, 05°, . . ., 90°)

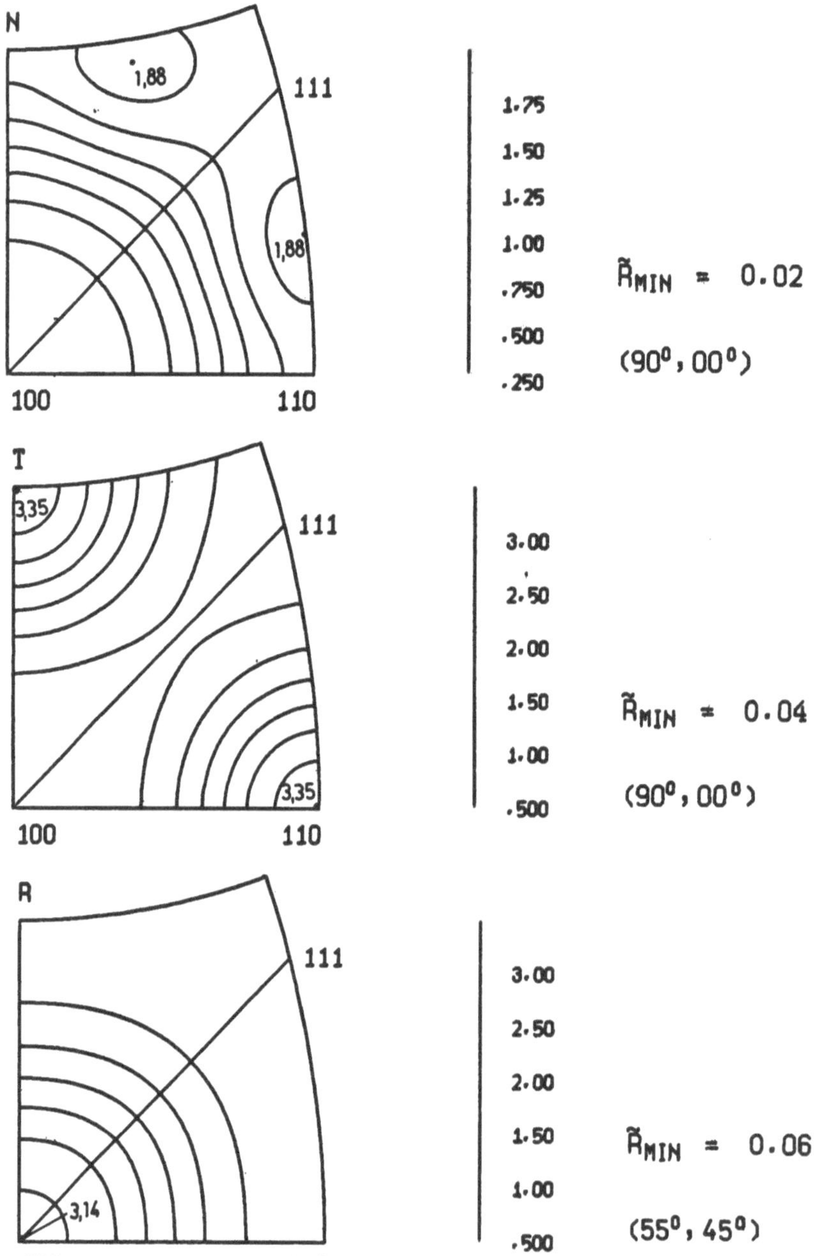

$\tilde{R}$, G, 30.0°, {525}<151>

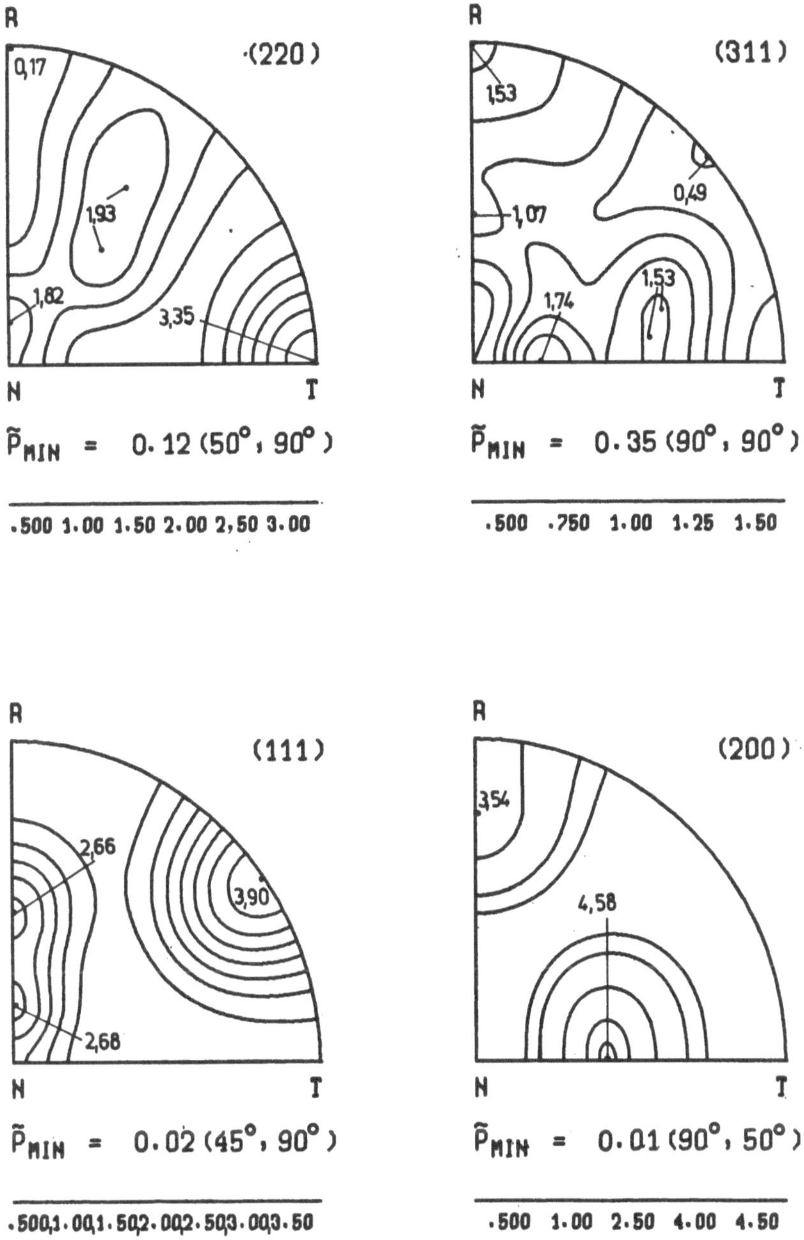

$\tilde{P}$, 6, 30.0°, {525}⟨151⟩

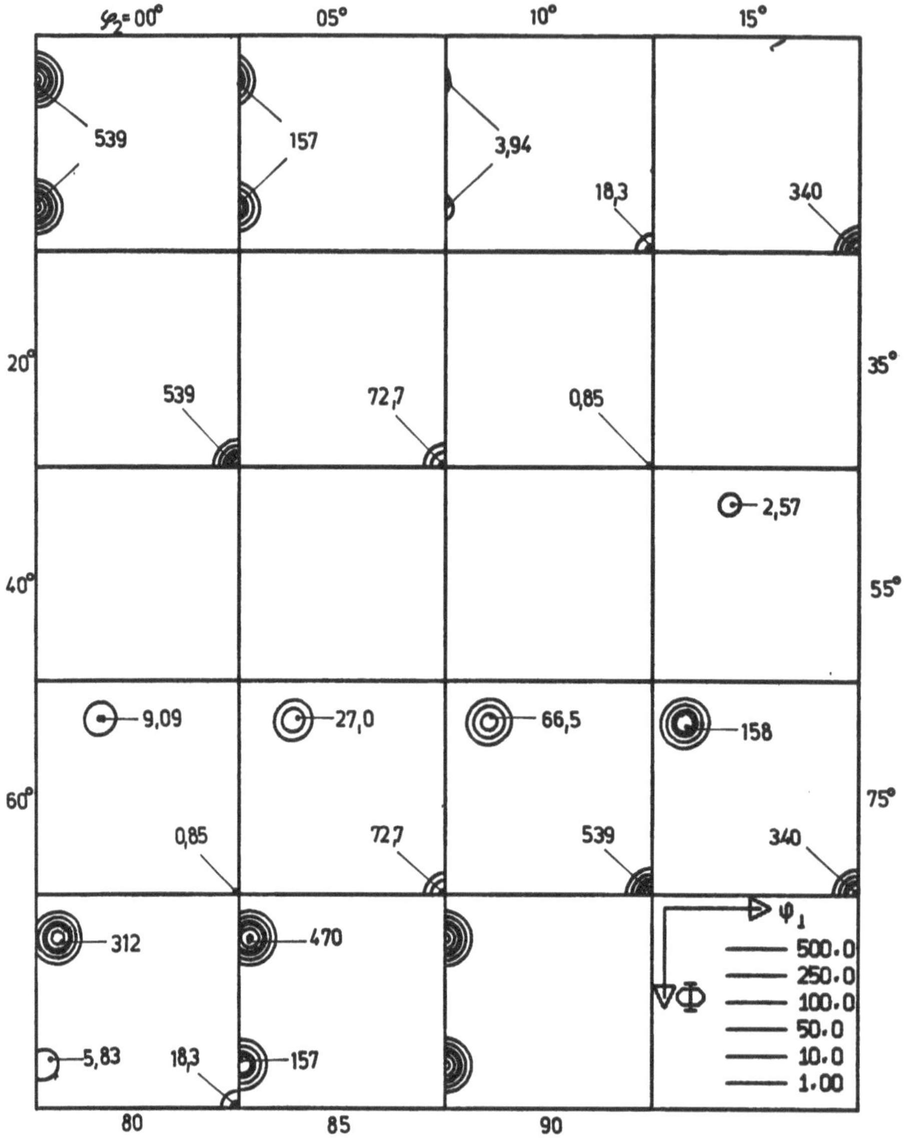

F, G, 7.50° , {013}<100>

F_{MAX} = 538.54 (00°, 20°, 70°, 90°)

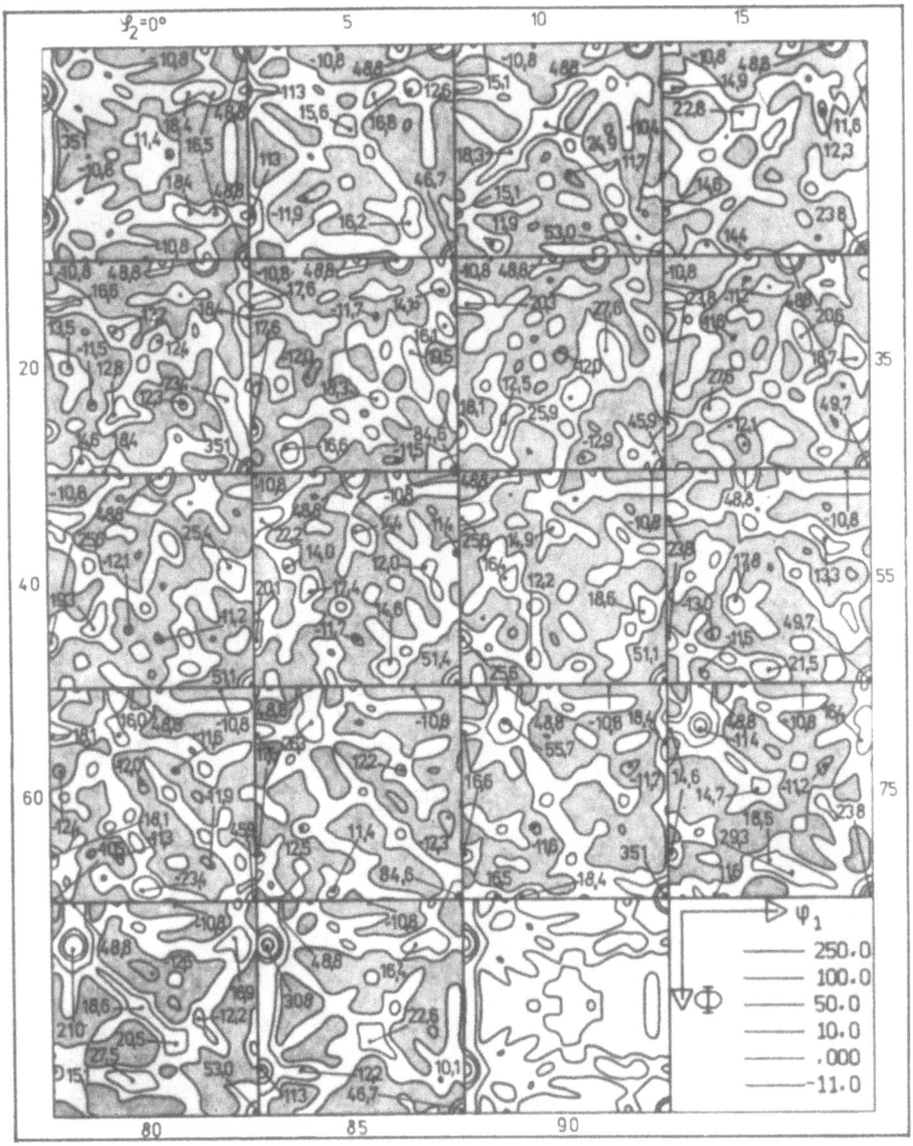

$\tilde{F}$, G, 7.50° , {013}<100>

$\tilde{F}_{MAX}$ = 351.19 (00°, 20°, 70°, 90°)

$\tilde{F}_{MIN}$ = −13.00 (55°)

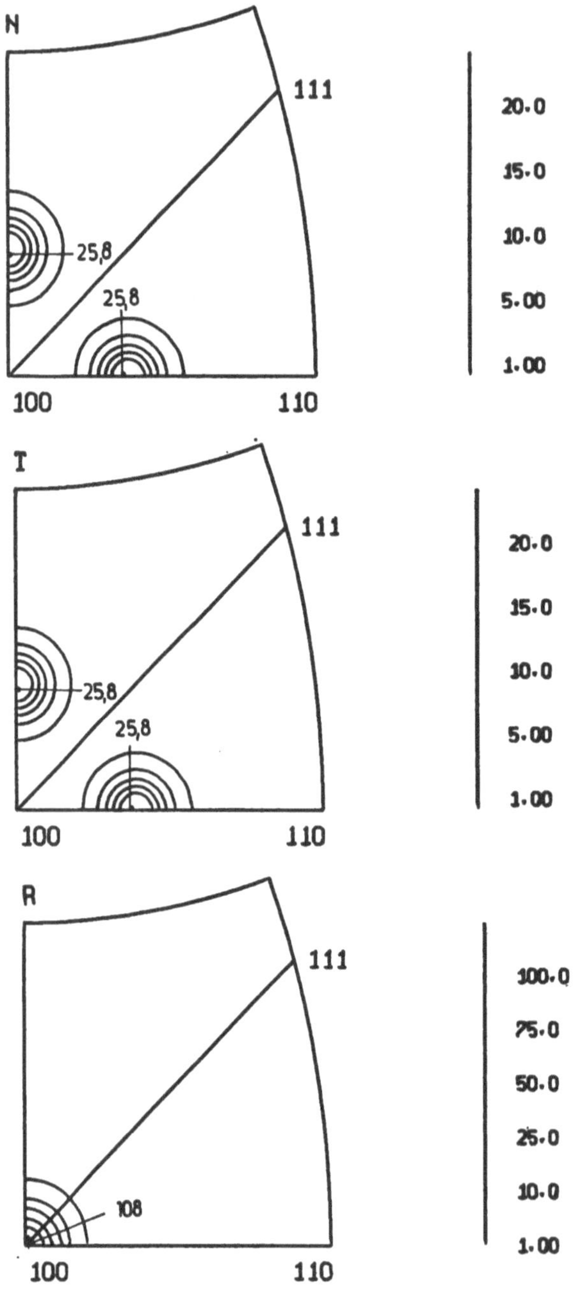

$\tilde{R}$, G, 7.50°, {013}⟨100⟩

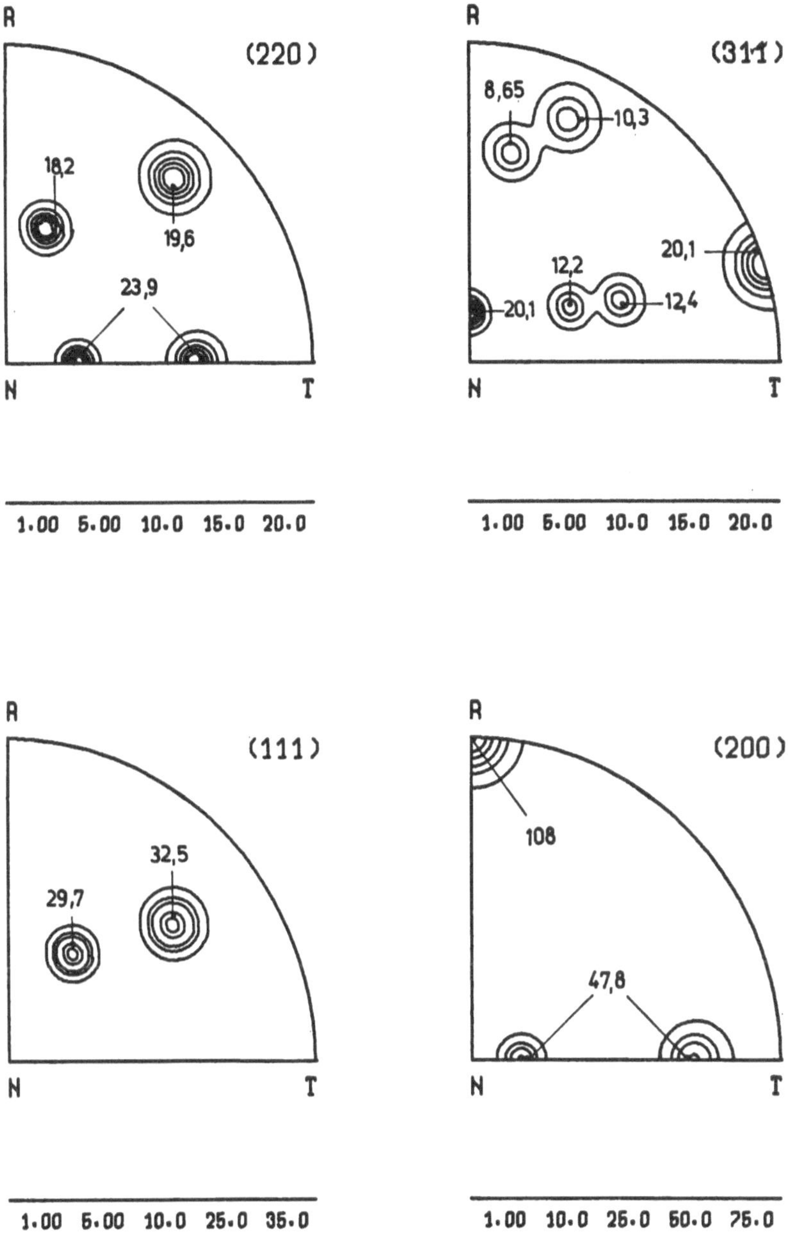

$\tilde{P}$, G, 7.50°, $\{013\}\langle 100\rangle$

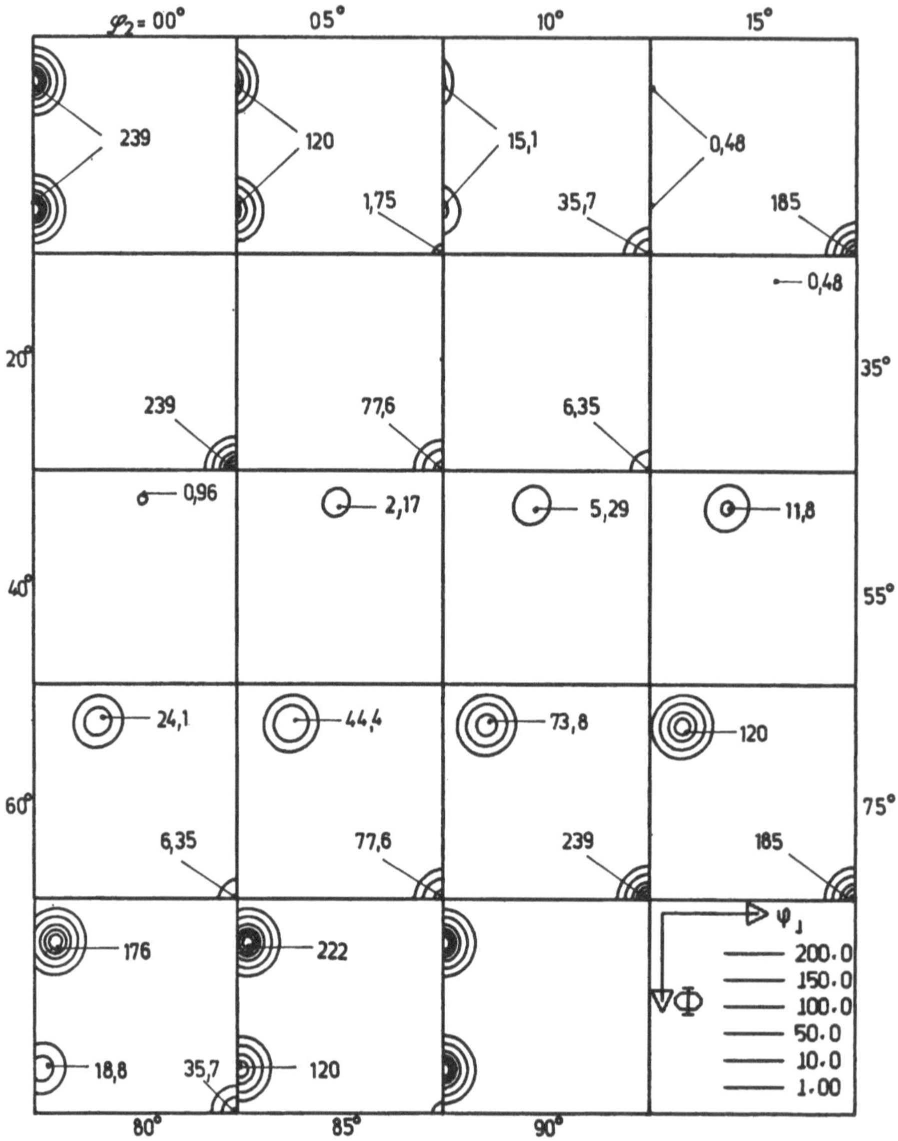

F, G, 10.0°, {013}<100>

F_{MAX} = 239.40 (00°, 20°, 70°, 90°)

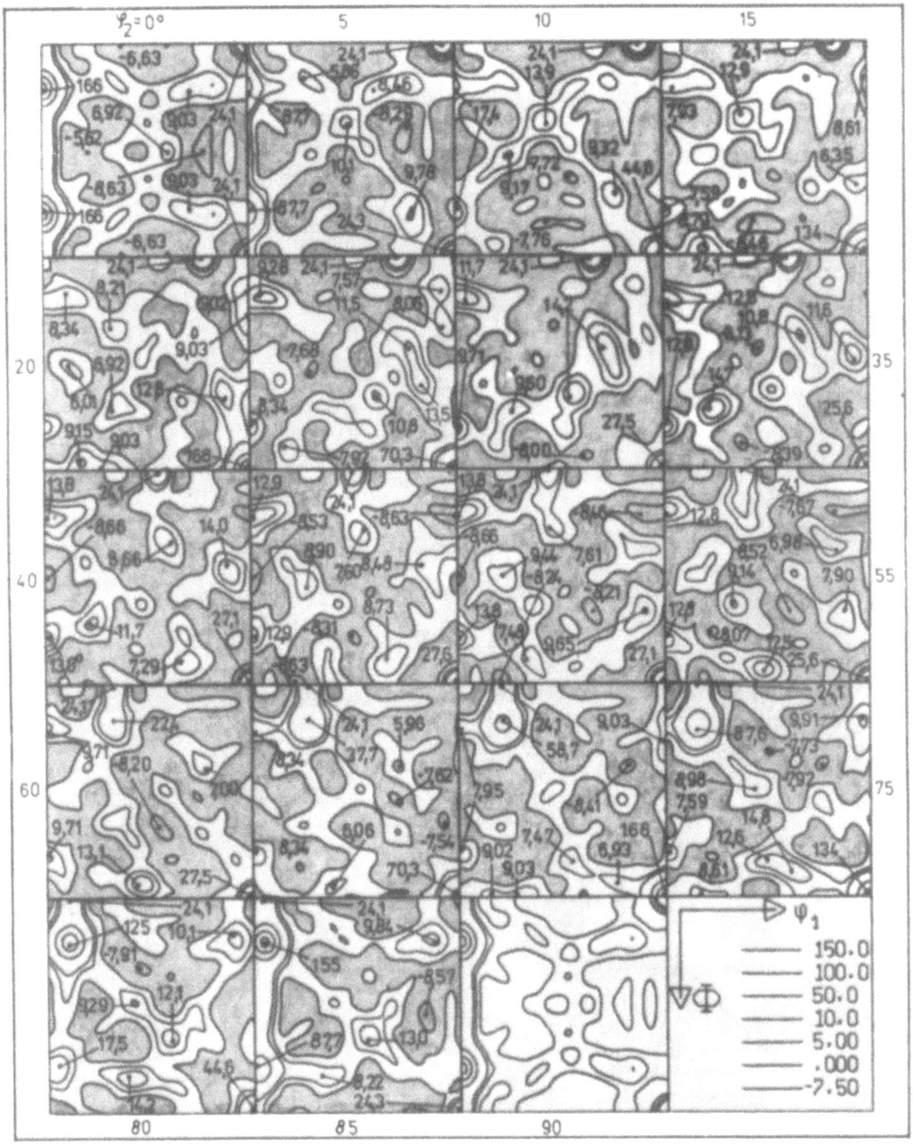

$\tilde{F}$, G, 10.0°, $\{013\}\langle 100\rangle$

$\tilde{F}_{MAX}$ = 166.39 (00°, 20°, 70°, 90°)

$\tilde{F}_{MIN}$ = −8.66 (40°, 50°)

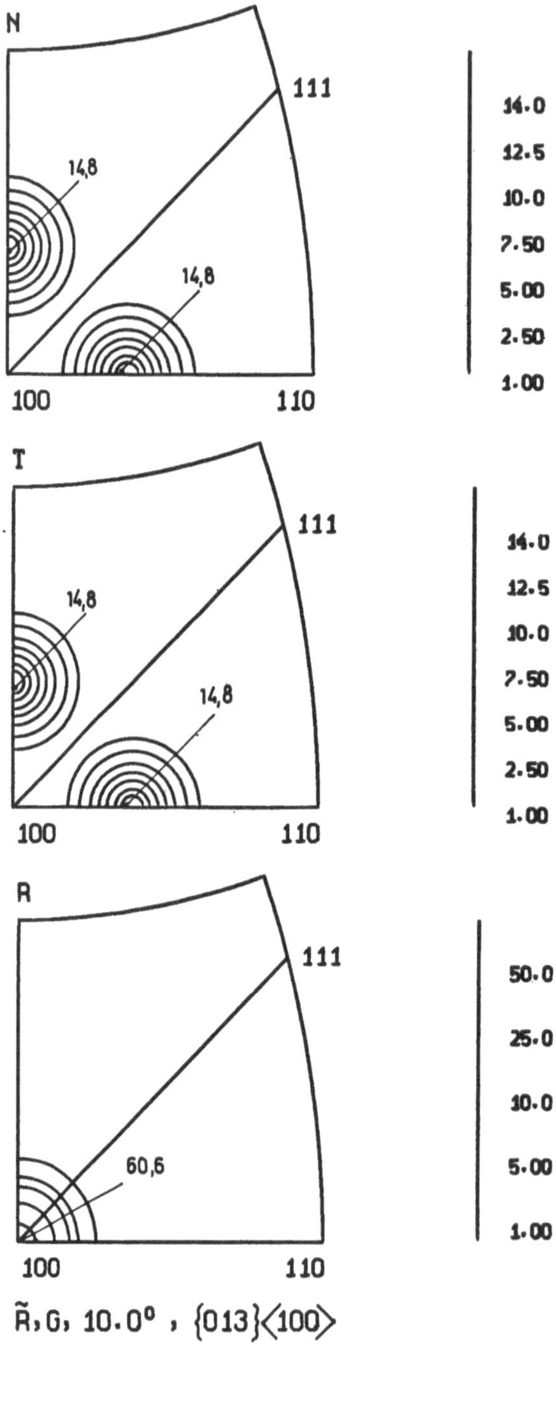

$\tilde{R}$, G, 10.0°, {013}⟨100⟩

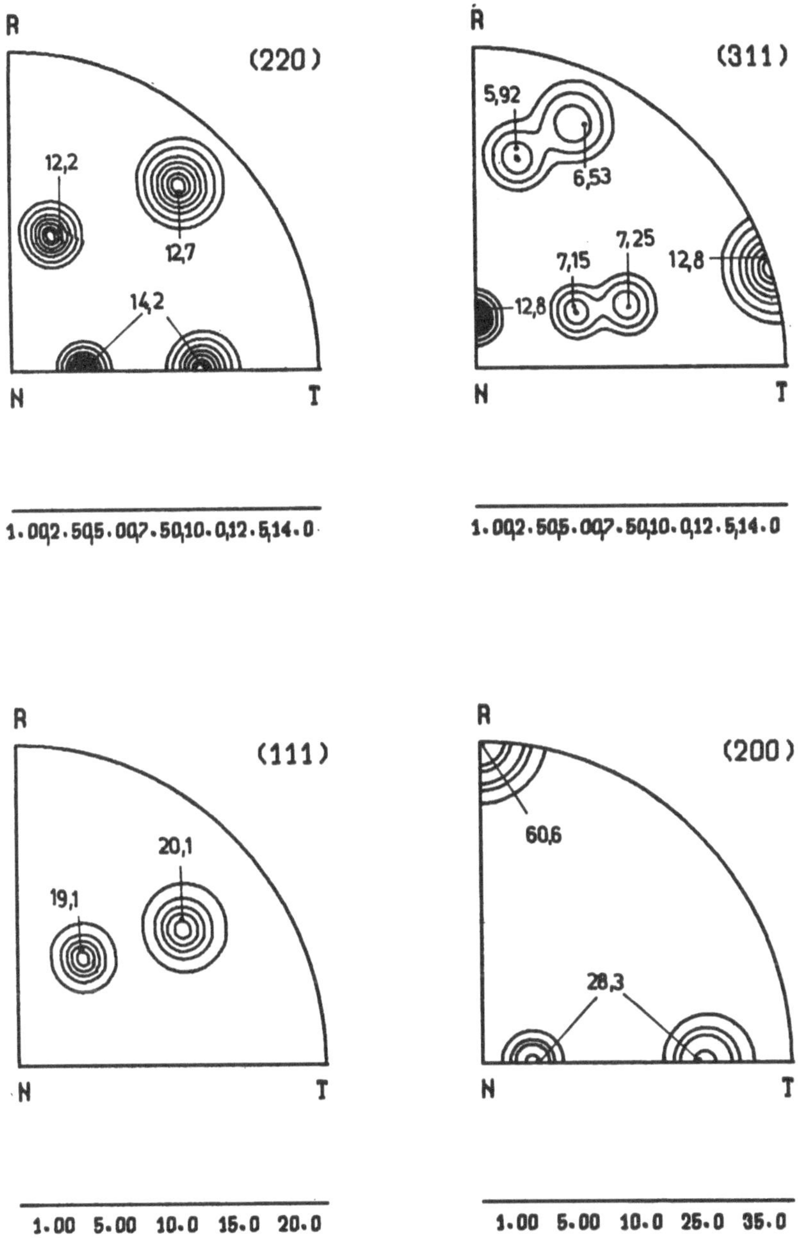

$\tilde{P}$, G, 10.0°, $\{0\dot{1}3\}\langle 100\rangle$

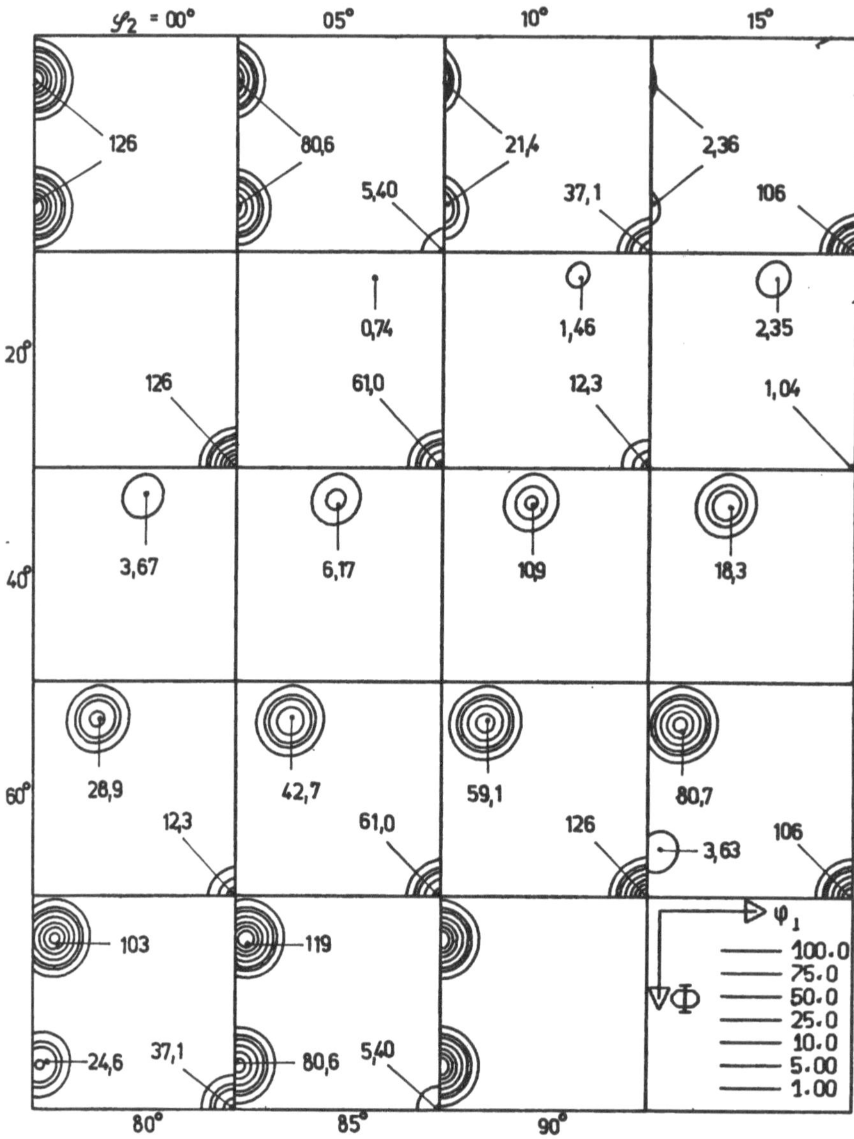

F, G, 12.5°, {013}<100>

F_{MAX} = 125.53 (00°, 20°, 70°, 90°)

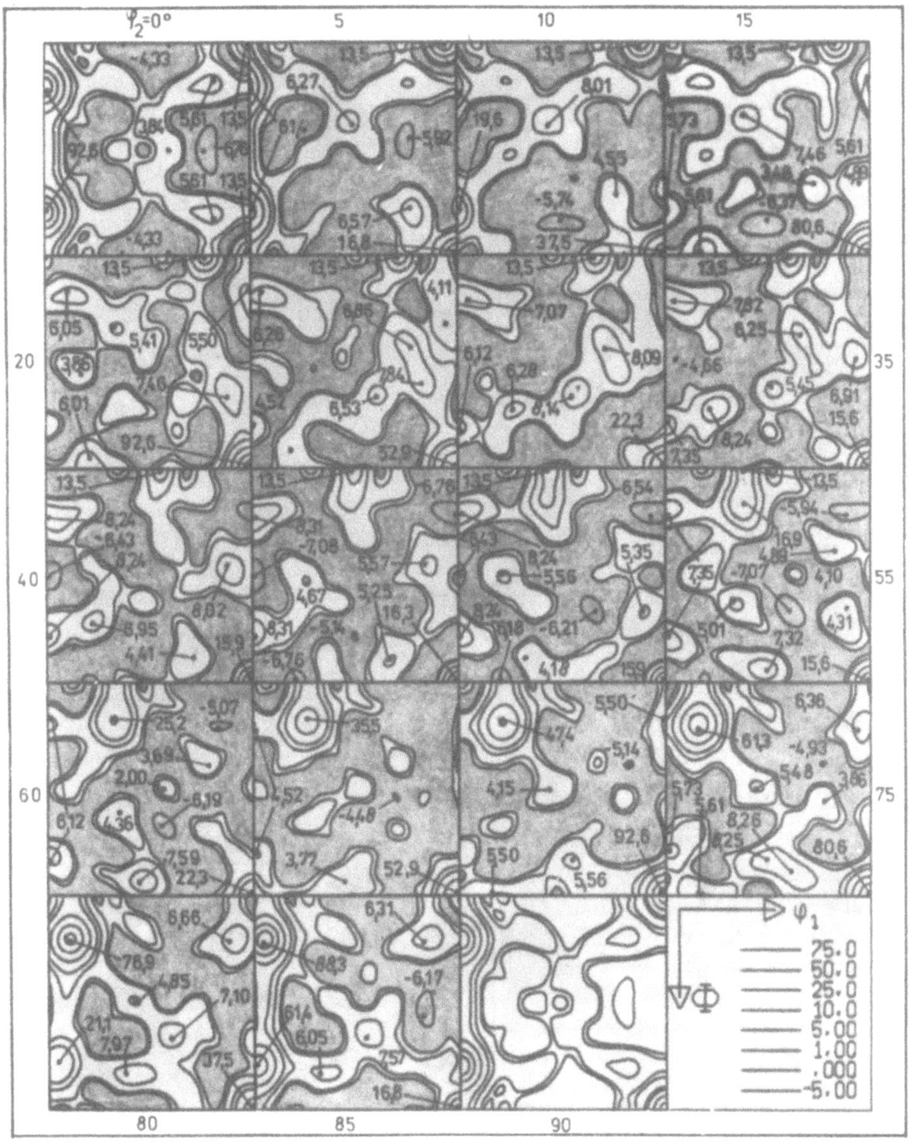

$\tilde{F}$, G, 12.5°, $\{013\}\langle 100\rangle$

$\tilde{F}_{MAX}$ = 92.55 (00°, 20°, 70°, 90°)

$\tilde{F}_{MIN}$ = -7.08 (45°)

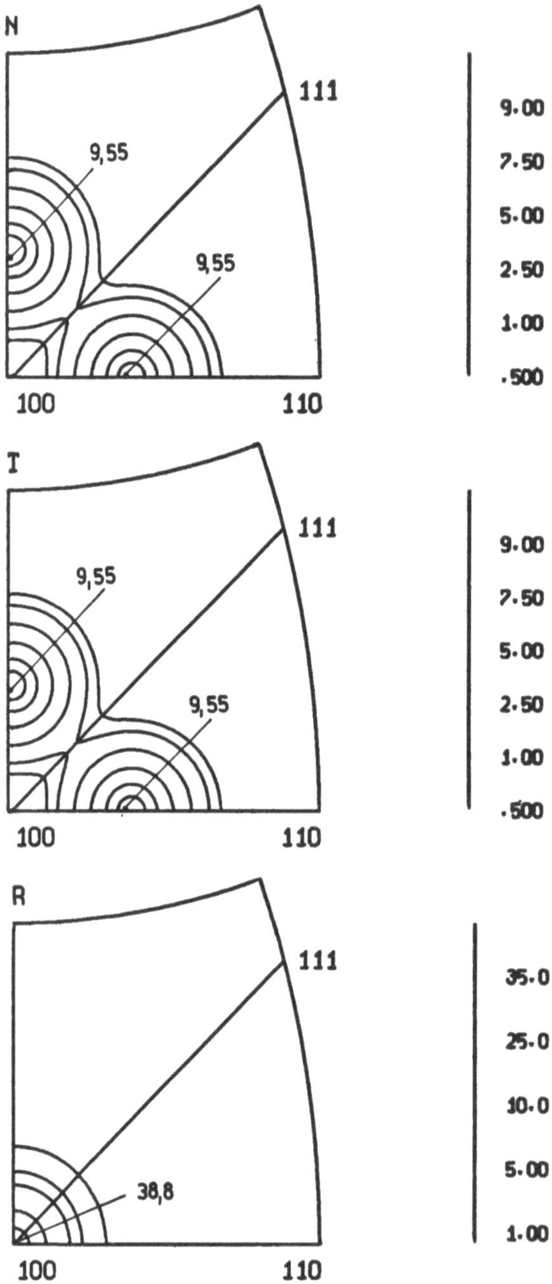

R̃, G, 12.5° , {013}<100>

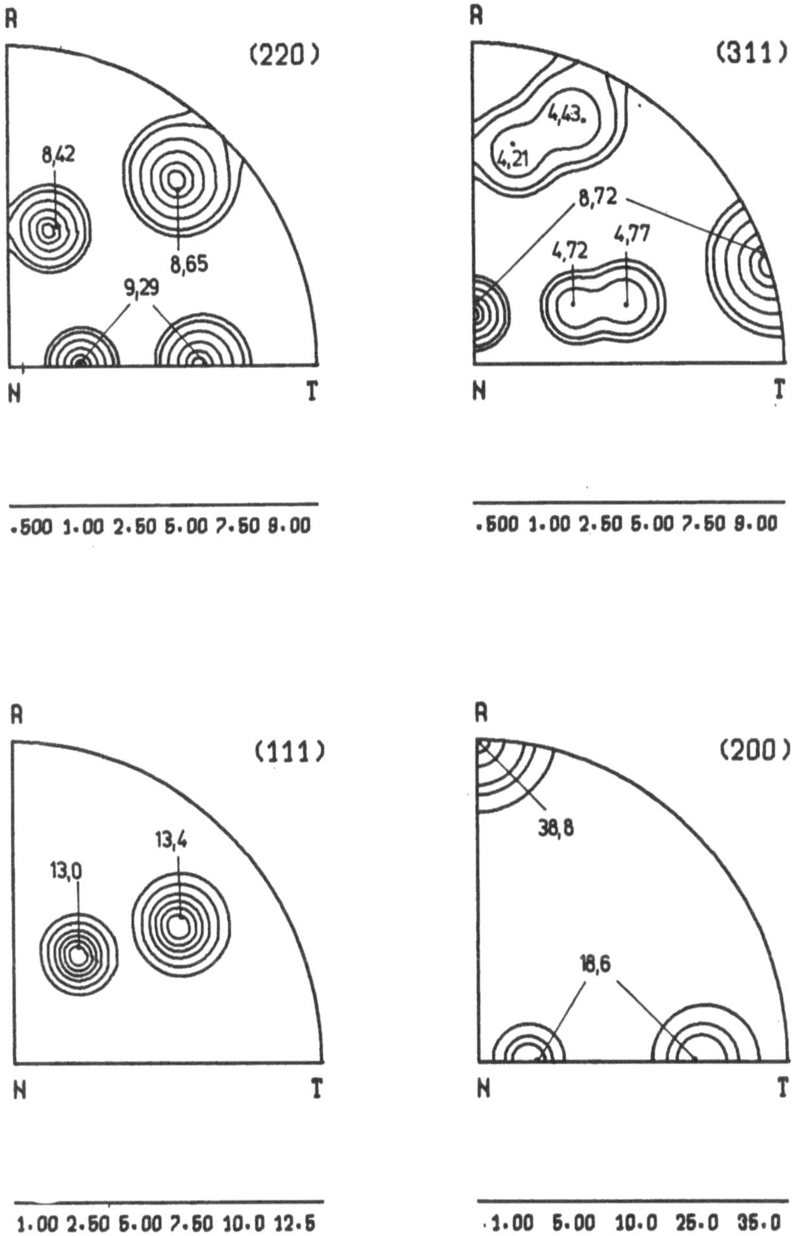

$\tilde{P}$, G, 12.5°, {013}⟨100⟩

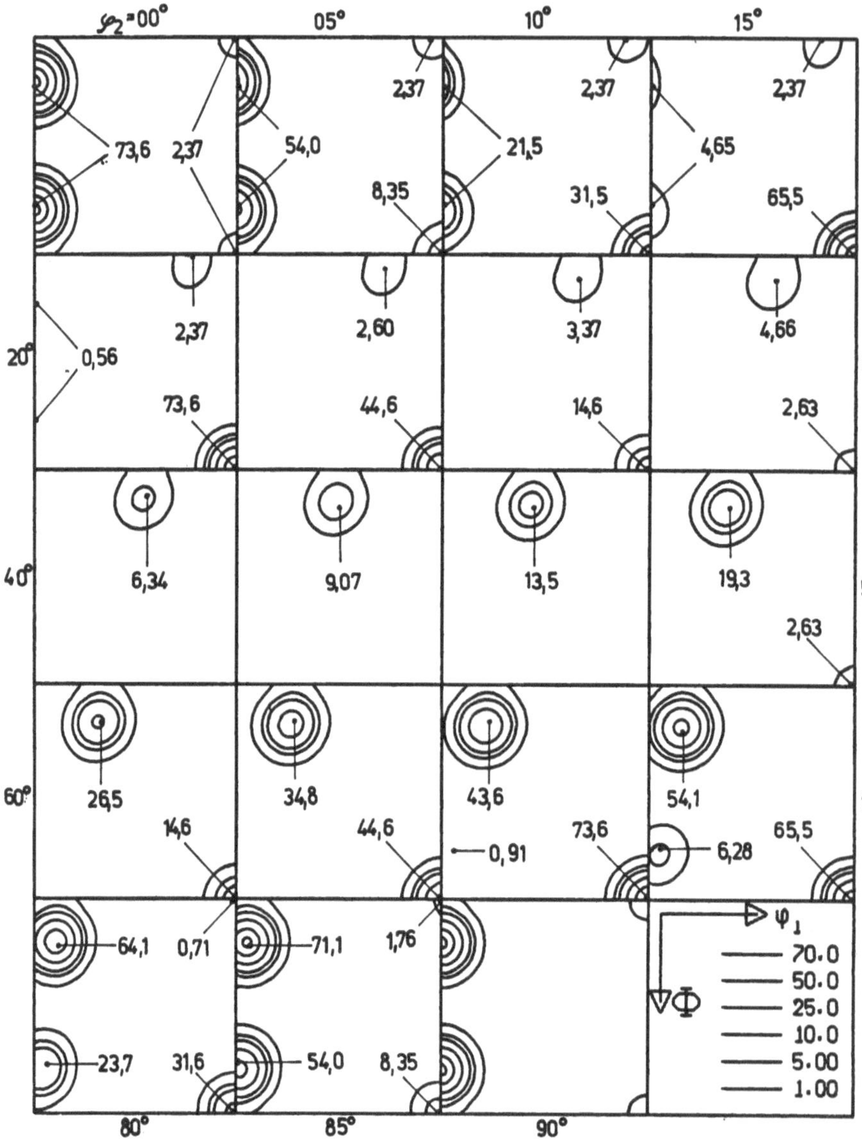

F, G, 15.0°, {013}<100>

F_{MAX} = 73.56 (00°, 20°, 70°, 90°)

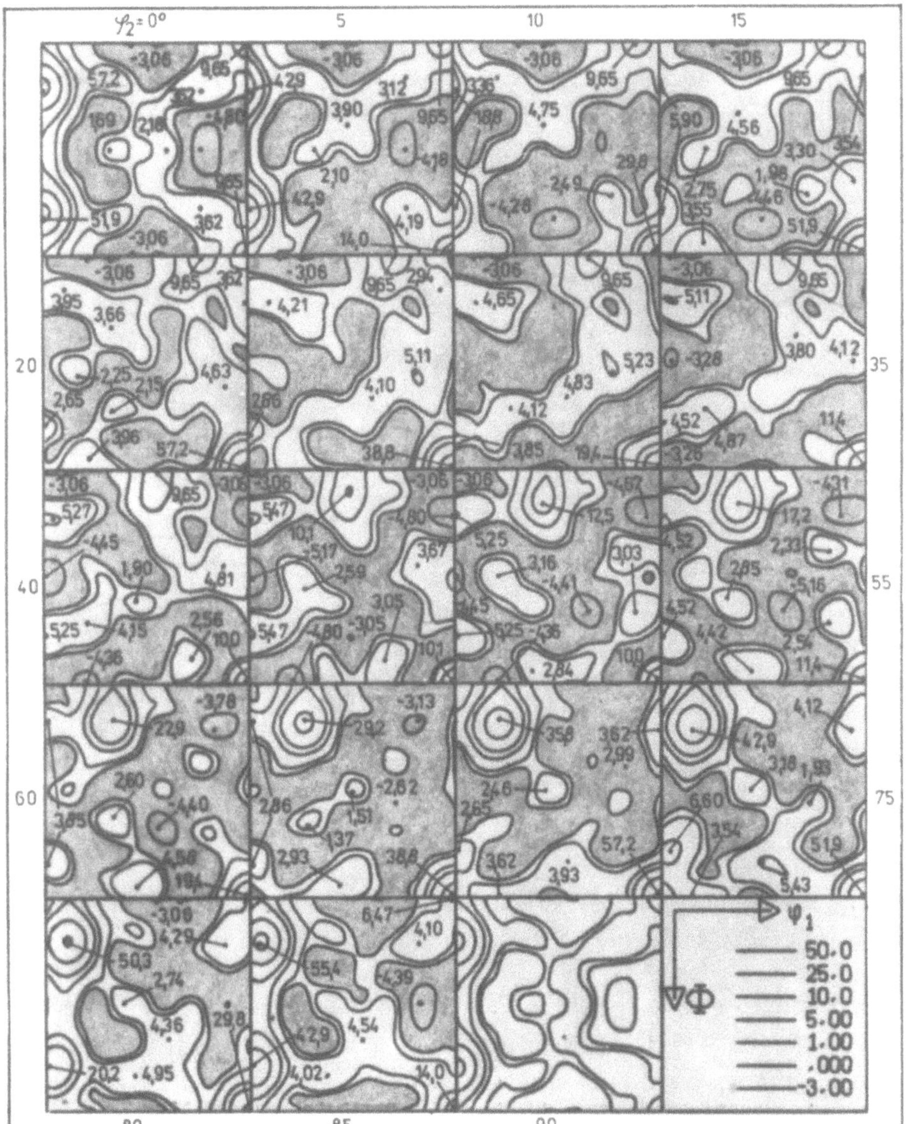

$\tilde{F}$, G, 15.0° , {013}<100>

$\tilde{F}_{MAX}$ = 57.18 (00°, 20°, 70°, 90°)

$\tilde{F}_{MIN}$ = −5.17 (45°)

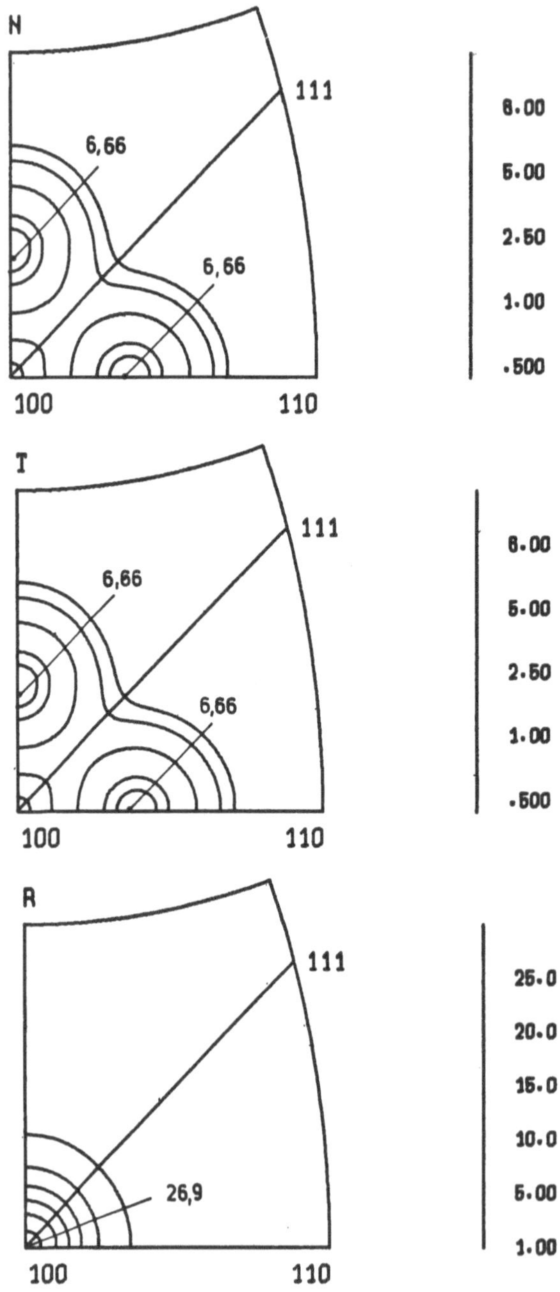

R̃, G, 15.0°, $\{013\}\langle 100\rangle$

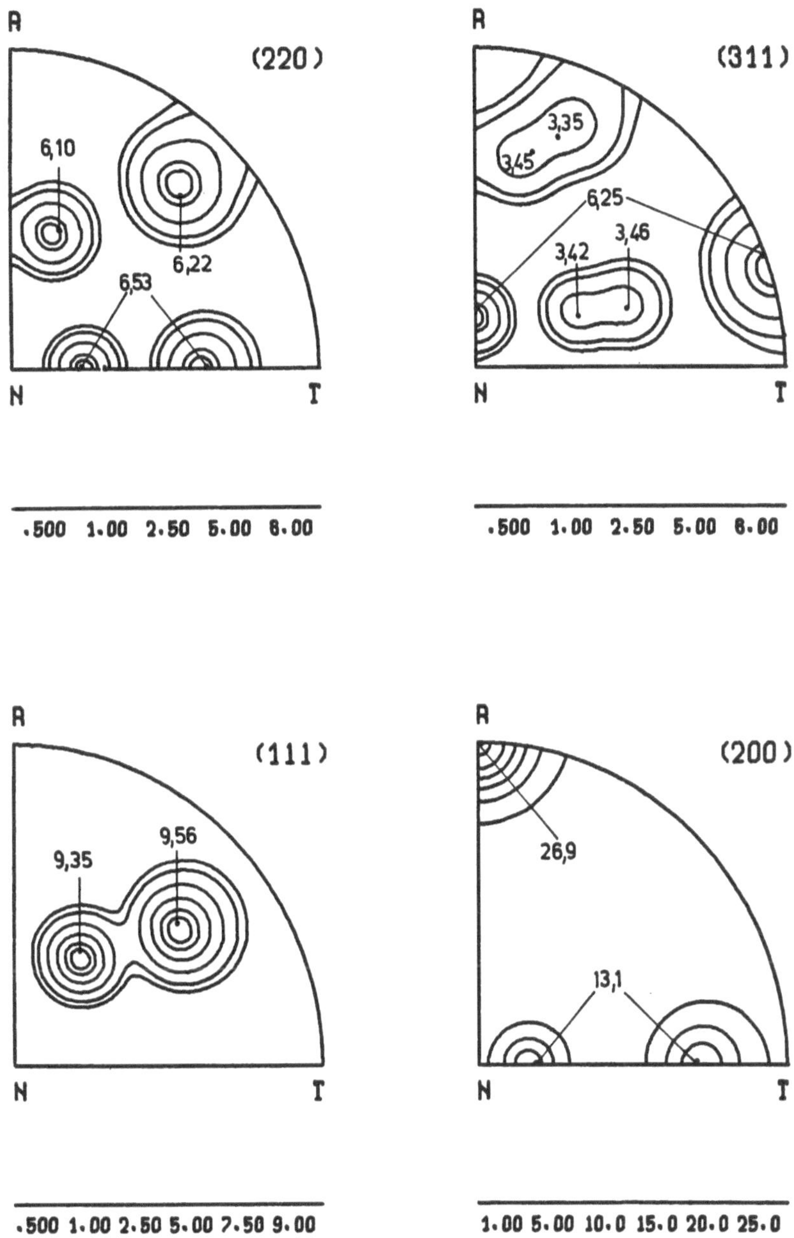

$\tilde{P}$, G, 15.0°, {013}⟨100⟩

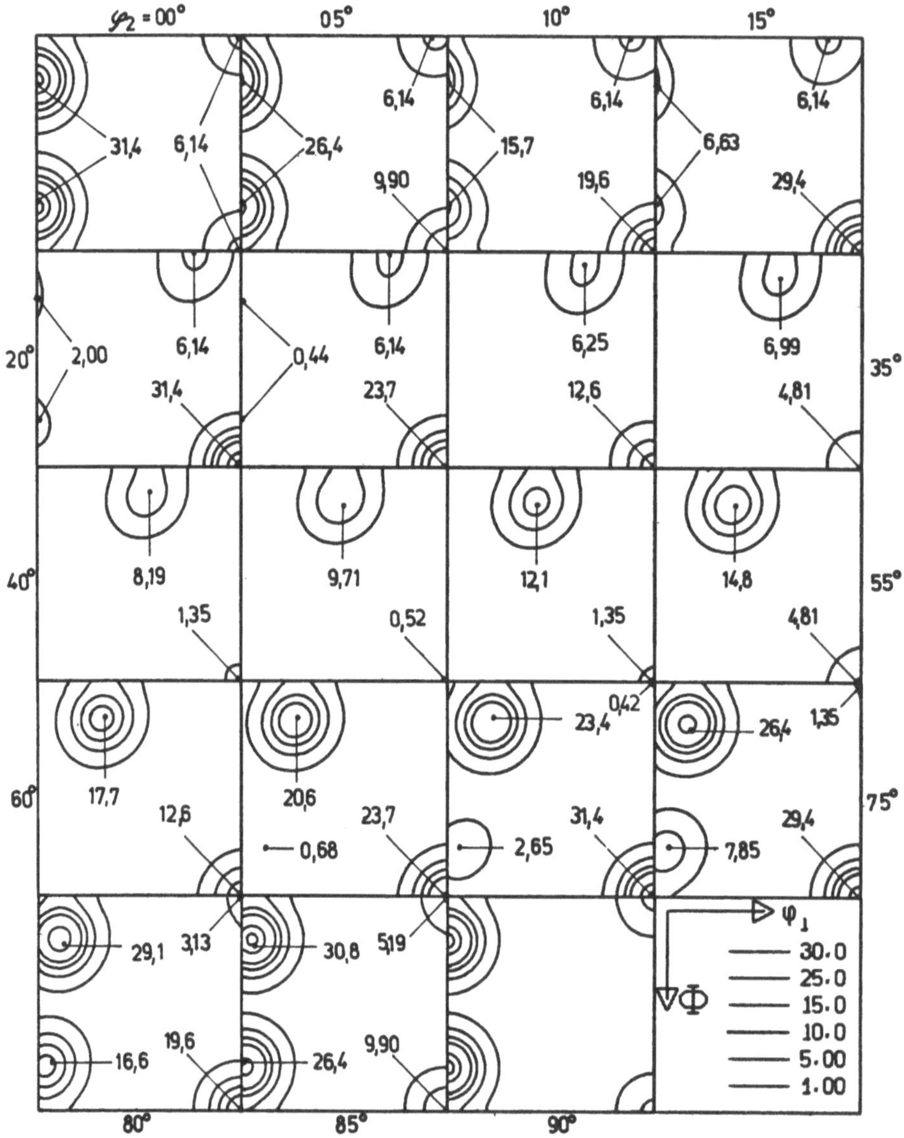

F, G, 20.0°, {013}<100>

F_{MAX} = 31.38 (00°, 20°, 70°, 90°)

$\tilde{F}$, G, 20.0°, {013}<100>

$\tilde{F}_{MAX}$ = 26.54 (00°, 20°, 70°, 90°)

$\tilde{F}_{MIN}$ = -2.58 (45°, 55°)

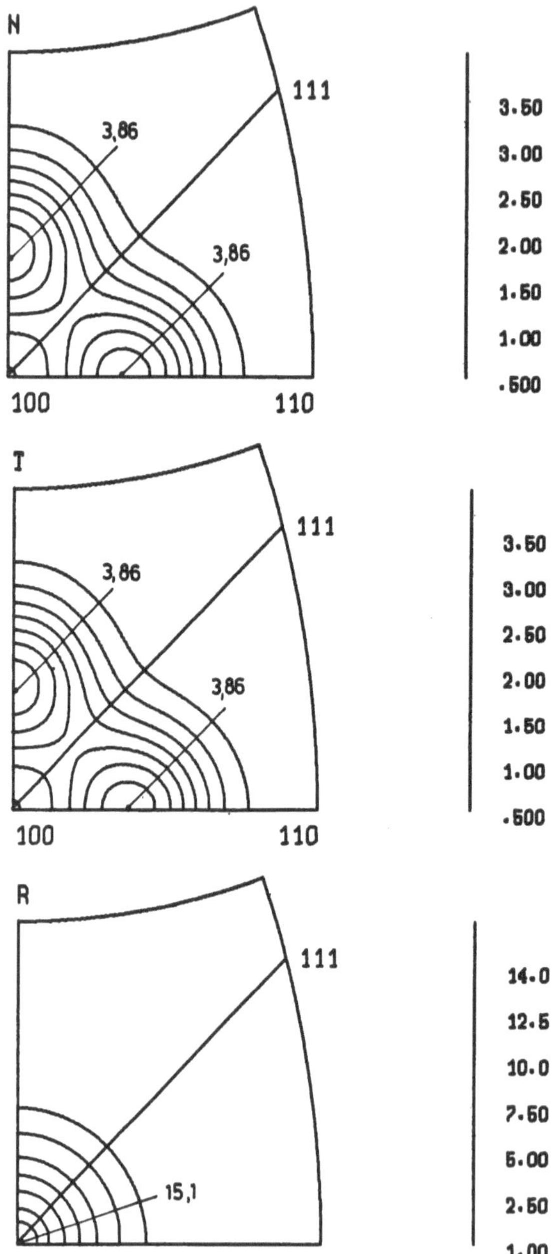

$\tilde{R}$, G, 20.0°, {013}⟨100⟩

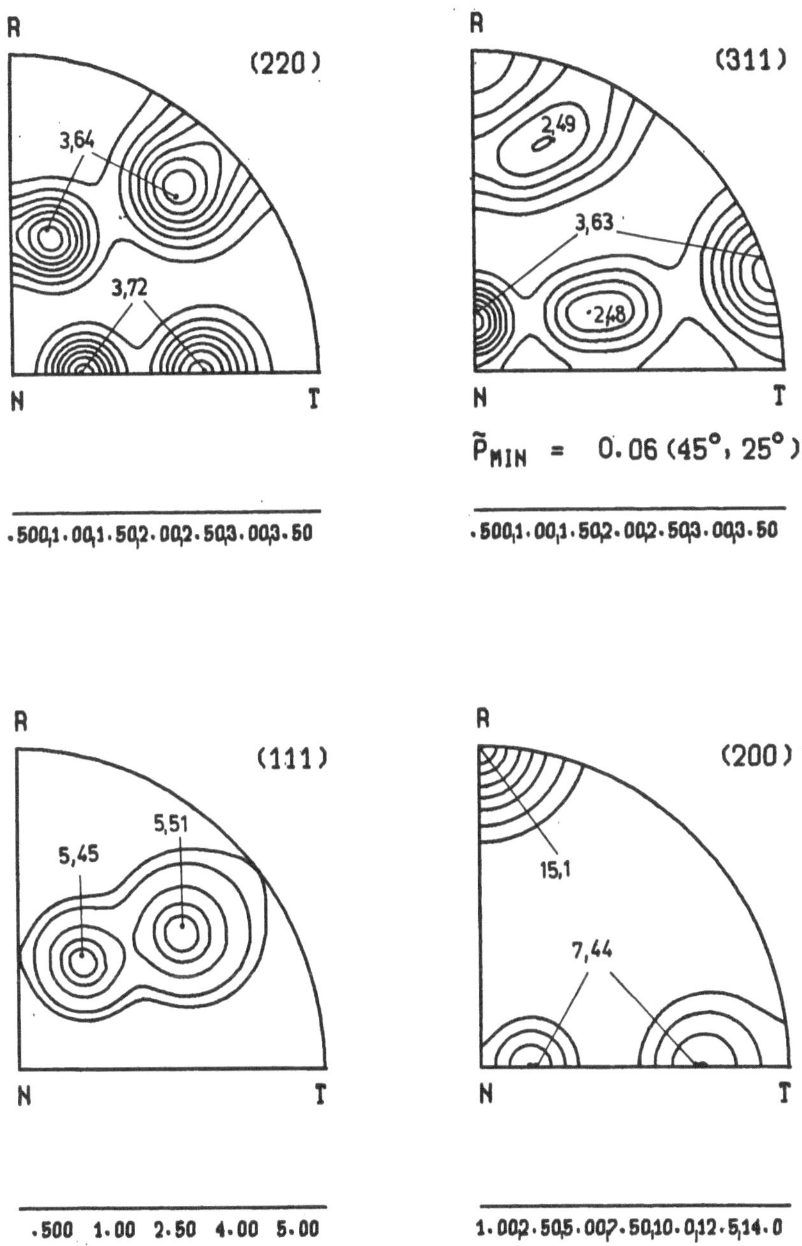

$\tilde{P}$, G, 20.0°, {013}⟨100⟩

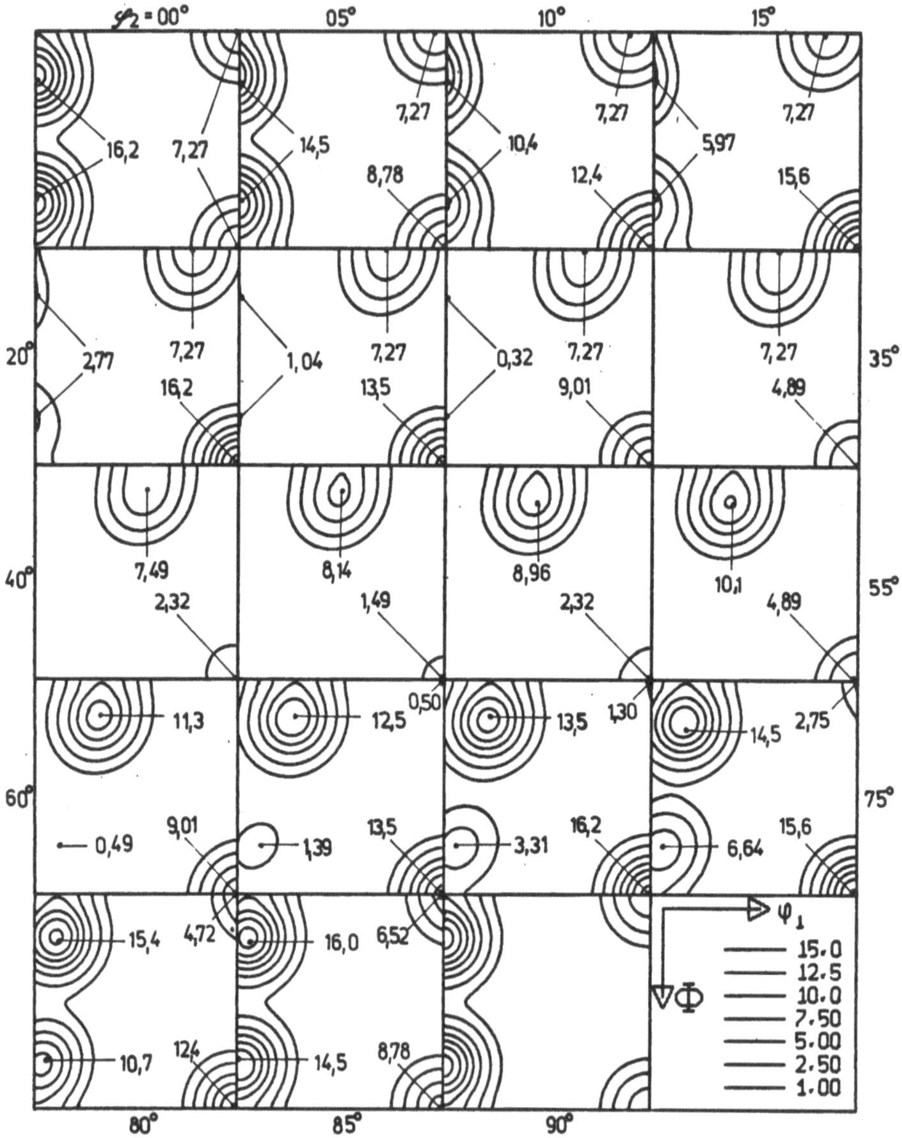

F, G, 25.0°, {013}<100>

F_{MAX} = 16.15 (00°, 20°, 70°, 90°)

$\tilde{F}$, G, 25.0°, {013}<100>

$\tilde{F}_{MAX}$ = 14.46 (00°, 20°, 70°, 90°)

$\tilde{F}_{MIN}$ = -1.35 (00°, 45°, 90°)

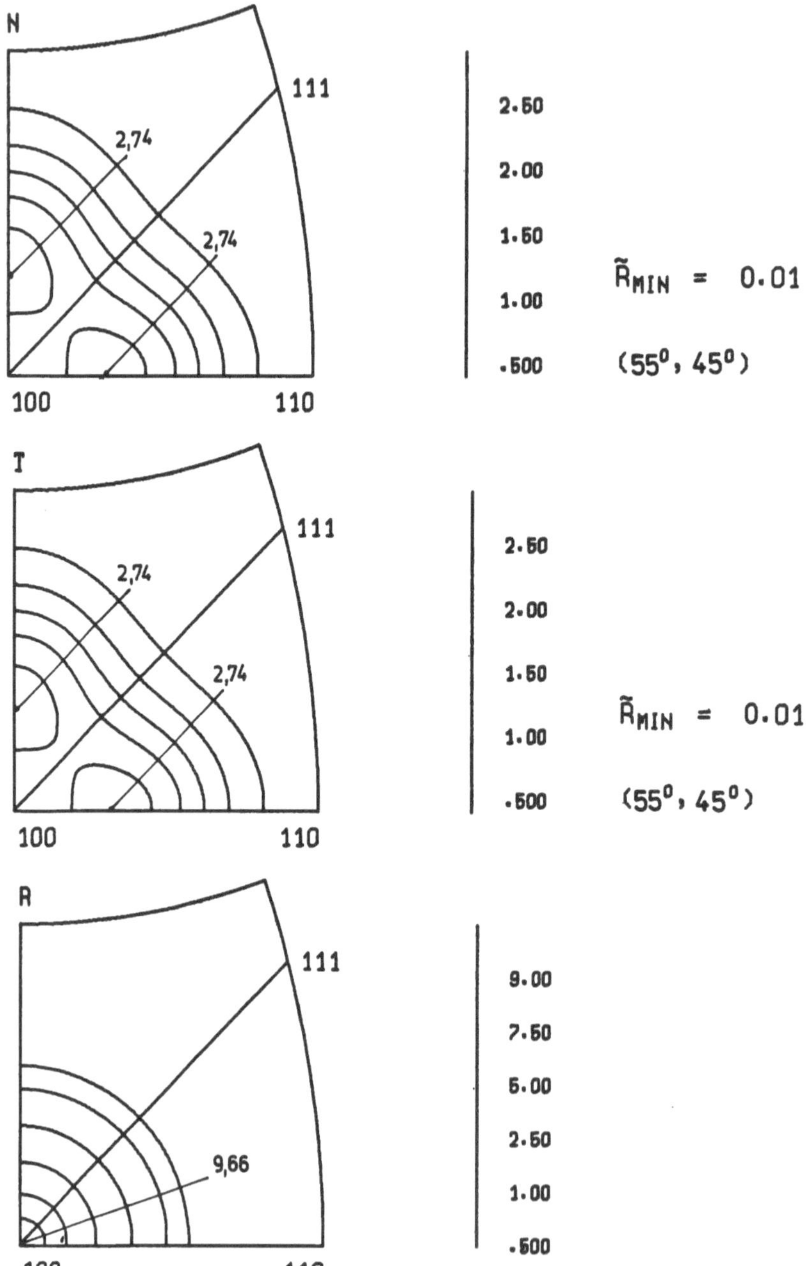

$\tilde{R}$, G, 25.0^0 , $\{013\}\langle 100 \rangle$

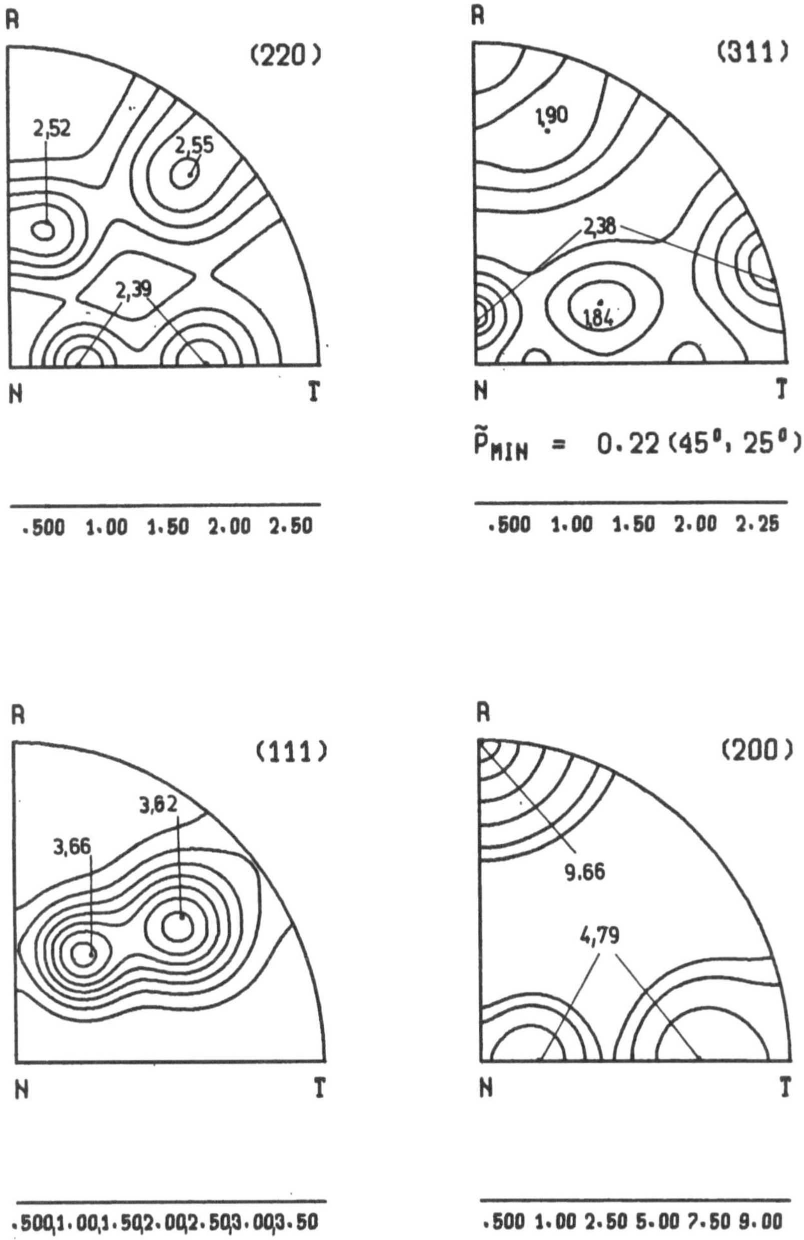

$\tilde{P}$, G, 25.0°, {013}⟨100⟩

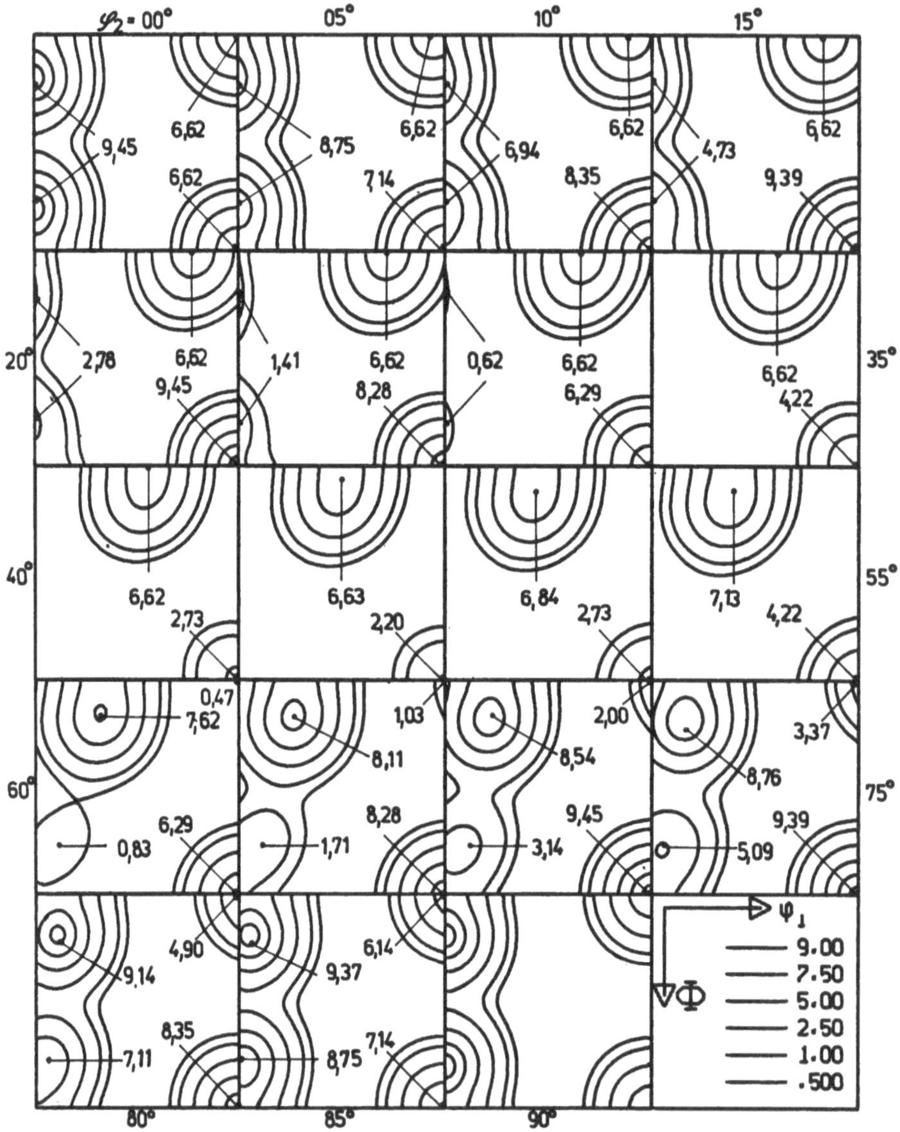

F, G, 30.0°, {013}<100>

F_{MAX} = 9.45 (00°, 20°, 70°, 90°)

$\tilde{F}$, G, 30.0°, {013}<100>

$\tilde{F}_{MAX}$ = 8.79 (00°, 15°, 20°, 70°, 75°, 90°)

$\tilde{F}_{MIN}$ = -.63 (00°, 45°, 90°)

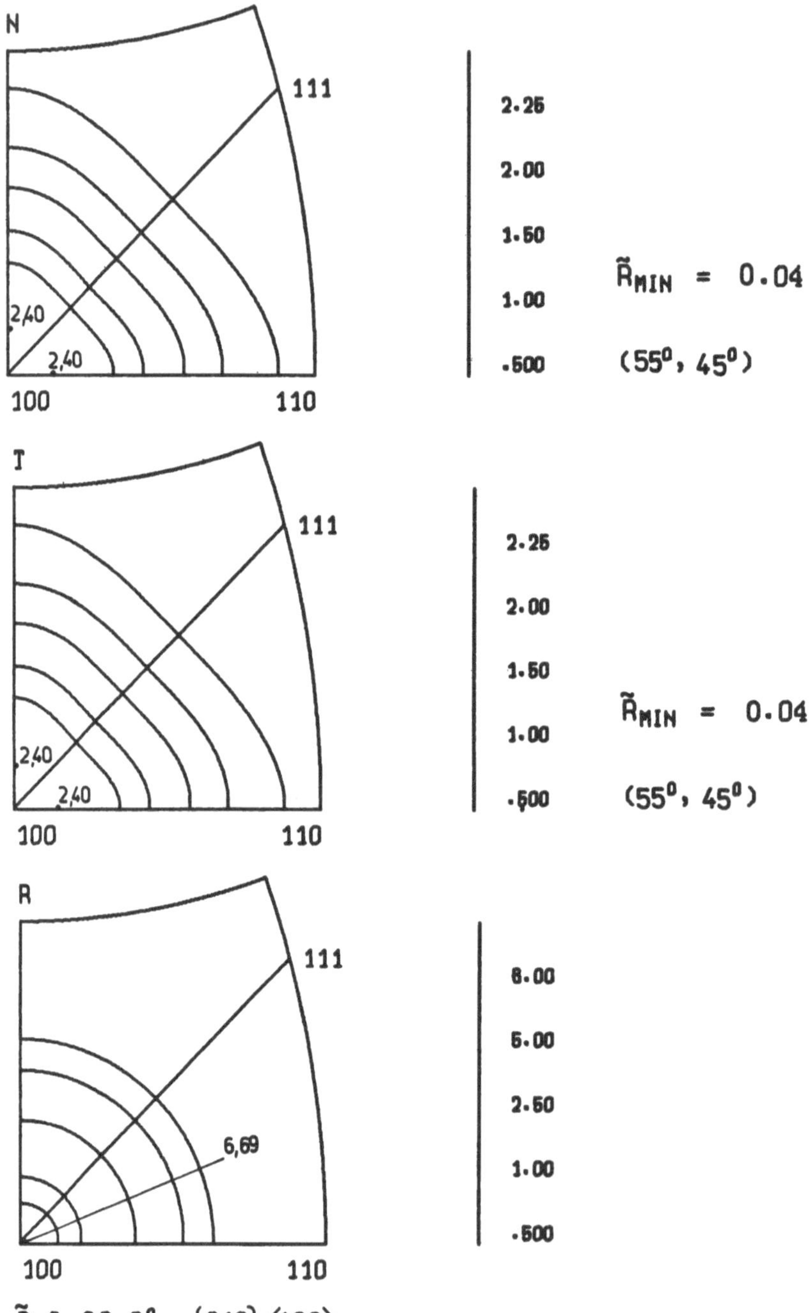

R̃, G, 30.0°, {013}<100>

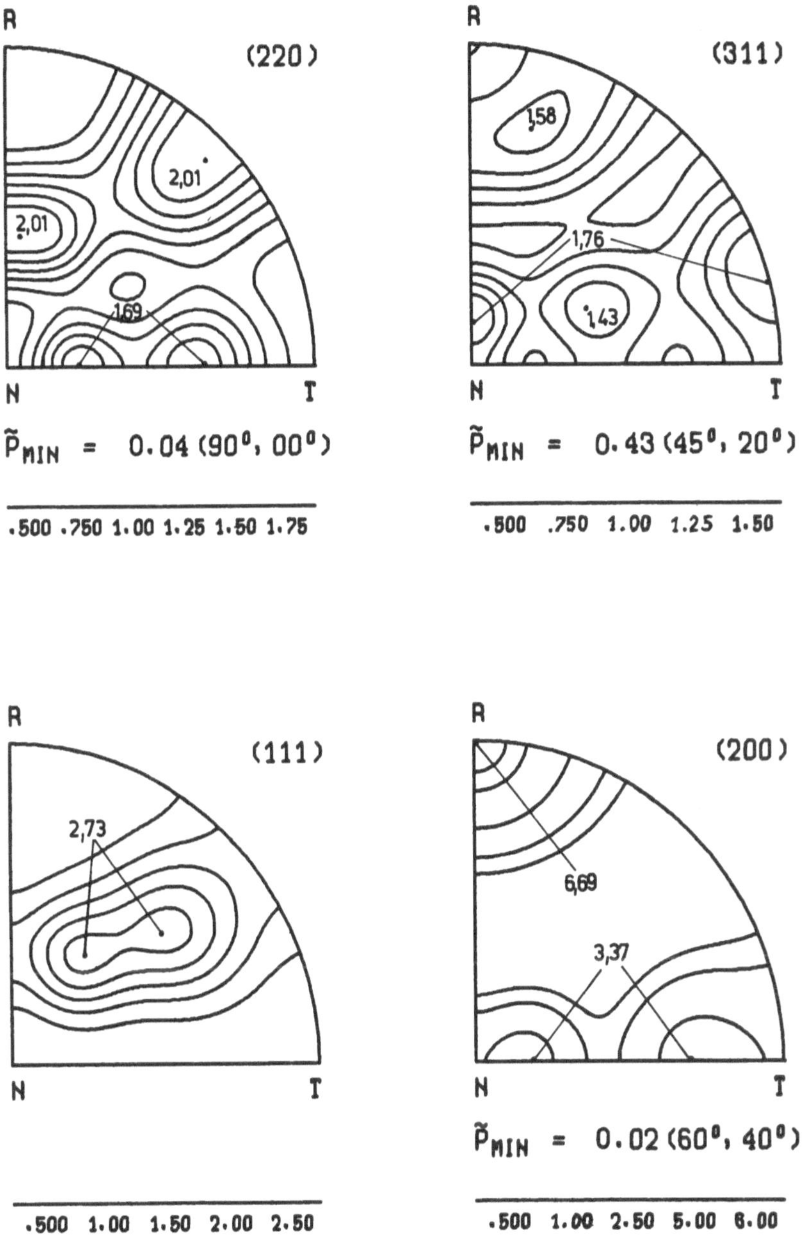

$\tilde{P}$, G, 30.0° , {013}⟨100⟩

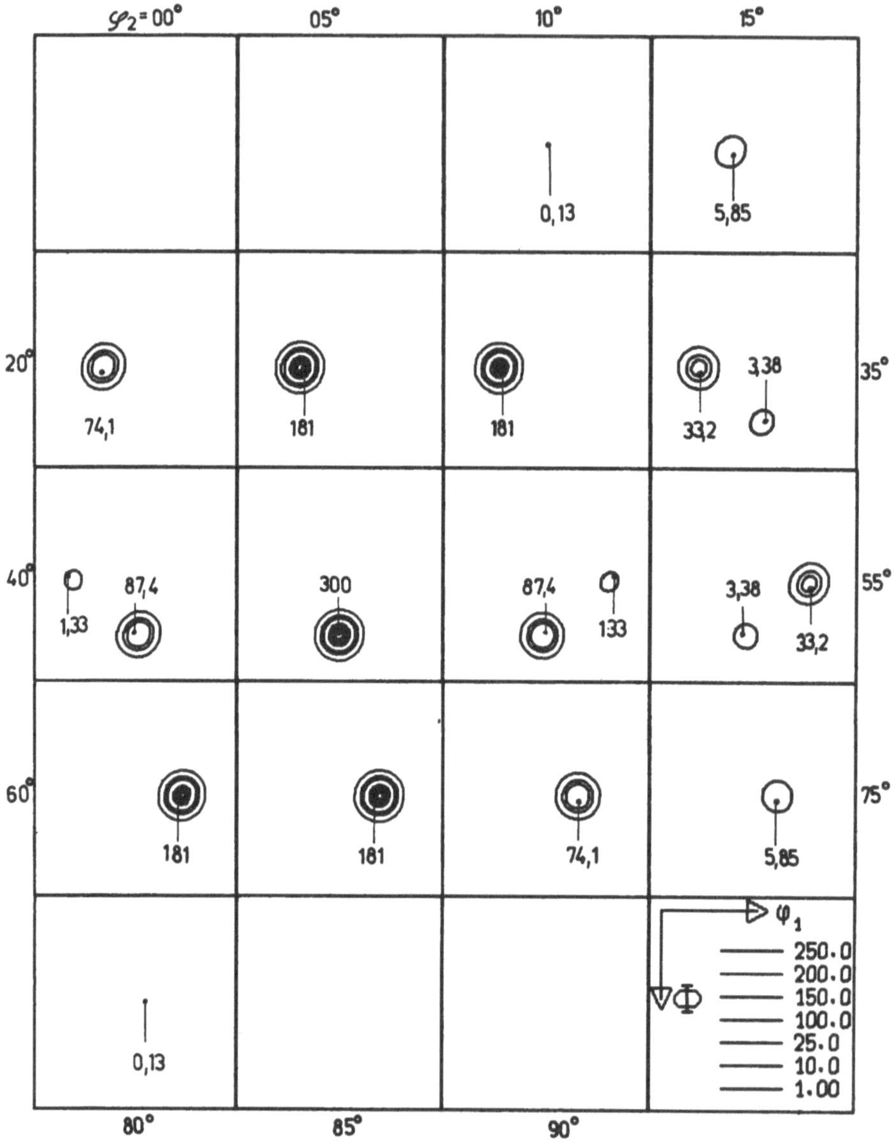

F, G, 7.50°, {122}<221>

F_{MAX} = 299.67 (45°)

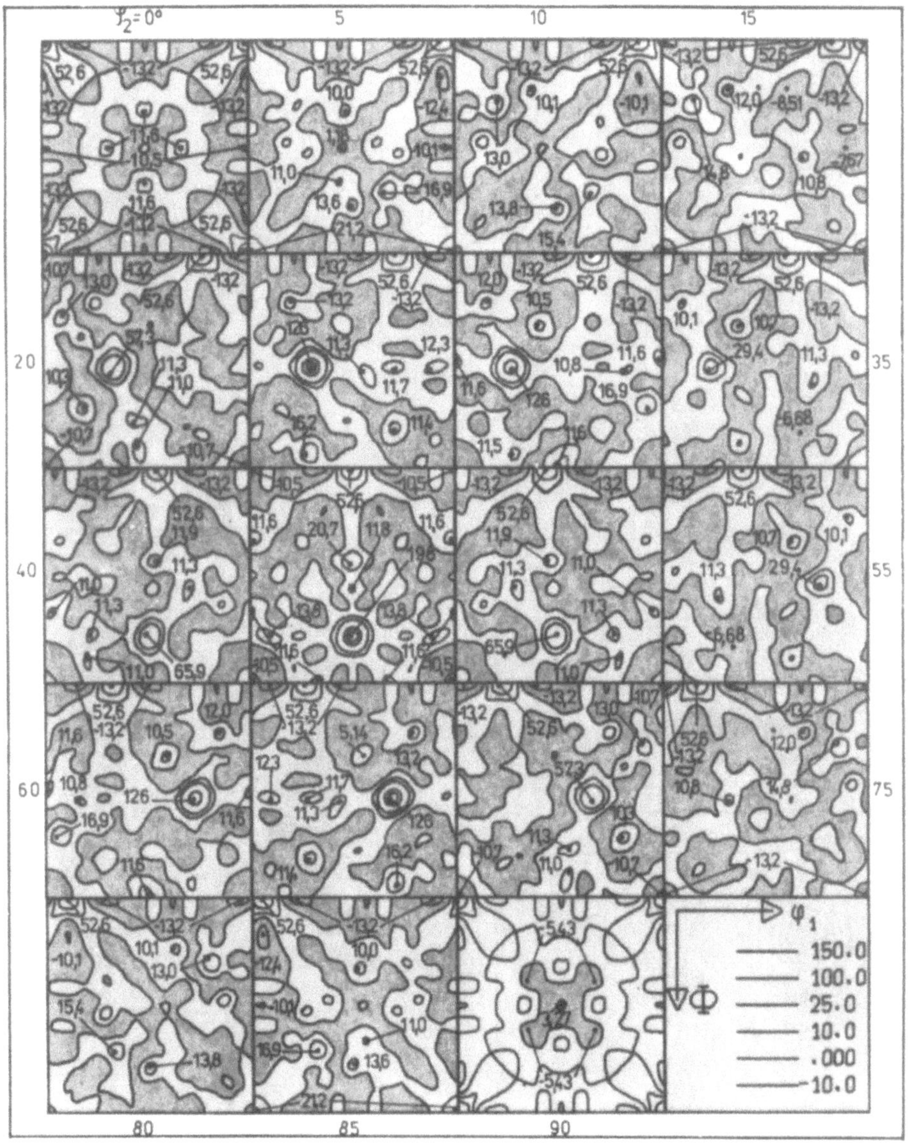

$\tilde{F}$, G, 7.50° , {122}<221>

$\tilde{F}_{MAX}$ = 197.71 (45°)

$\tilde{F}_{MIN}$ = −13.16 (00°, 05°, . . . , 90°)

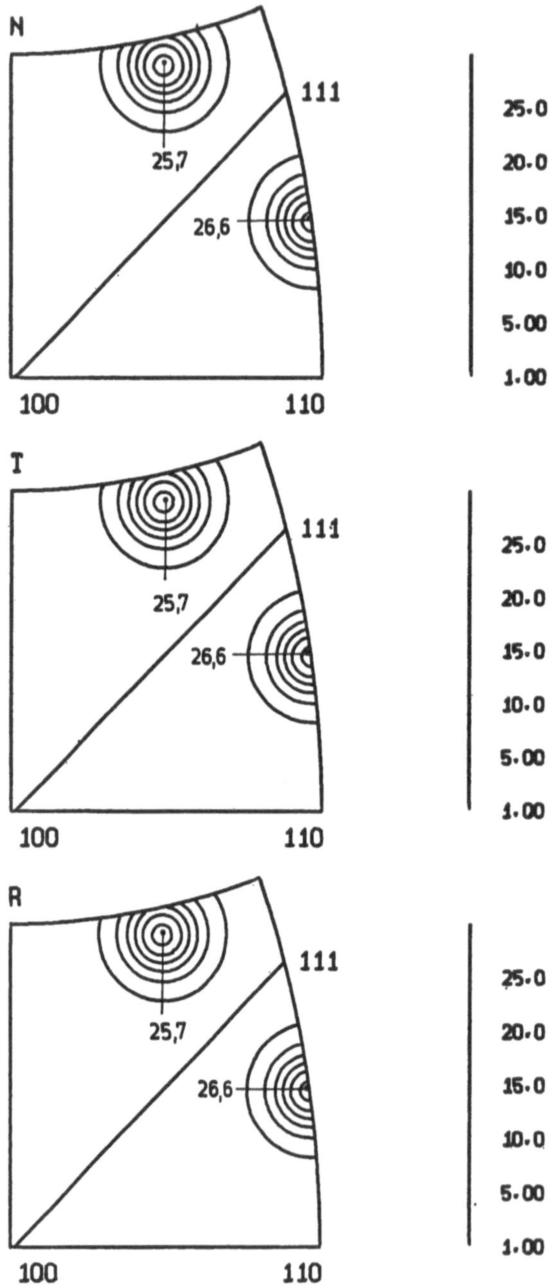

$\tilde{R}$, G, 7.50°, {122}⟨221⟩

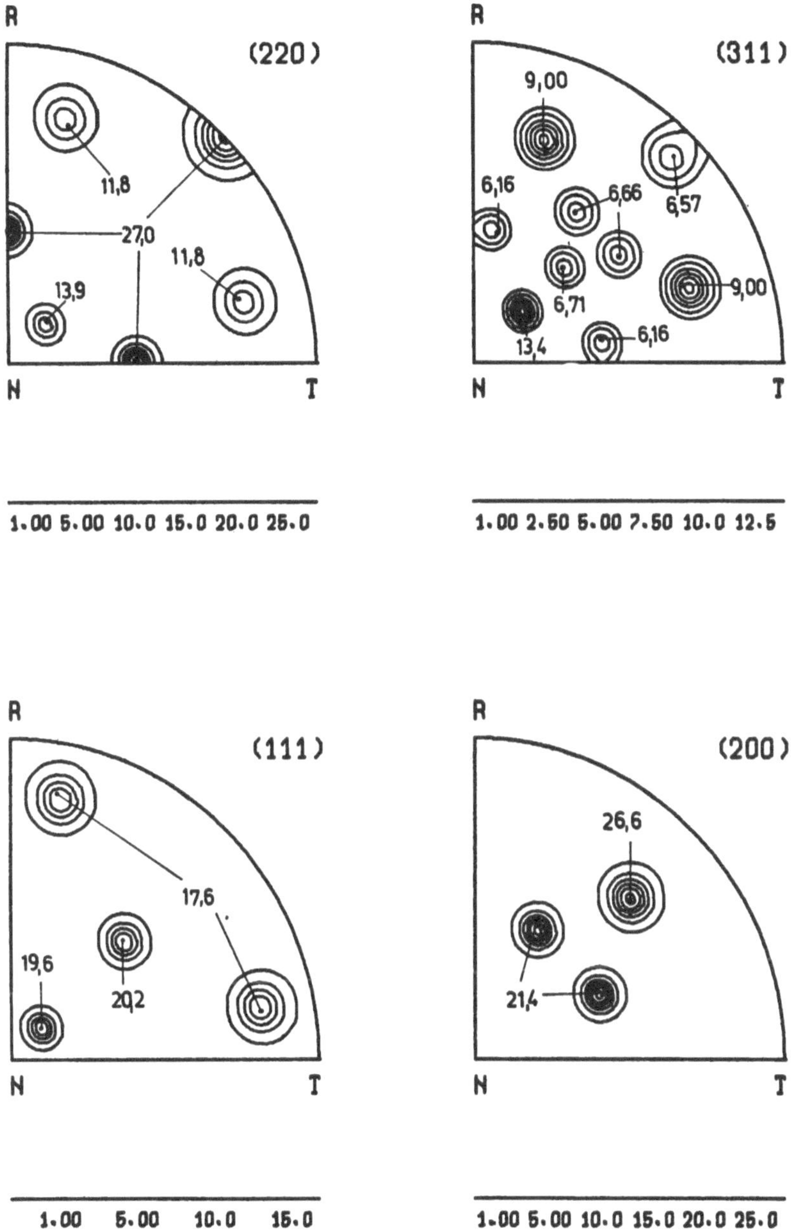

$\tilde{P}$, G, 7.50°; $\{122\}\langle 221\rangle$

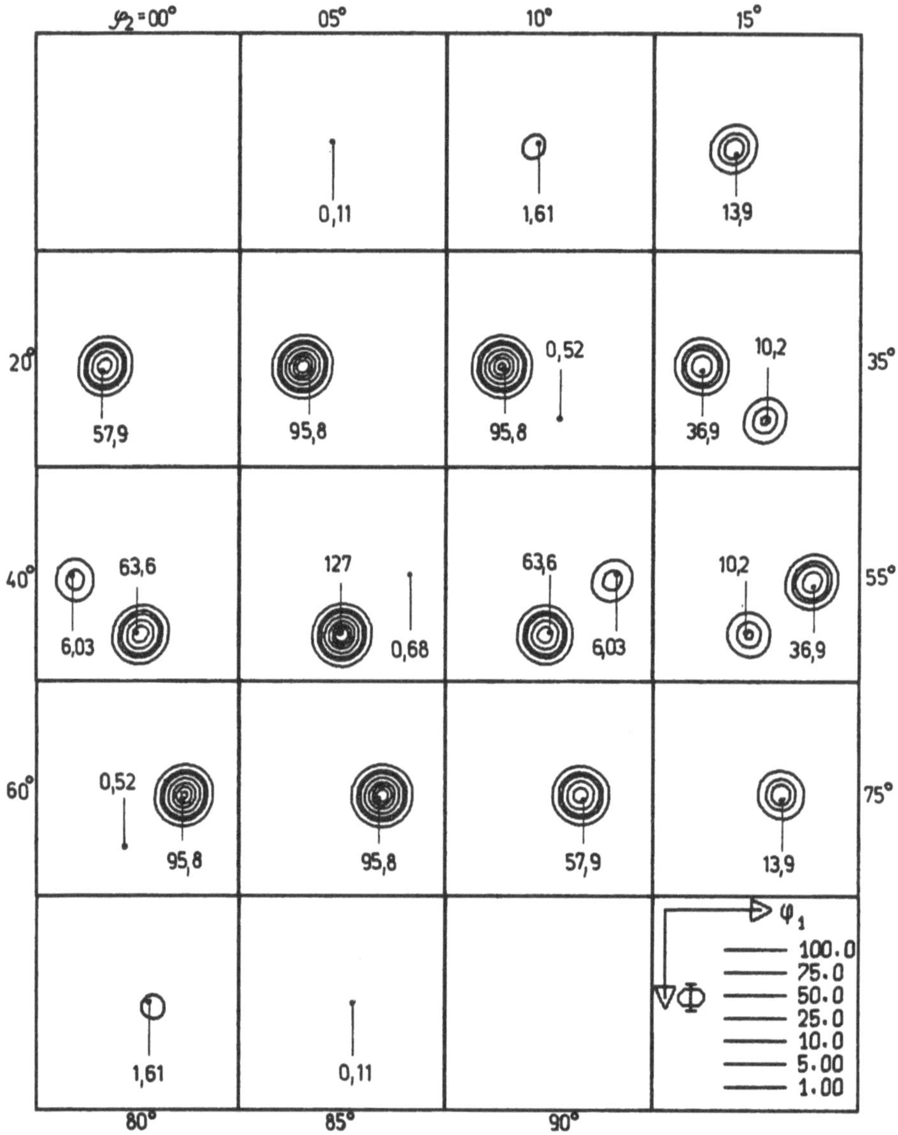

F, G, 10.0°, {122}<221>

F_{MAX} = 127.13 (45°)

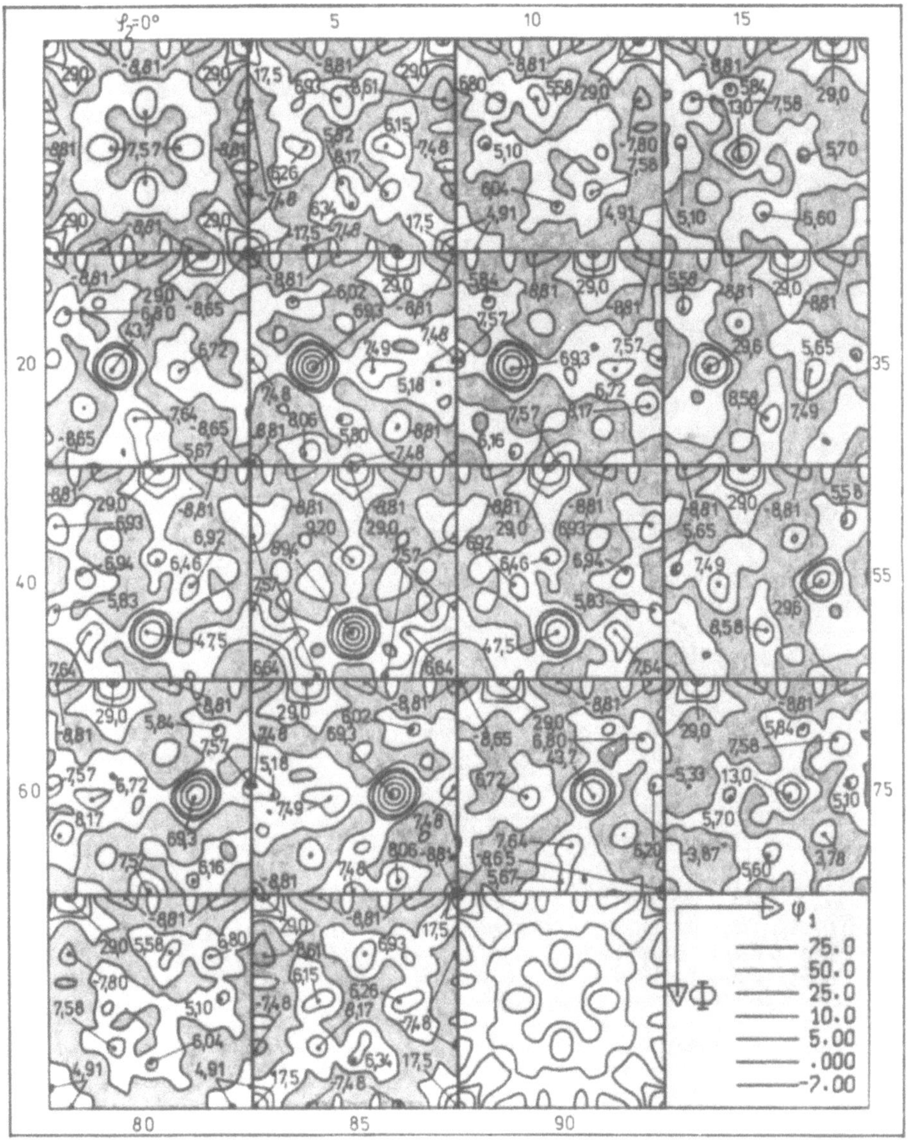

$\tilde{F}$, G, 10.0°, {122}<221>

$\tilde{F}_{MAX}$ = 89.39 (45°)

$\tilde{F}_{MIN}$ = -8.81 (00°, 05°, . . ., 90°)

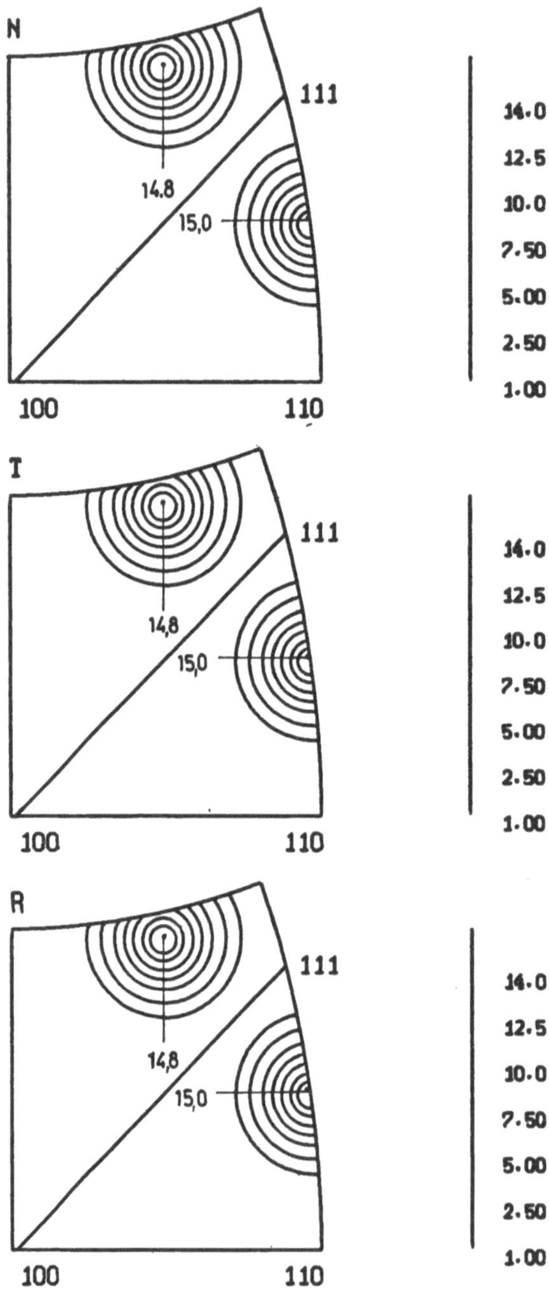

$\tilde{R}$, G, 10.0°, {122}$\langle 221 \rangle$

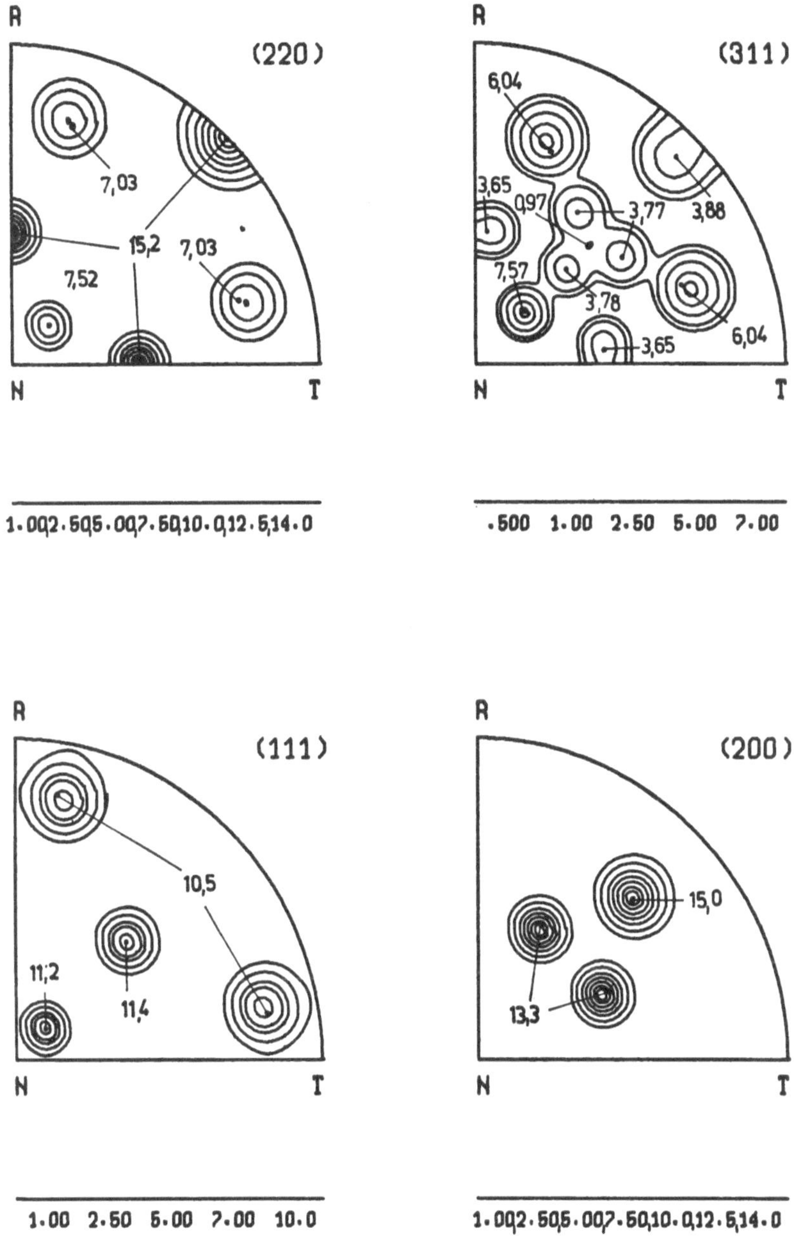

$\tilde{P}$, G, 10.0°, {122}⟨221⟩

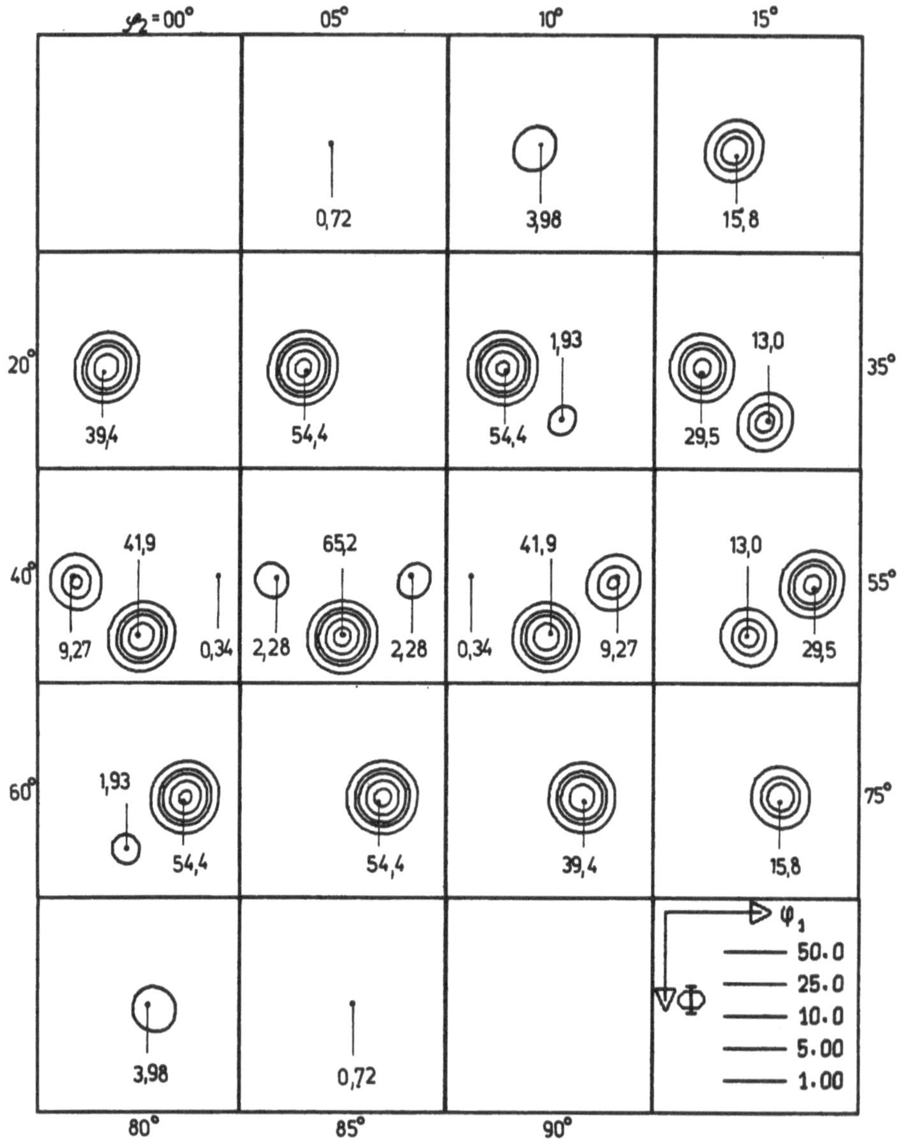

F, G, 12.5°, {122}<221>

F_{MAX} = 65.23 (45°)

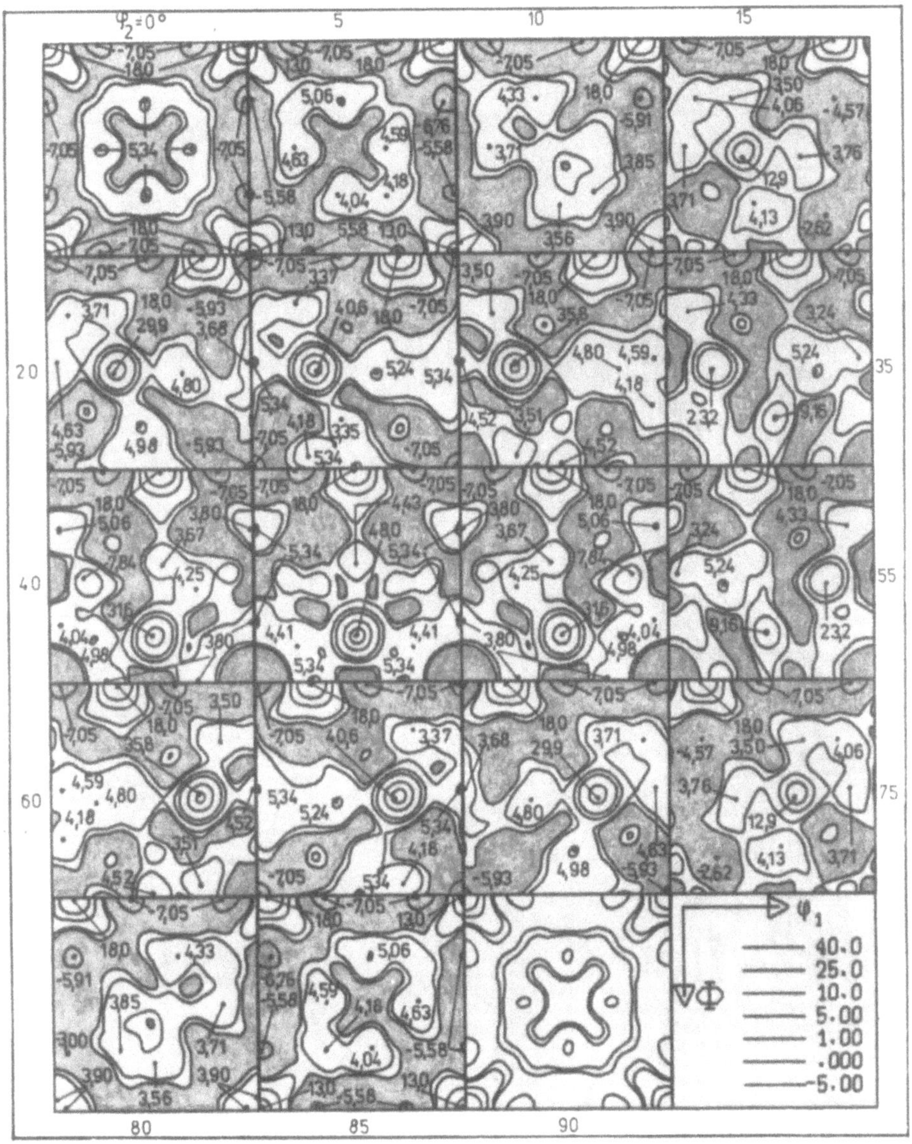

$\tilde{F}$, G, 12.5°, {122}<221>

$\tilde{F}_{MAX}$ = 47.99 (45°)

$\tilde{F}_{MIN}$ = -7.05 (00°, 05°, . . ., 90°)

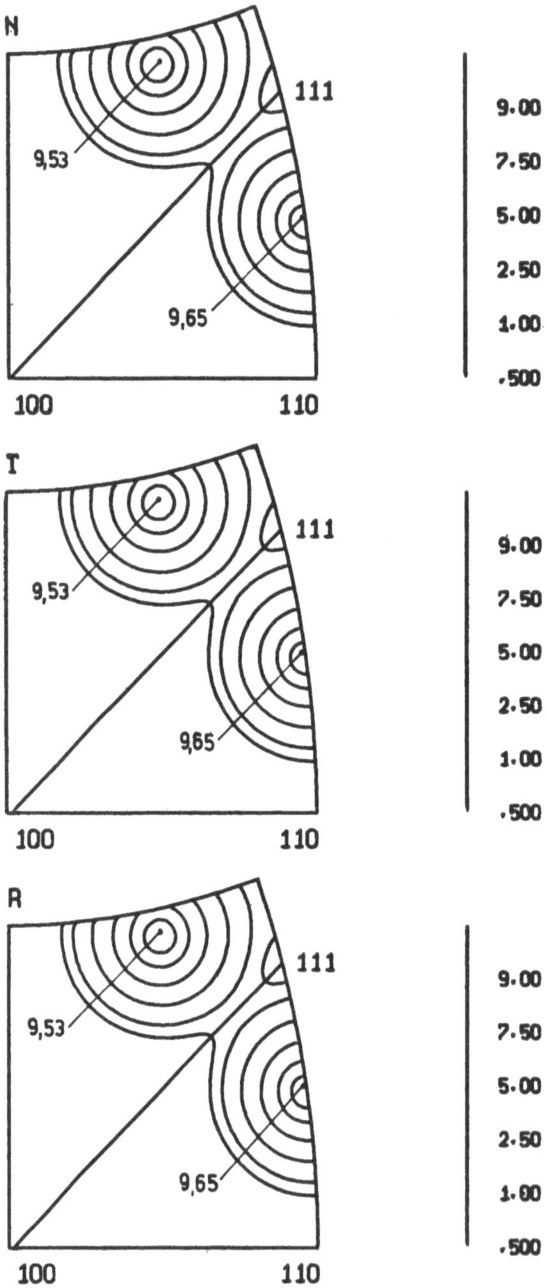

$\tilde{R}$, G, 12.5°, $\{122\}\langle 221\rangle$

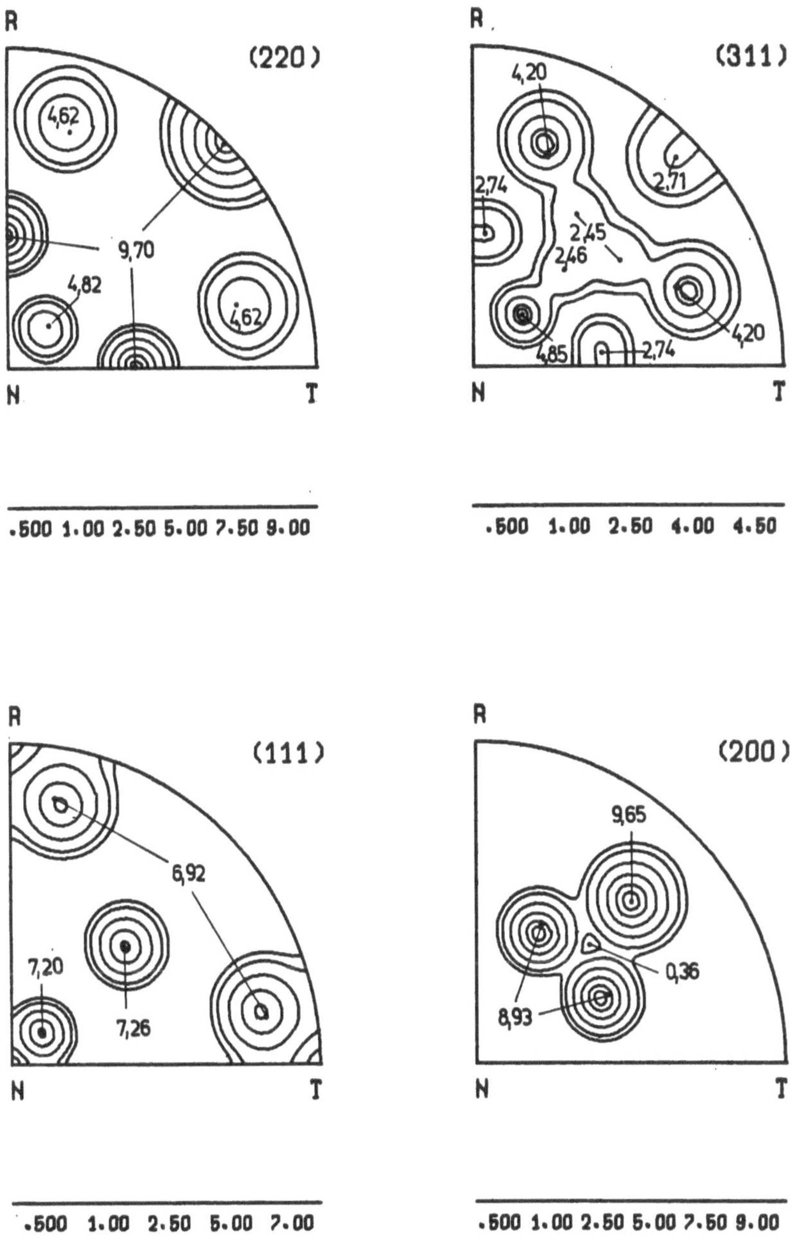

$\tilde{P}$, G, 12.5°, $\{122\}\langle 221\rangle$

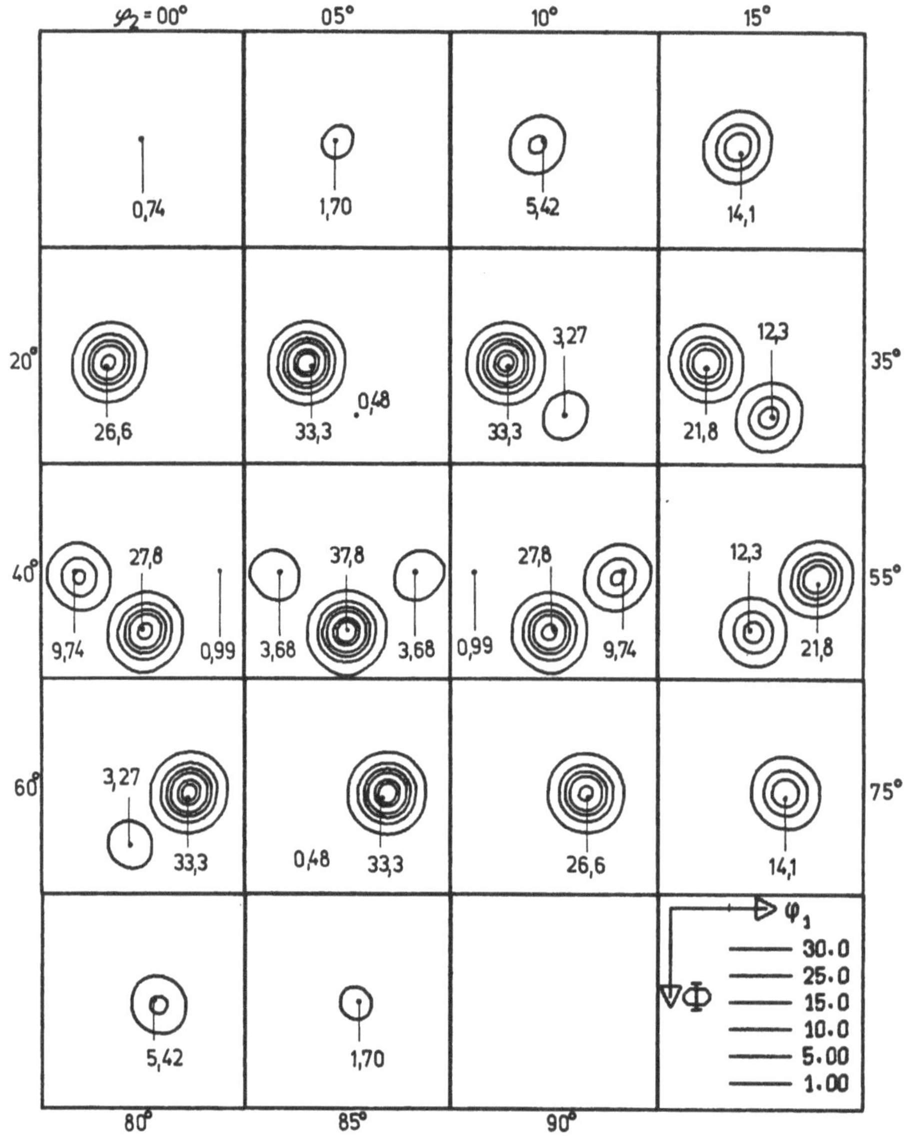

F, G, 15.0°, {122}<221>

F_{MAX} = 37.78 (45°)

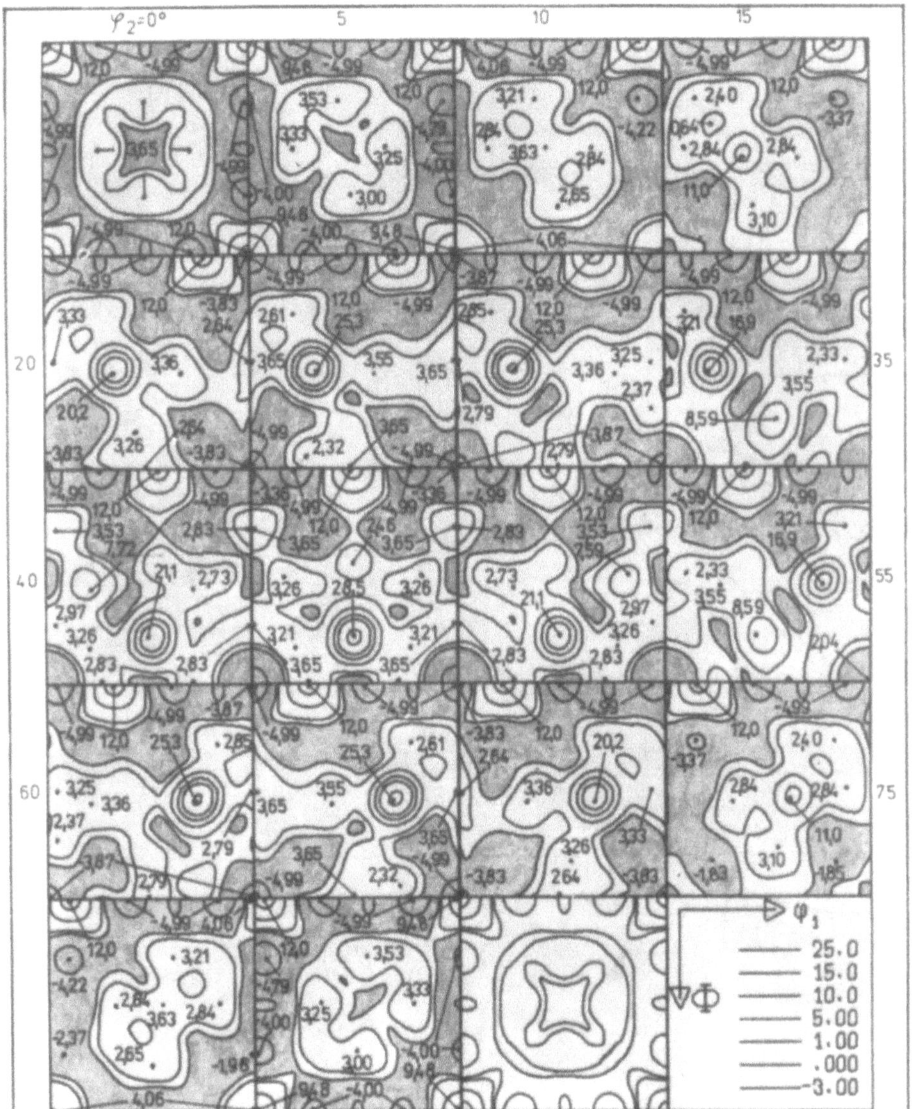

$\tilde{F}$, G, 15.0°, {122}<221>

$\tilde{F}_{MAX}$ = 28.45 (45°)

$\tilde{F}_{MIN}$ = -4.99 (00°, 05°, . . ., 90°)

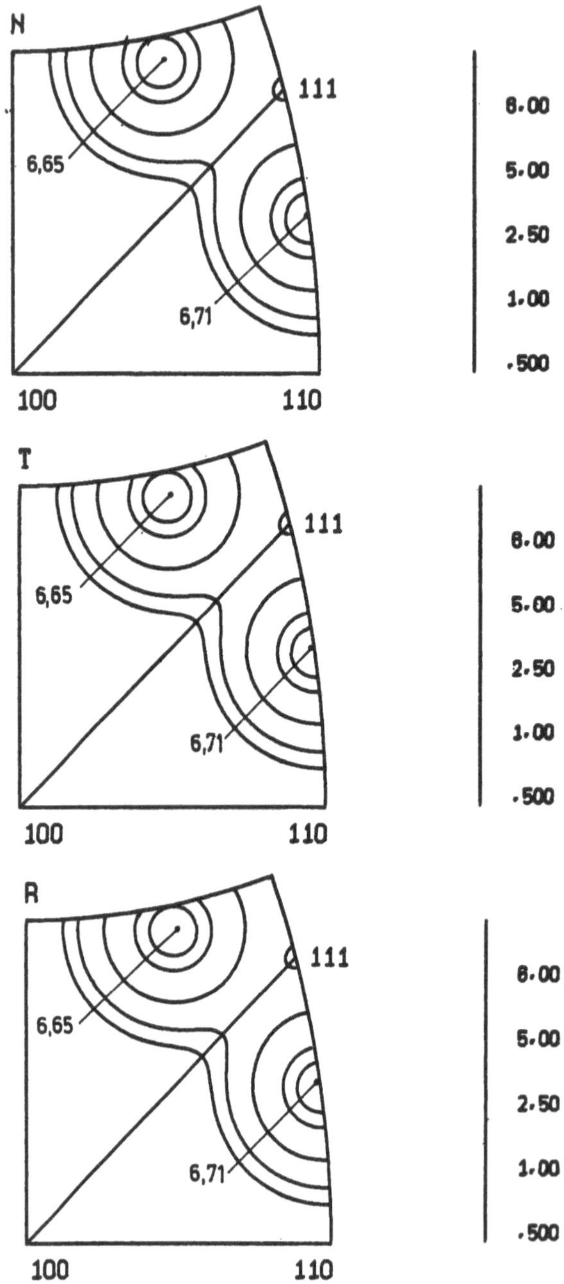

R̃, G, 15.0°, {122}⟨221⟩

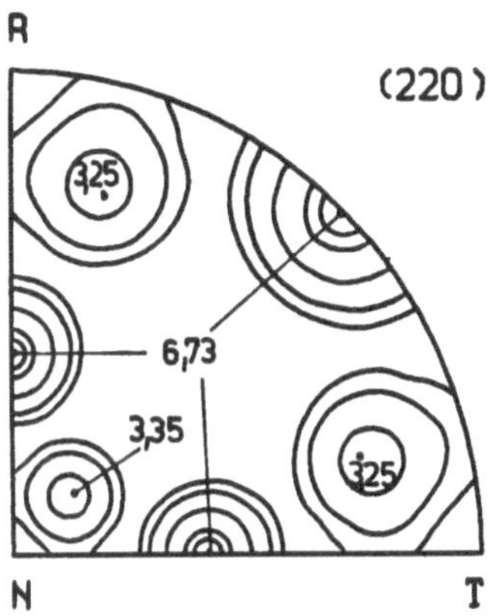

.500 1.00 2.50 5.00 6.00

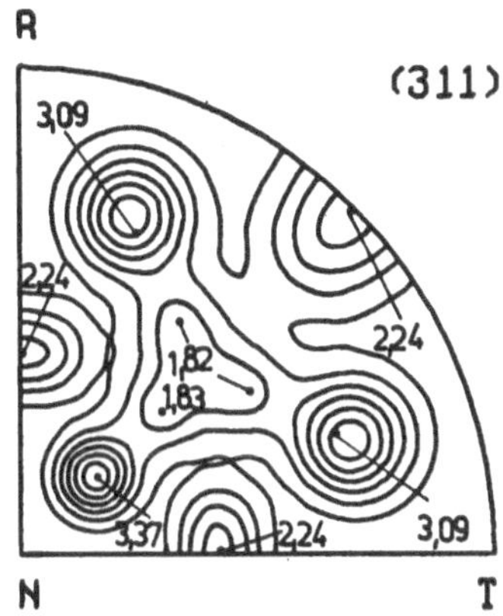

$\tilde{P}_{MIN}$ = 0.01 (90°, 90°)

.500 1.00 1.50 2.00 2.50 3.00

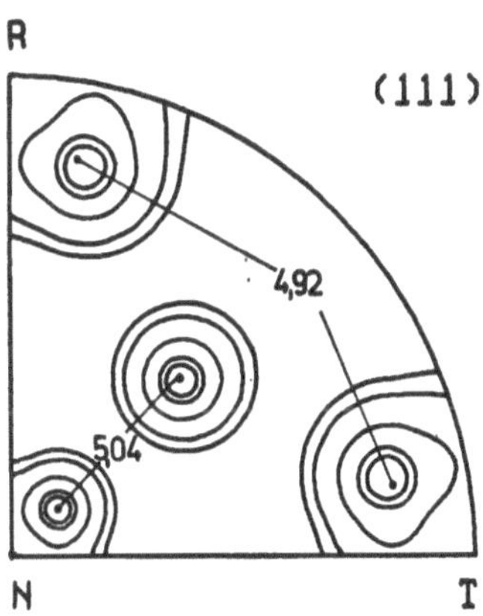

.500 1.00 2.50 4.00 4.50

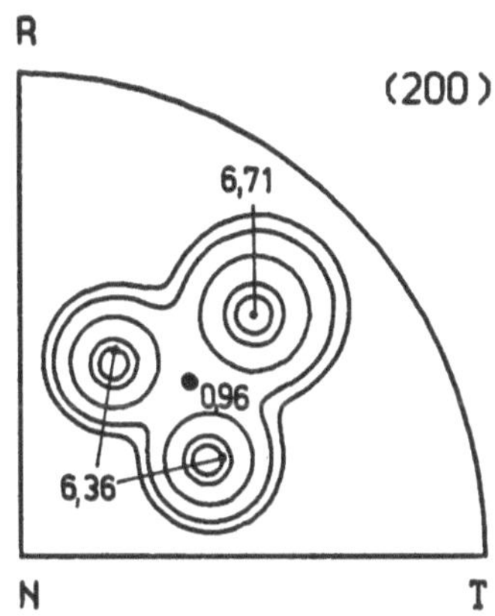

.500 1.00 2.50 5.00 6.00

$\tilde{P}$, G, 15.0°, {122}⟨221⟩

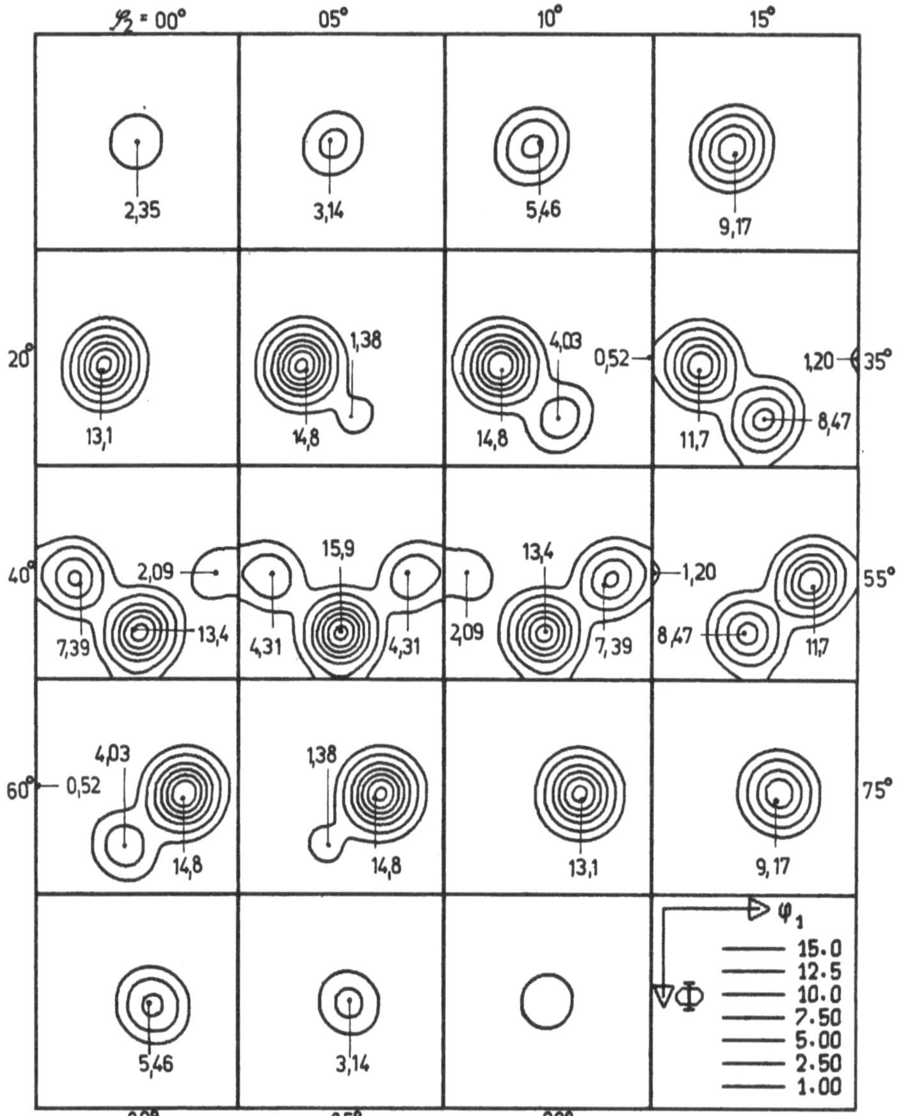

F, G, 20.0°, {122}<221>

F_{MAX} = 15.93 (45°)

$\tilde{F}$, G, 20.0°, {122}<221>

$\tilde{F}_{MAX}$ = 12.04 (45°)

$\tilde{F}_{MIN}$ = −2.37 (00°, 05°, . . ., 90°)

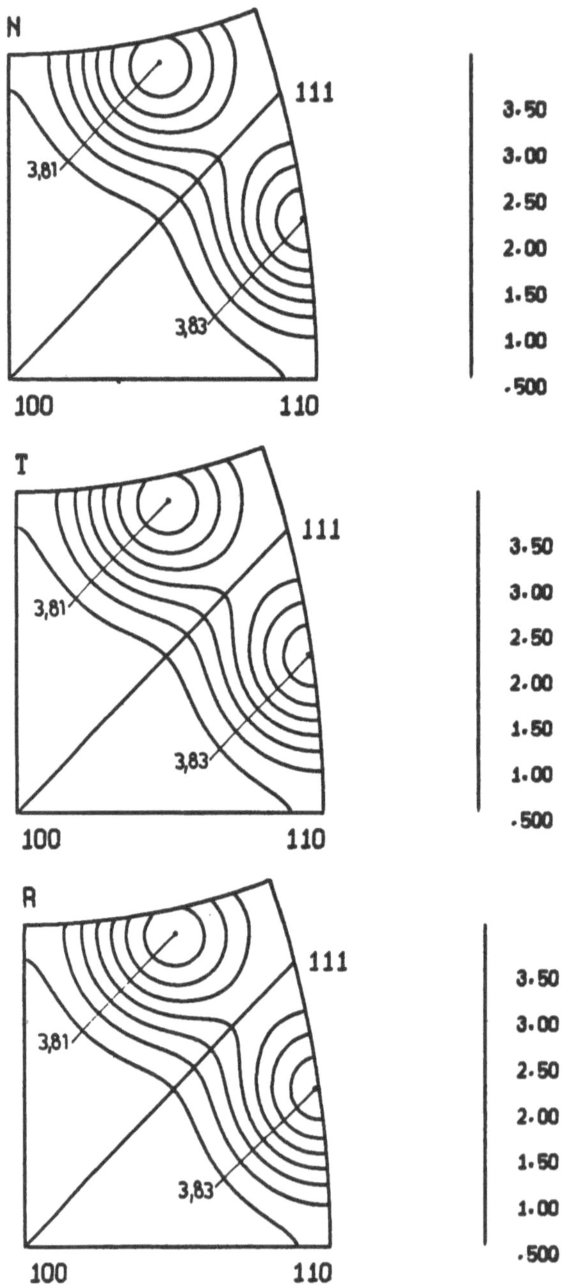

$\tilde{R}$, G, 20.0°, $\{122\}\langle 221\rangle$

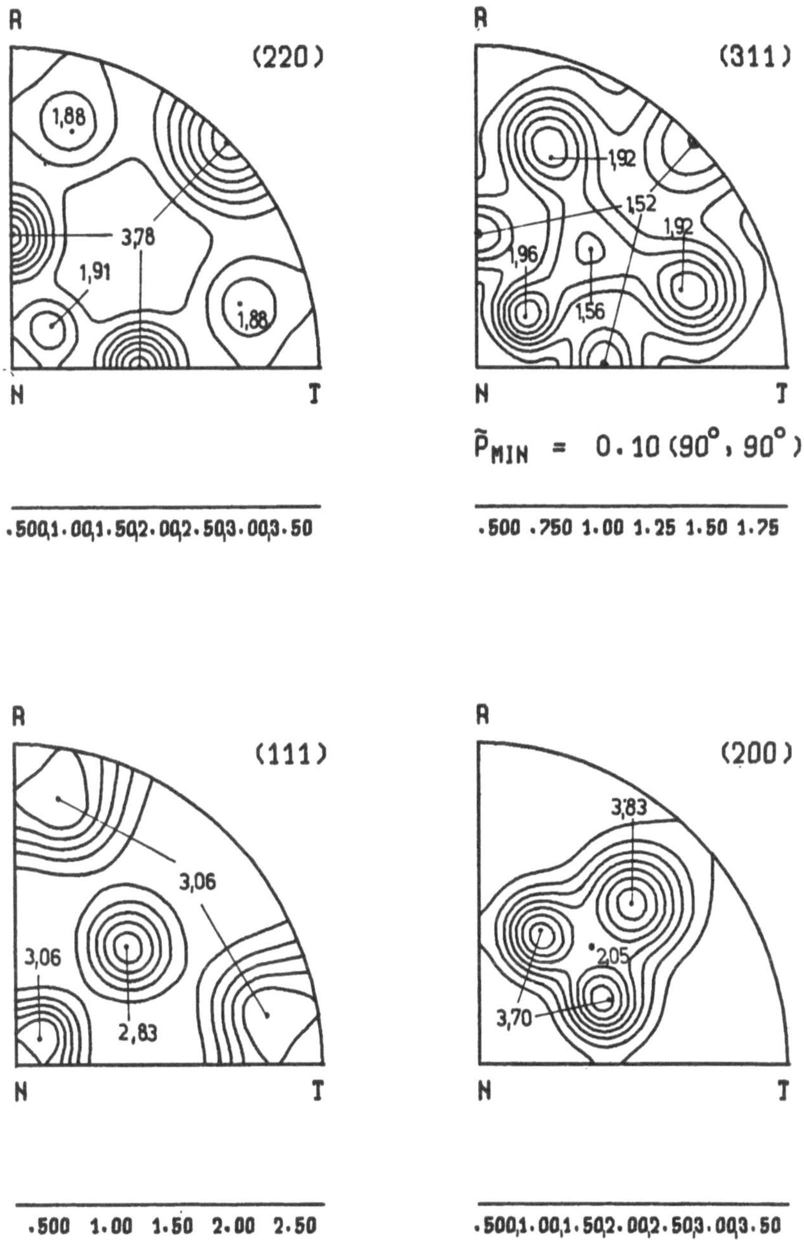

$\tilde{P}$, G, 20.0°, {122}⟨221⟩

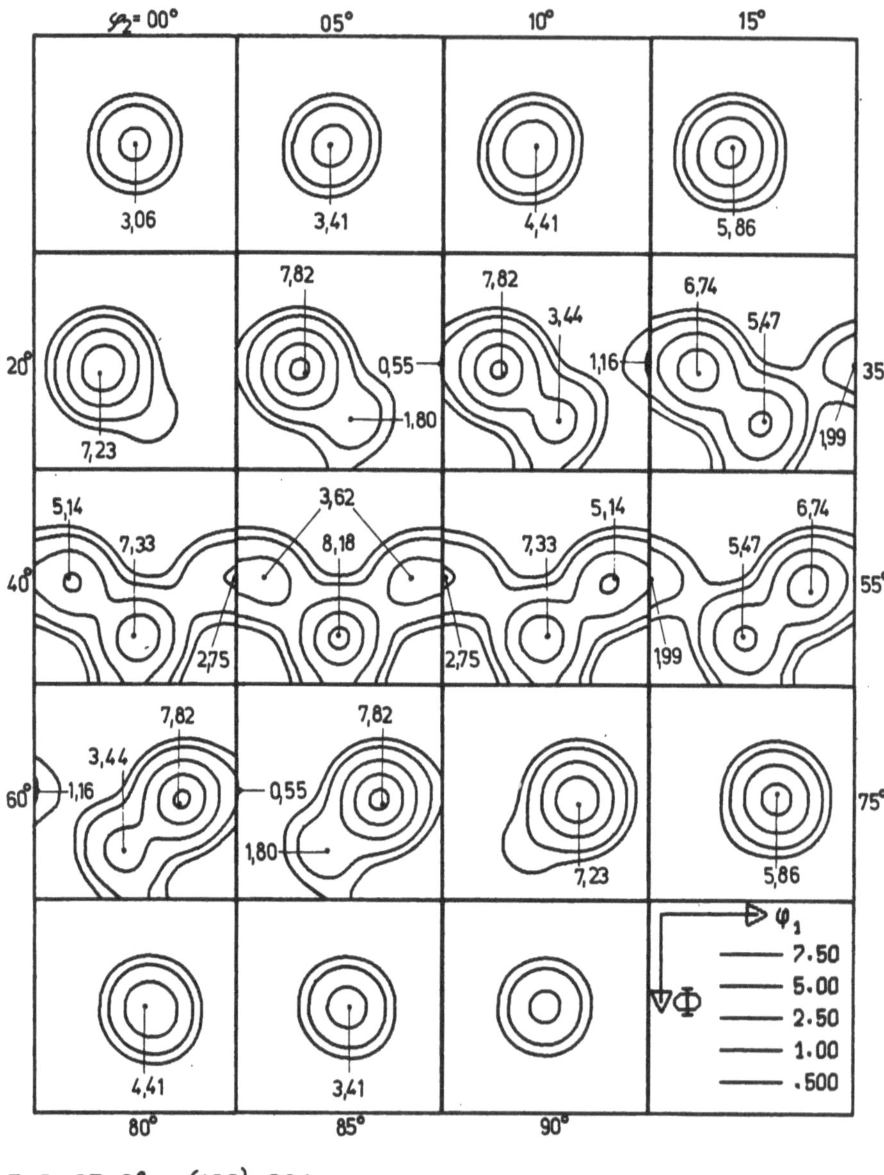

F, G, 25.0° , {122}<221>

F_{MAX} = 8.18 (45°)

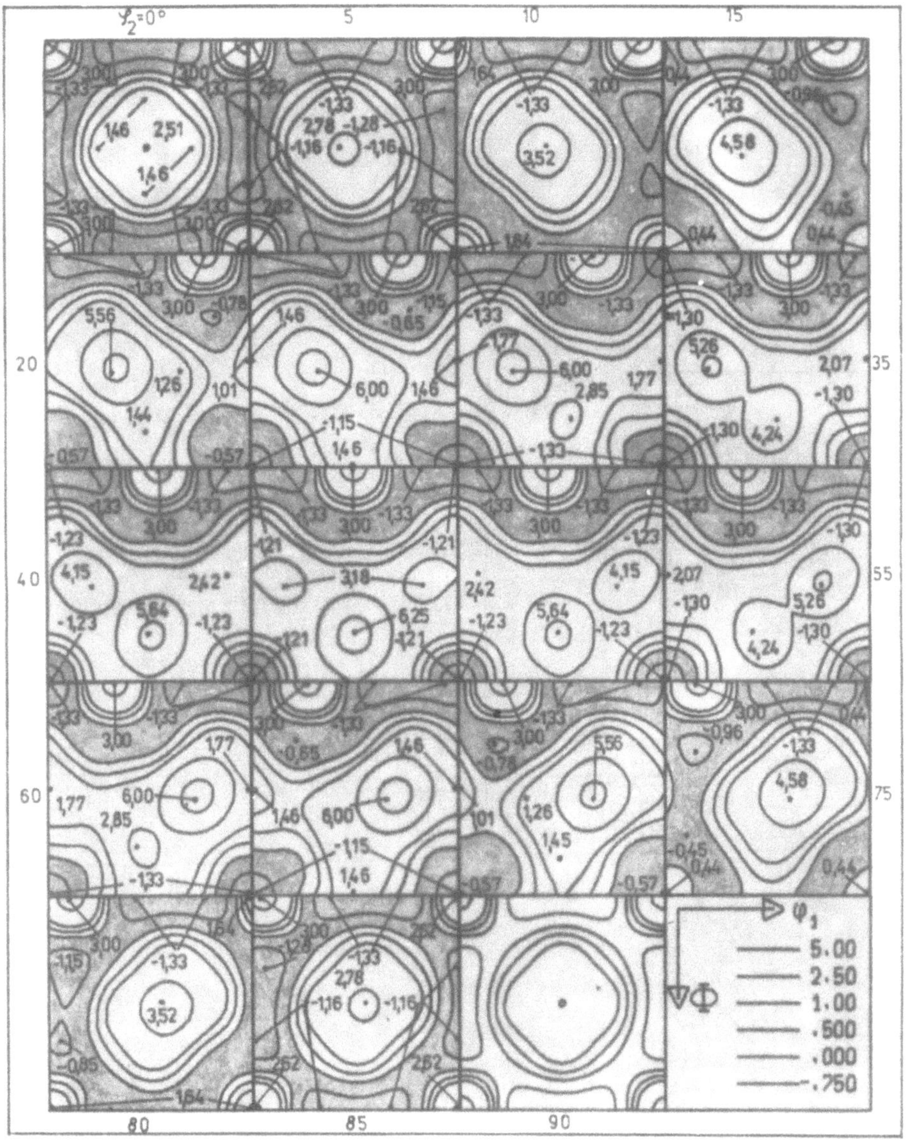

$\tilde{F}$, G, 25.0°, {122}<221>

$\tilde{F}_{MAX}$ = 6.25 (45°)

$\tilde{F}_{MIN}$ = −1.33 (00°, 05°, . . ., 90°)

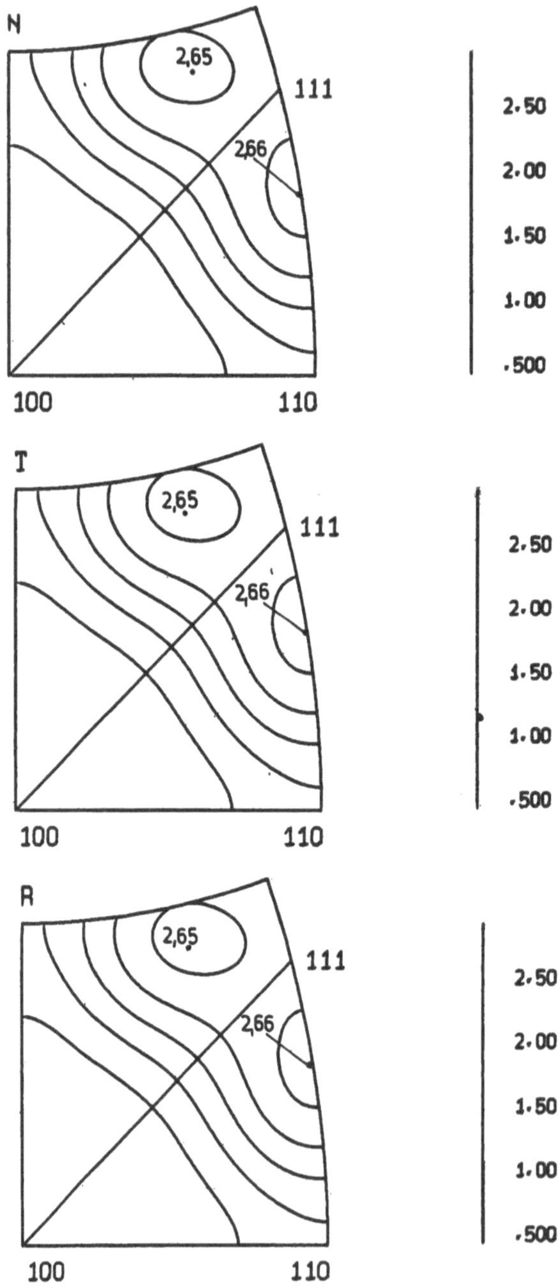

$\tilde{R}$, G, 25.0^{0} , $\{122\}\langle 221\rangle$

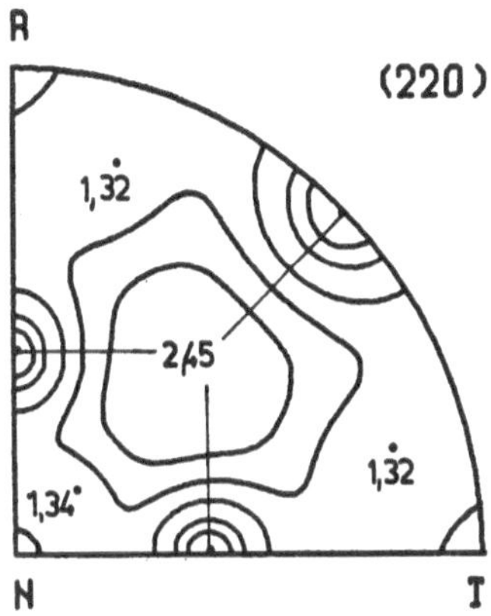

$\tilde{P}_{MIN}$ = 0.05 (55°, 45°)

.500 1.00 1.50 2.00 2.25

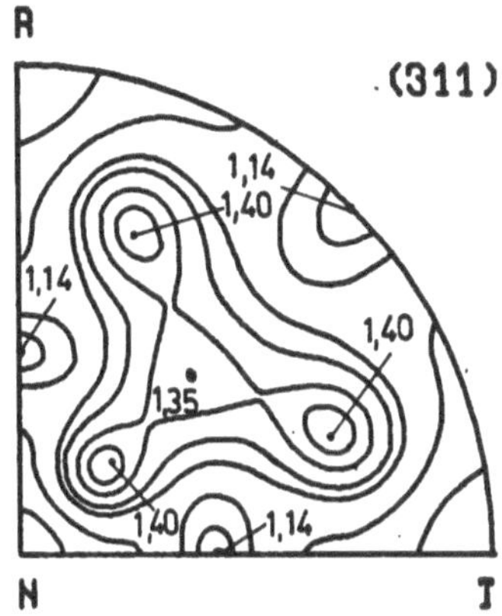

$\tilde{P}_{MIN}$ = 0.30 (90°, 90°)

.500 .750 1.00 1.10 1.25 1.35

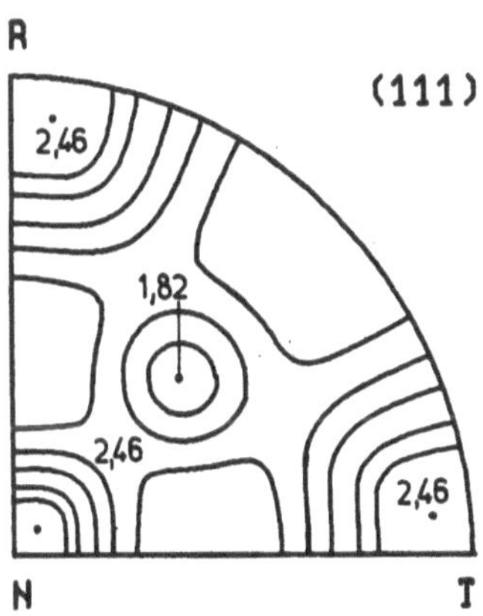

$\tilde{P}_{MIN}$ = 0.05 (90°, 45°)

.500 1.00 1.50 2.00 2.25

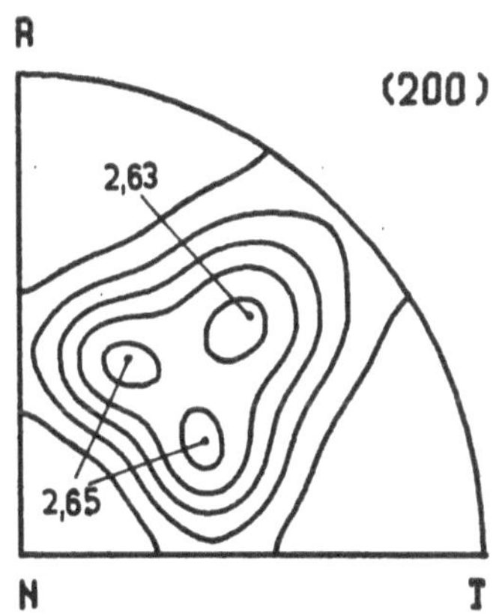

.500 1.00 1.50 2.00 2.50

$\tilde{P}$, G, 25.0°, {122}⟨221⟩

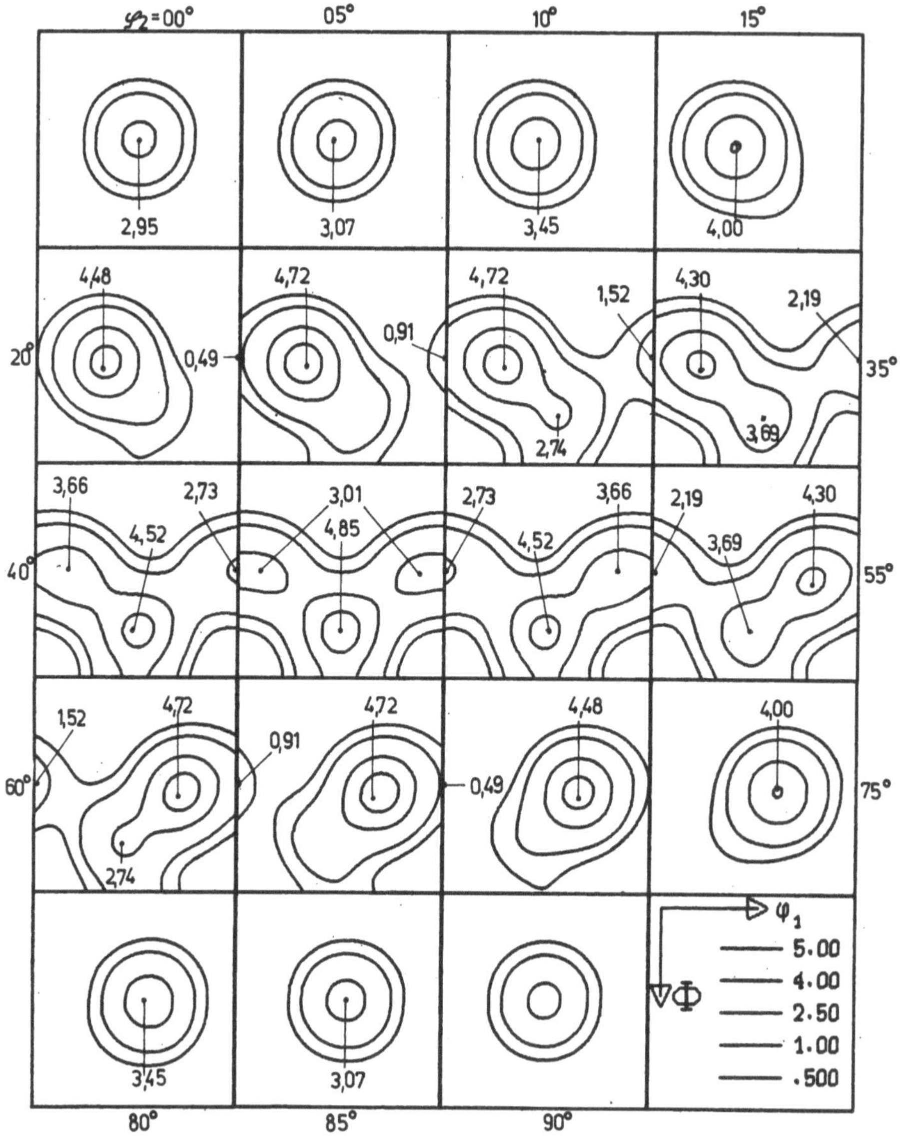

F, G, 30.0°, {122}<221>

F_{MAX} = 4.85 (45°)

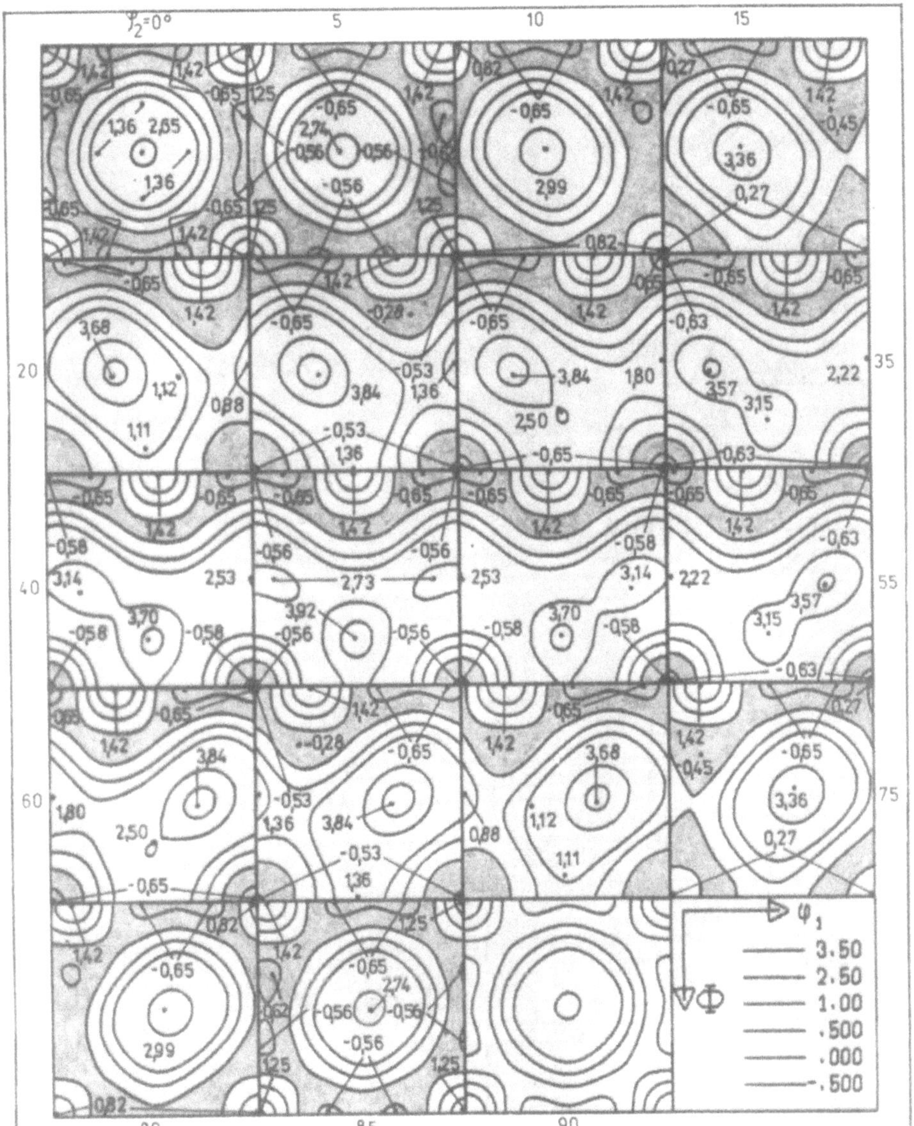

$\tilde{F}$, G, 30.0°, {122}<221>

$\tilde{F}_{MAX}$ ≐ 3.92 (45°)

$\tilde{F}_{MIN}$ = −.65 (00°, 05°, . . . , 90°)

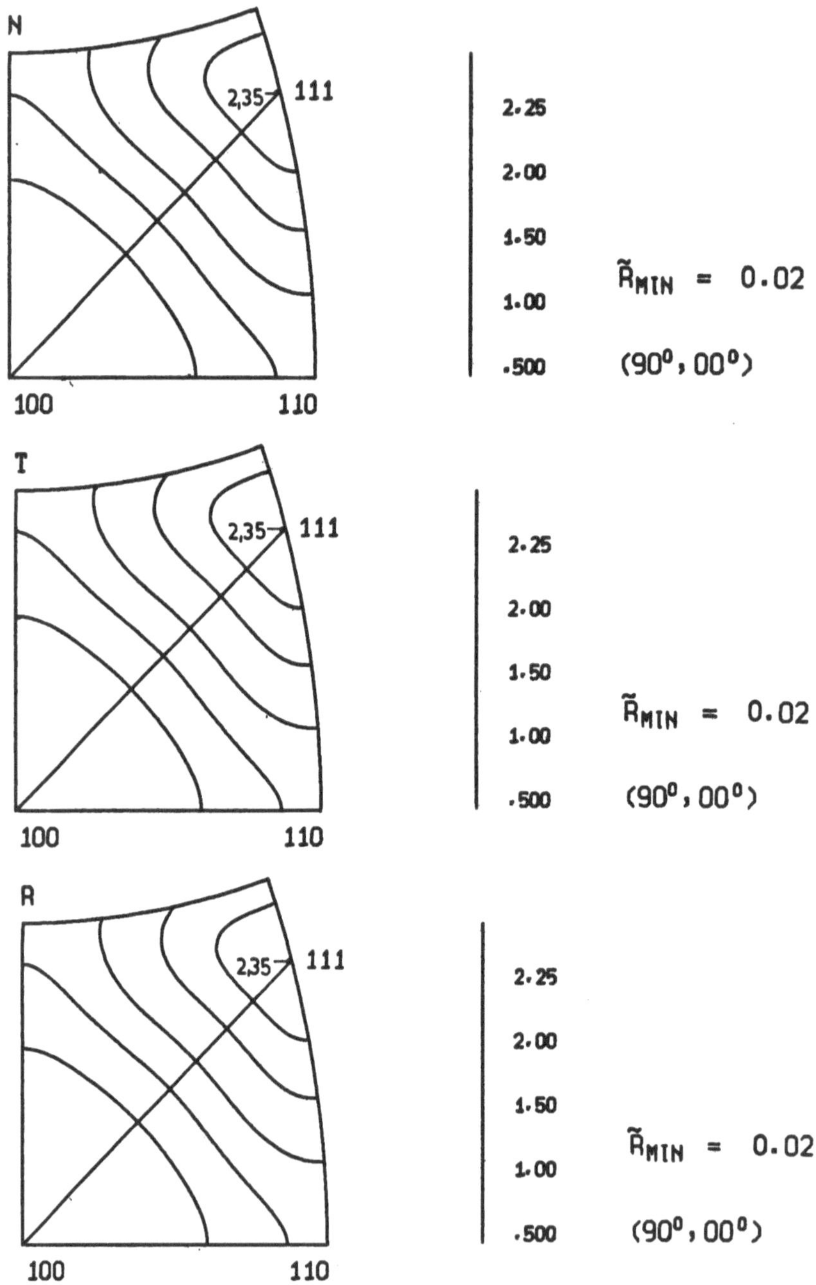

$\tilde{R}$, G, 30.0°, $\{122\}\langle 221\rangle$

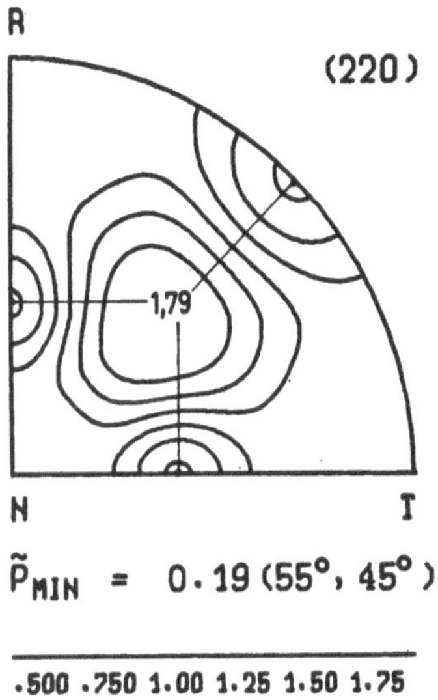

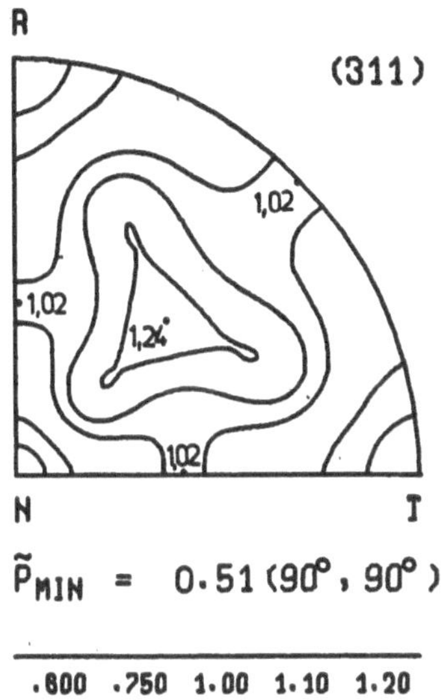

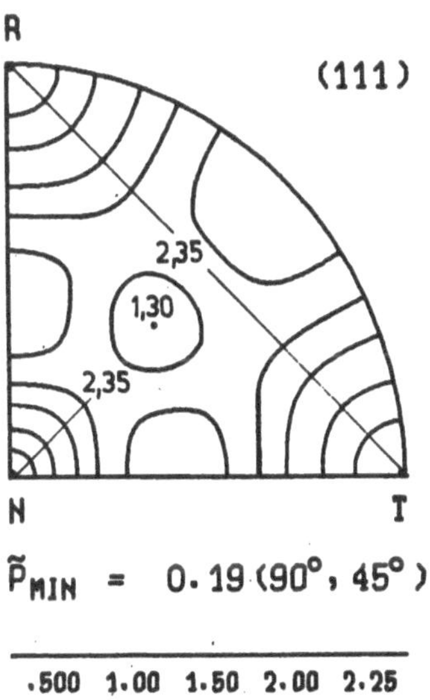

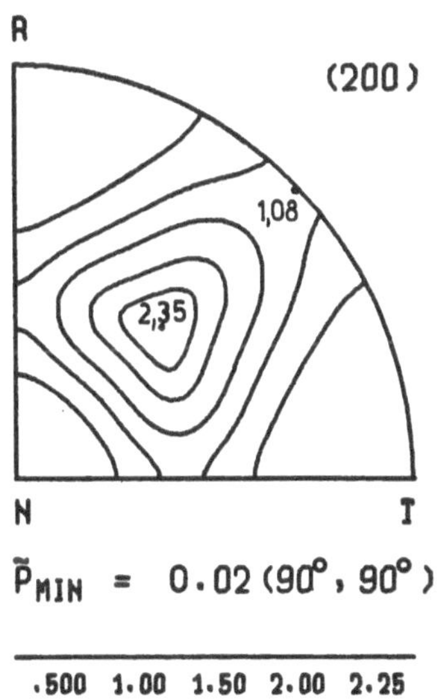

$\tilde{P}$, G, 30.0°, {122}⟨221⟩

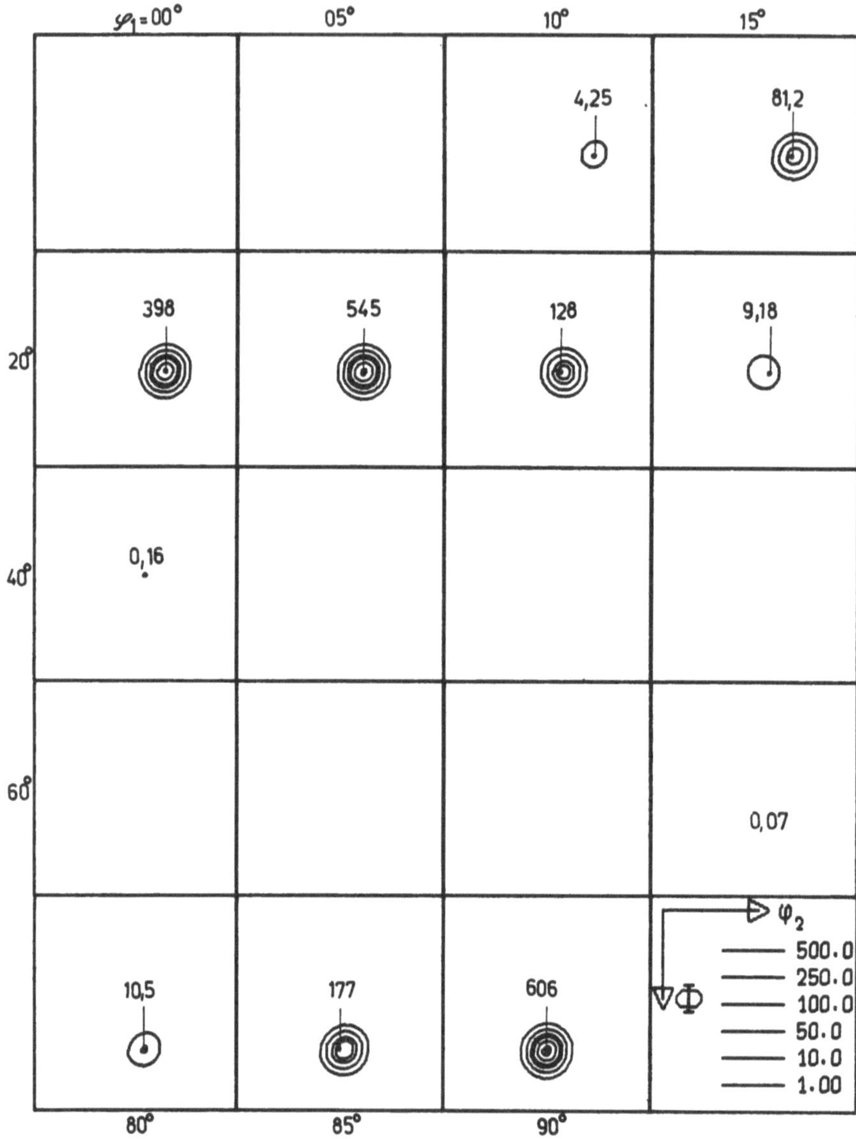

F, G, 7.50°, {323}<131>

F_{MAX} = 605.95 (90°)

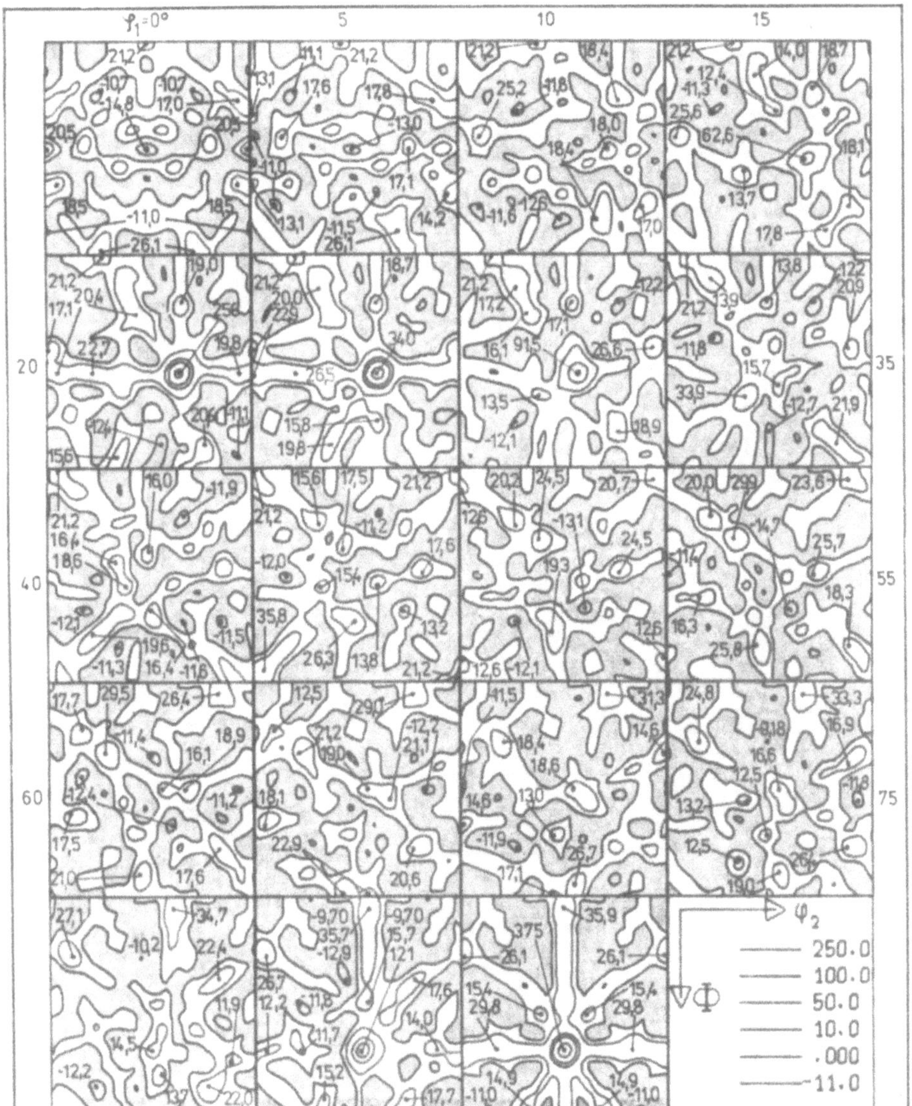

$\tilde{F}$, G, 7.50°, {323}<131>

$\tilde{F}_{MAX}$ = 375.45 (90°)

$\tilde{F}_{MIN}$ = -14.79 (00°)

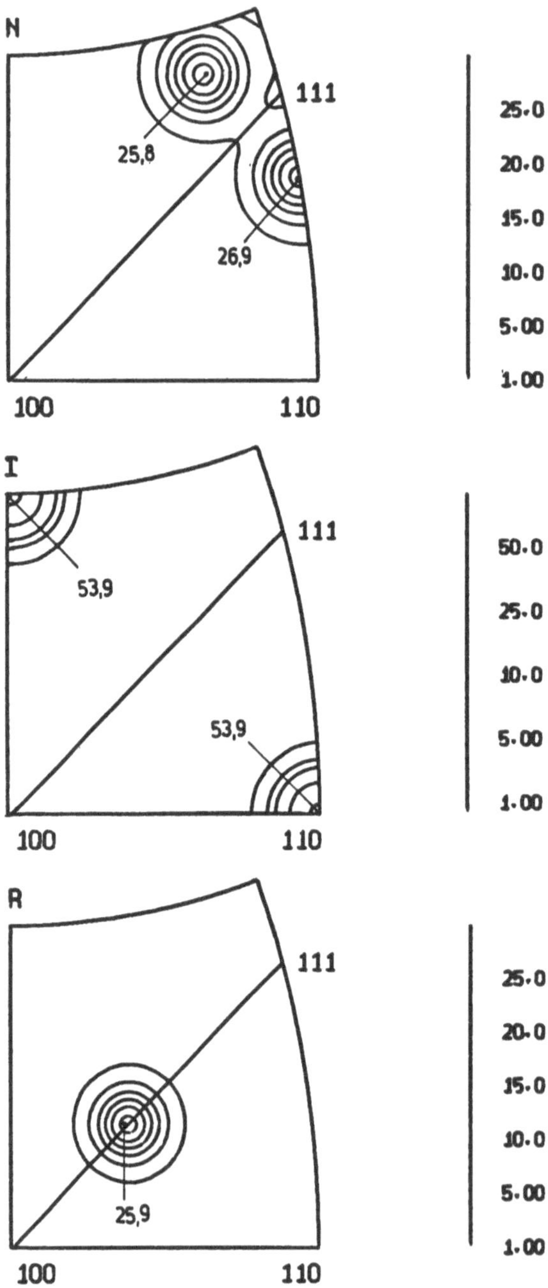

$\tilde{R}$, G, 7.50° , $\{323\}\langle 131\rangle$

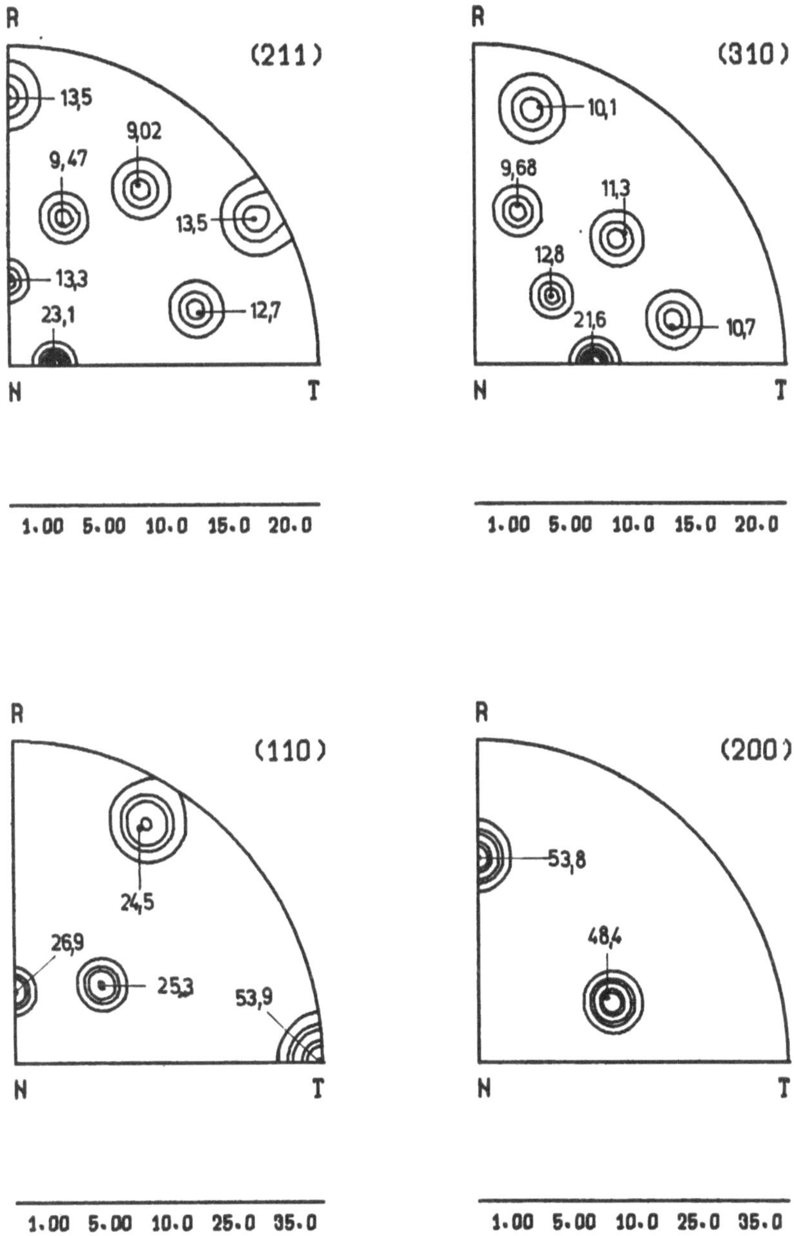

$\tilde{P}$, G, 7.50°, $\{323\}\langle 131\rangle$

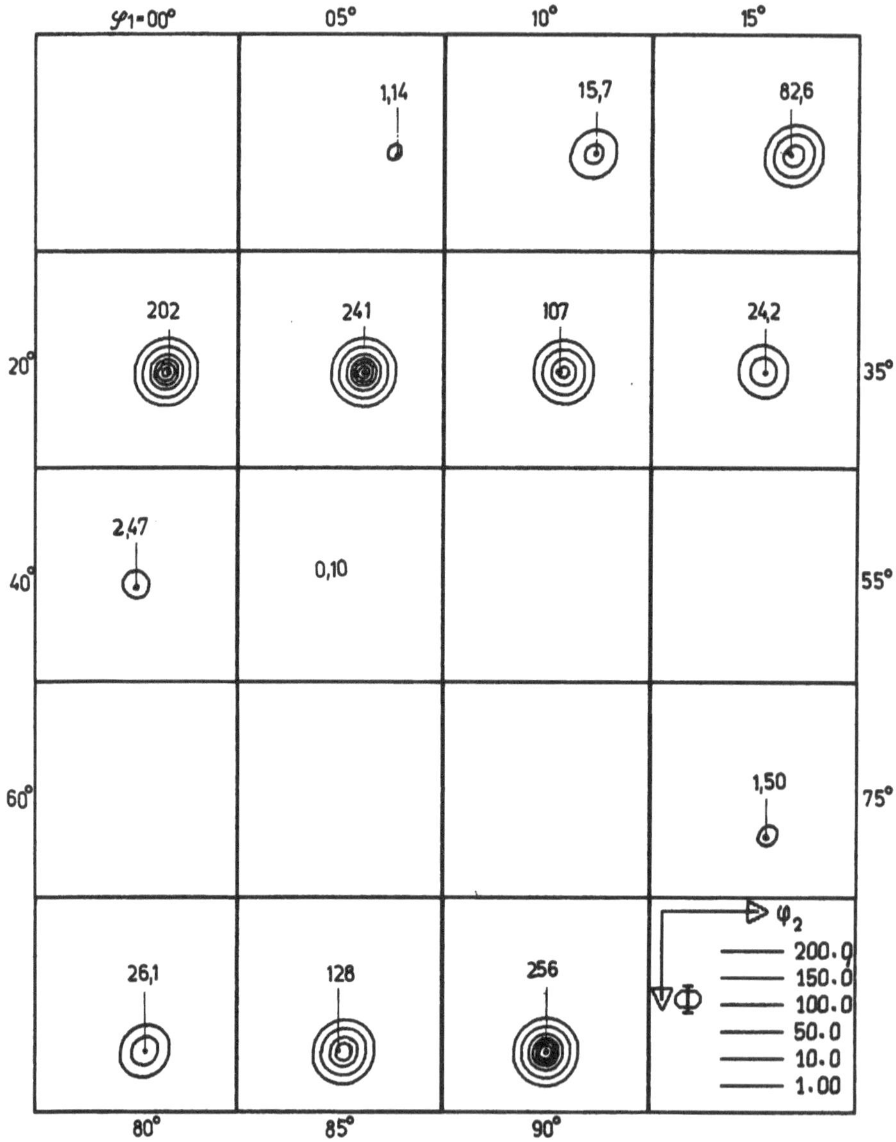

F, G, 10.0°, {323}<131>

F_{MAX} = 255.83 (90°)

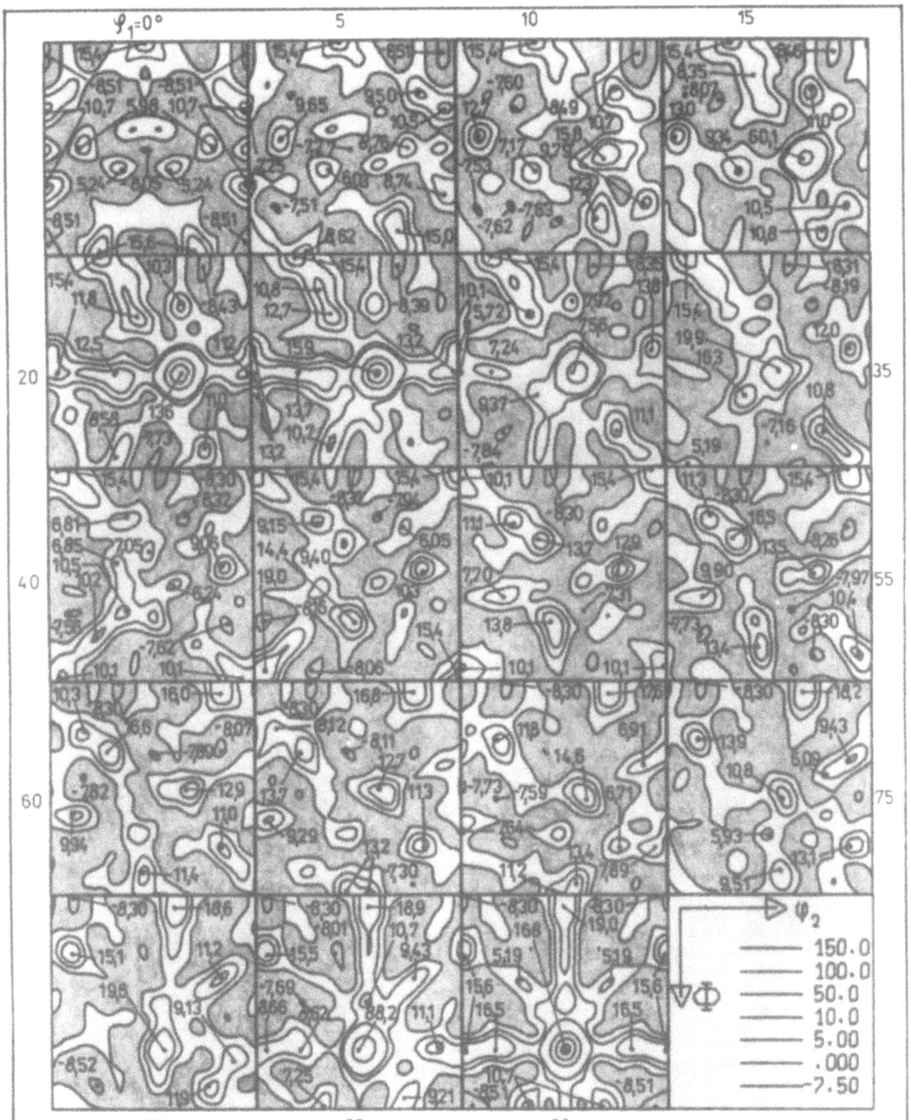

$\tilde{F}$, G, 10.0°, {323}<131>

$\tilde{F}_{MAX}$ = 167.87 (90°)

$\tilde{F}_{MIN}$ = -8.52 (80°)

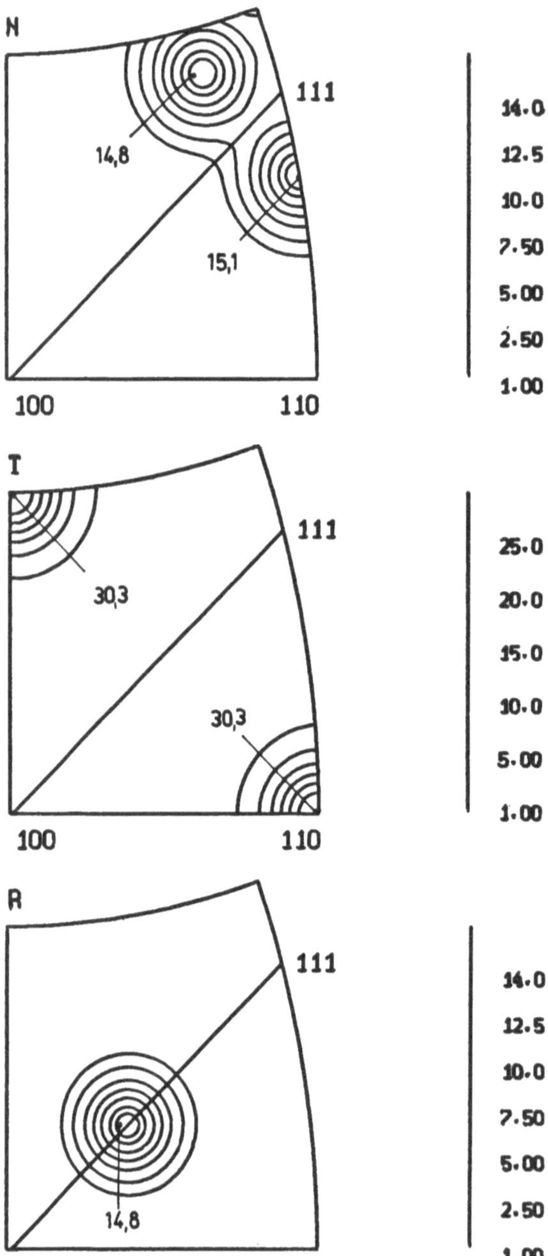

$\tilde{R}$, G, 10.0°, $\{323\}\langle 131\rangle$

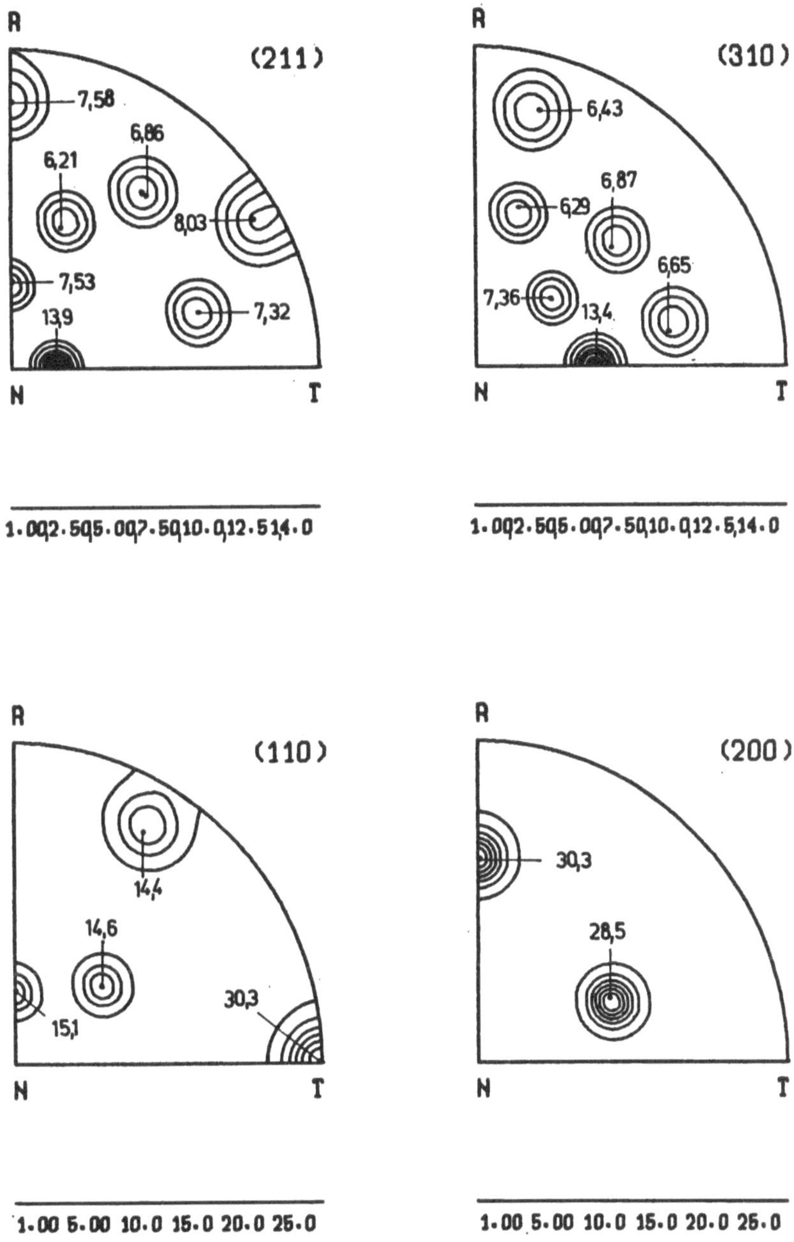

$\tilde{P}$, G, 10.0°, {323}⟨131⟩

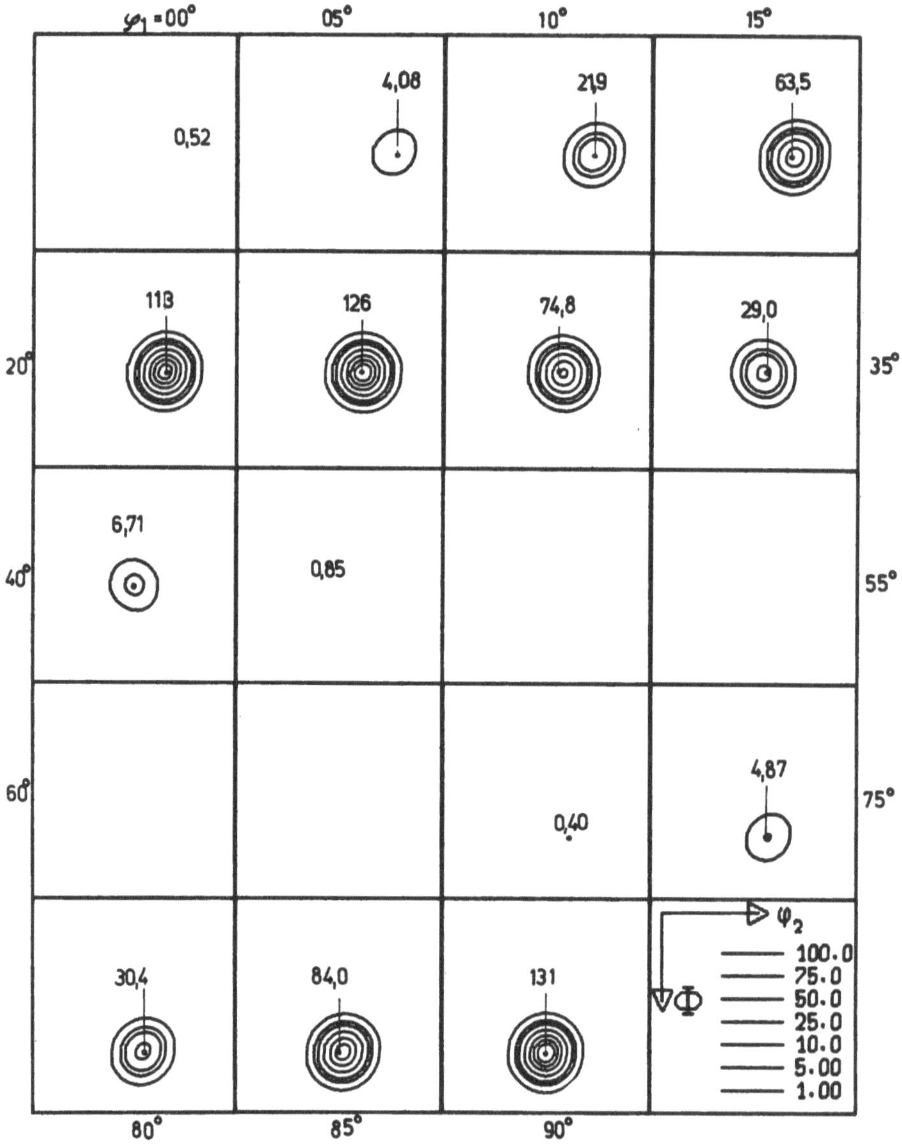

F, G, 12.5°, {323}<131>

F_{MAX} = 130.97 (90°)

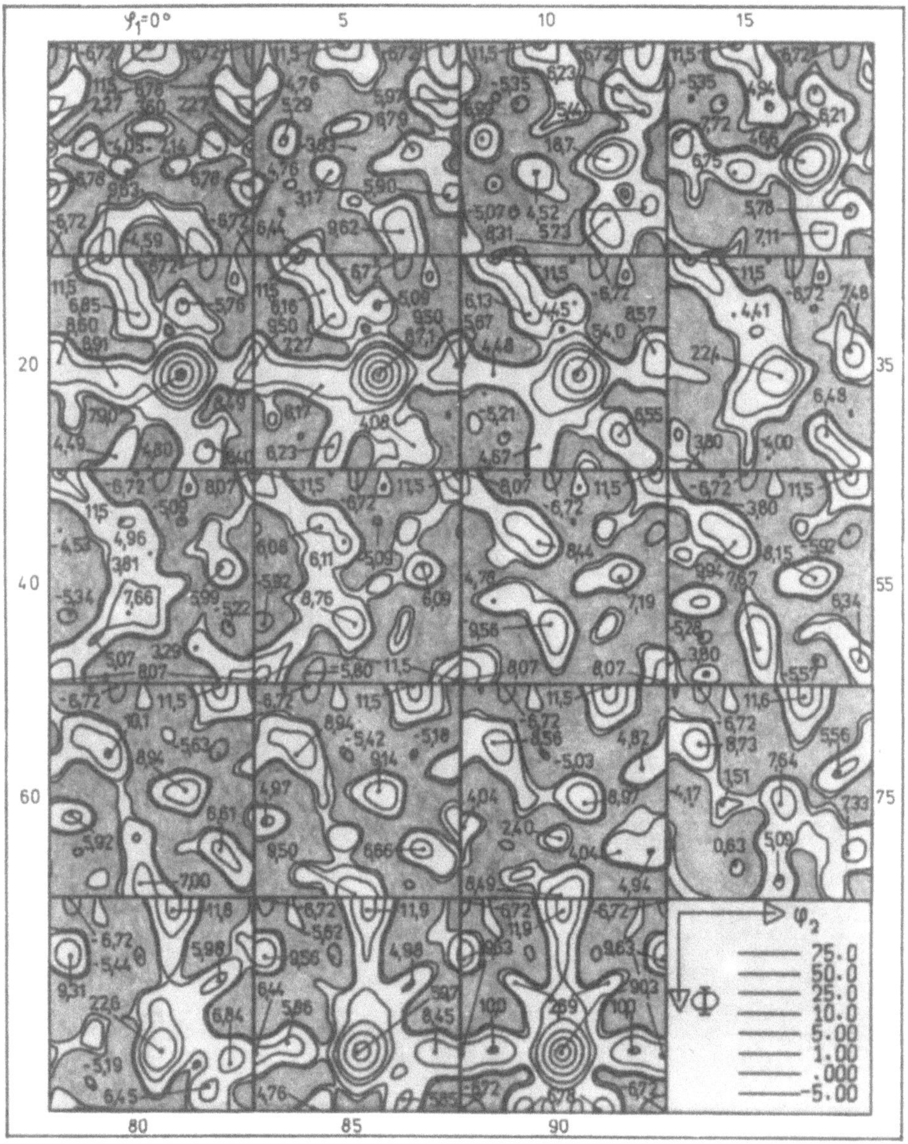

$\tilde{F}$, G, 12.5°, $\{323\}\langle 131\rangle$

$\tilde{F}_{MAX}$ = 90.28 (90°)

$\tilde{F}_{MIN}$ = −6.72 (00°, 05°, . . ., 90°)

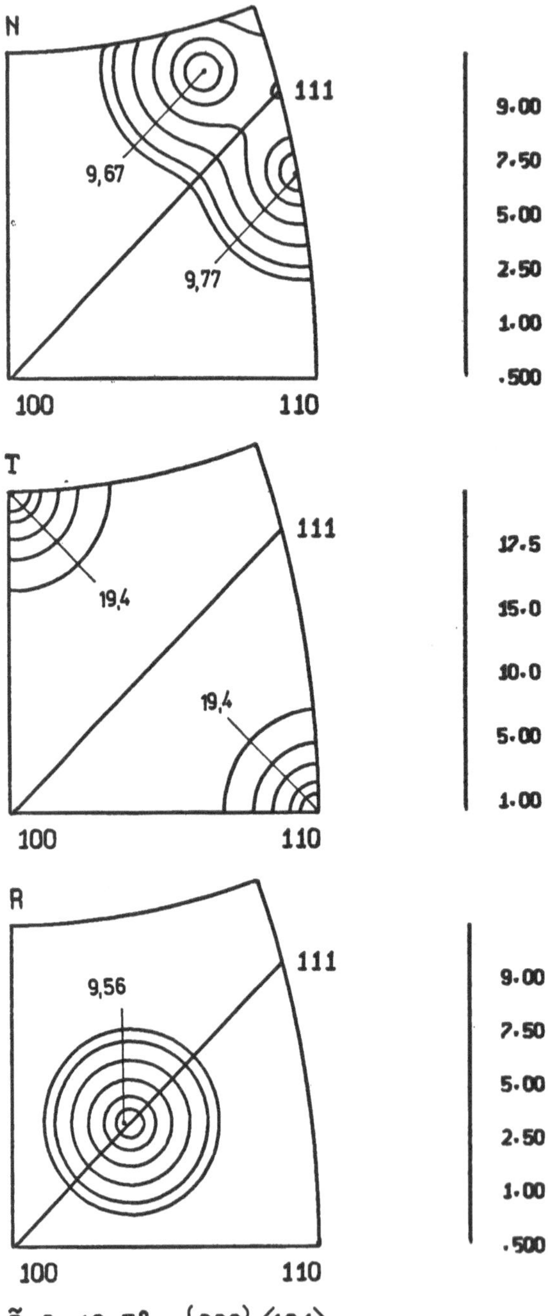

$\tilde{R}$, G, 12.5°, $\{323\}\langle 131\rangle$

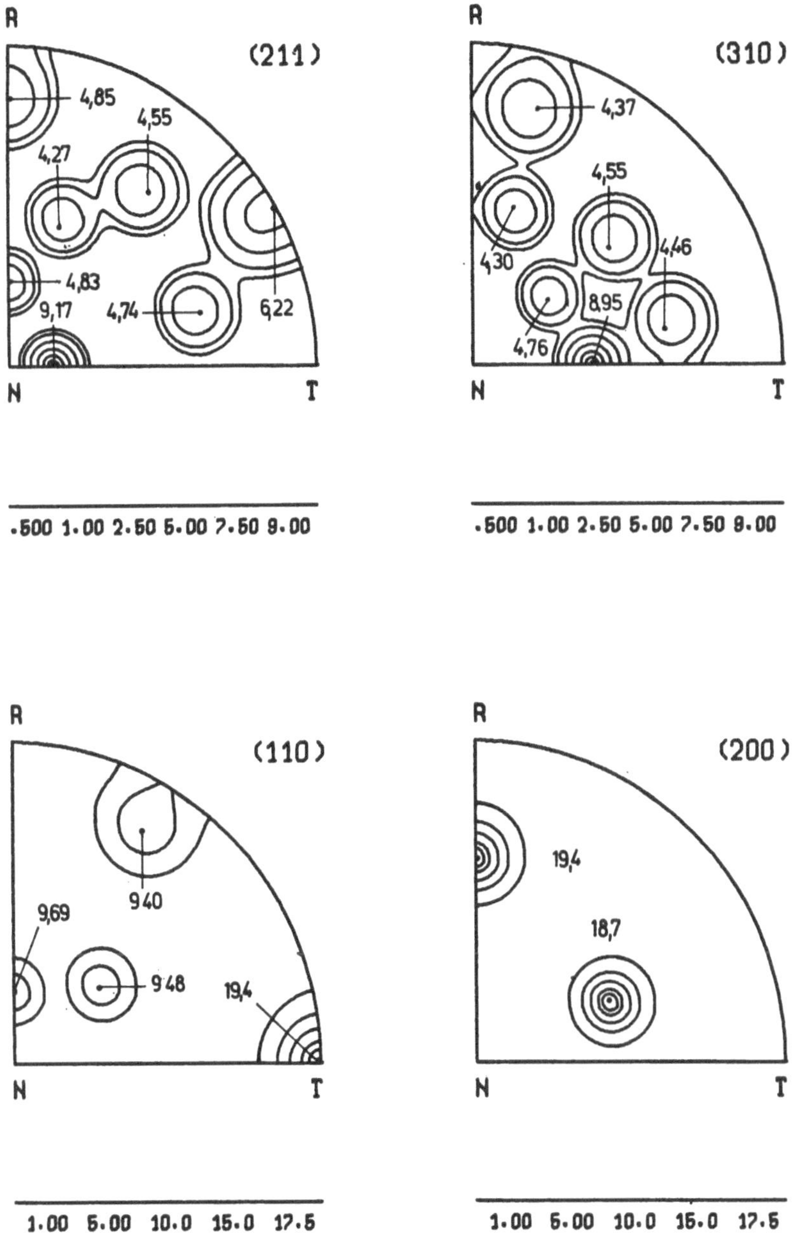

$\tilde{P}$, G, 12.5°, $\{323\}\langle 131\rangle$

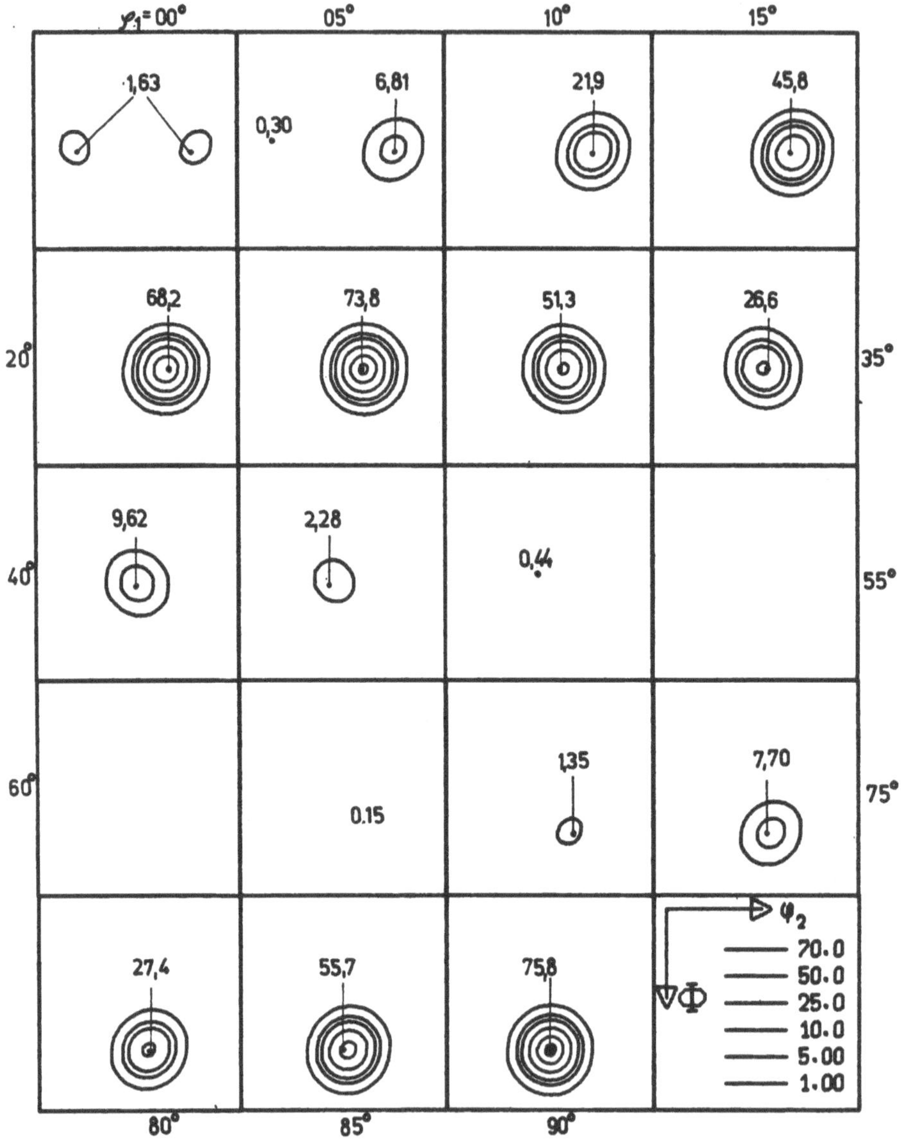

F, G, 15.0°, {323}<131>

F_{MAX} = 75.76 (90°)

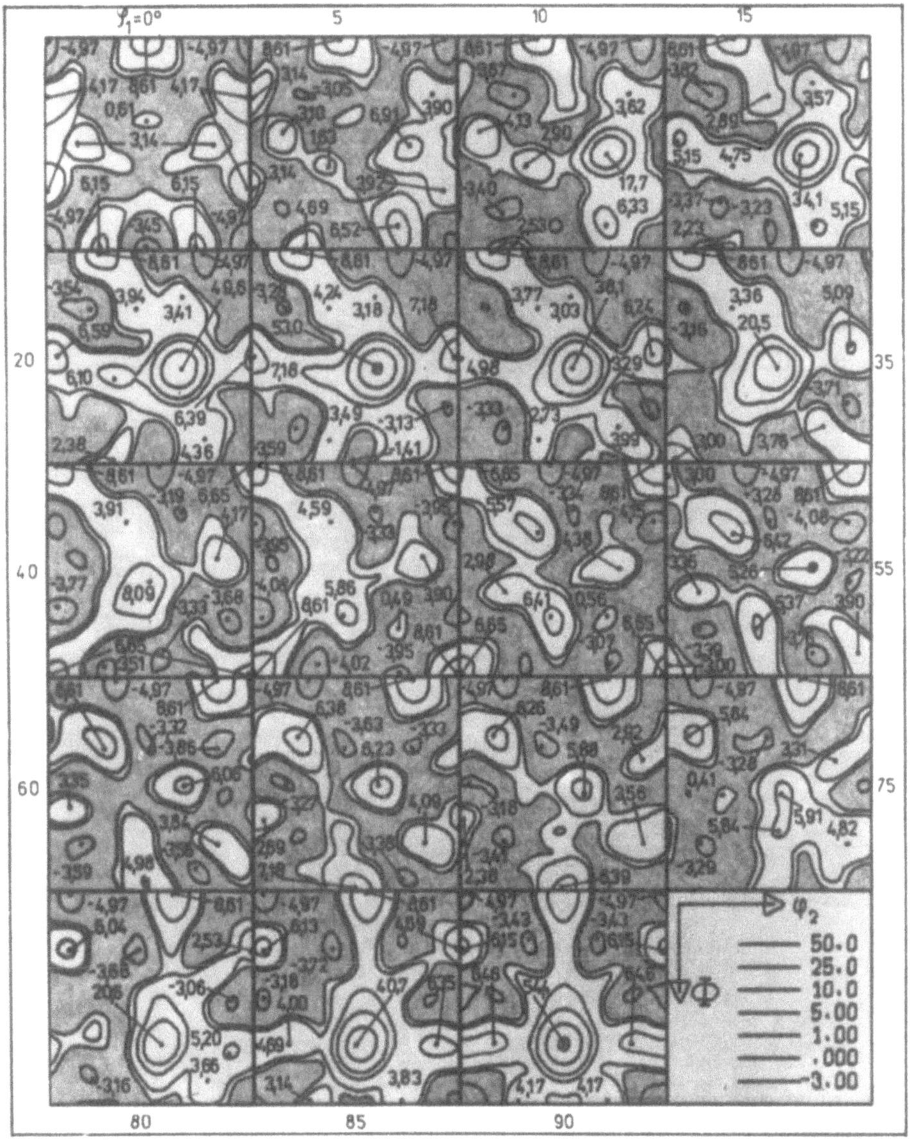

$\tilde{F}$, G, 15.0°, {323}<131>

$\tilde{F}_{MAX}$ = 54.38 (90°)

$\tilde{F}_{MIN}$ = -4.97 (00°, 05°, . . ., 90°)

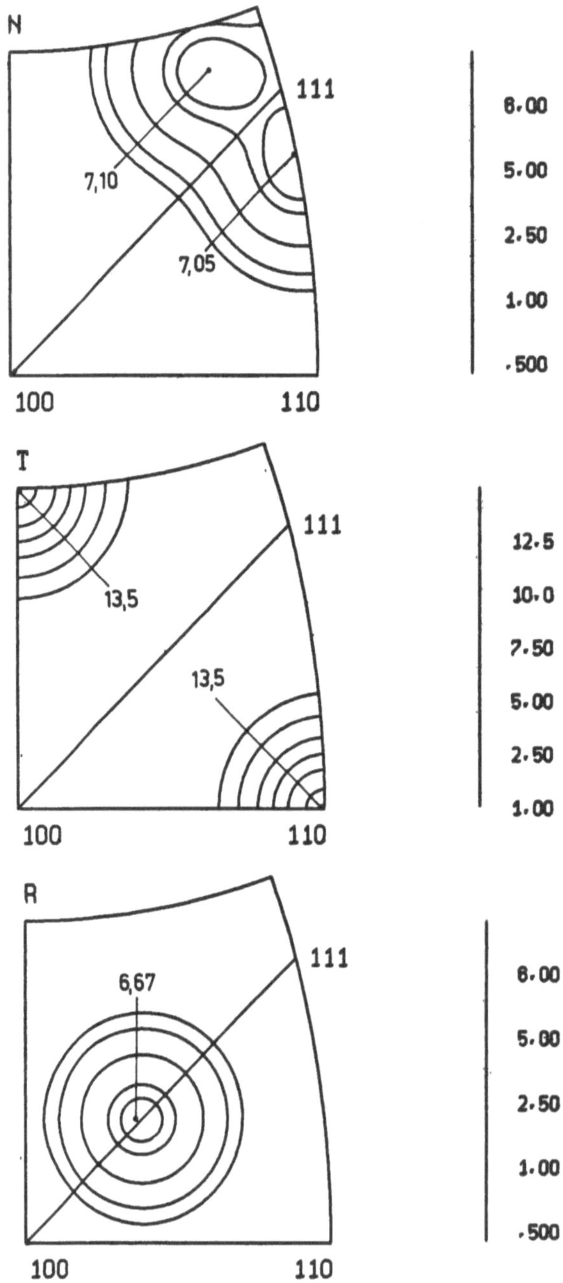

$\tilde{R}$, G, 15.0°, $\{323\}\langle 131\rangle$

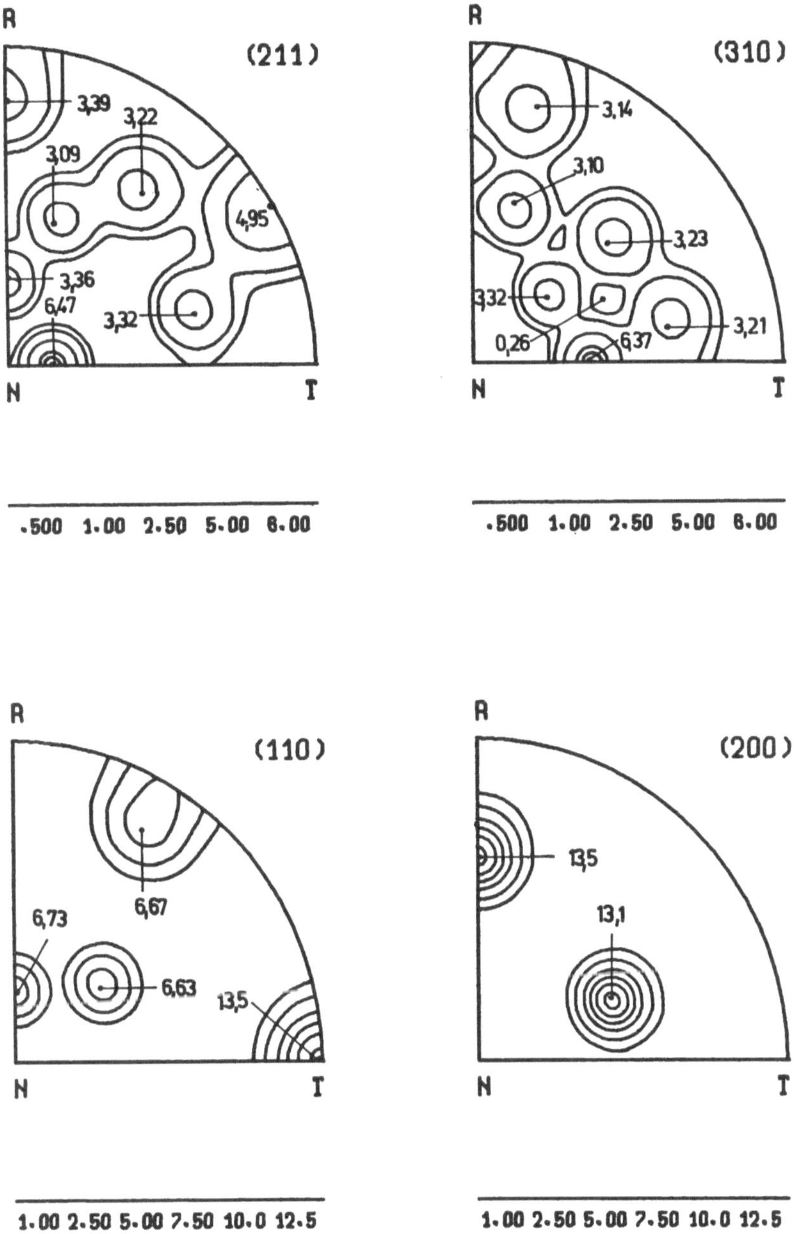

$\tilde{P}$, G, 15.0°, $\{323\}\langle 131\rangle$

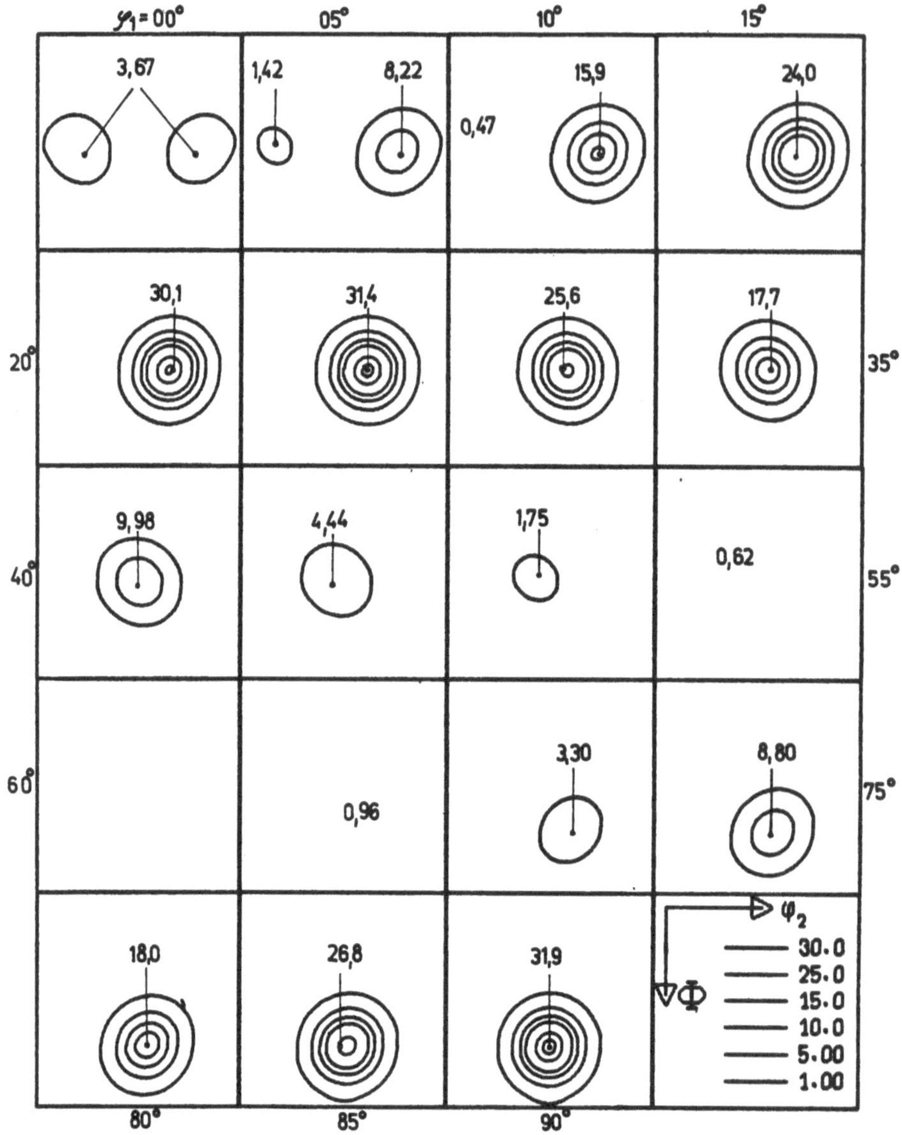

F, G, 20.0°, {323}<131>

F_{MAX} = 31.91 (90°)

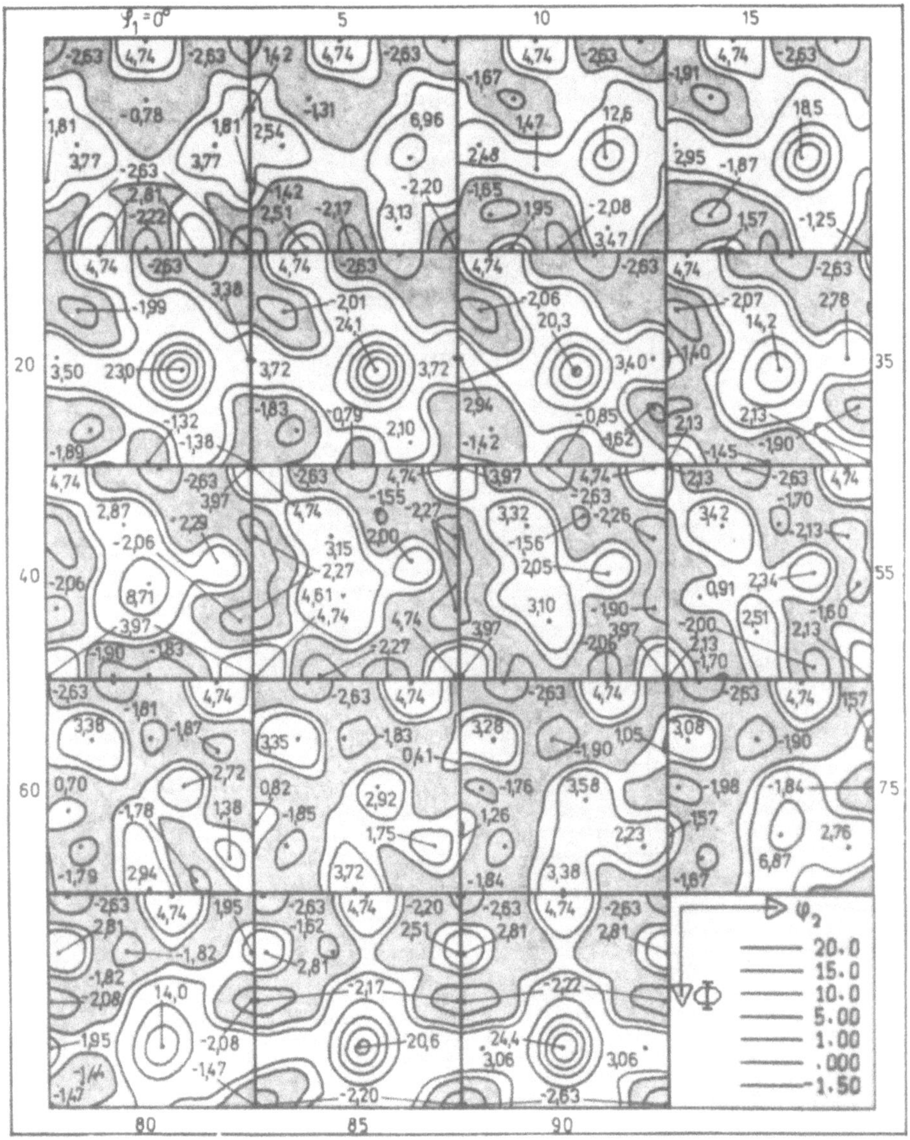

$\tilde{F}$, G, 20.0°, {323}<131>

$\tilde{F}_{MAX}$ = 24.38 (90°)

$\tilde{F}_{MIN}$ = −2.63 (00°, 05°, . . . , 90°)

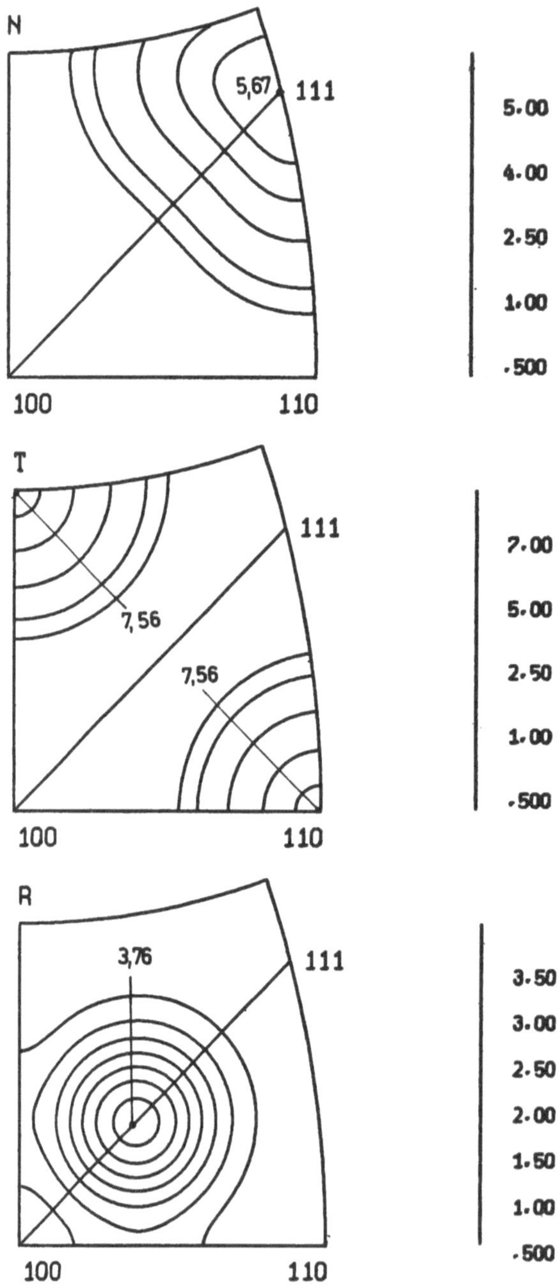

$\tilde{R}_{MIN} = 0.02$

(90°, 45°)

$\tilde{R}$, G, 20.0° , {323}<131>

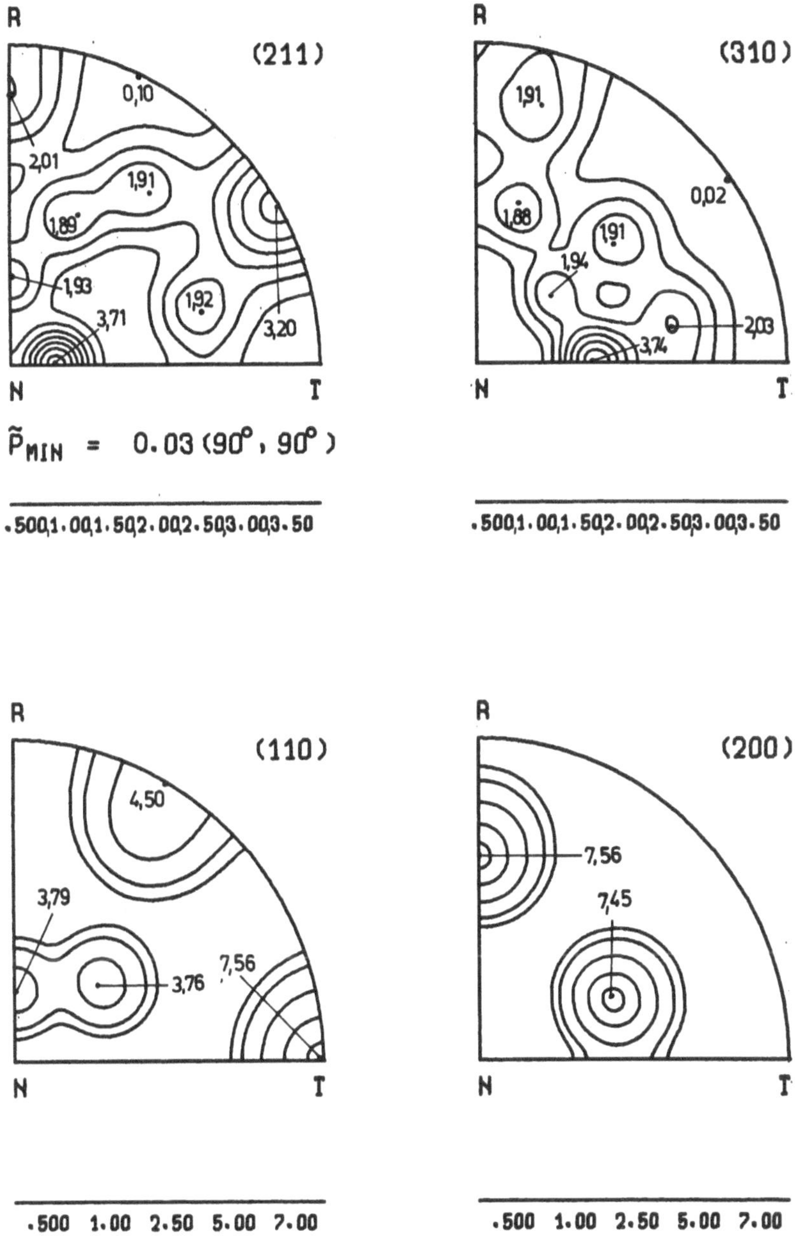

$\tilde{P}$, 6, 20.0°, {323}⟨131⟩

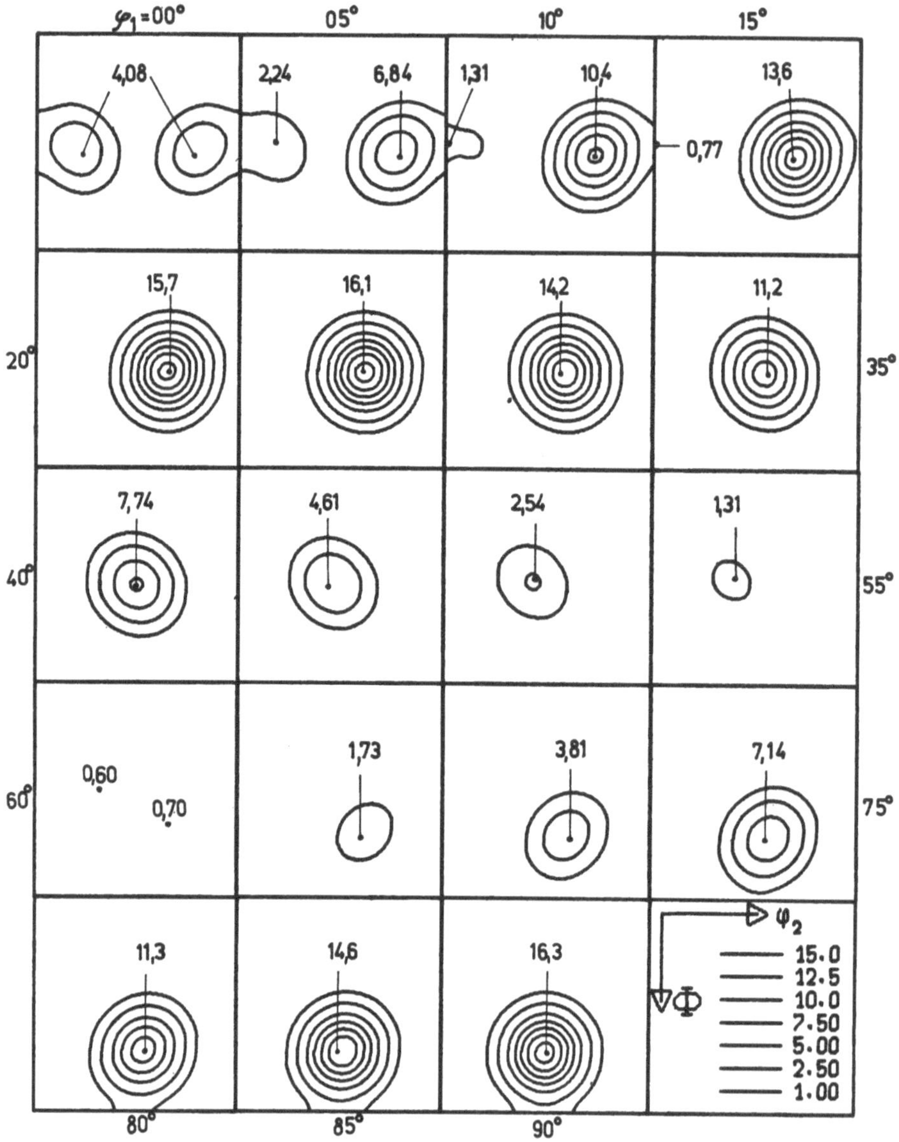

F, G, 25.0°, {323}<131>

F_{MAX} = 16.30 (90°)

$\tilde{F}$, G, 25.0°, {323}<131>

$\tilde{F}_{MAX}$ = 13.15 (90°)

$\tilde{F}_{MIN}$ = −1.37 (00°, 05°, . . . , 90°)

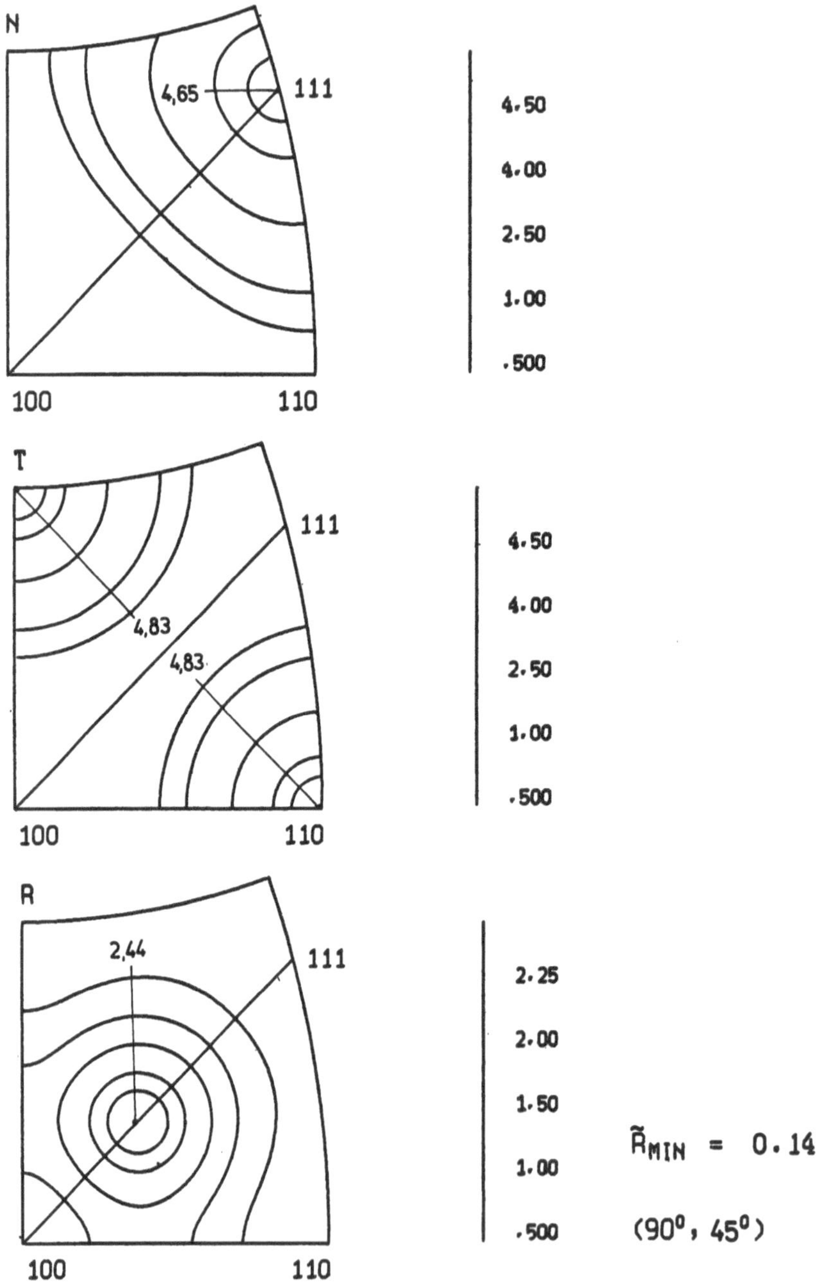

$\tilde{R}$, G, 25.0°, $\{323\}\langle 131\rangle$

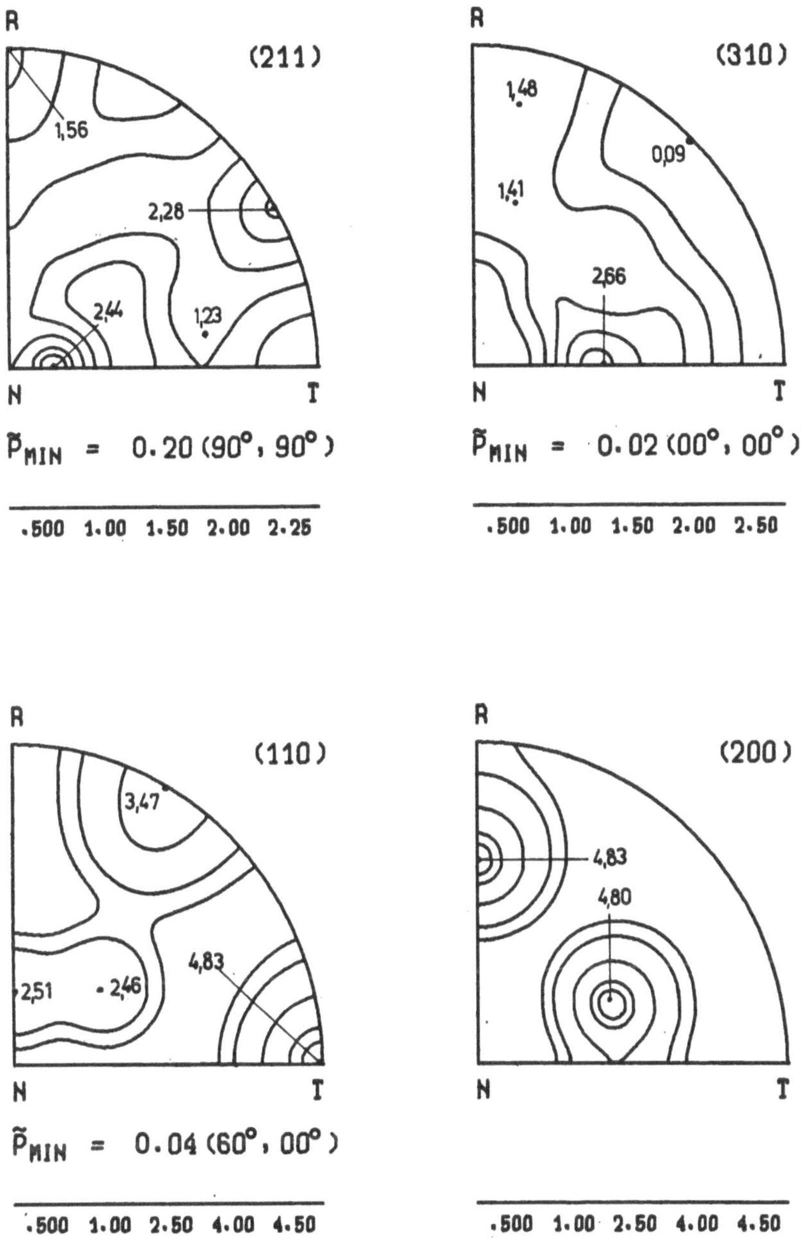

$\tilde{P}$, G, 25.0°, {323}⟨131⟩

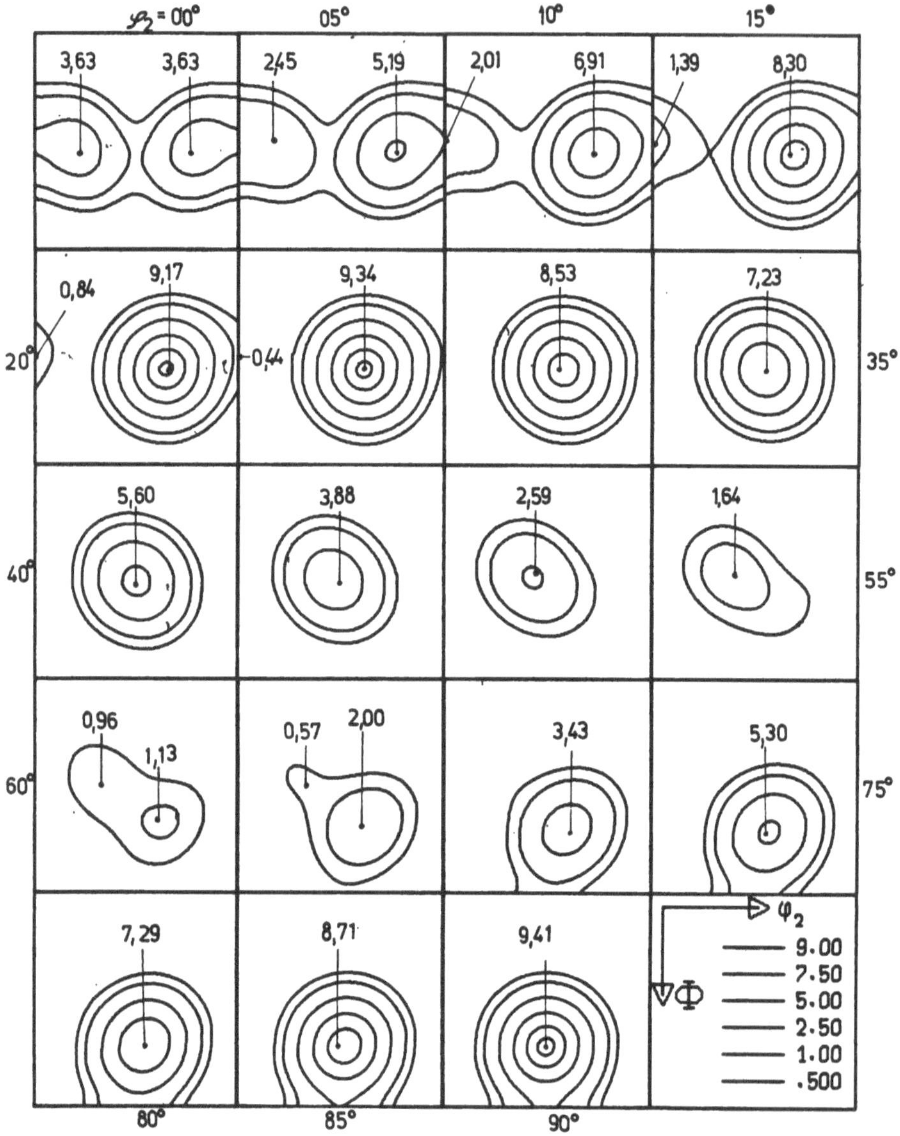

F, G, 30.0°, {323}<131>

F_{MAX} = 9.41 (90°)

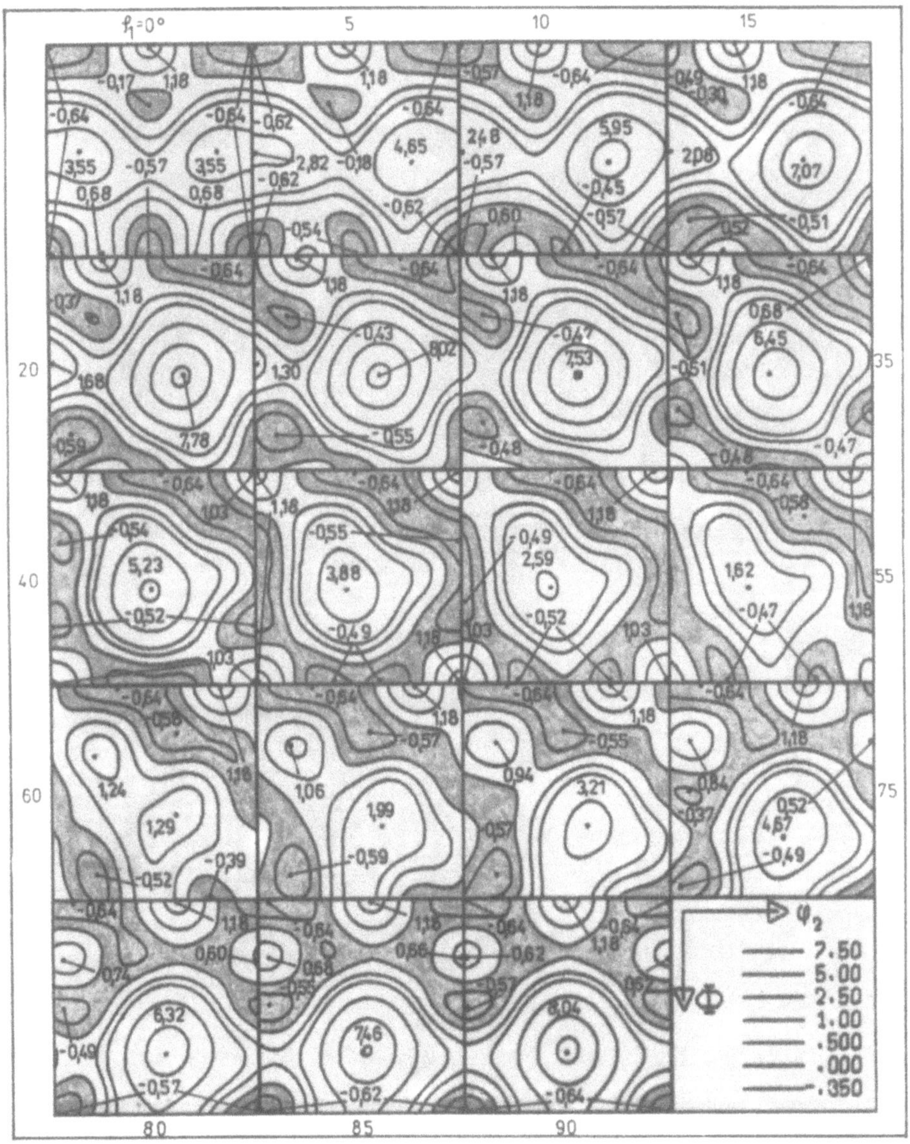

$\tilde{F}$, G, 30.0°, {323}<131>

$\tilde{F}_{MAX}$ = 8.04 (90°)

$\tilde{F}_{MIN}$ = −.64 (00°, 05°, . . . , 90°)

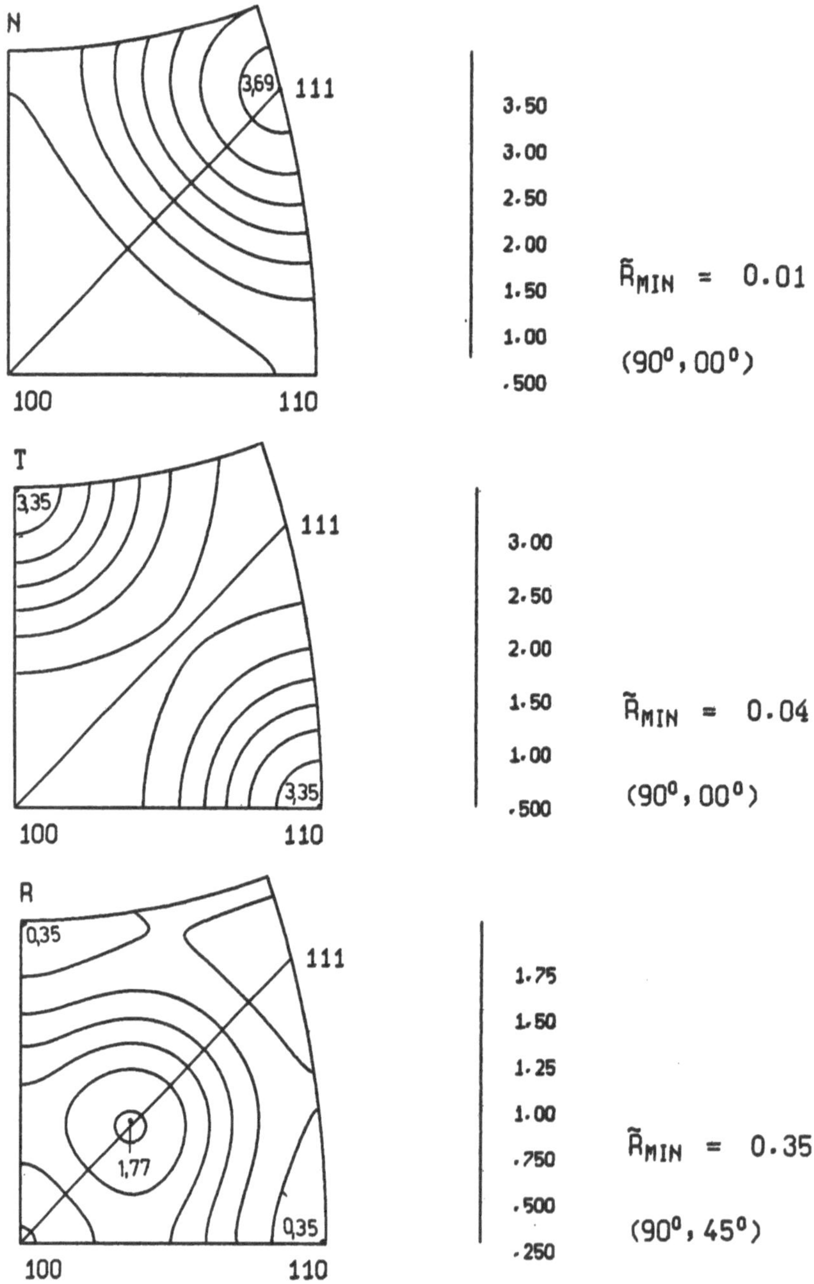

$\tilde{R}$, G, 30.0° , {323}⟨131⟩

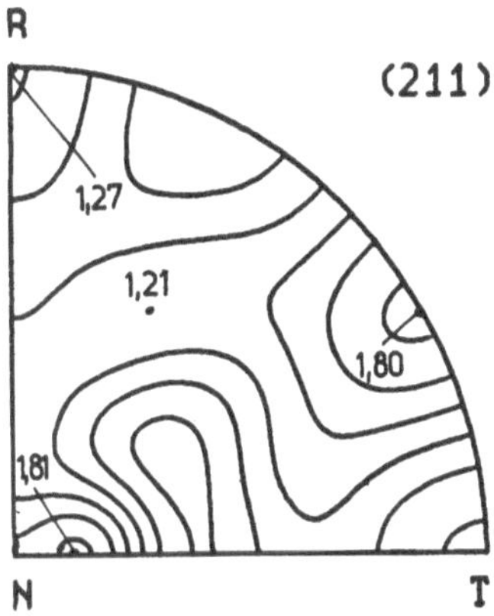

$\tilde{P}_{MIN}$ = 0.41 (45°, 60°)

.500 .750 1.00 1.25 1.50 1.75

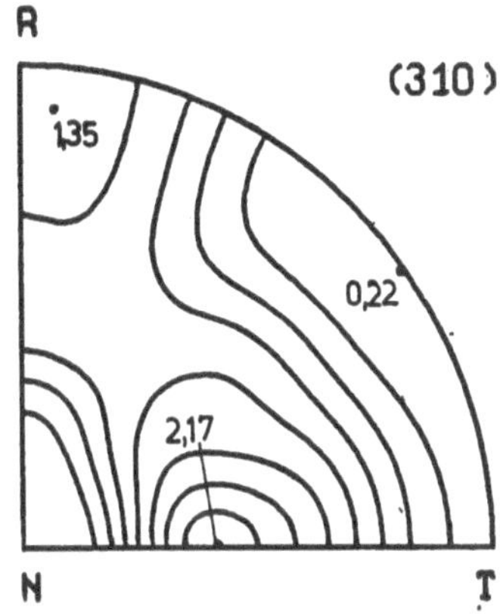

$\tilde{P}_{MIN}$ = 0.09 (00°, 00°)

.500, .750, 1.00, 1.25, 1.50, 1.75, 2.00

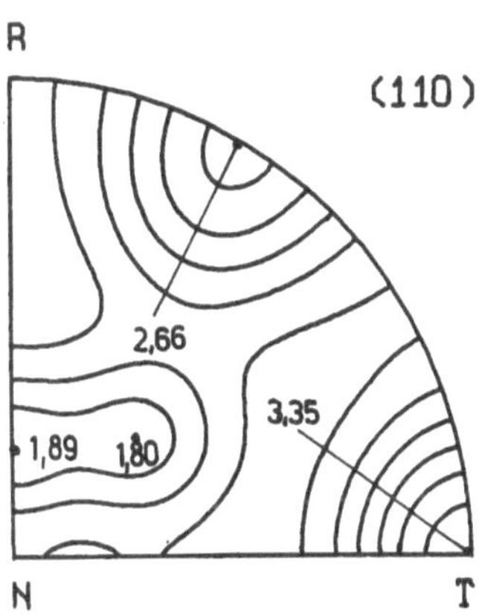

$\tilde{P}_{MIN}$ = 0.15 (60°, 00°)

.500 1.00 1.50 2.00 2.50 3.00

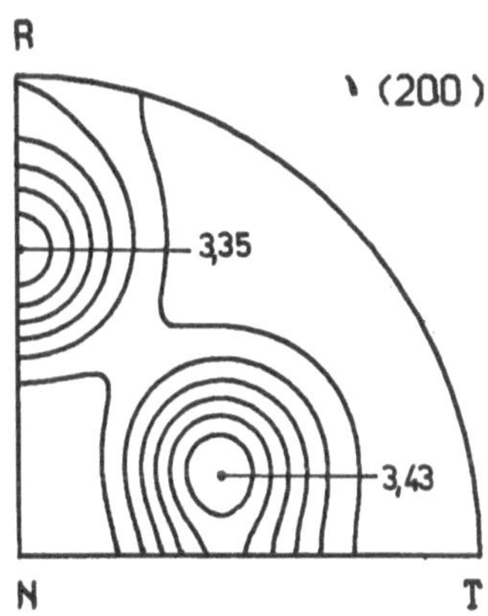

$\tilde{P}_{MIN}$ = 0.01 (00°, 00°)

.500 1.00 1.50 2.00 2.50 3.00

$\tilde{P}$, G, 30.0°, {323}⟨131⟩

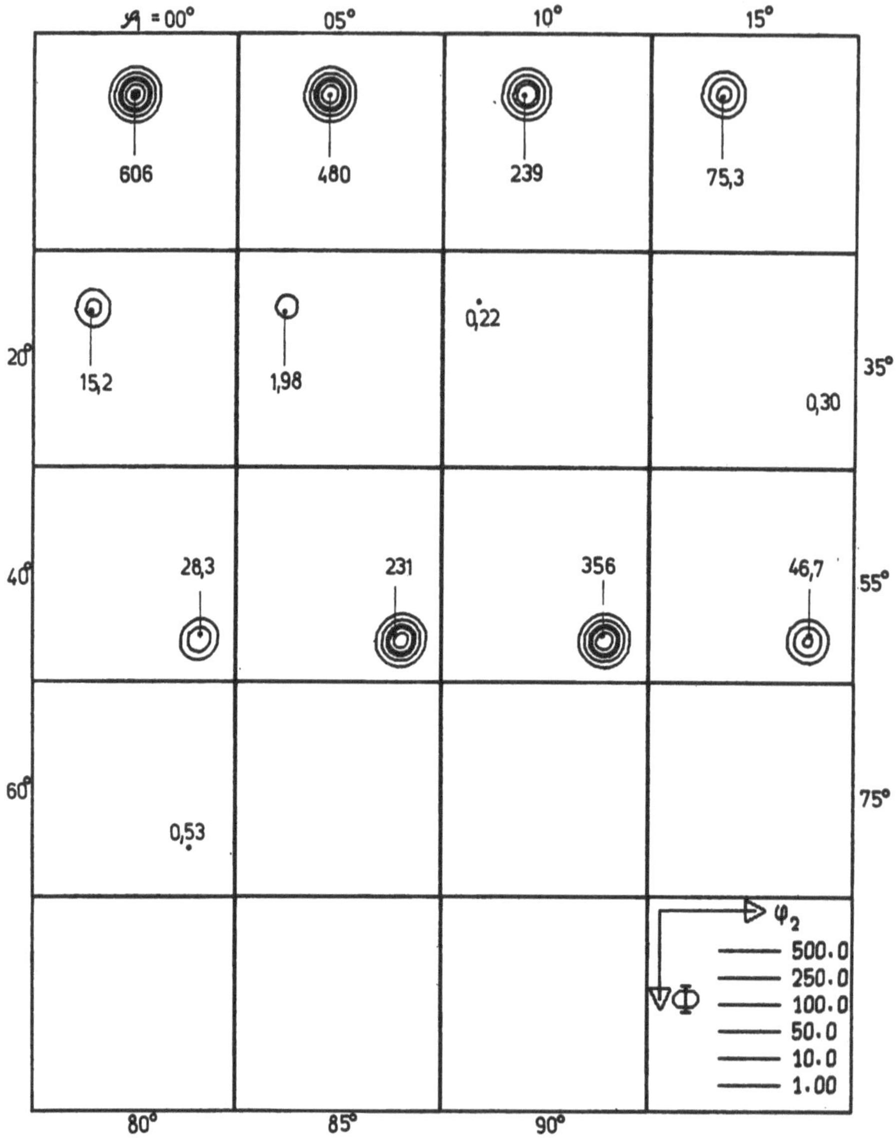

F, G, 7.50°, {113}<110>

F_{MAX} = 605.95 (00°)

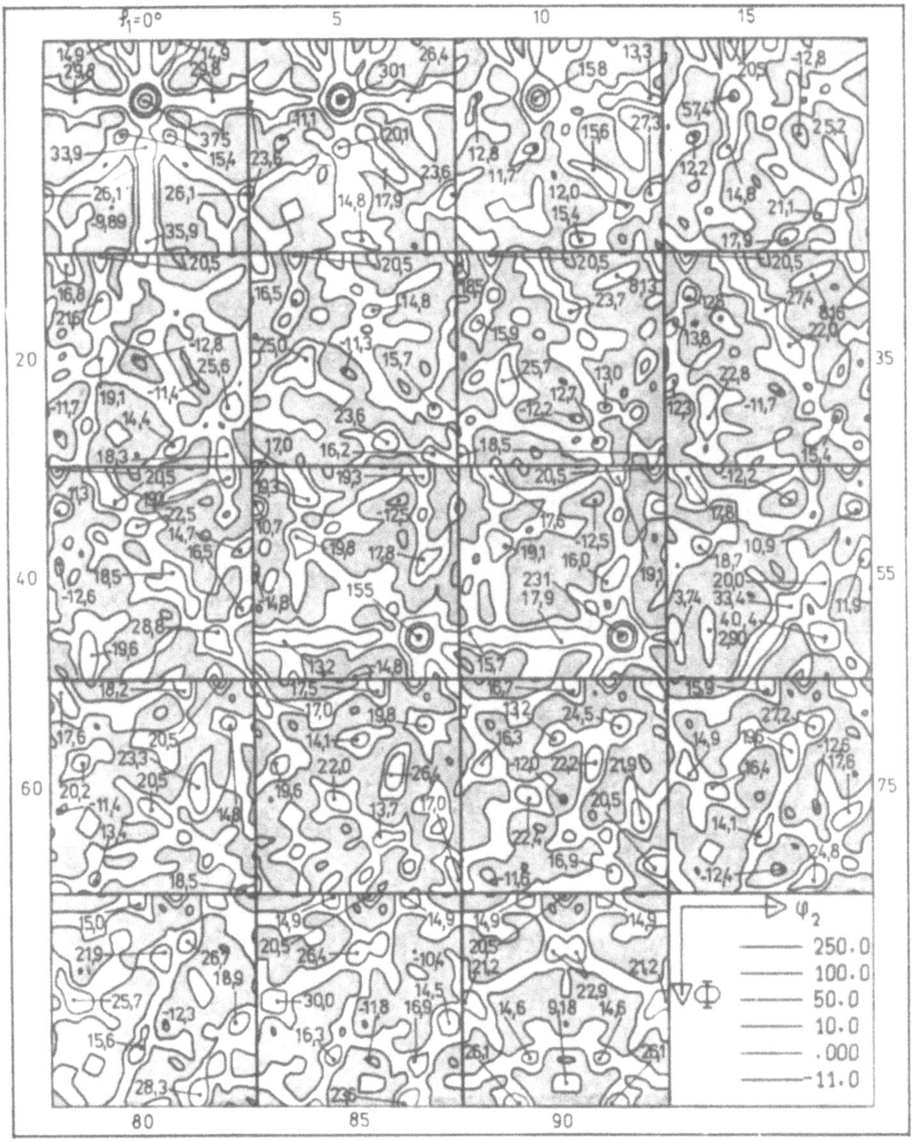

$\tilde{F}$, G, 7.50°, {113}<110>

$\tilde{F}_{MAX}$ = 375.45 (00°)

$\tilde{F}_{MIN}$ = −14.79 (45°)

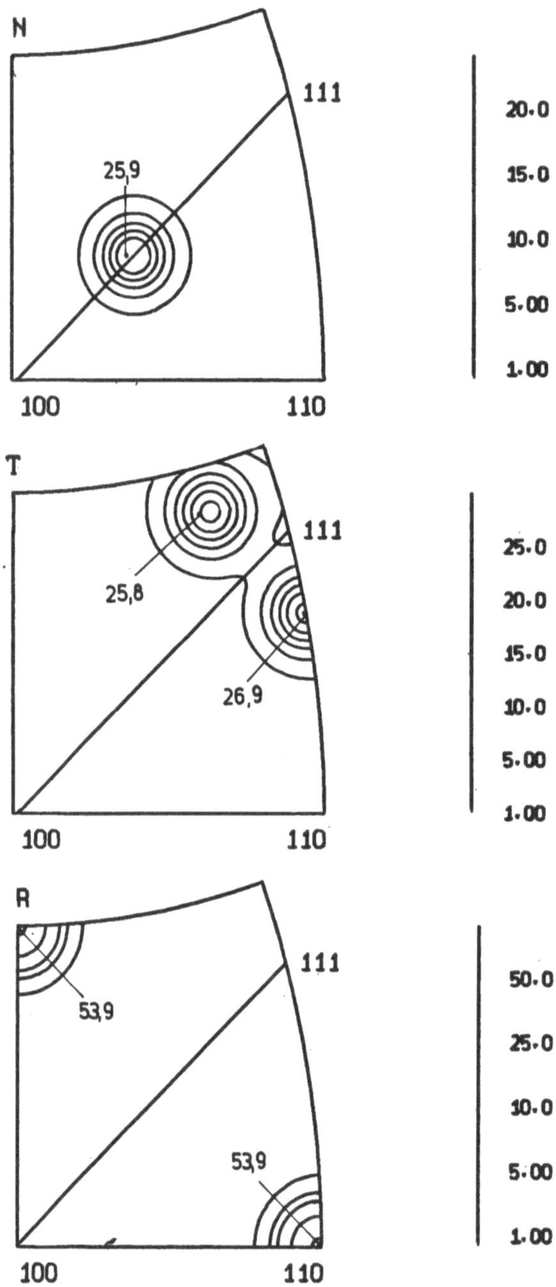

$\tilde{R}$, G, 7.50°, {113}⟨110⟩

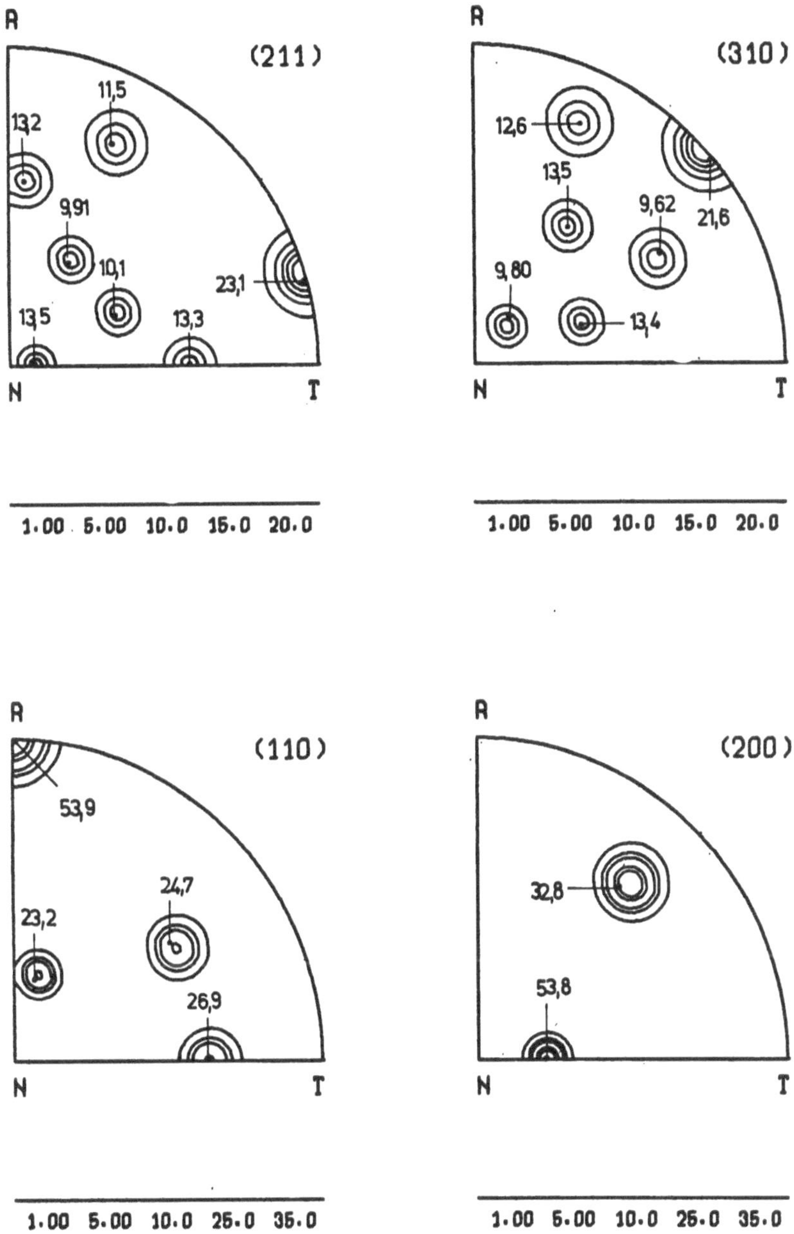

$\tilde{P}$, 6, 7.50°, $\{113\}\langle 110\rangle$

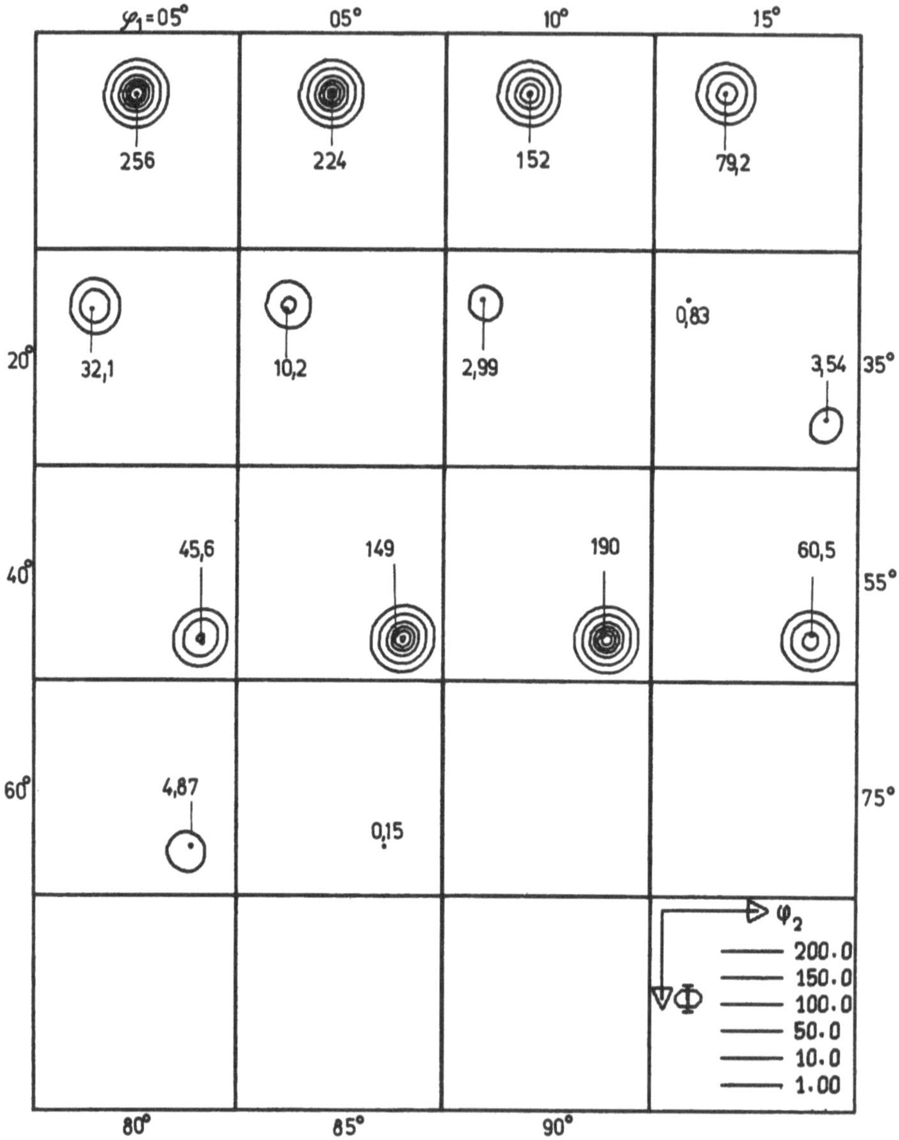

F, G, 10.0° , {113}<110>

F_{MAX} = 255.83 (00°)

$\tilde{F}$, G, 10.0°, {113}<110>

$\tilde{F}_{MAX}$ = 167.87 (00°)

$\tilde{F}_{MIN}$ = -8.51 (00°, 05°, . . . , 90°)

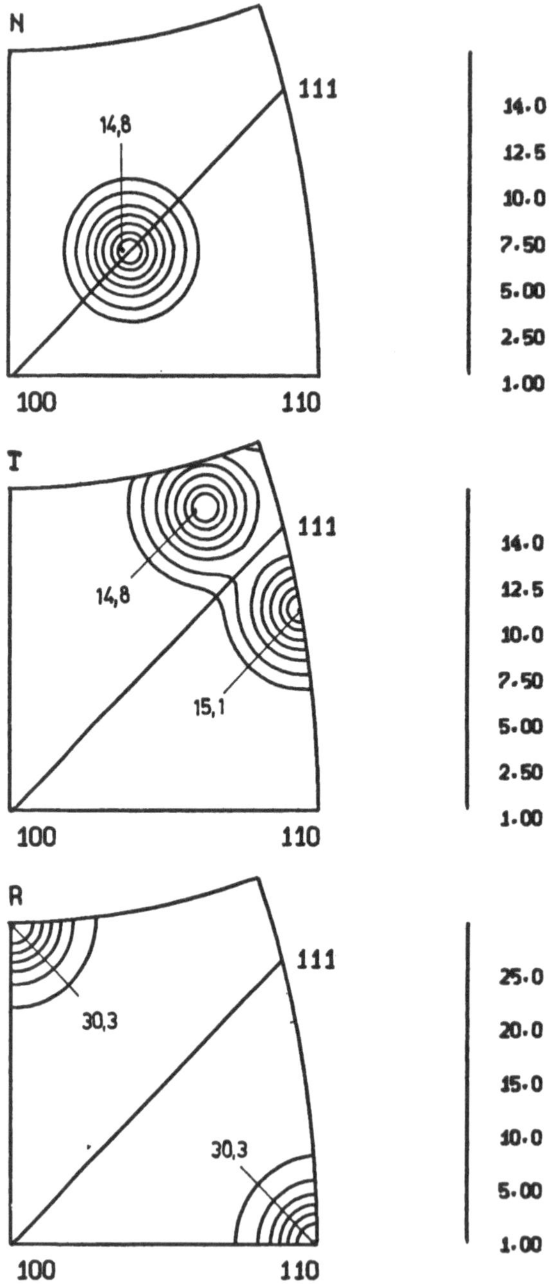

$\tilde{R}$, G, 10.0°, $\{113\}\langle 110\rangle$

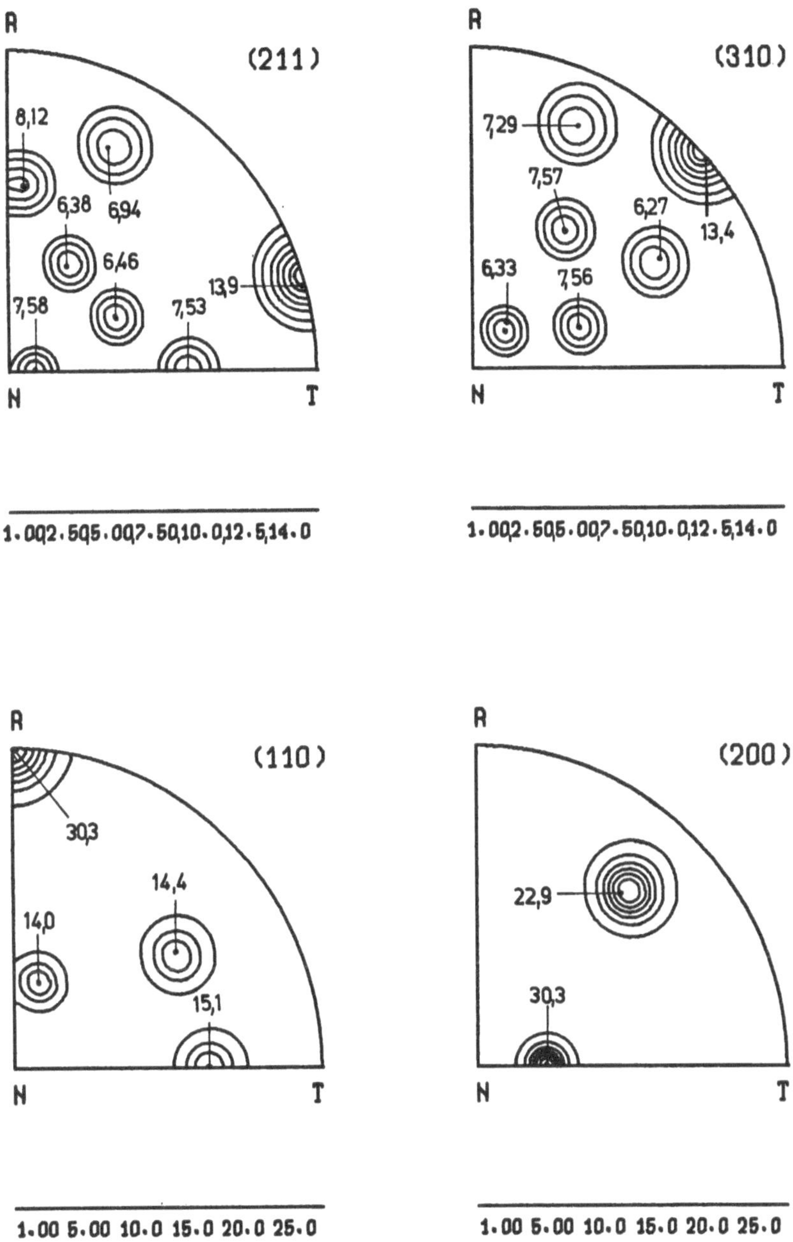

$\tilde{P}$, G, 10.0°, {113}⟨110⟩

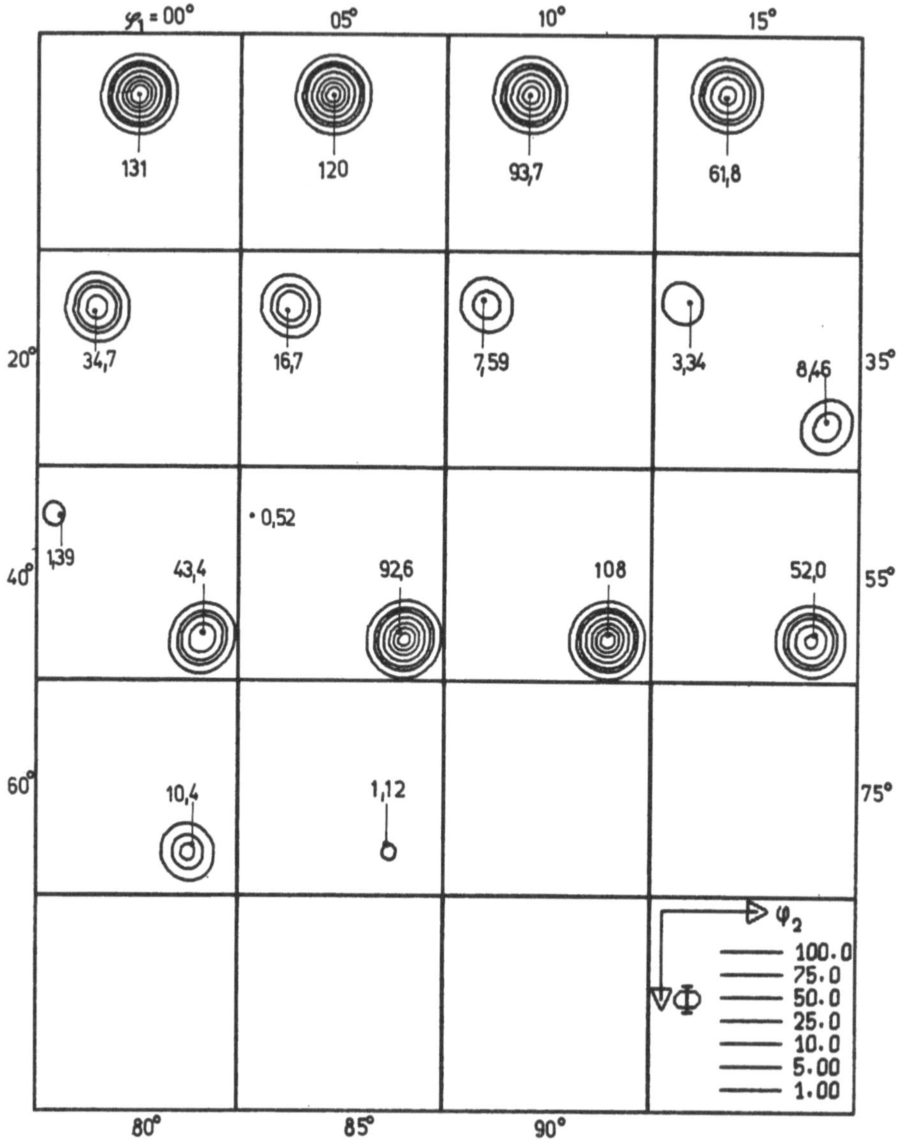

F, G, 12.5°, {113}<110>

F_{MAX} = 130.97 (00°)

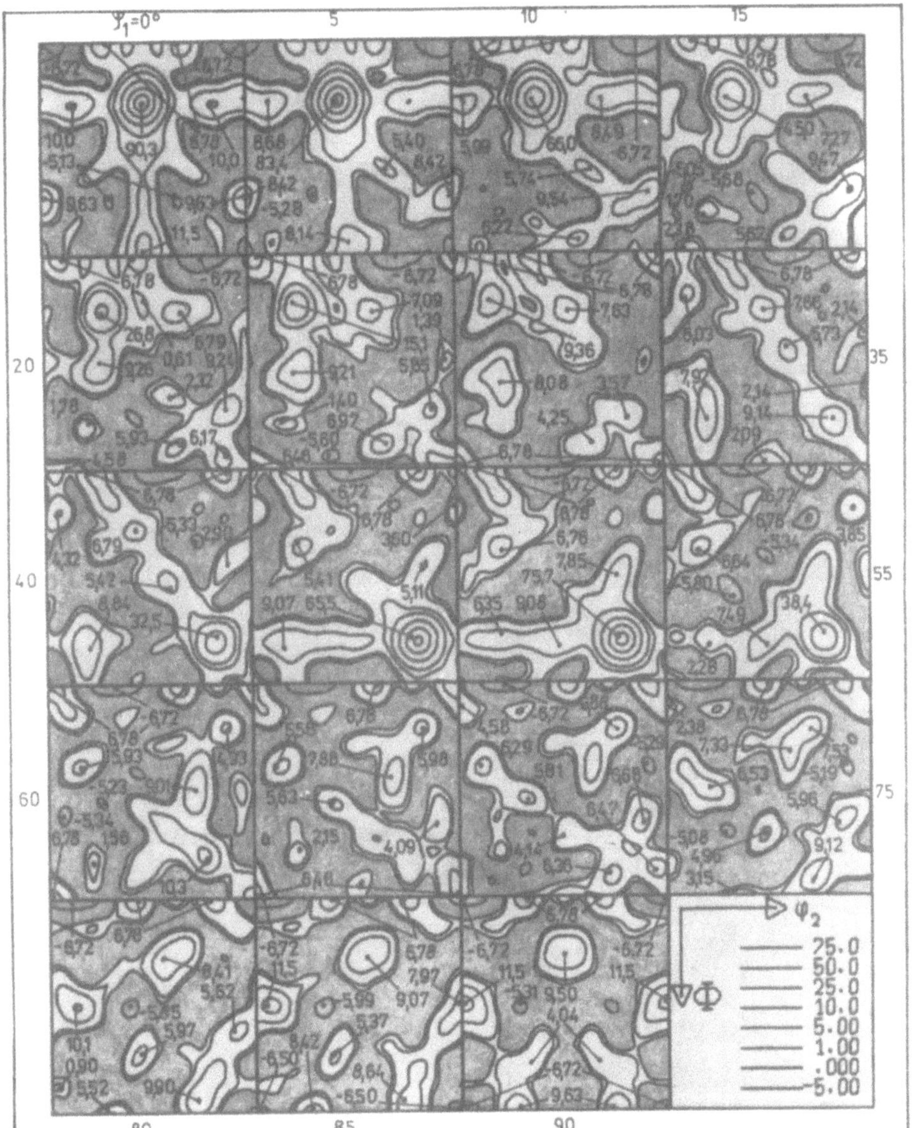

$\tilde{F}$, G, 12.5°, {113}<110>

$\tilde{F}_{MAX}$ = 90.28 (00°)

$\tilde{F}_{MIN}$ = −6.72 (00°, 05°, . . . , 90°)

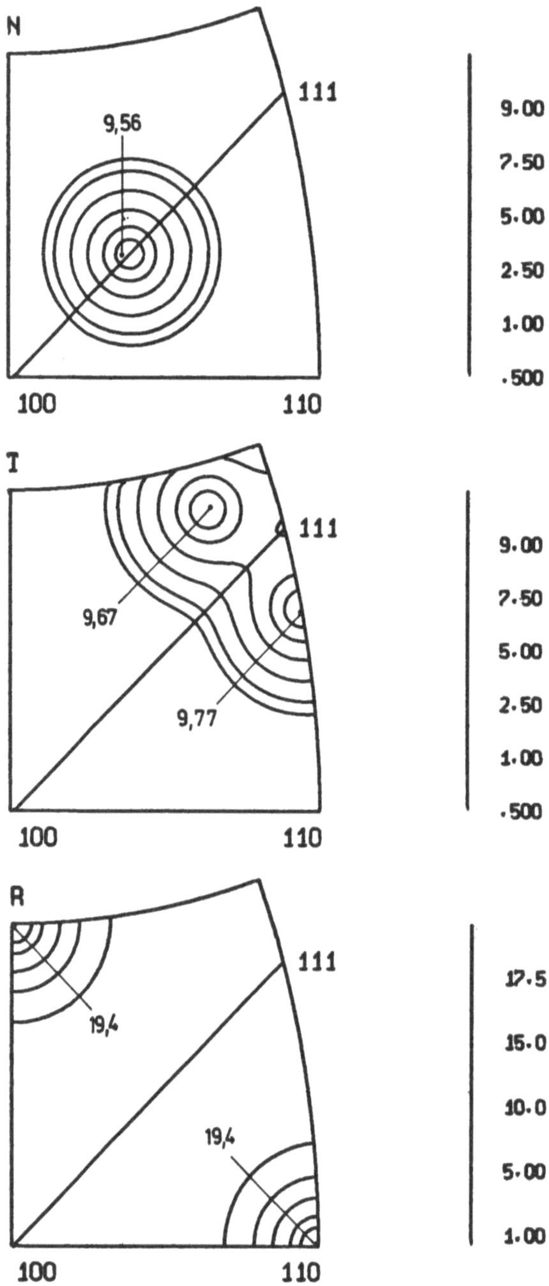

R̃, G, 12.5°, {113}⟨110⟩

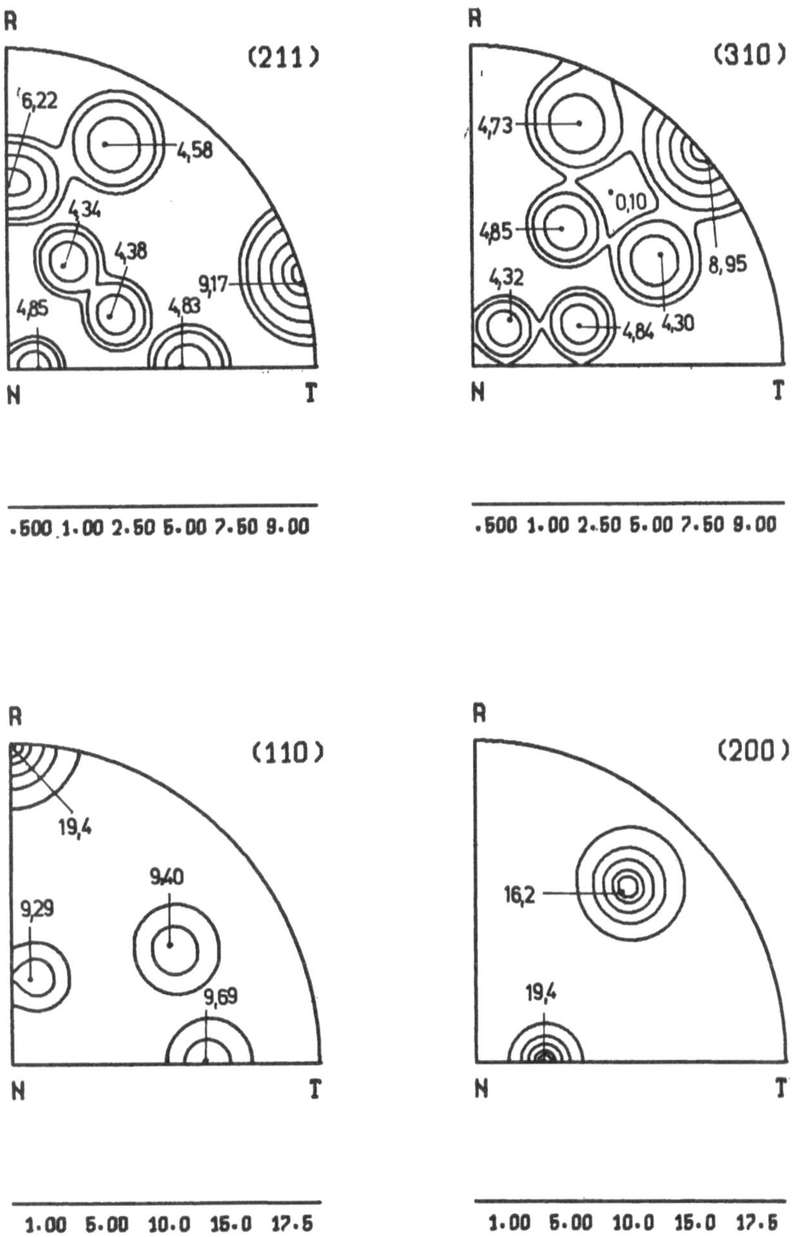

$\tilde{P}$, G, 12.5^{0}, $\{113\}\langle 110\rangle$

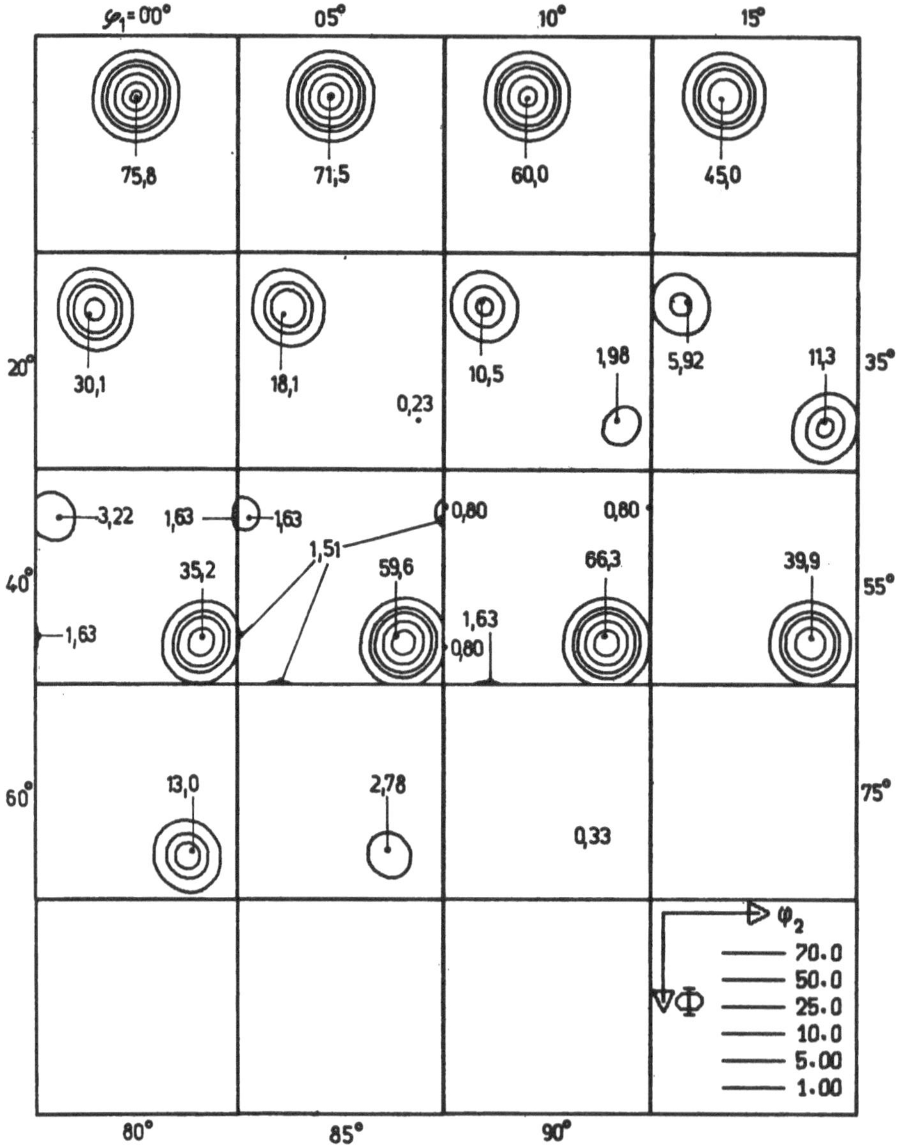

F, G, 15.0°, {113}<110>

F_{MAX} = 75.76 (00°)

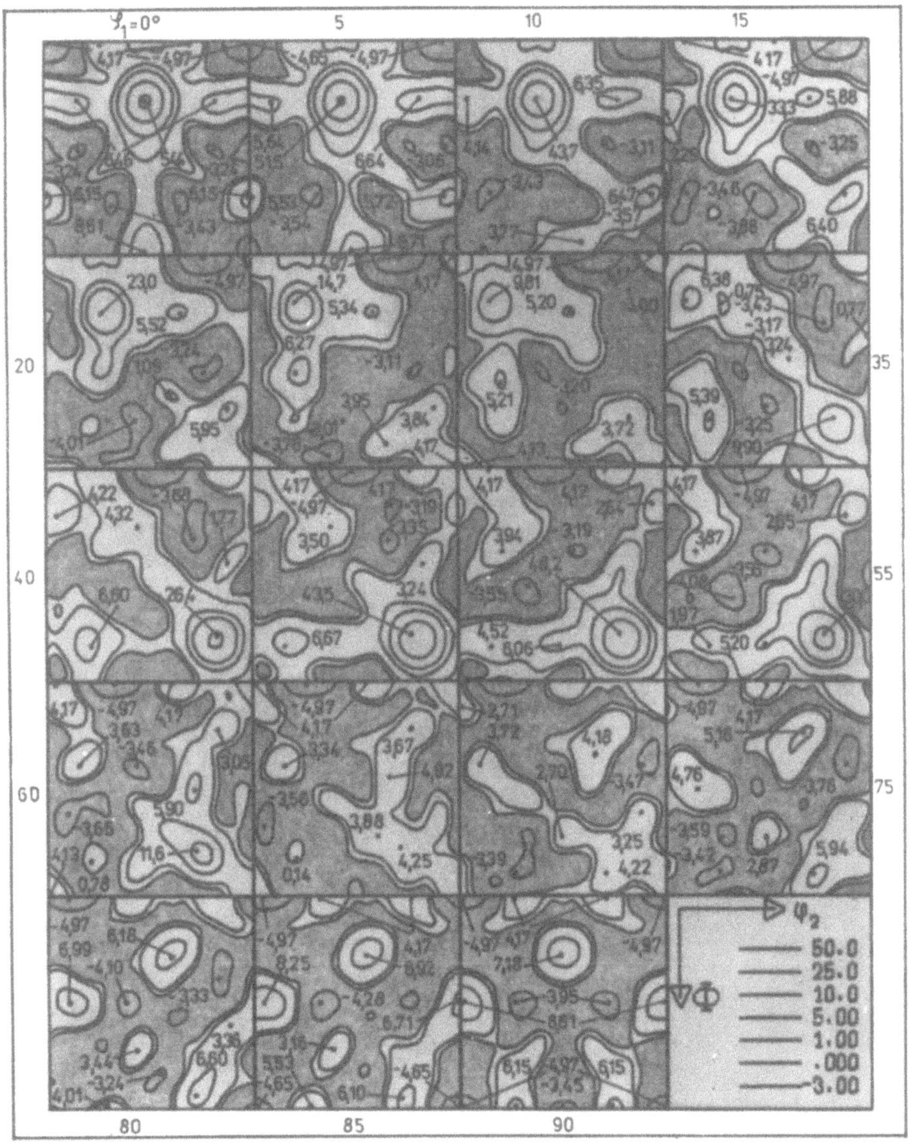

$\tilde{F}$, G, 15.0° , {113}<110>

$\tilde{F}_{MAX}$ = 54.38 (00°)

$\tilde{F}_{MIN}$ = -4.97 (00°, 05°, . . . , 90°)

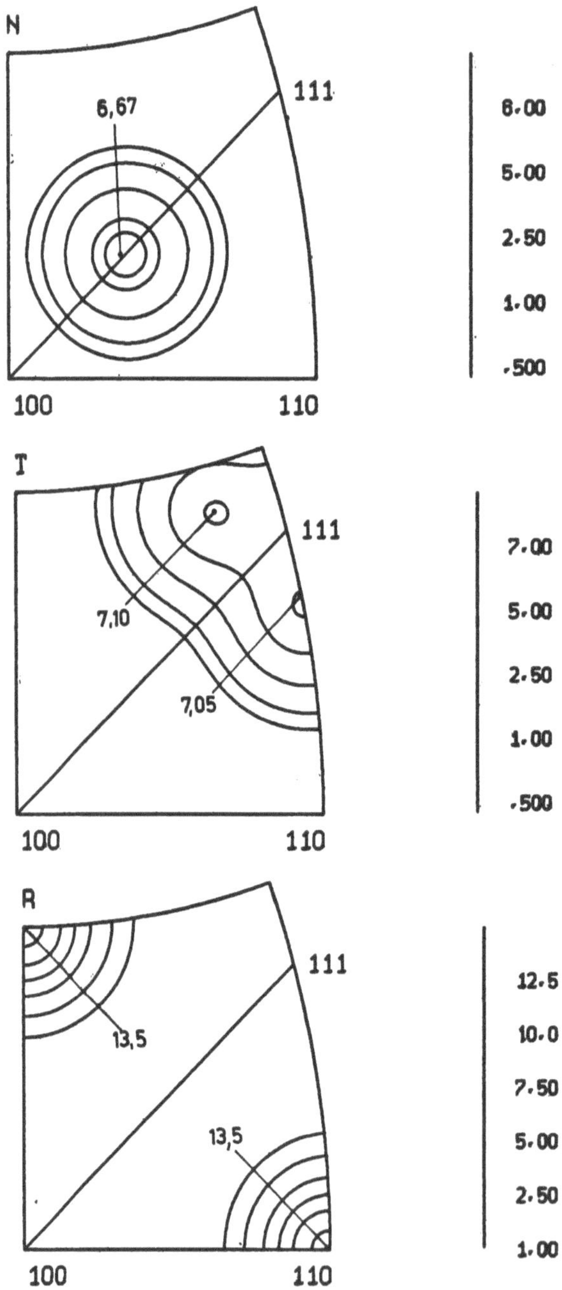

R̃, G, 15.0°, {113}<110>

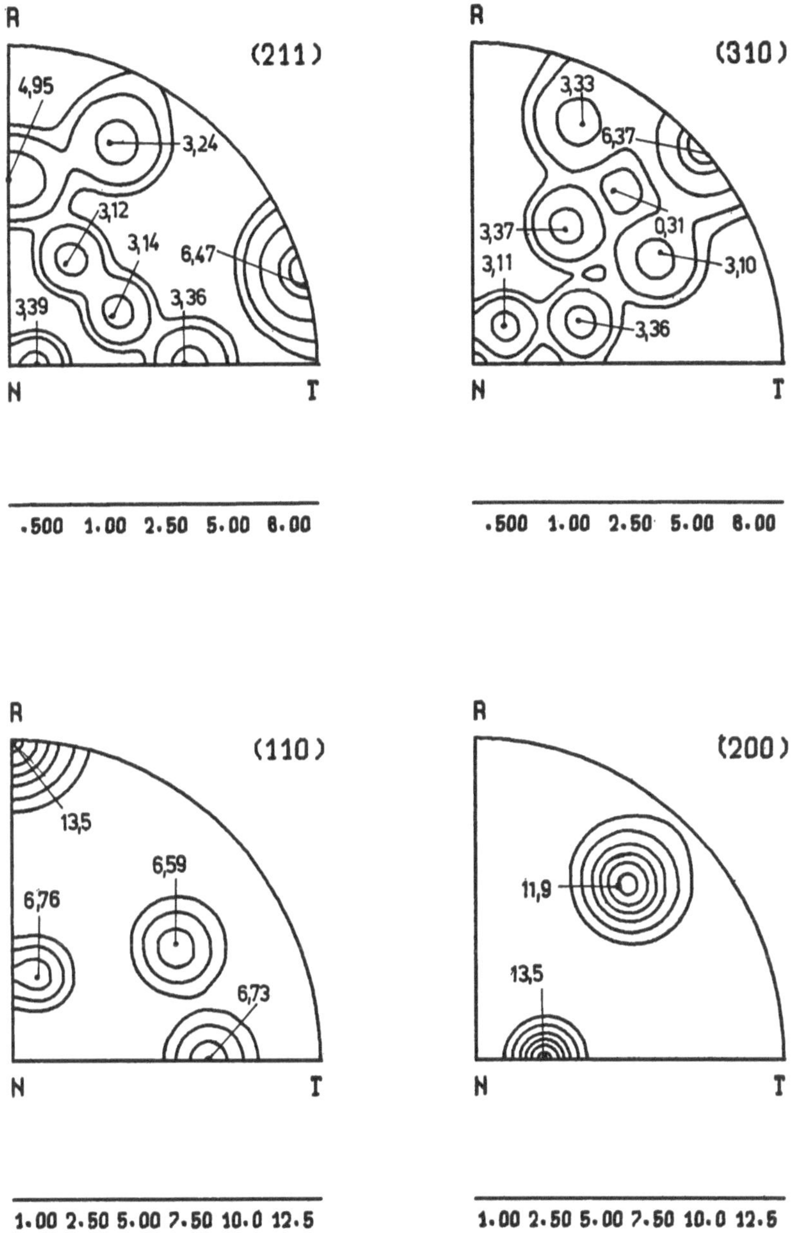

$\tilde{P}$, G, 15.0°, $\{113\}\langle 110\rangle$

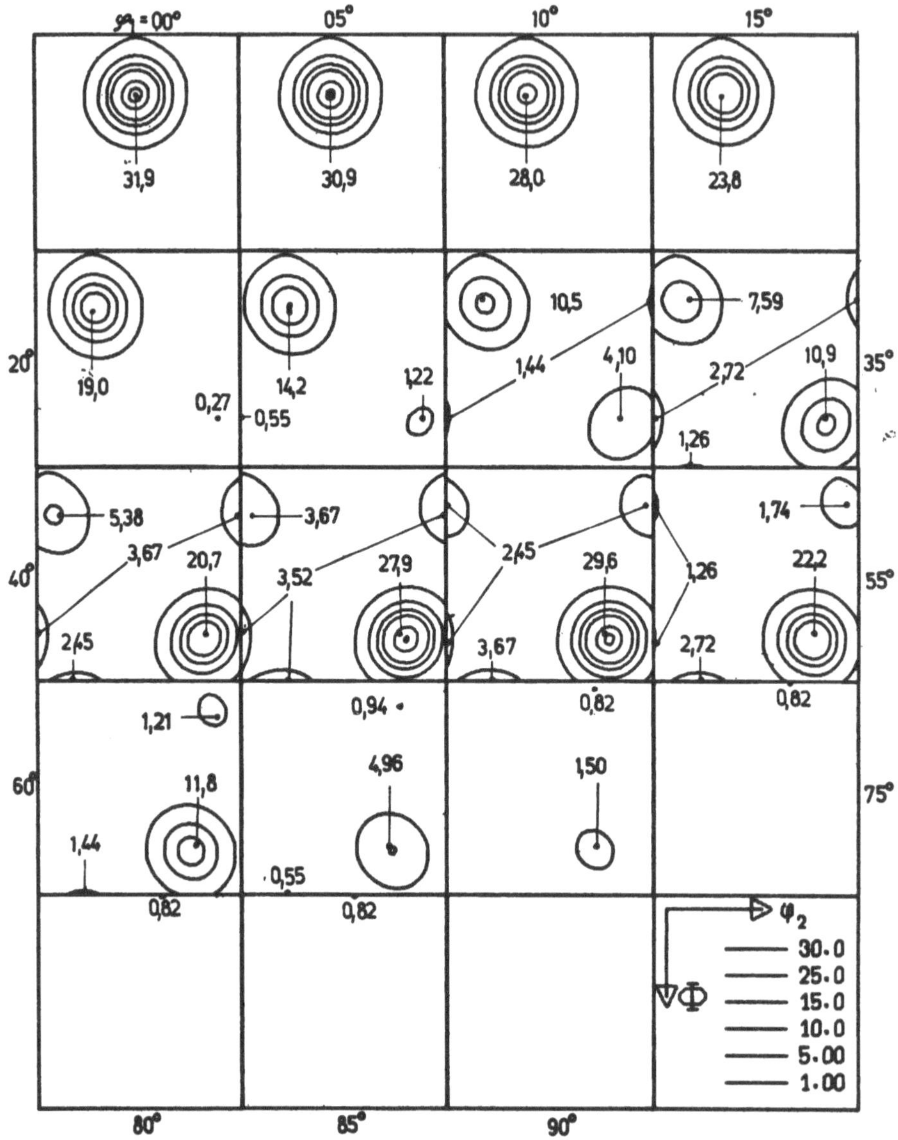

F, G, 20.0°, {113}<110>

F_{MAX} = 31.91 (00°)

$\tilde{F}$, G, 20.0° , {113}<110>

$\tilde{F}_{MAX}$ = 24.38 (00°)

$\tilde{F}_{MIN}$ = −2.63 (00°, 05°, . . . , 90°)

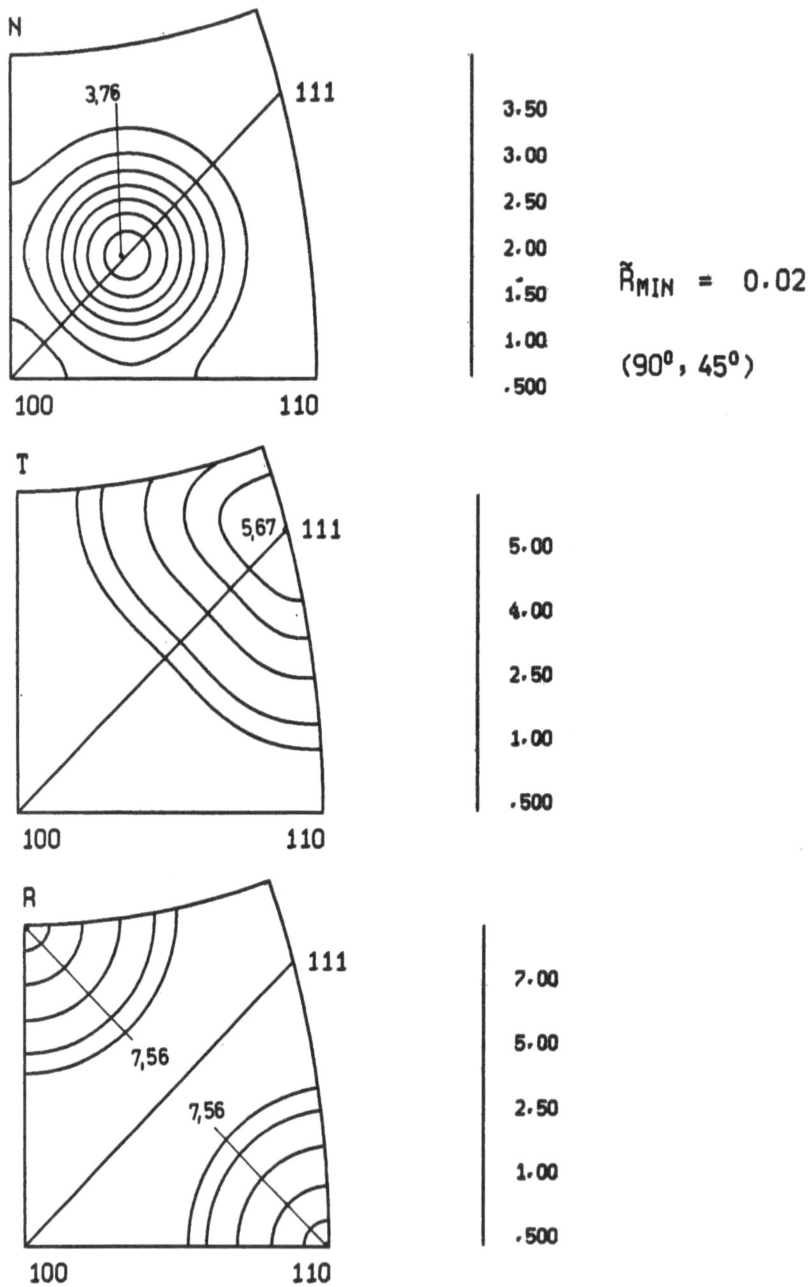

R̃, G, 20.0°, {113}<110>

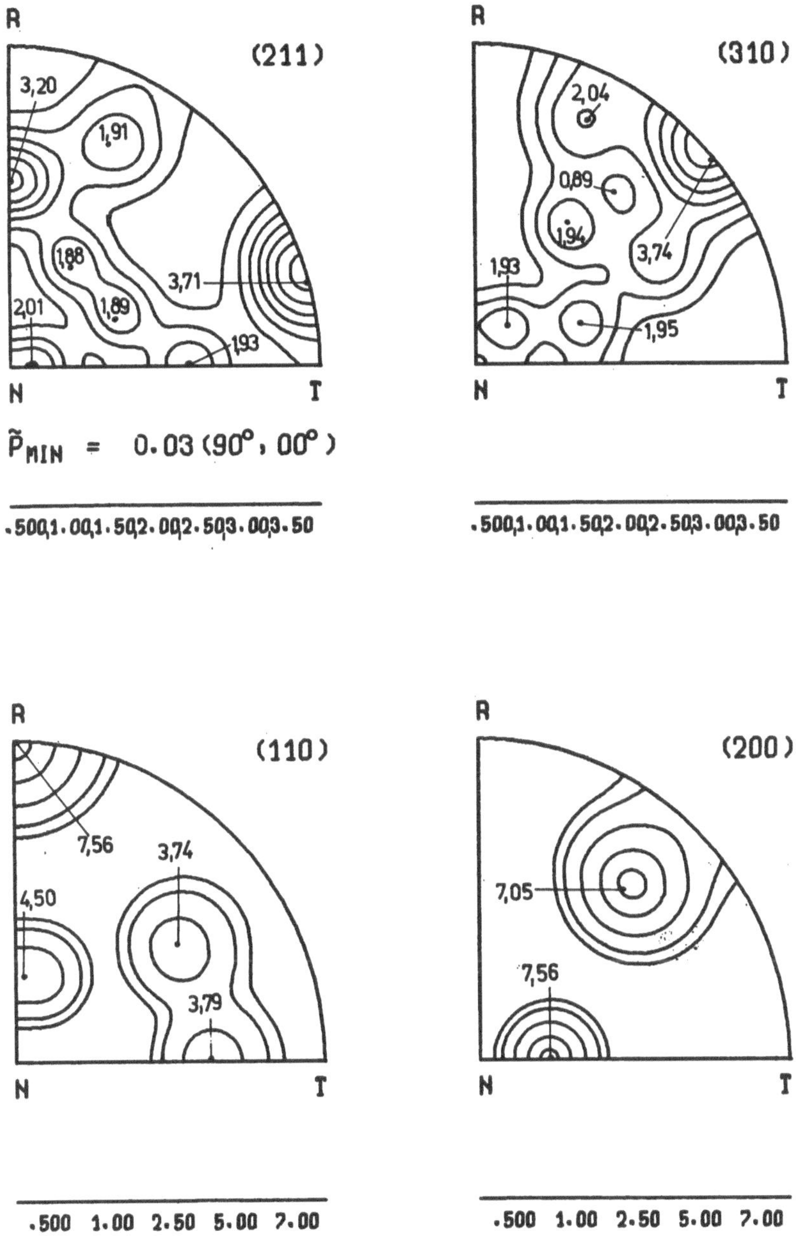

$\tilde{P}$, 6, 20.0°, {113}⟨110⟩

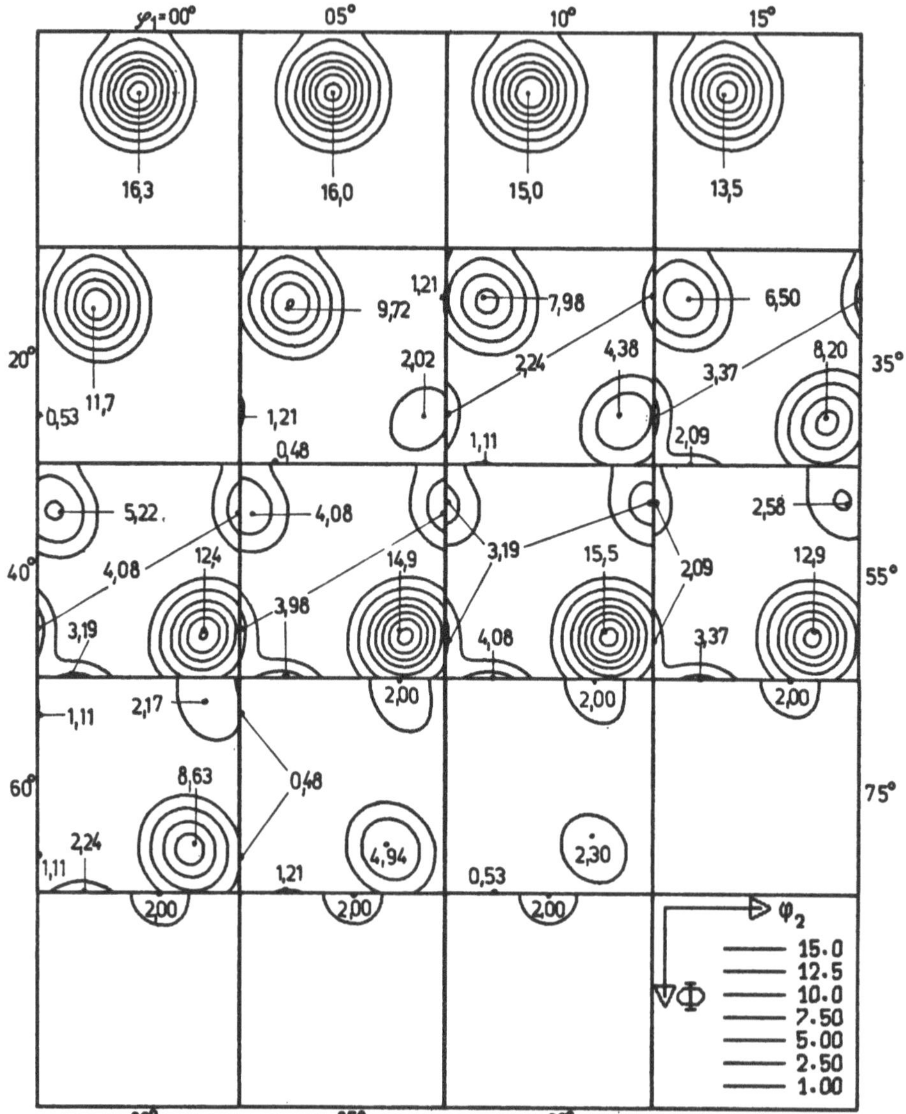

F, G, 25.0°, {113}<110>

F_{MAX} = 16.30 (00°)

$\tilde{F}$, G, 25.0°, {113}<110>

$\tilde{F}_{MAX}$ = 13.15 (00°)

$\tilde{F}_{MIN}$ = −1.37 (00°, 05°, . . ., 90°)

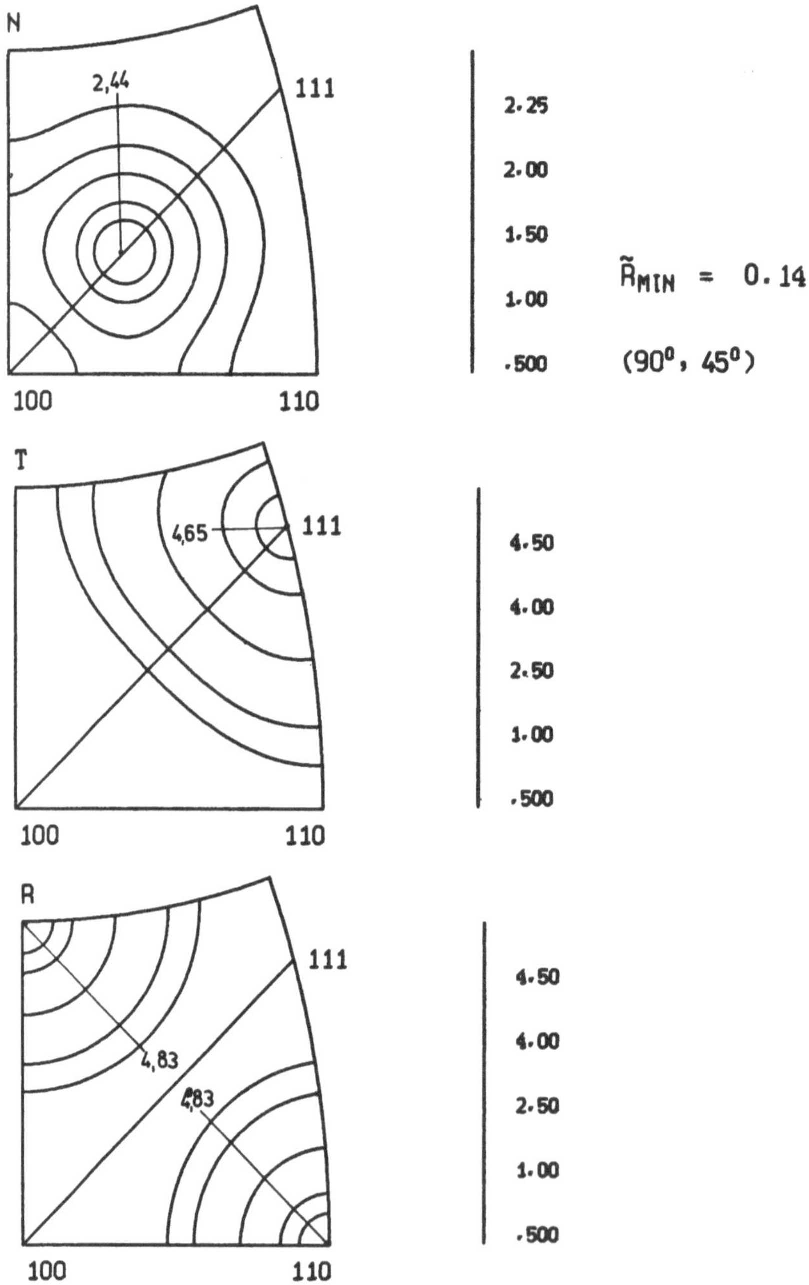

$\tilde{R}$, G, 25.0° , $\{113\}\langle 110\rangle$

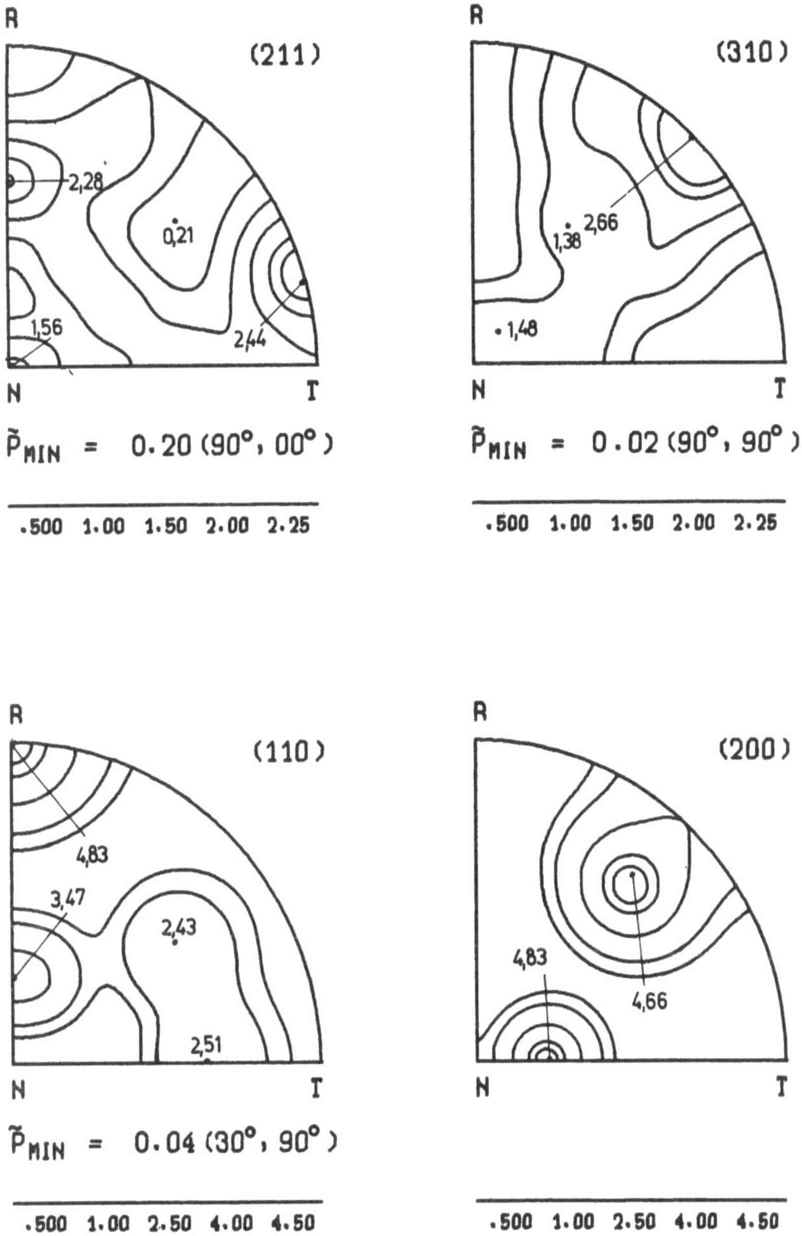

P̃, G, 25.0°, {113}⟨110⟩

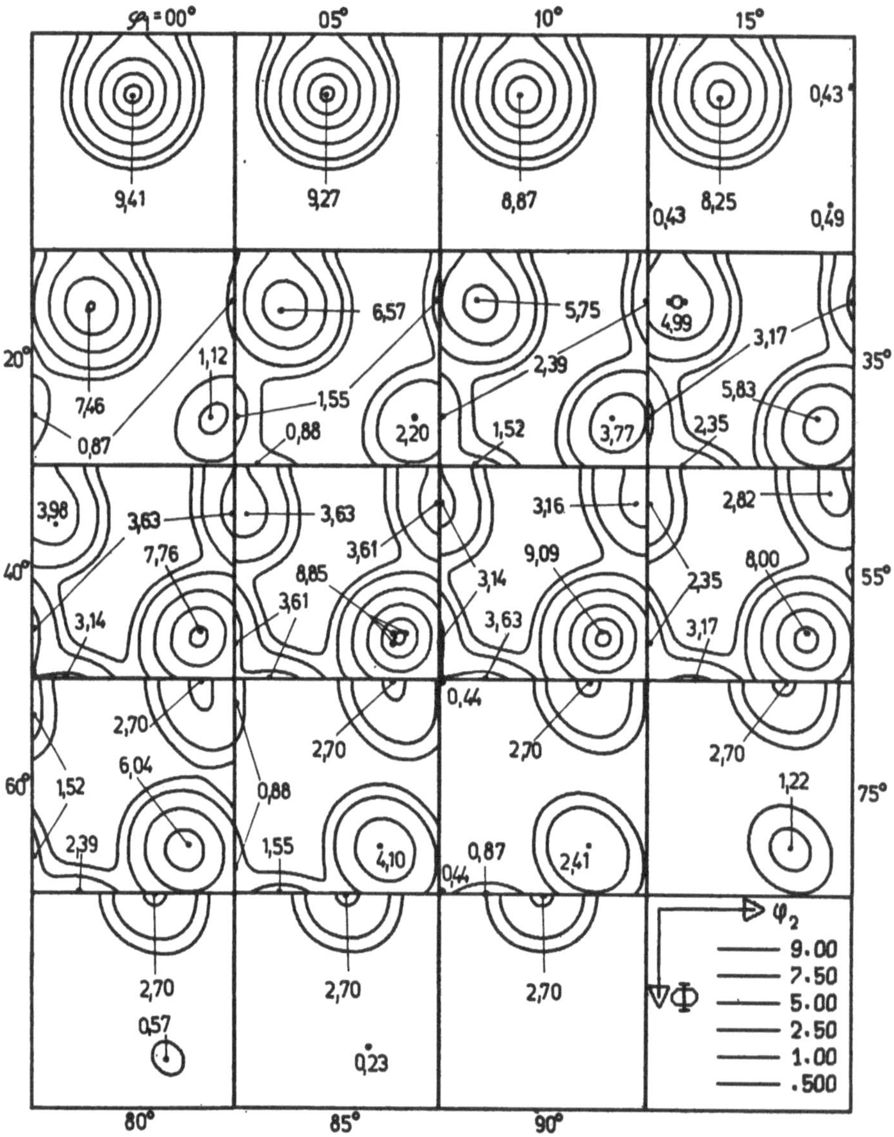

F, G. 30.0°, {113}<111>

F_{MAX} = 9.41 (00°)

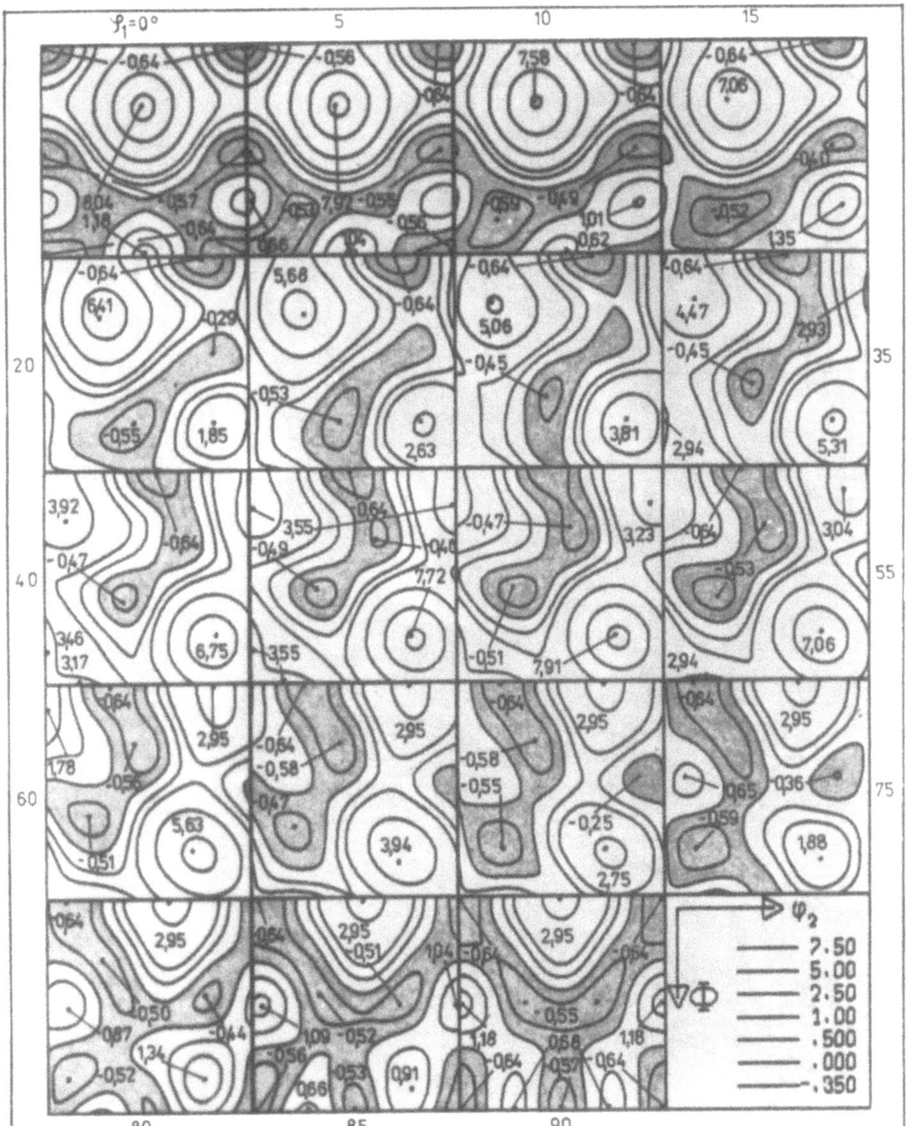

$\tilde{F}$, G, 30.0°, {113}<110>

$\tilde{F}_{MAX}$ = 8.04 (00°)

$\tilde{F}_{MIN}$ = -.64 (00°, 05°, . . . , 90°)

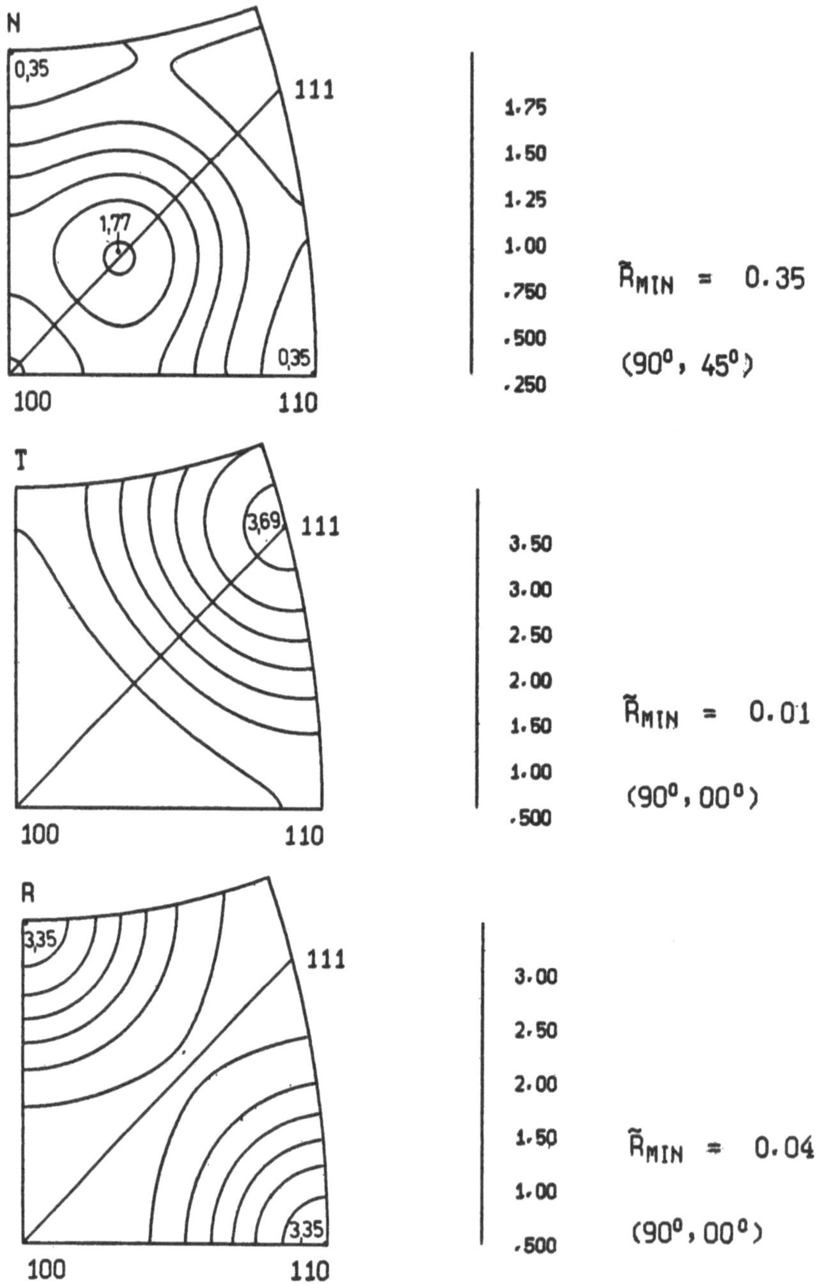

R̃, G, 30.0°, {113}<110>

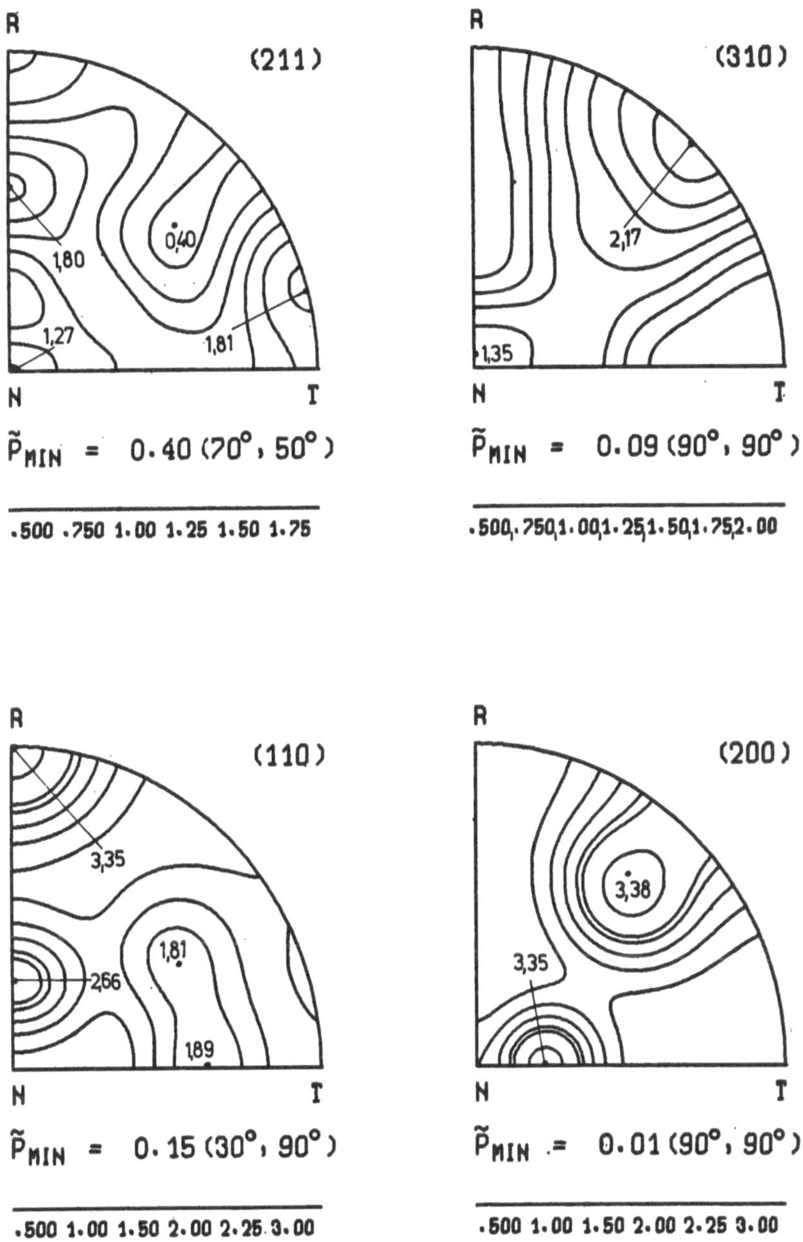

$\tilde{P}$, G, 30.0°, {113}⟨110⟩

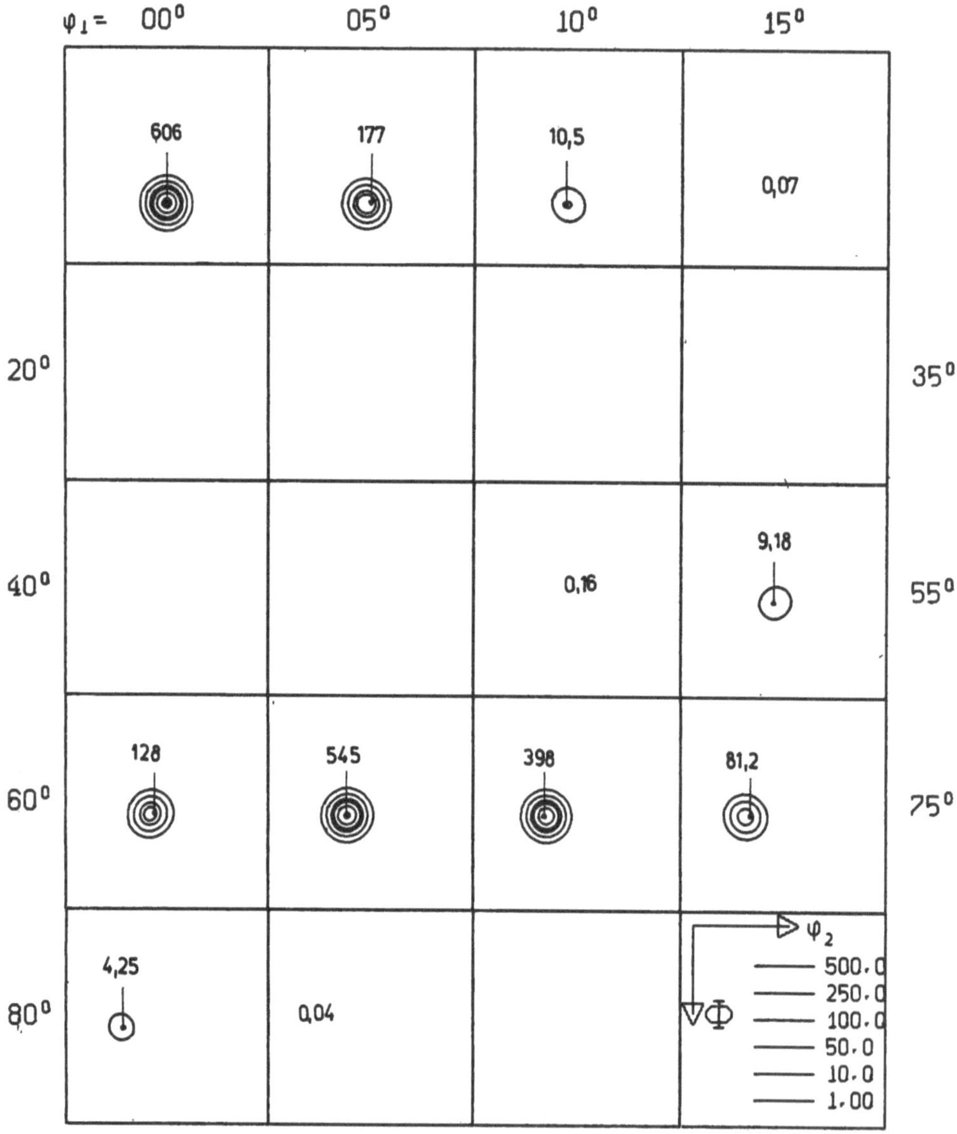

F, G, 7.50° , {233}<011>

F_{MAX} = 606.06 (00°)

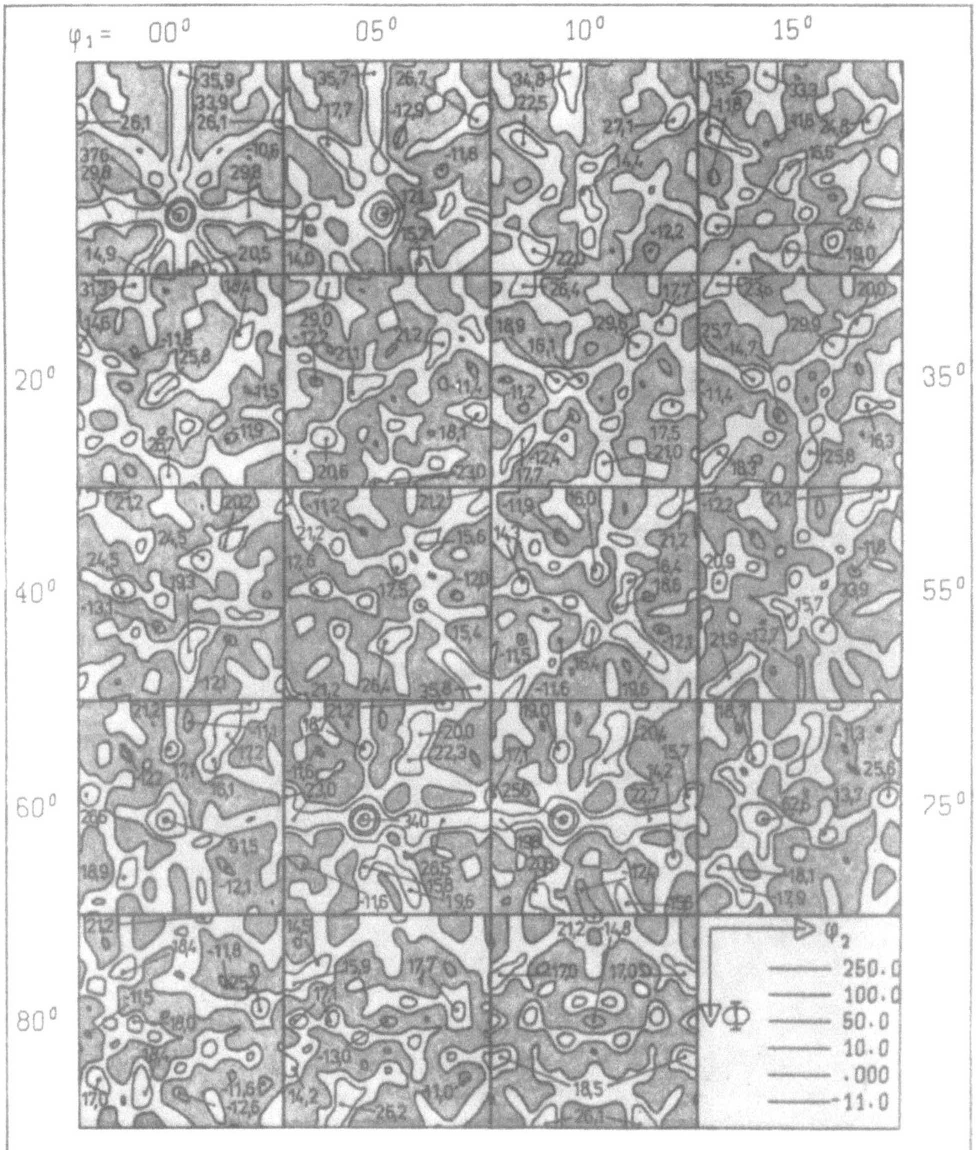

$\tilde{F}$, G, 7.50°, {233}$\langle 011 \rangle$

$\tilde{F}_{MAX}$ = 375.52 (00°)

$\tilde{F}_{MIN}$ = −14.80 (90°)

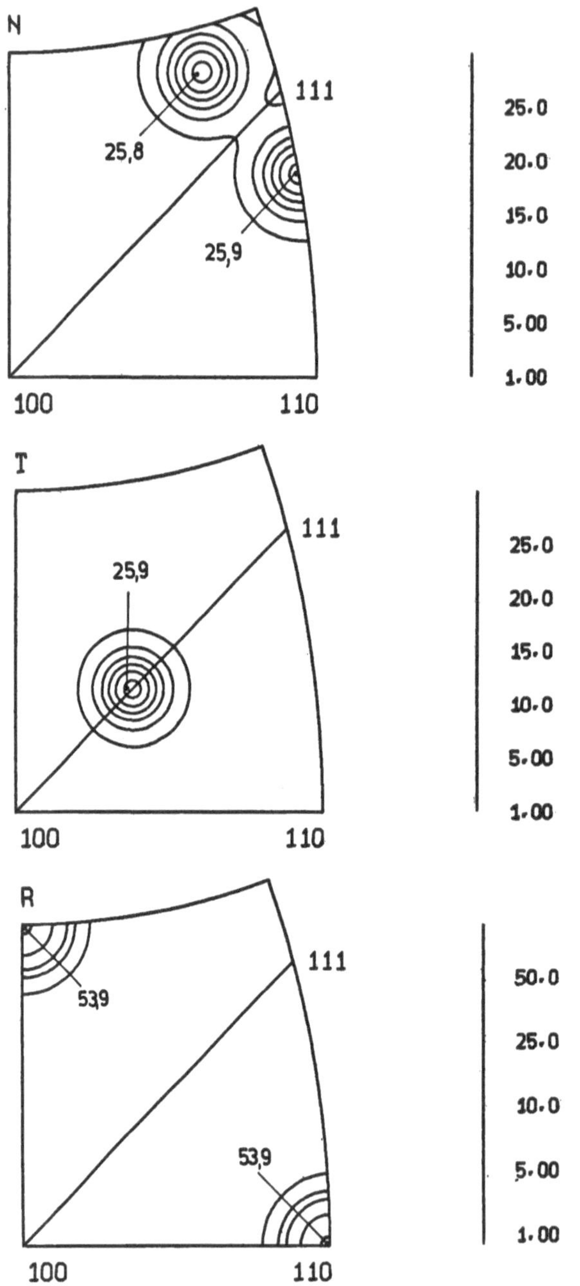

$\tilde{R}$, G, 7.50°, {233}⟨011⟩

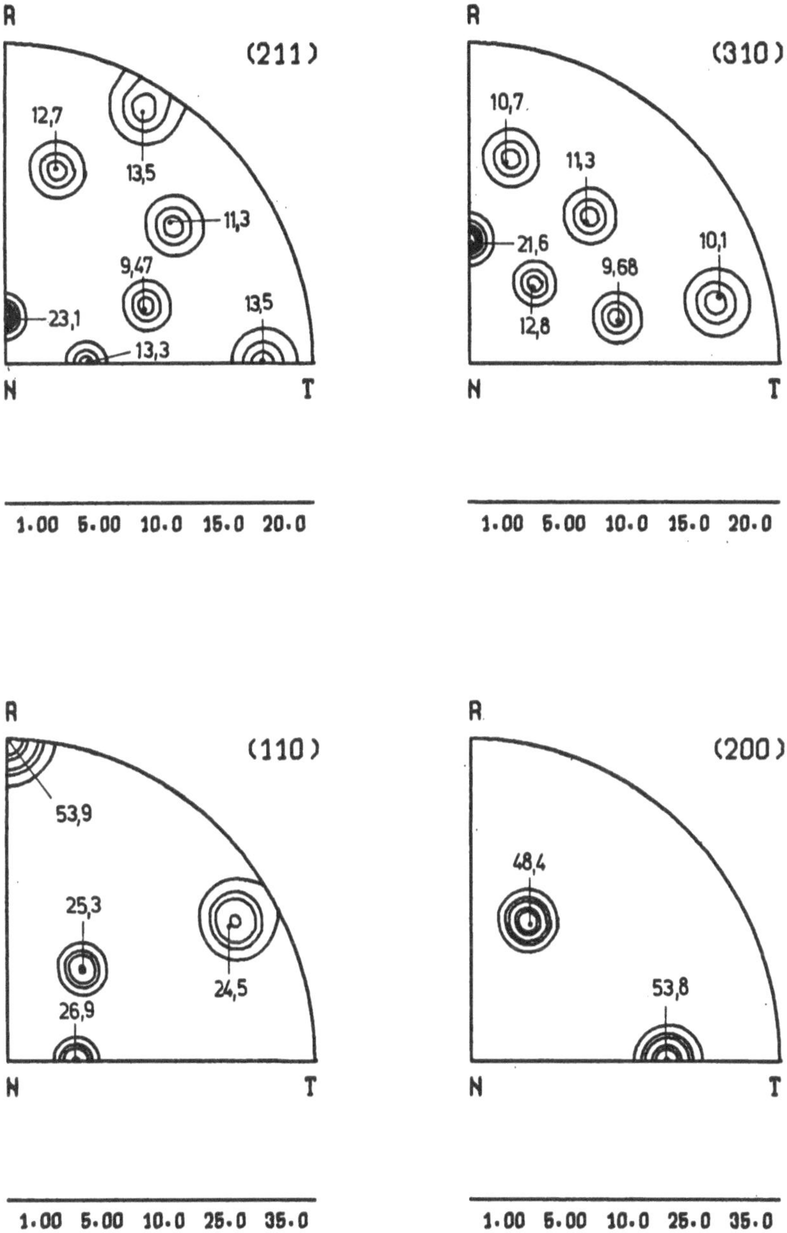

$\tilde{P}$, G, 7.50°, {233}⟨011⟩

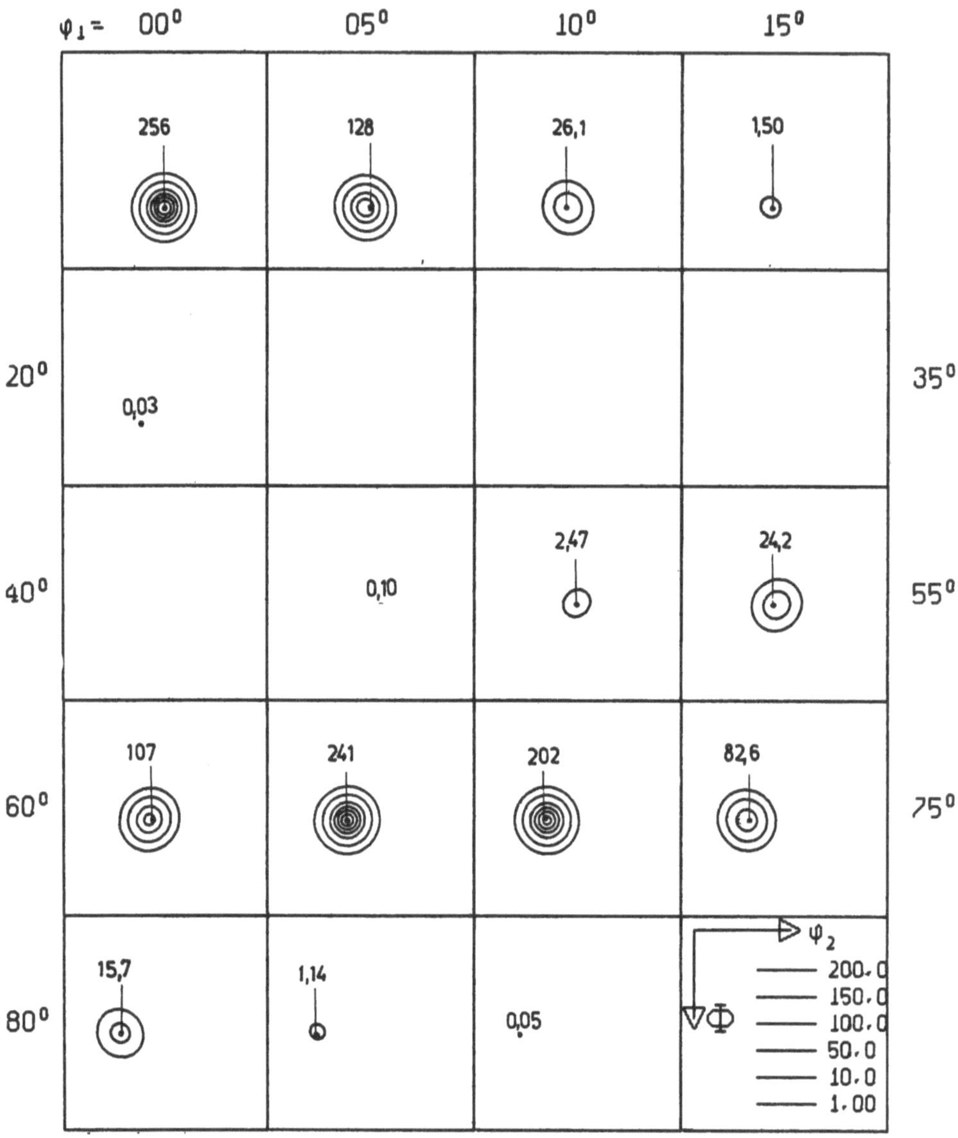

F, G, 10.0°, {233}<011>

F_{MAX} = 255.81 (00°)

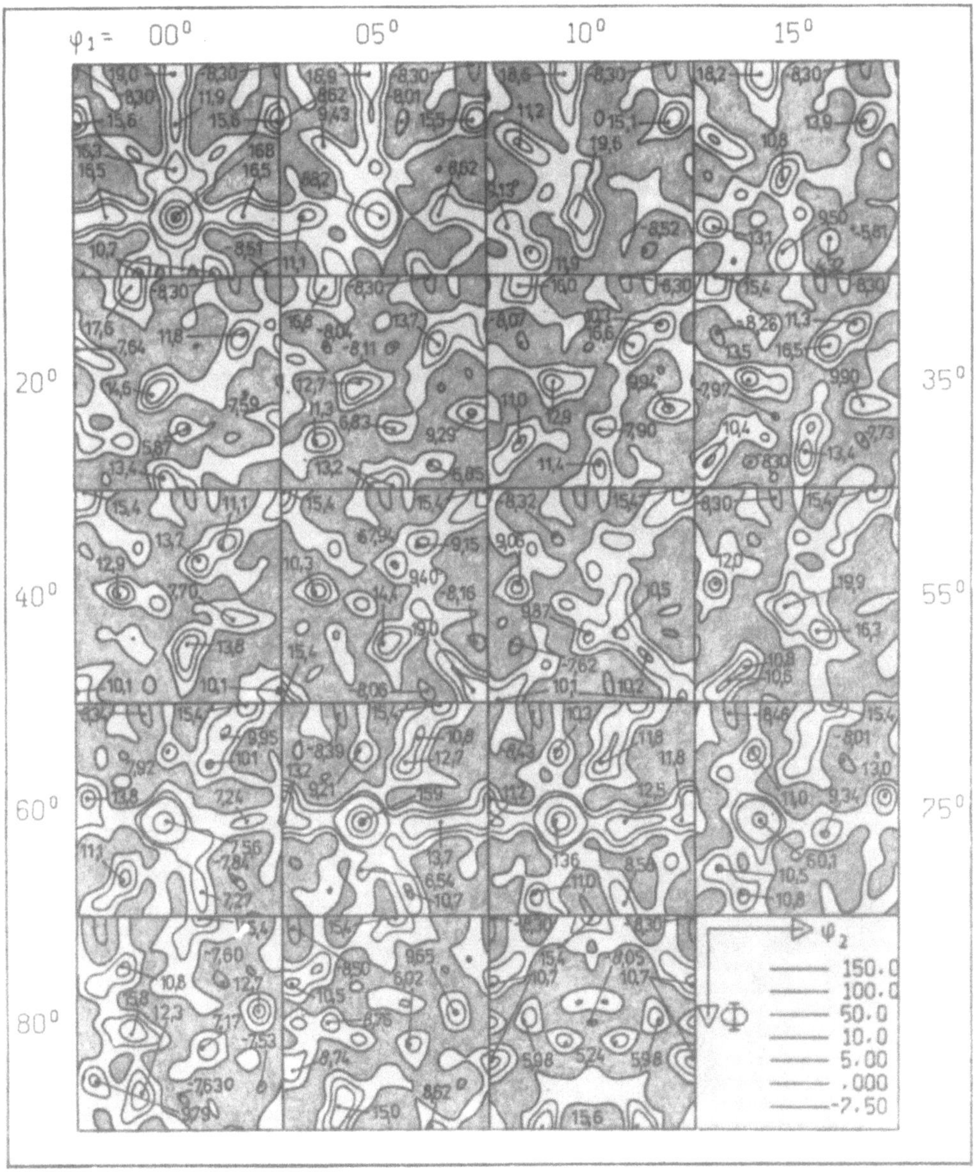

$\tilde{F}$, G, 10.0°, {233}<011>

$\tilde{F}_{MAX}$ = 167.86 (00°)

$\tilde{F}_{MIN}$ = -8.52 (10°)

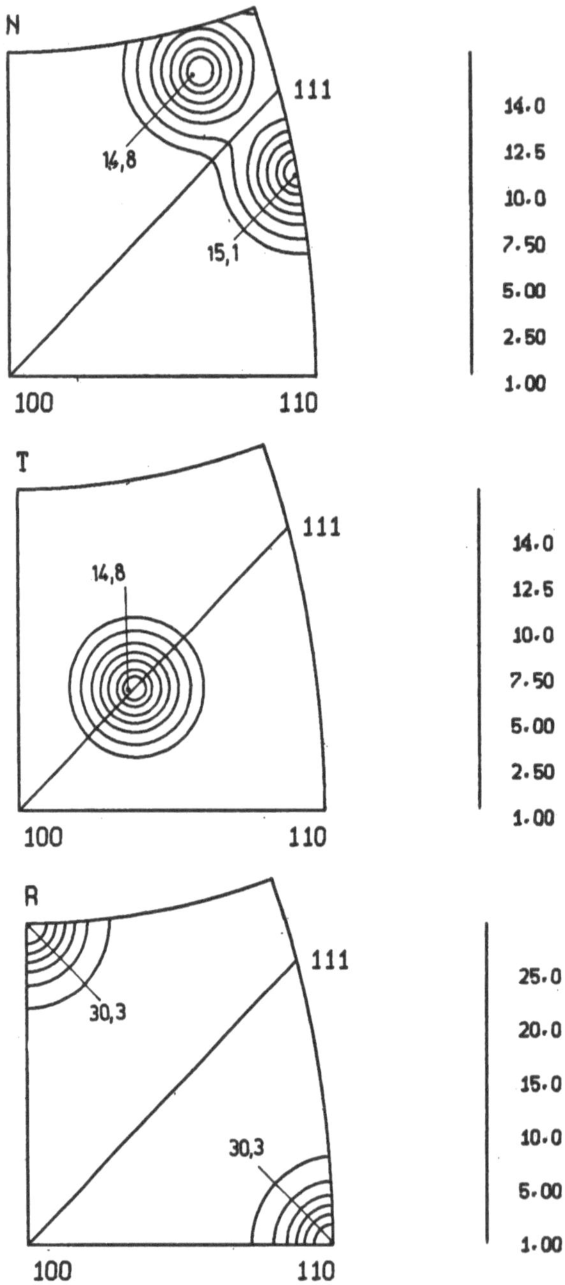

$\tilde{R}$, G, 10.0°, {233}<011>

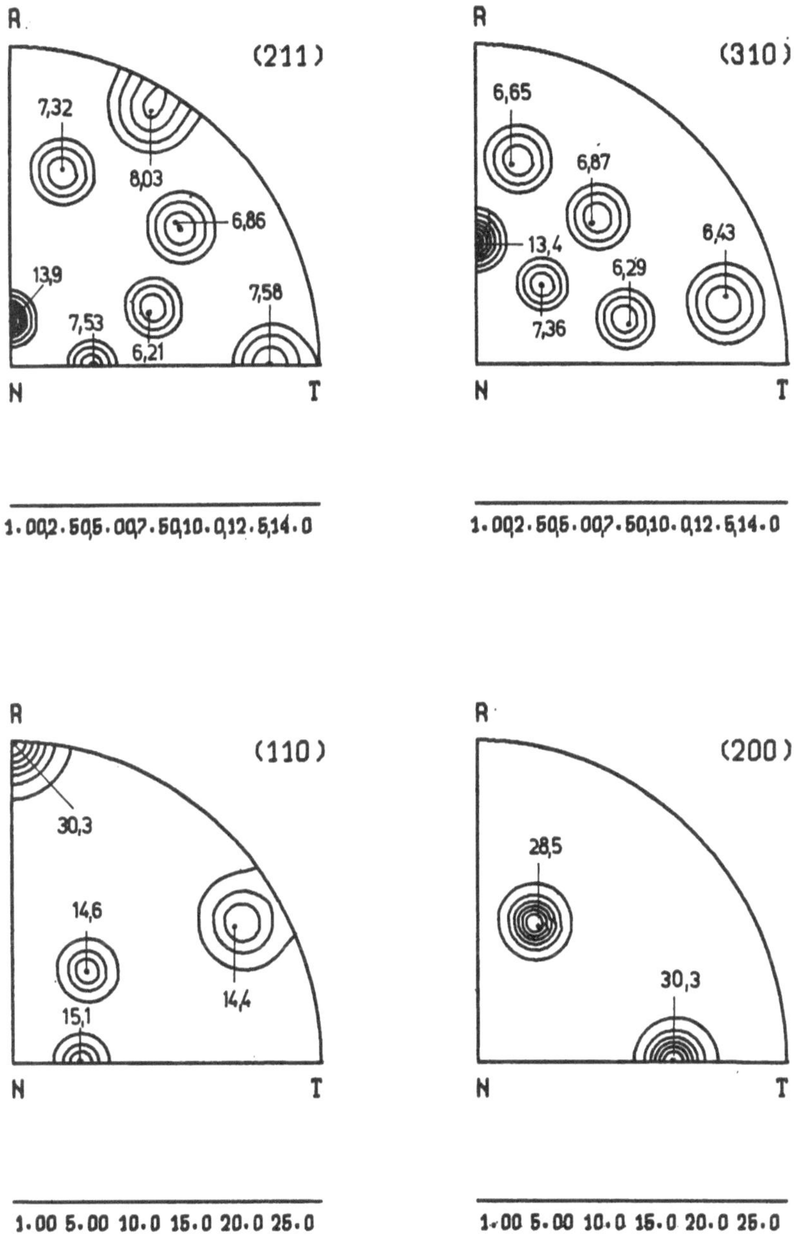

$\tilde{P}$, G, 10.0°, $\{233\}\langle 011\rangle$

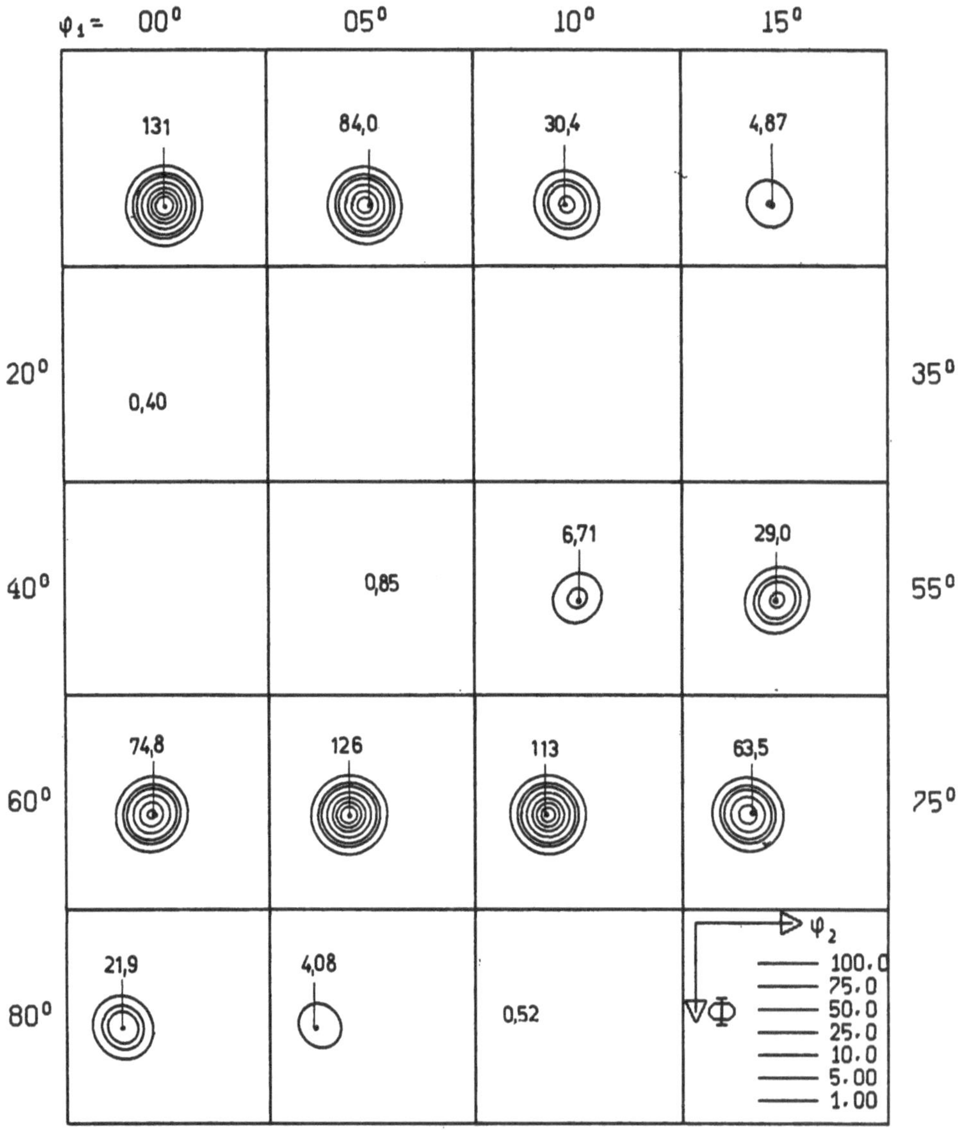

F, G, 12.5°, {233}<011>

F_{MAX} = 130.97 (00°)

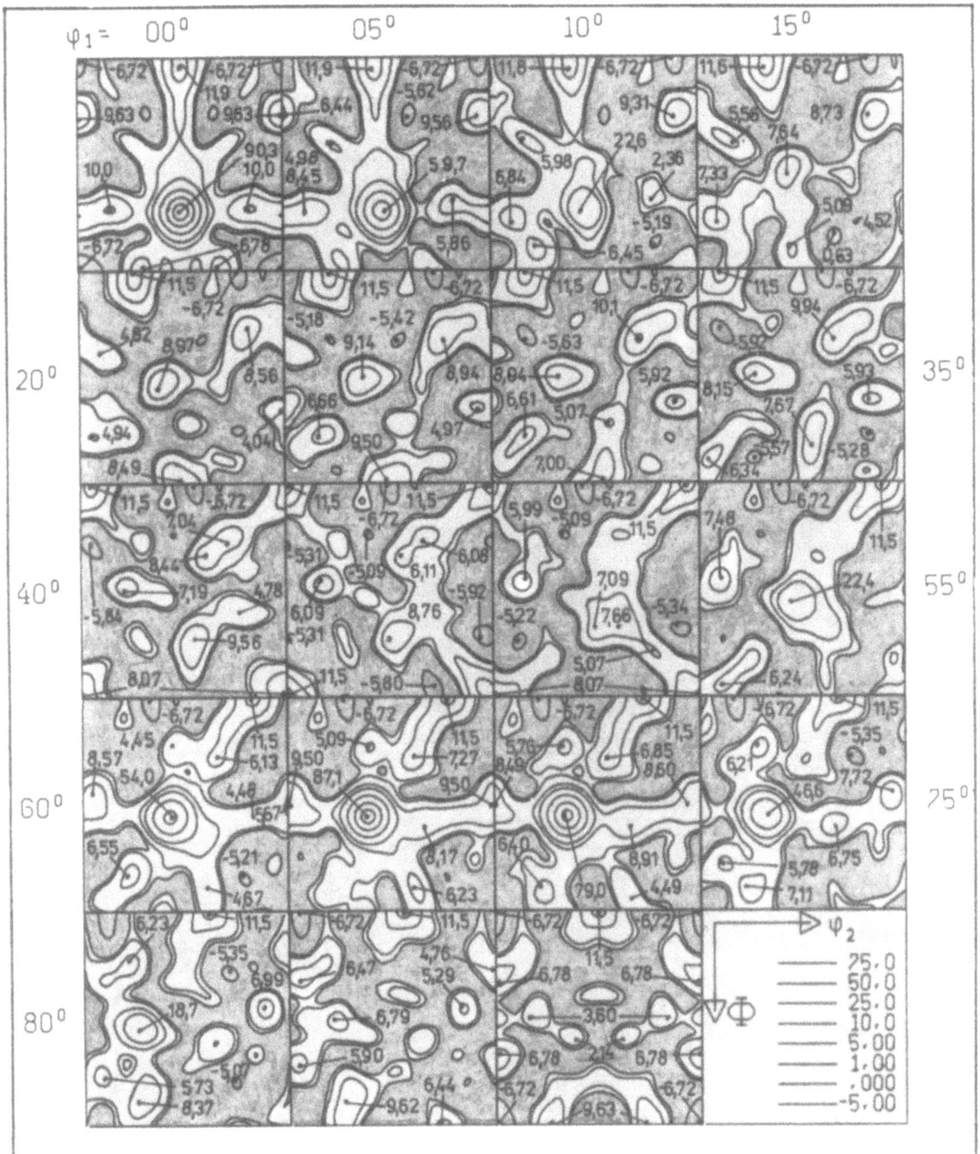

$\tilde{F}$, G, 12.5°, {233}<011>

$\tilde{F}_{MAX}$ = 90.28 (00°)

$\tilde{F}_{MIN}$ = -6.72 (00°, 05°, . . . , 90°)

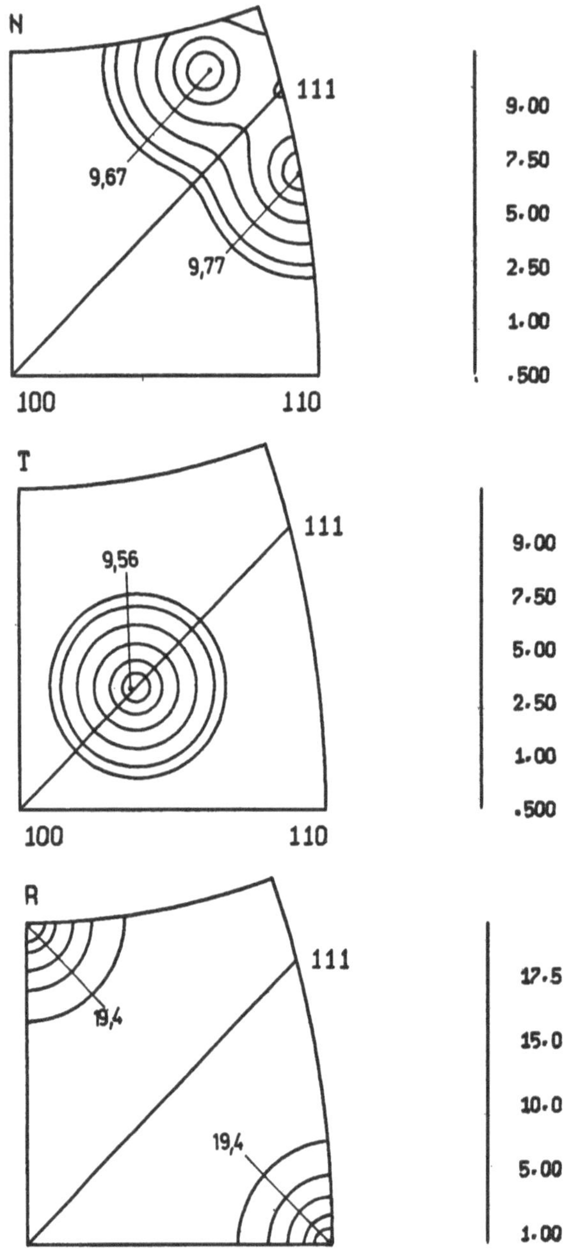

R̃, G, 12.5°, {233}<011>

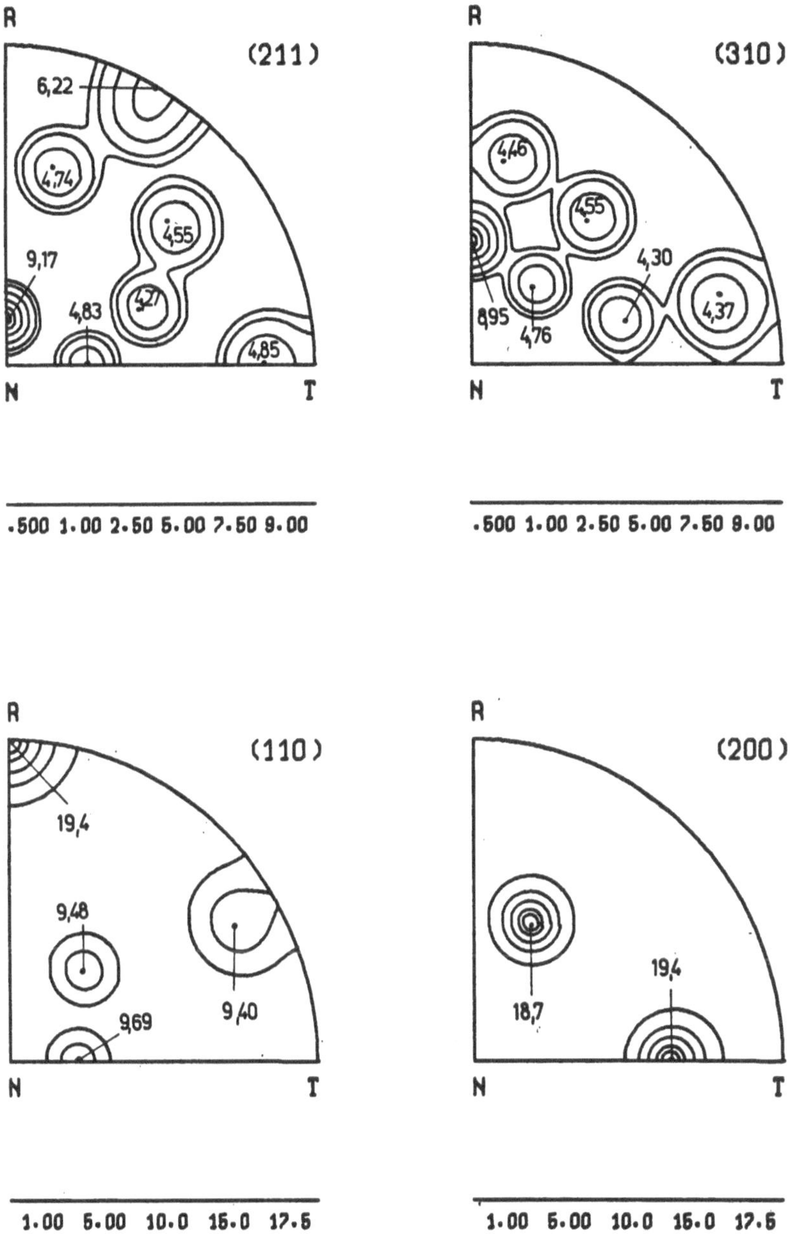

$\tilde{P}$, G, 12.5°, $\{233\}\langle 011\rangle$

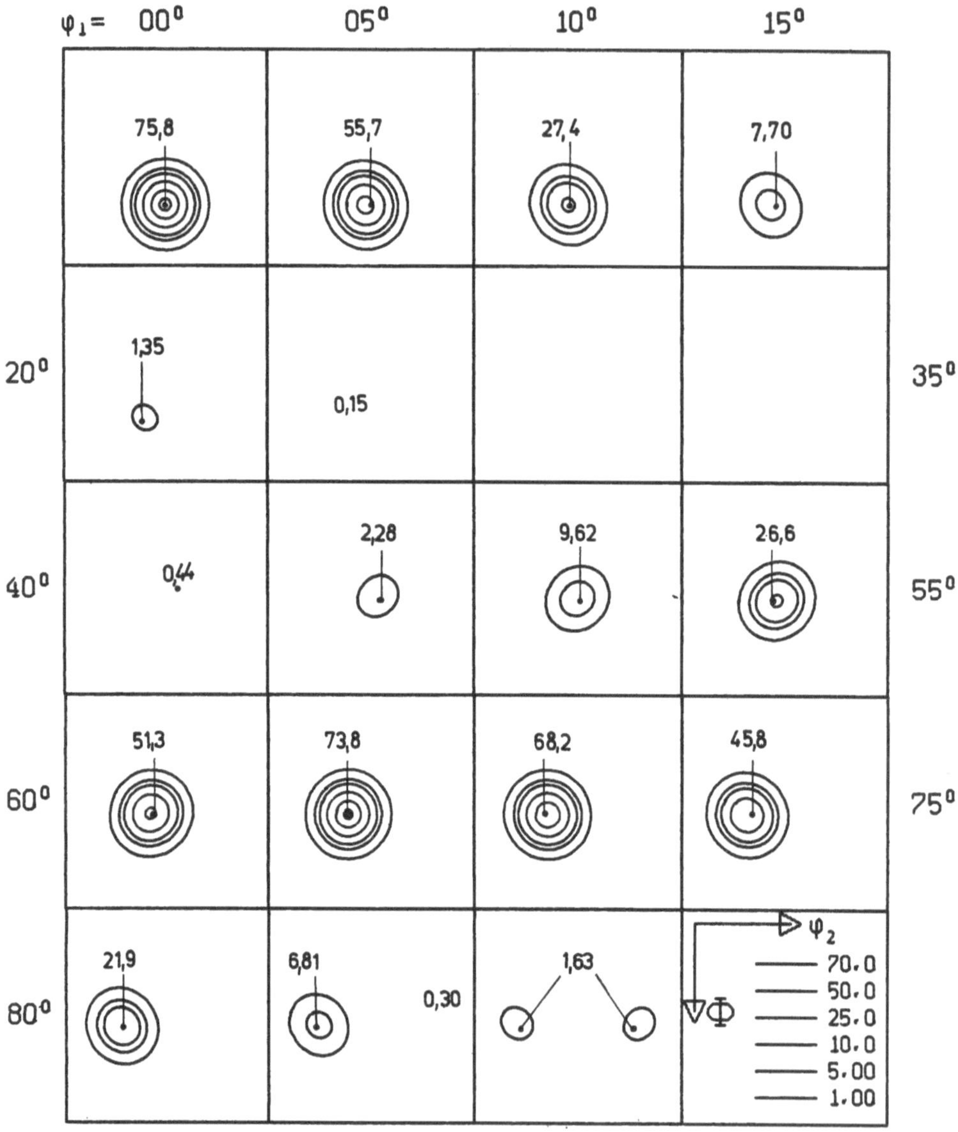

F, G, 15.0° , {233}<011>

F_{MAX} = 75.76 (00°)

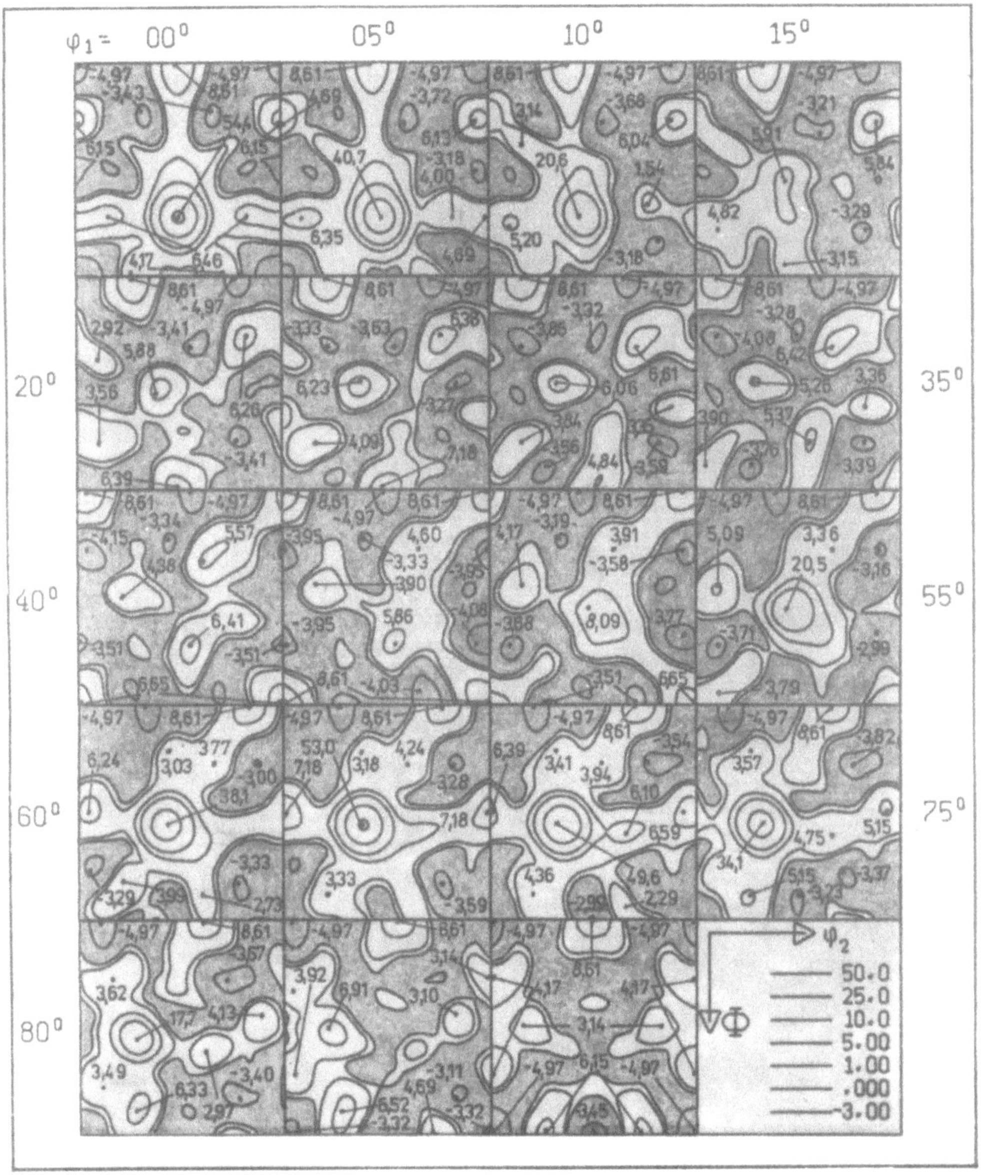

$\tilde{F}$, G, 15.0°, {233}<011>

$\tilde{F}_{MAX}$ = 54.38 (00°)

$\tilde{F}_{MIN}$ = -4.97 (00°, 05°, . . . , 90°)

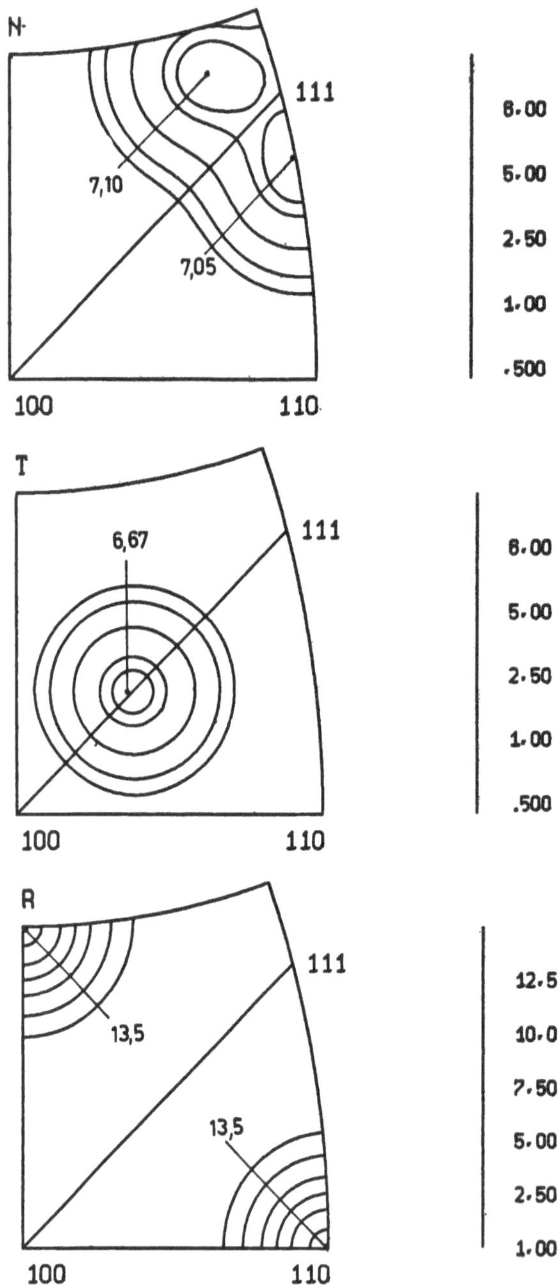

$\tilde{R}$, G, 15.0°, {233}$\langle 011\rangle$

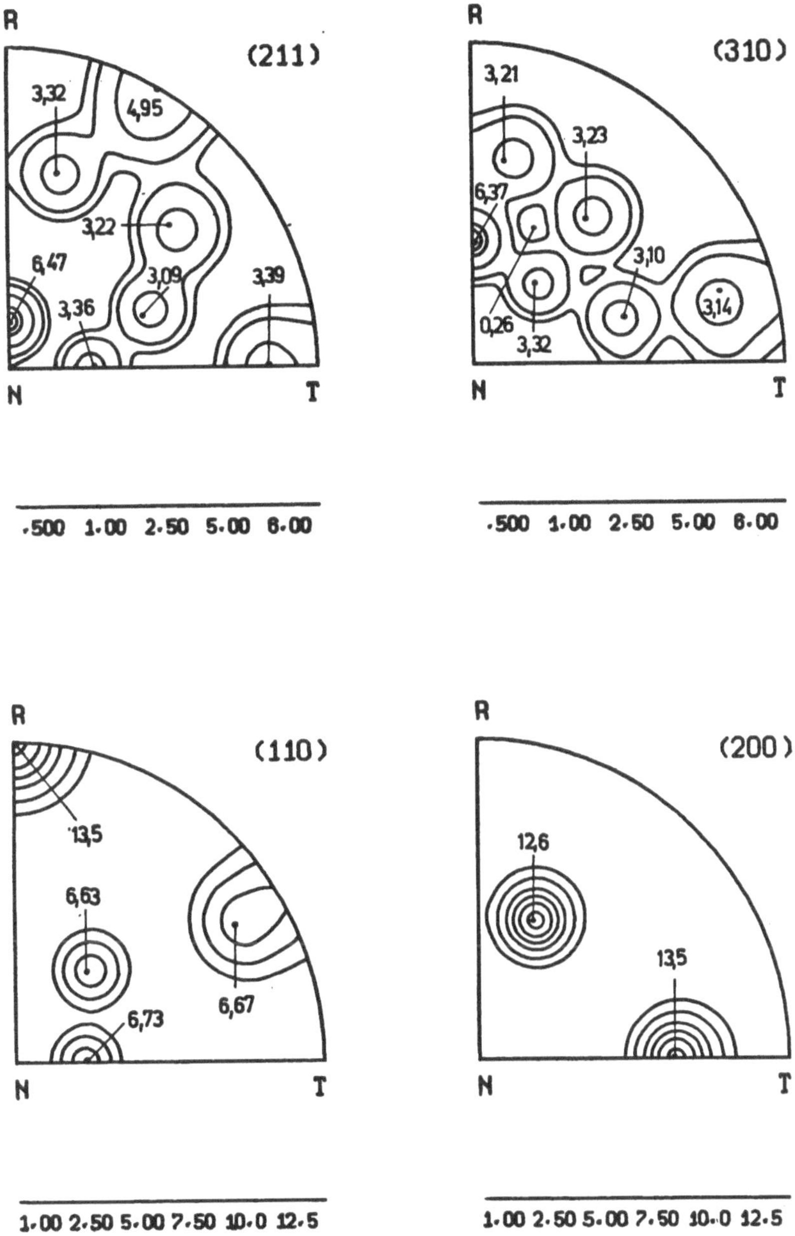

$\tilde{P}$, G, 15.0°, {233}⟨011⟩

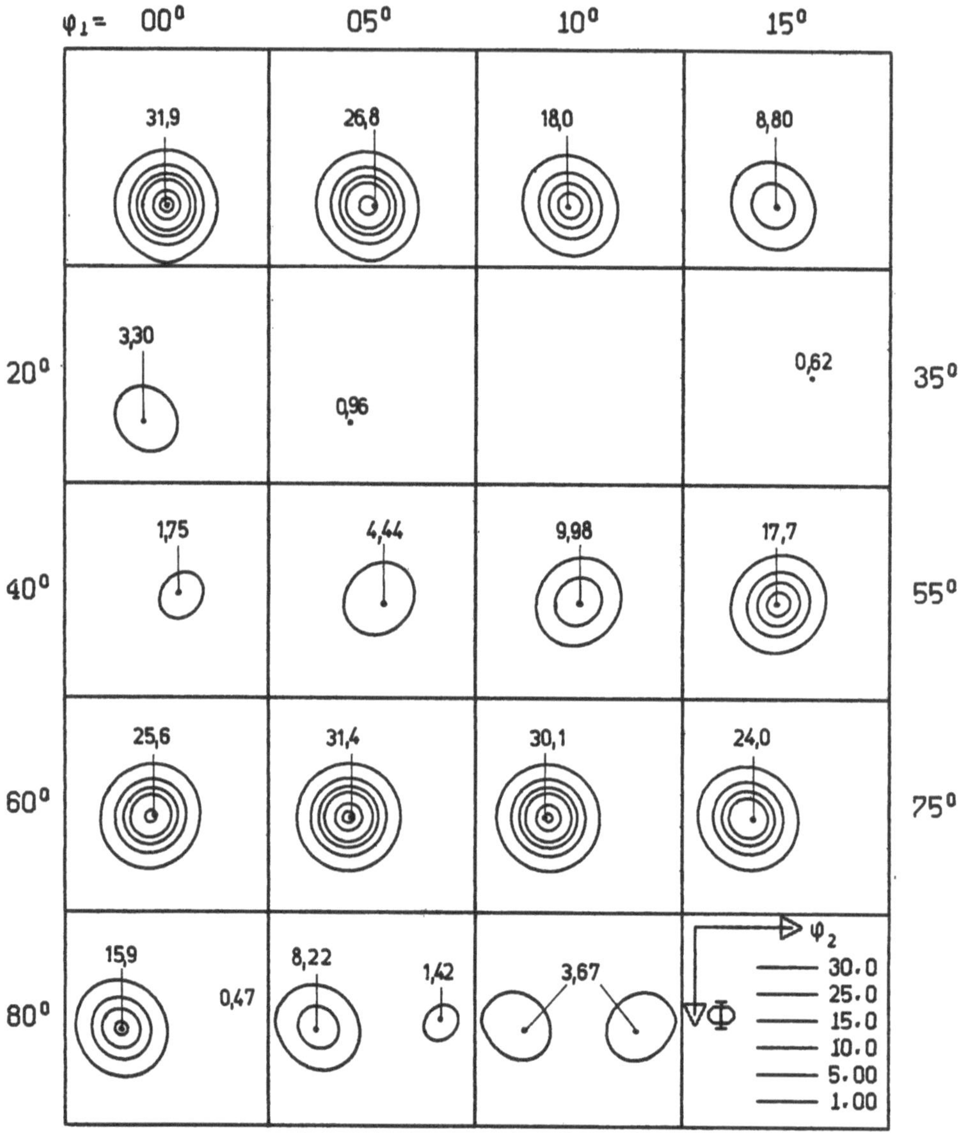

F, G, 20.0°, {233}<011>

F_{MAX} = 31.91 (00°)

$\tilde{F}$, G, 20.0°, {233}<011>

$\tilde{F}_{MAX}$ = 24.38 (00°)

$\tilde{F}_{MIN}$ = -2.63 (00°, 05°, . . . , 90°)

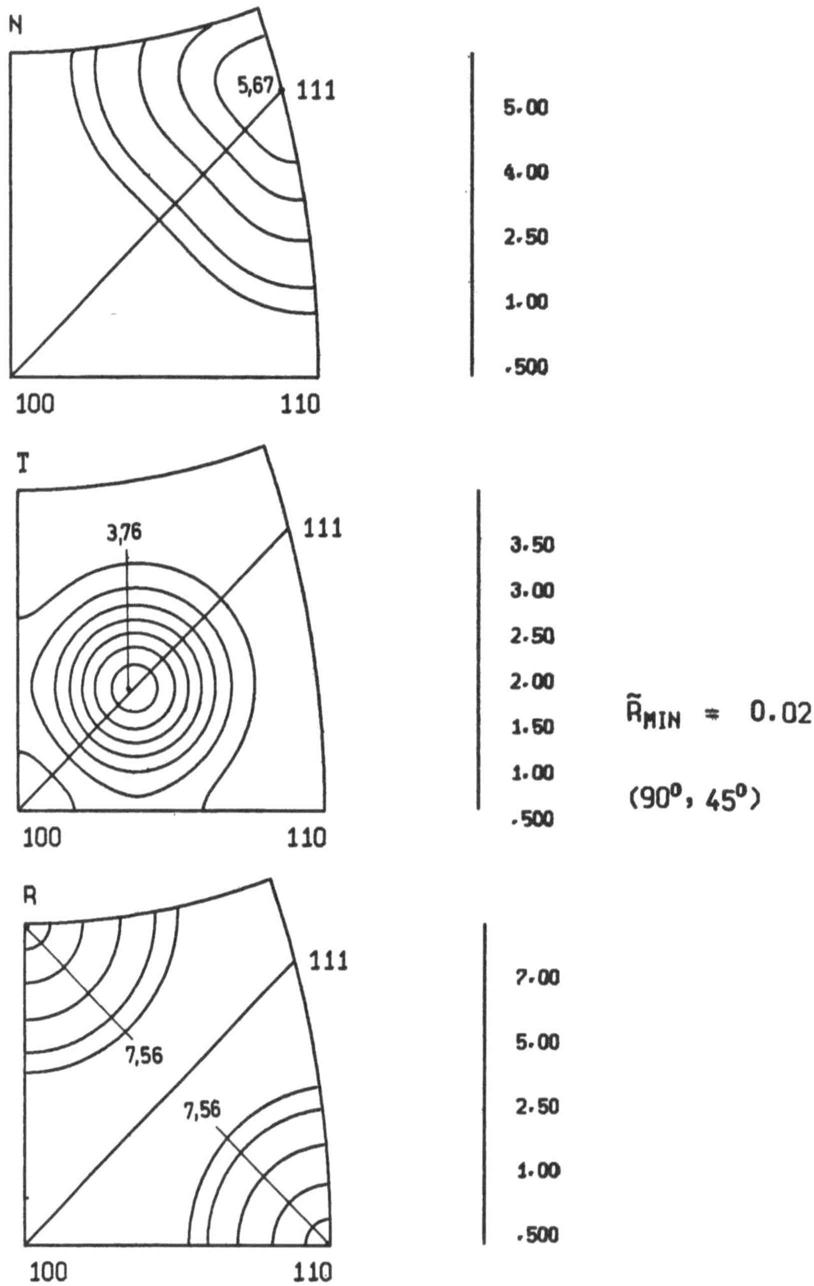

$\tilde{R}$, G, 20.0°, {233}⟨011⟩

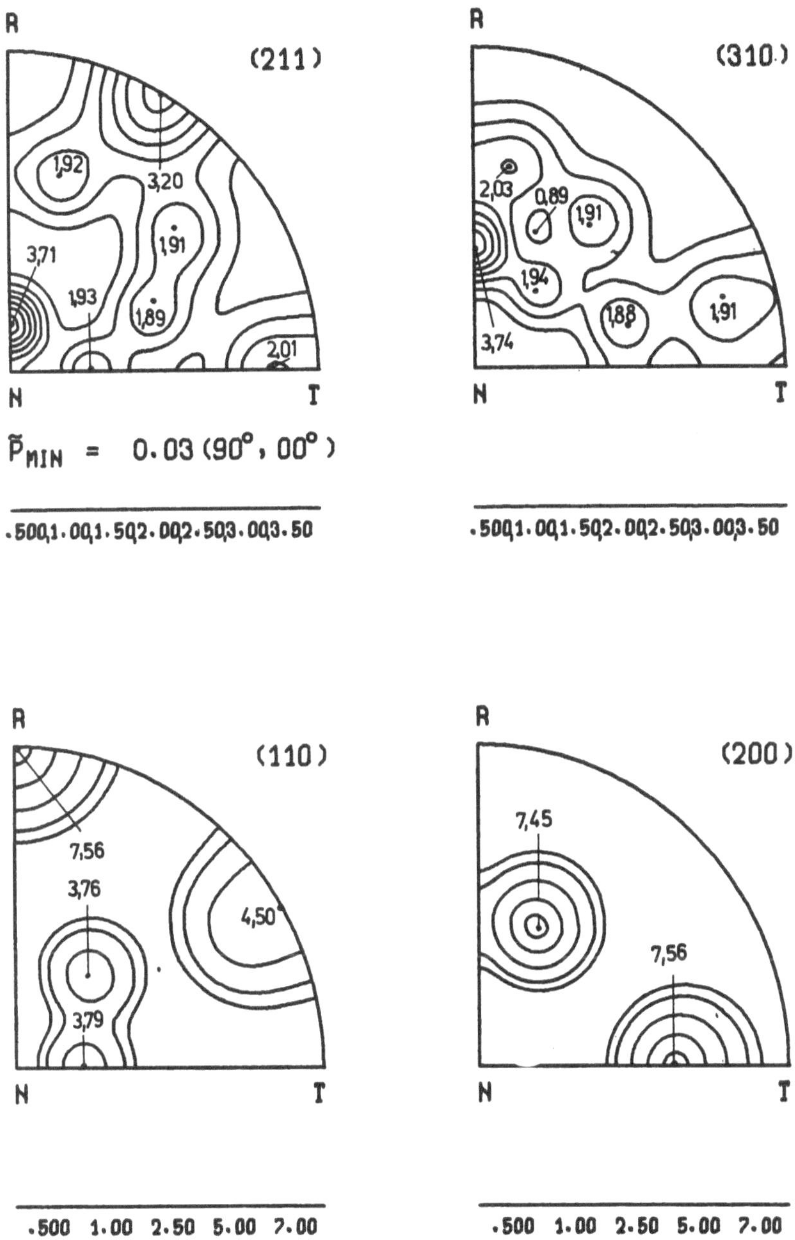

$\tilde{P}$, 6, 20.0°, {233}⟨011⟩

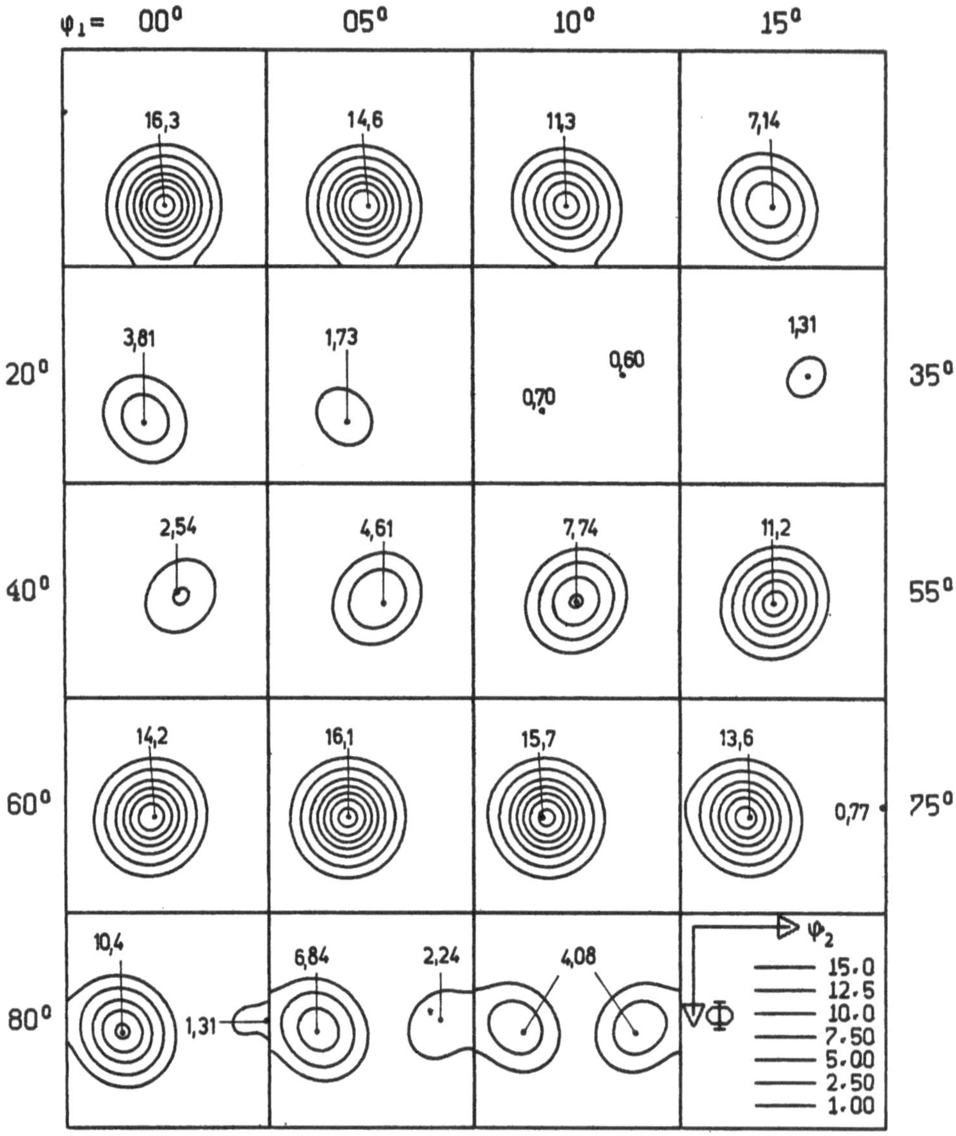

F, G, 25.0°, {233}<011>

F_{MAX} = 16.30 (00°)

$\tilde{F}$, G, 25.0°, {233}<011>

$\tilde{F}_{MAX}$ = 13.15 (00°)

$\tilde{F}_{MIN}$ = −1.37 (00°, 05°, . . . , 90°)

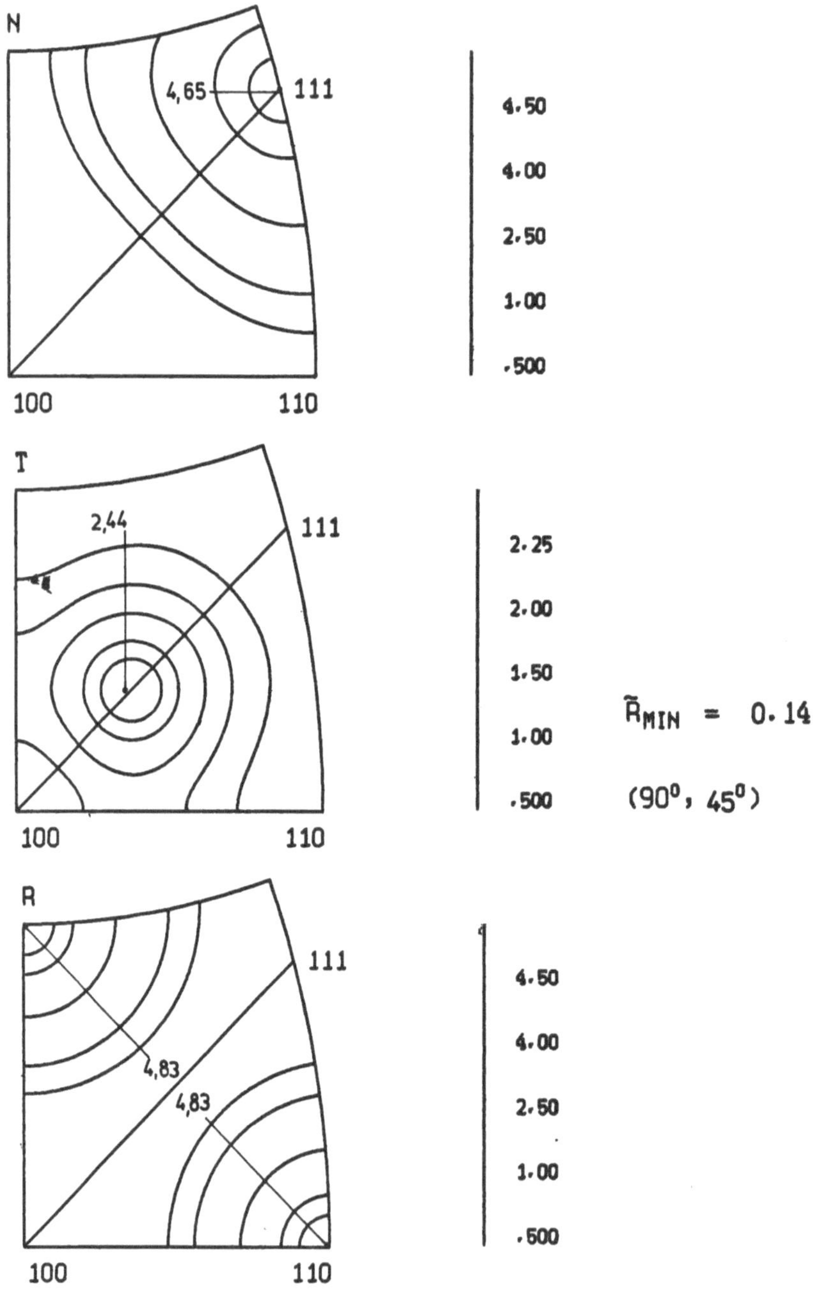

$\tilde{R}$, G, 25.0°, $\{233\}\langle 011\rangle$

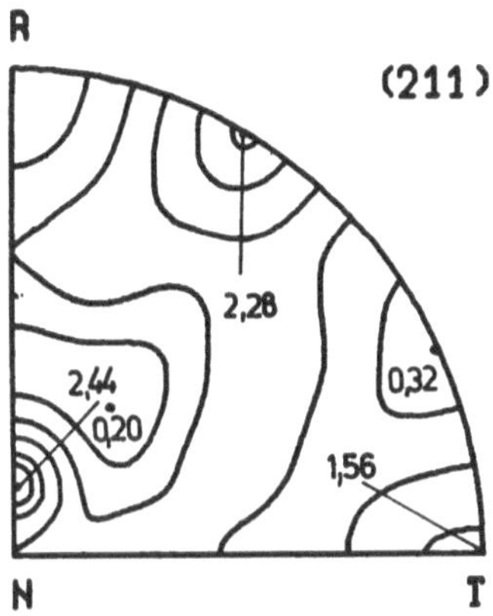

$\tilde{P}_{MIN}$ = 0.20 (90°, 00°)

.500 1.00 1.50 2.00 2.25

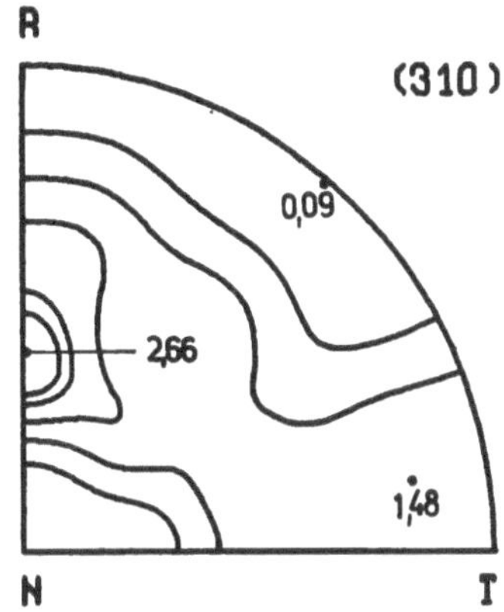

$\tilde{P}_{MIN}$ = 0.02 (00°, 00°)

.500 1.00 1.50 2.00 2.25

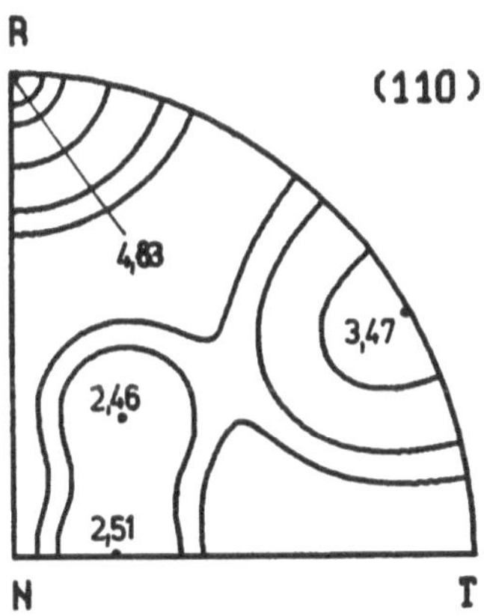

$\tilde{P}_{MIN}$ = 0.04 (60°, 90°)

.500 1.00 2.50 4.00 4.50

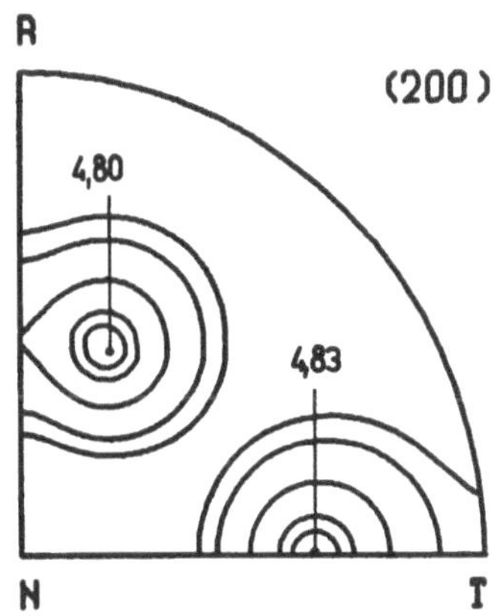

.500 1.00 2.50 4.00 4.50

$\tilde{P}$, 6, 25.0°, {233}⟨011⟩

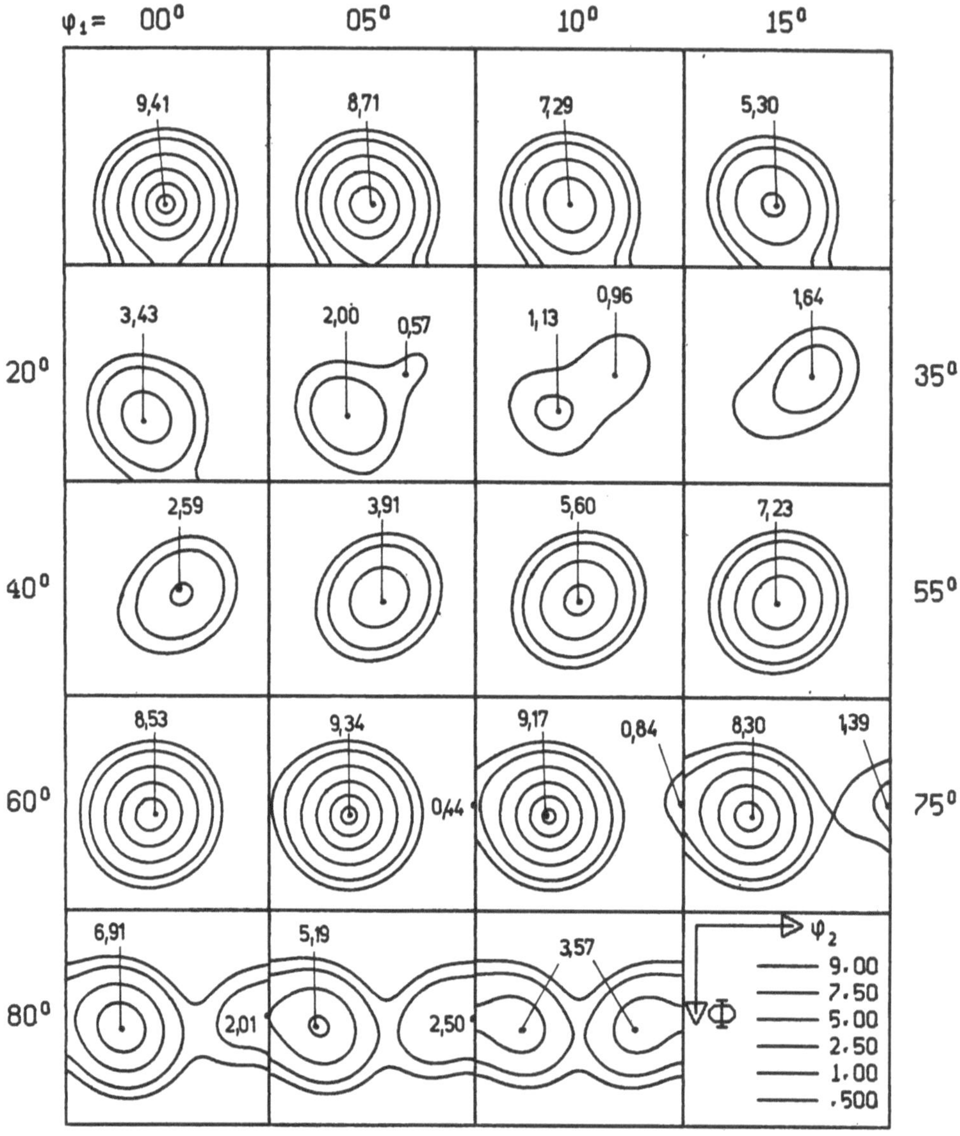

F, G, 30.0°, {233}<011>

F_{MAX} = 9.41 (00°)

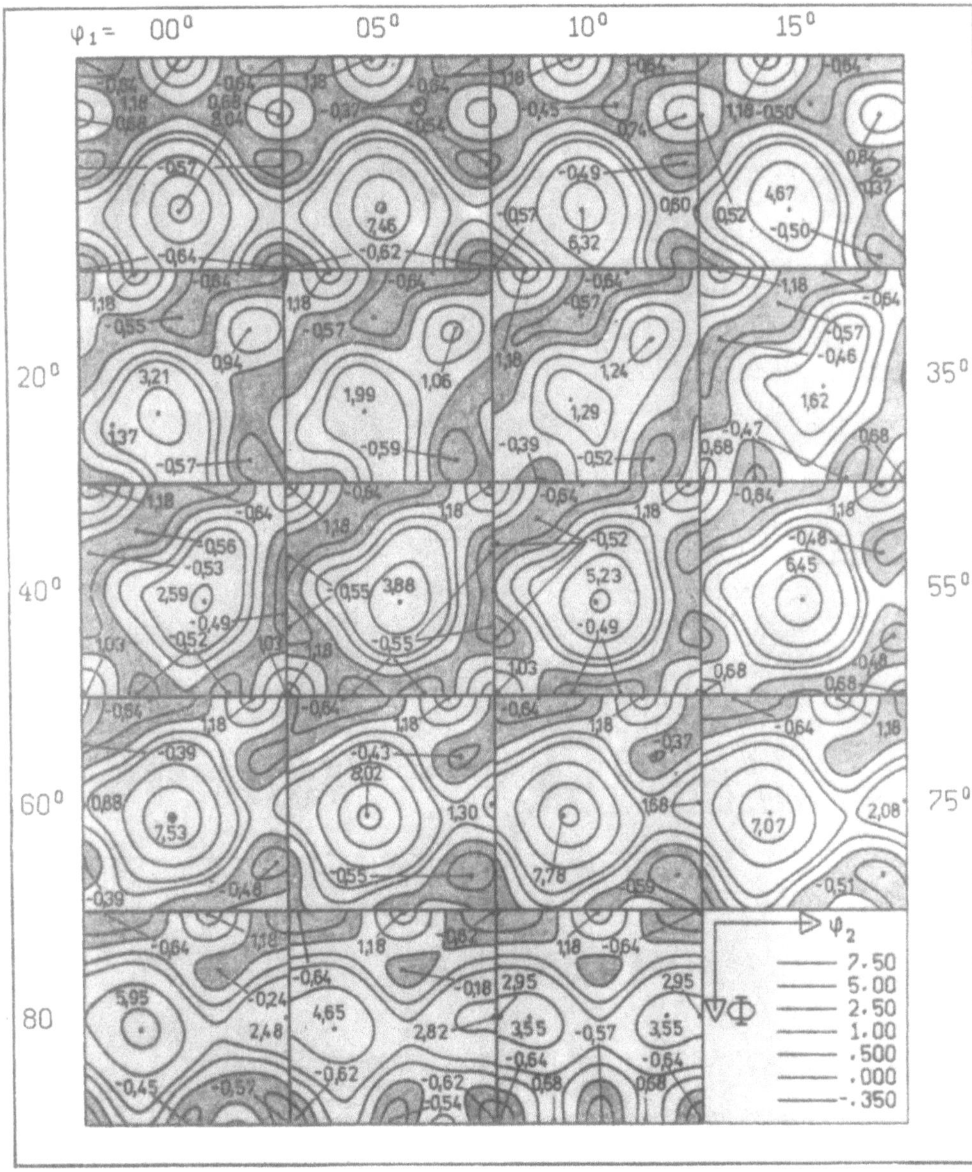

$\tilde{F}$, G, 30.0°, {233}<011>

$\tilde{F}_{MAX}$ = 8.04 (00°)

$\tilde{F}_{MIN}$ = -.64 (00°, 05°, . . . , 90°)

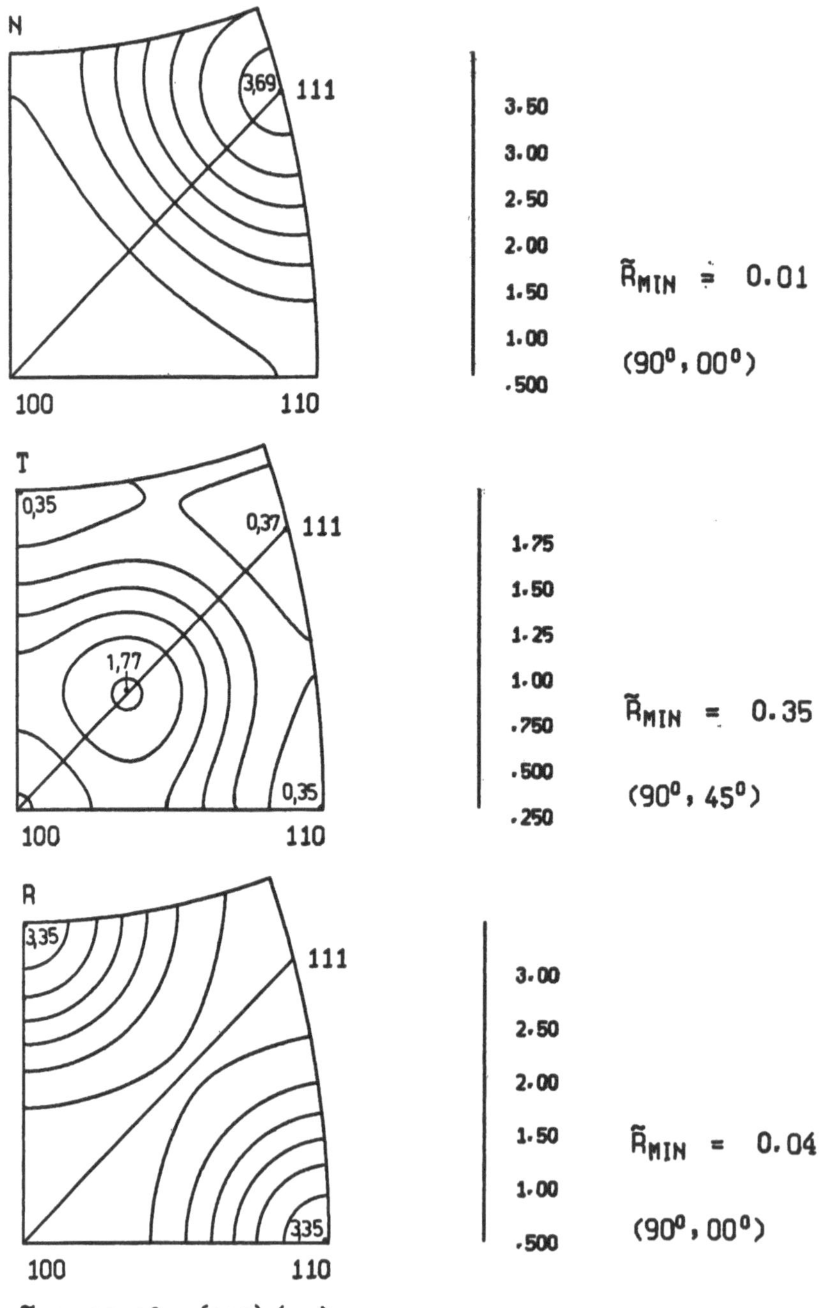

$\tilde{R}$, G, 30.0°, {233}<011>

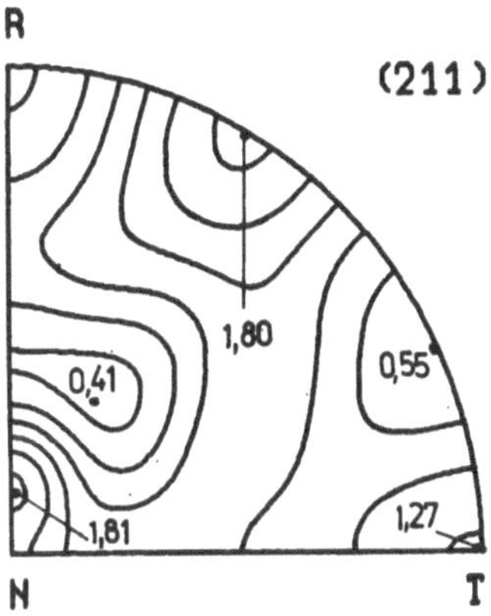

$\tilde{P}_{MIN}$ = 0.41 (45°, 30°)

.500 .750 1.00 1.25 1.50 1.75

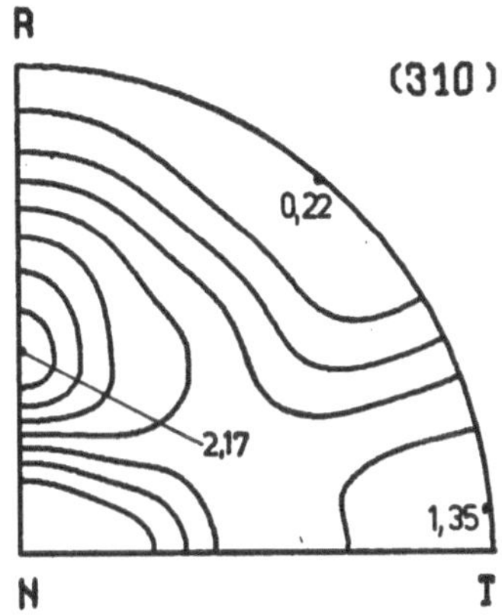

$\tilde{P}_{MIN}$ = 0.09 (00°, 00°)

.500 .750 1.00 1.25 1.50 1.75 2.00

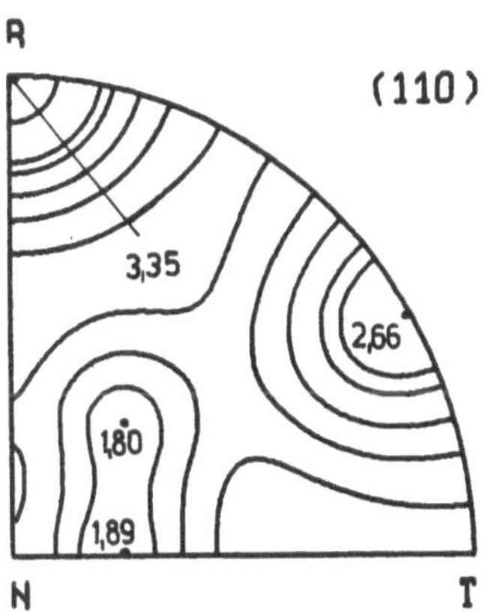

$\tilde{P}_{MIN}$ = 0.15 (60°, 90°)

.500 1.00 1.50 2.00 2.25 3.00

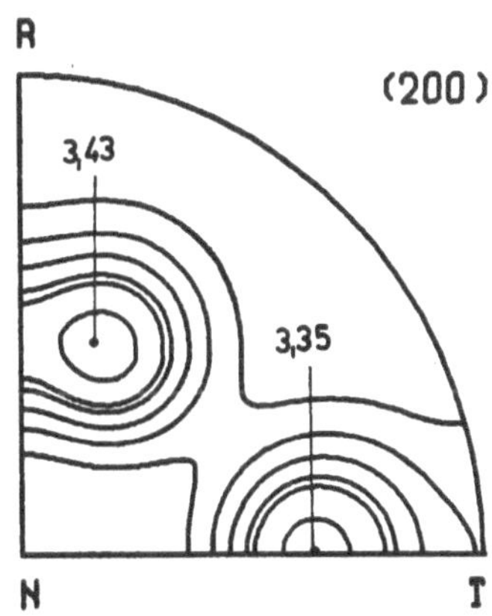

$\tilde{P}_{MIN}$ = 0.01 (00°, 00°)

.500 1.00 1.50 2.00 2.25 3.00

$\tilde{P}$, G, 30.0° , {233}⟨011⟩

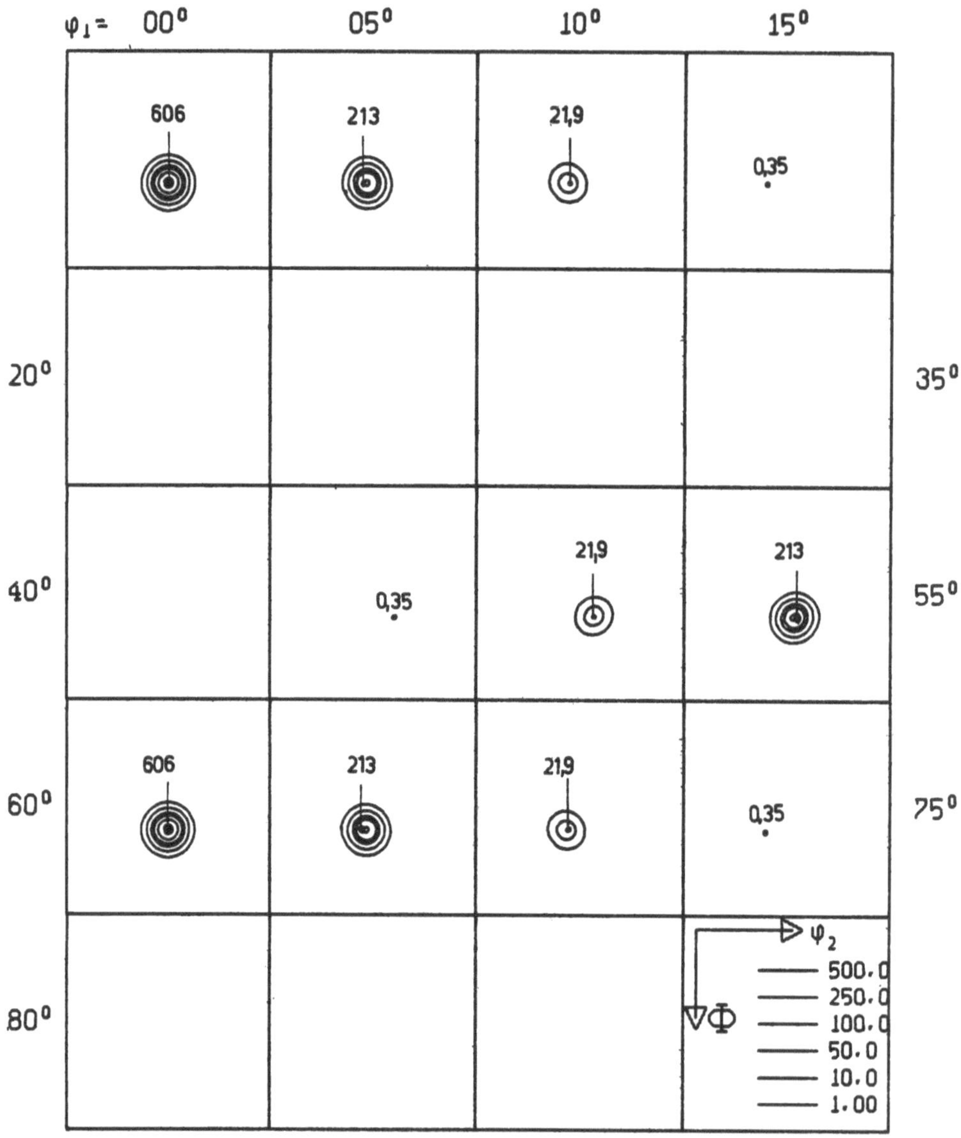

F, G, 7.50° , {111}<011>

F_{MAX} = 605.68 (00°, 60°)

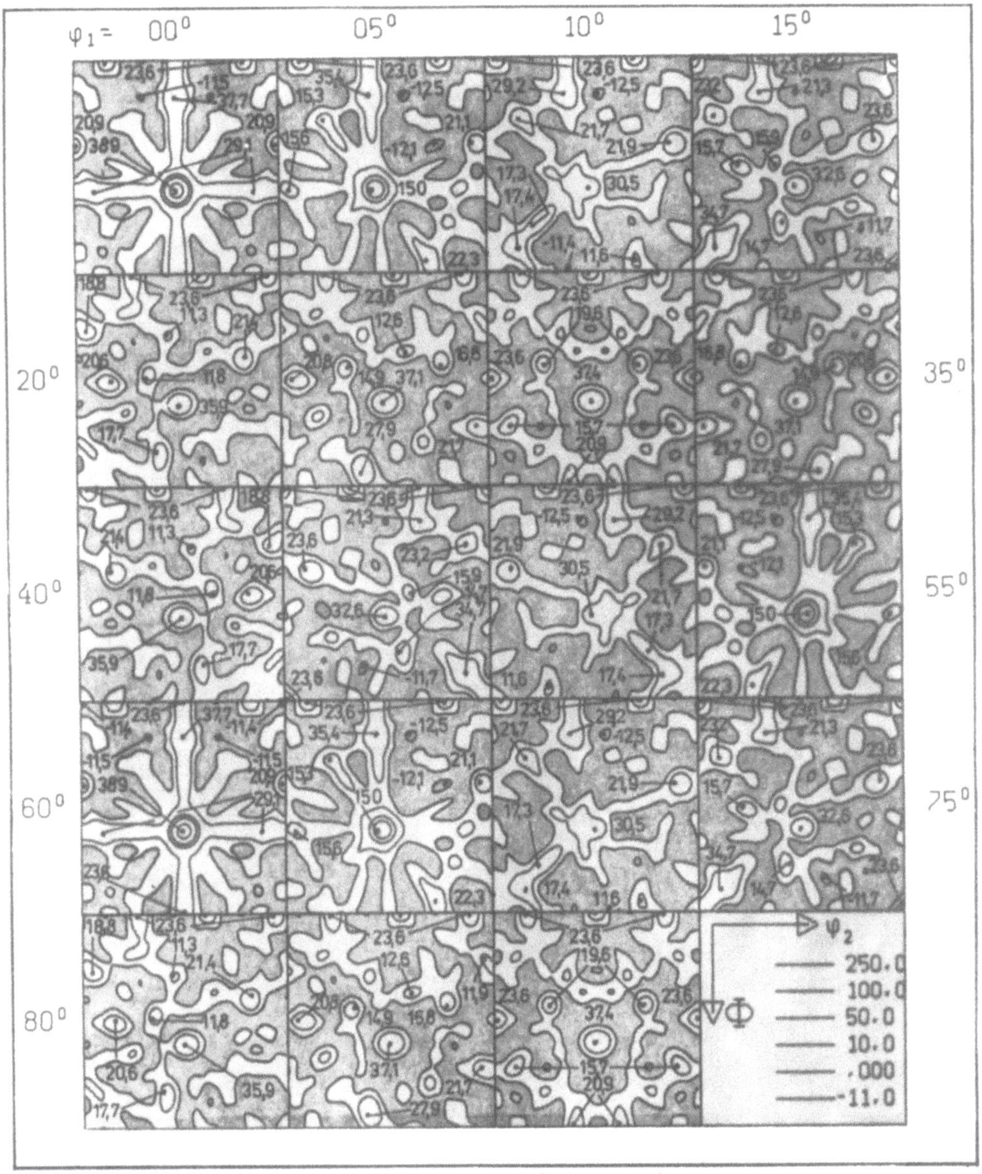

$\tilde{F}$, G, 7.50°, $\{111\}\langle 011\rangle$

$\tilde{F}_{MAX}$ = 389.45 (00°, 60°)

$\tilde{F}_{MIN}$ = −12.54 (05°, 55°, 65°)

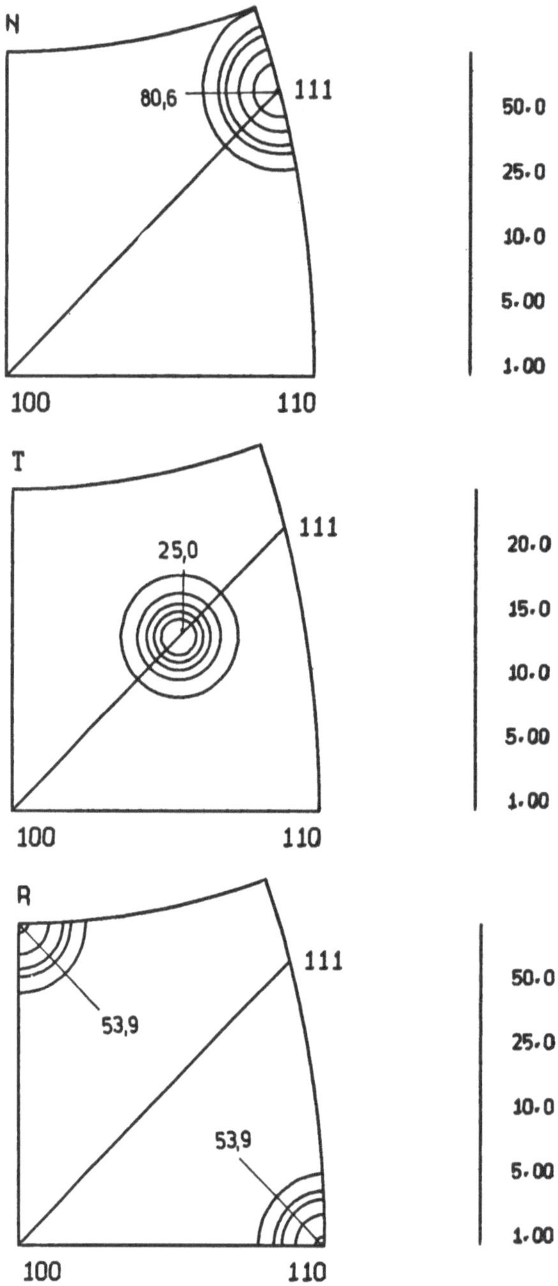

$\tilde{R}$, G, 7.50°, $\{111\}\langle 011\rangle$

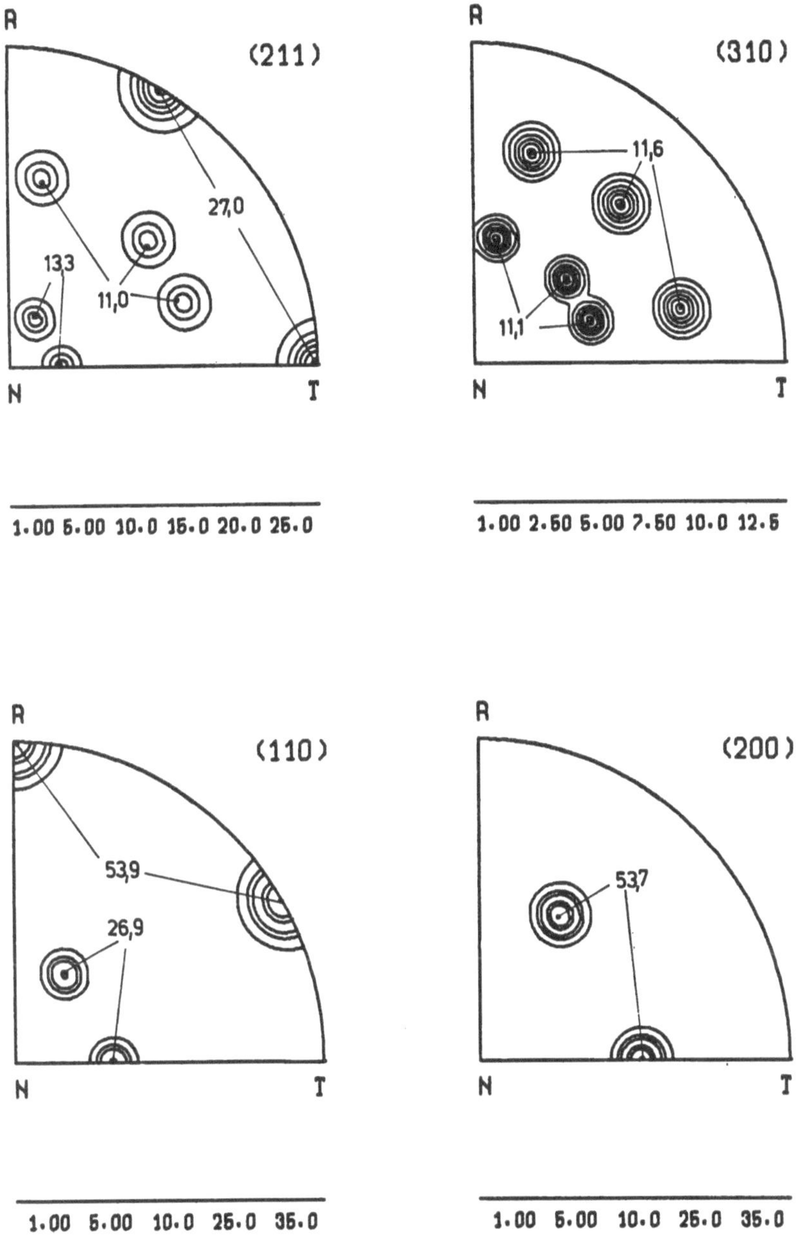

$\tilde{P}$, G, 7.50°, $\{111\}\langle 011\rangle$

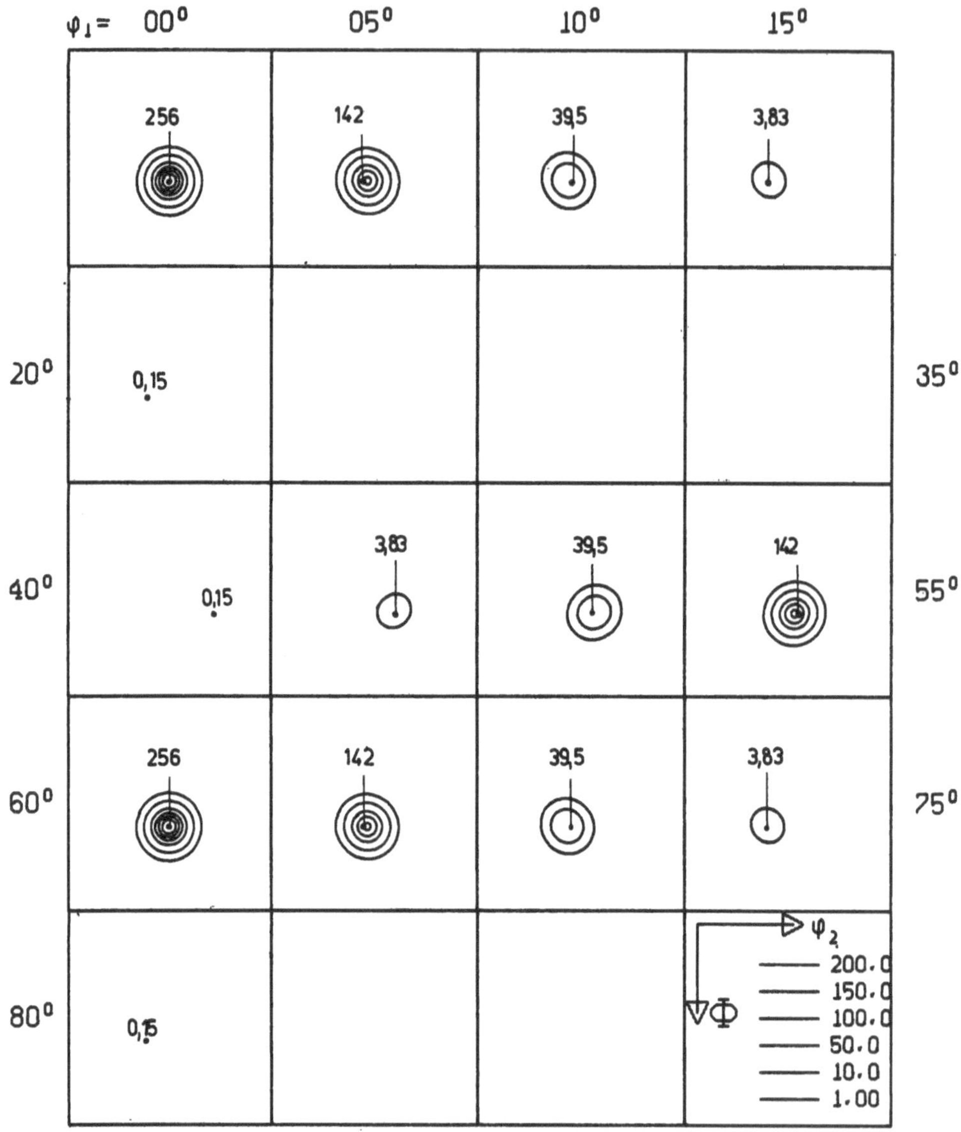

F, G, 10.0° , {111}<011>

F_{MAX} = 255.72 (00°, 60°)

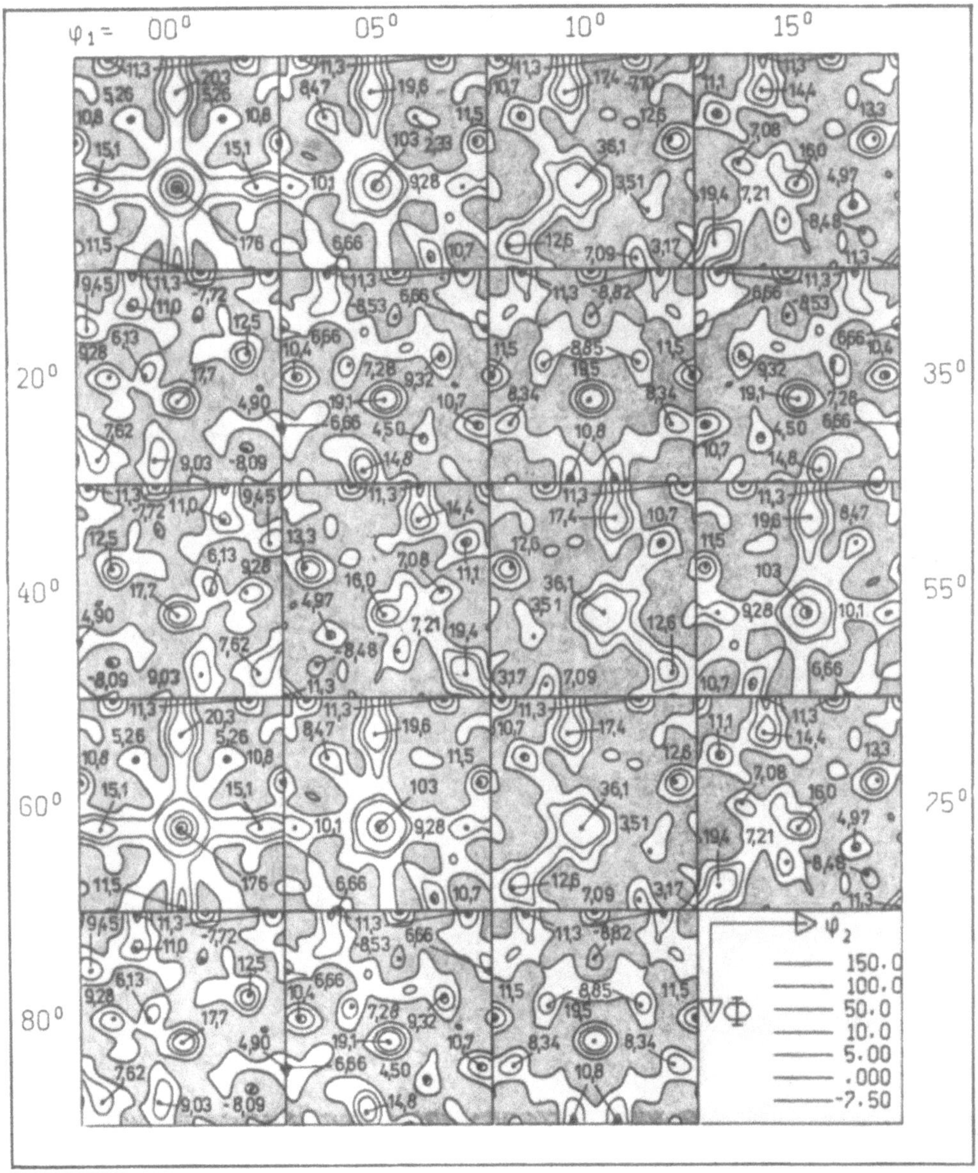

$\tilde{F}$, G, 10.0° ; {111}<011>

$\tilde{F}_{MAX}$ = 176.17 (00°, 60°)

$\tilde{F}_{MIN}$ = −8.82 (30°, 90°)

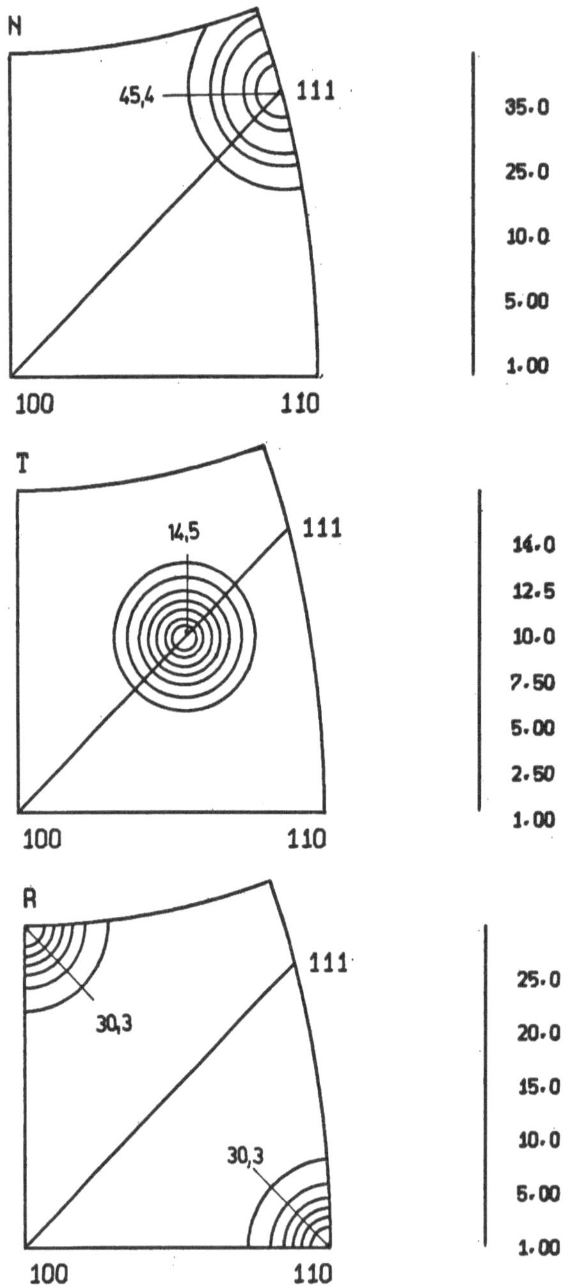

$\tilde{R}$, G, 10.0°, {111}⟨011⟩

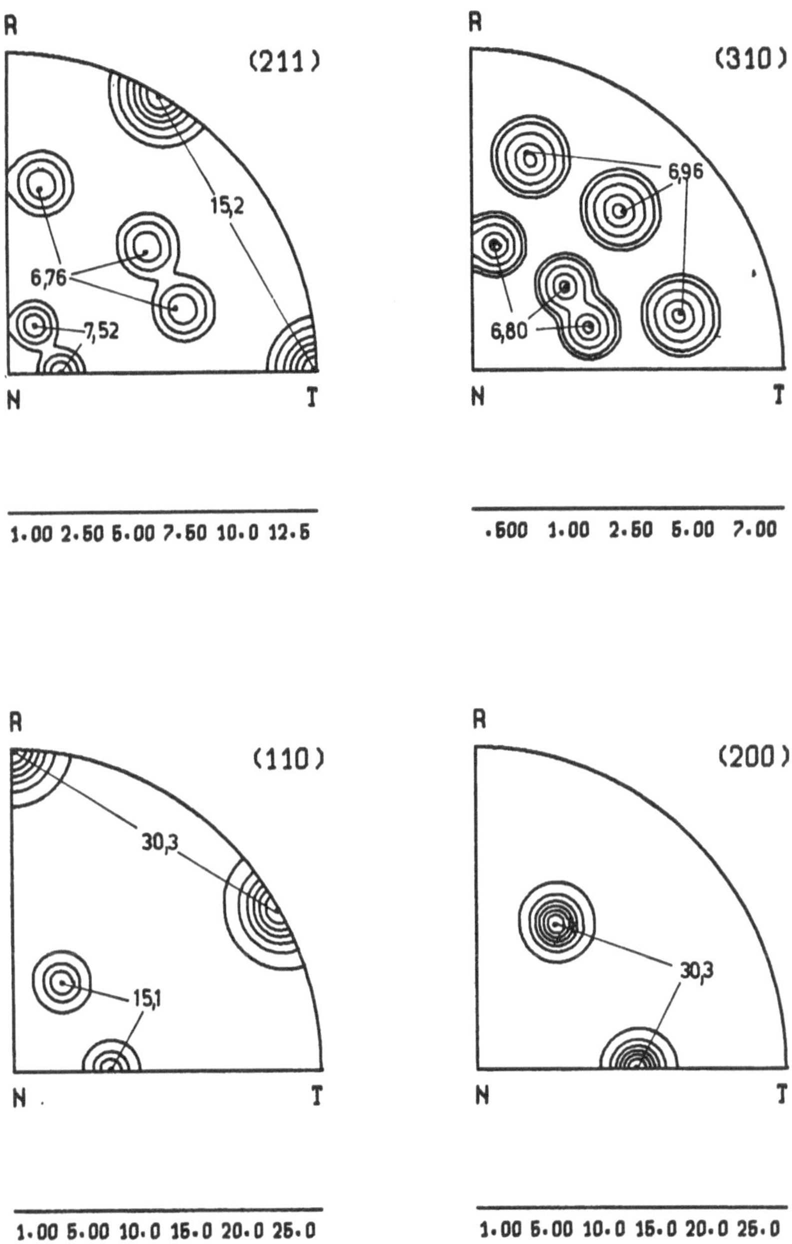

P,G, 10.0° , {111}⟨011⟩

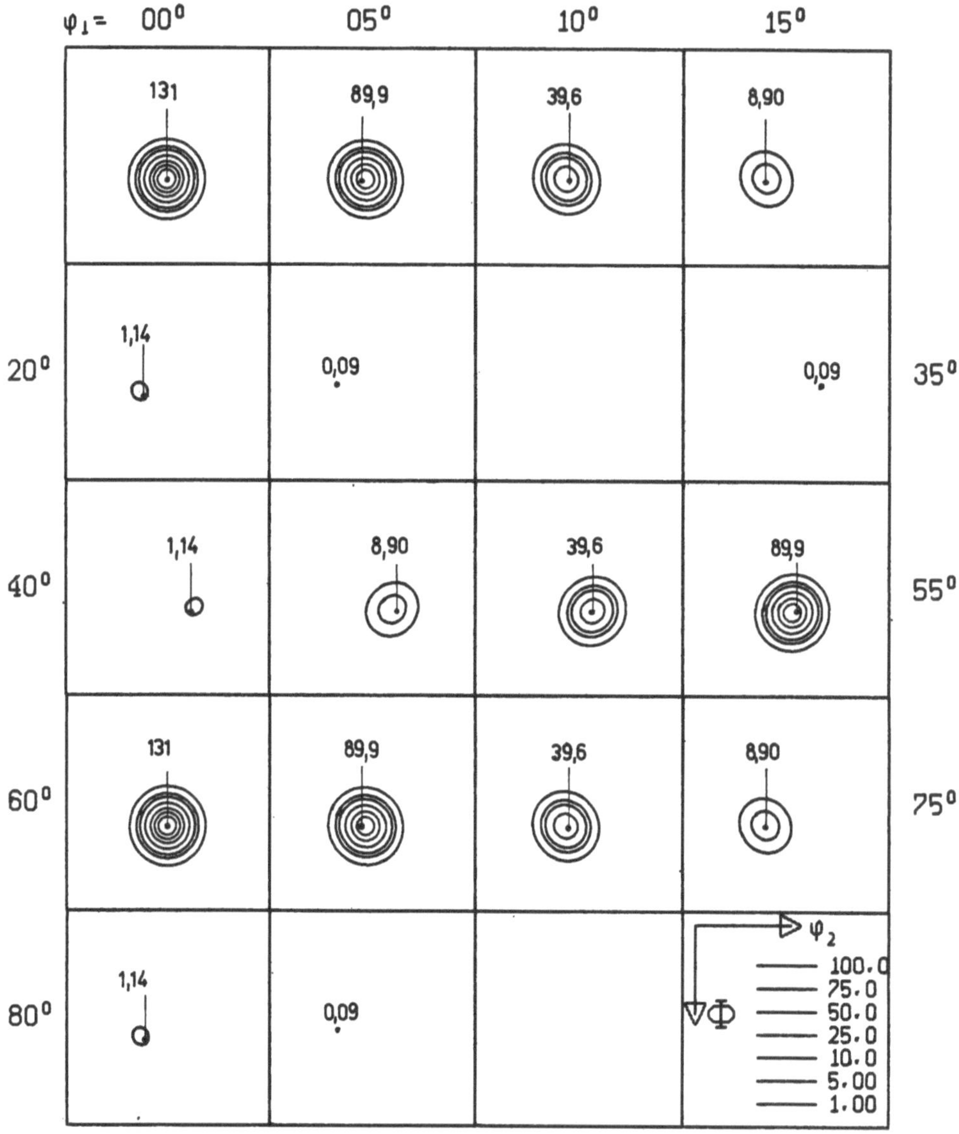

F, G, 12.5⁰ , {111}<011>

F_{MAX} = 130.94 (00⁰, 60⁰)

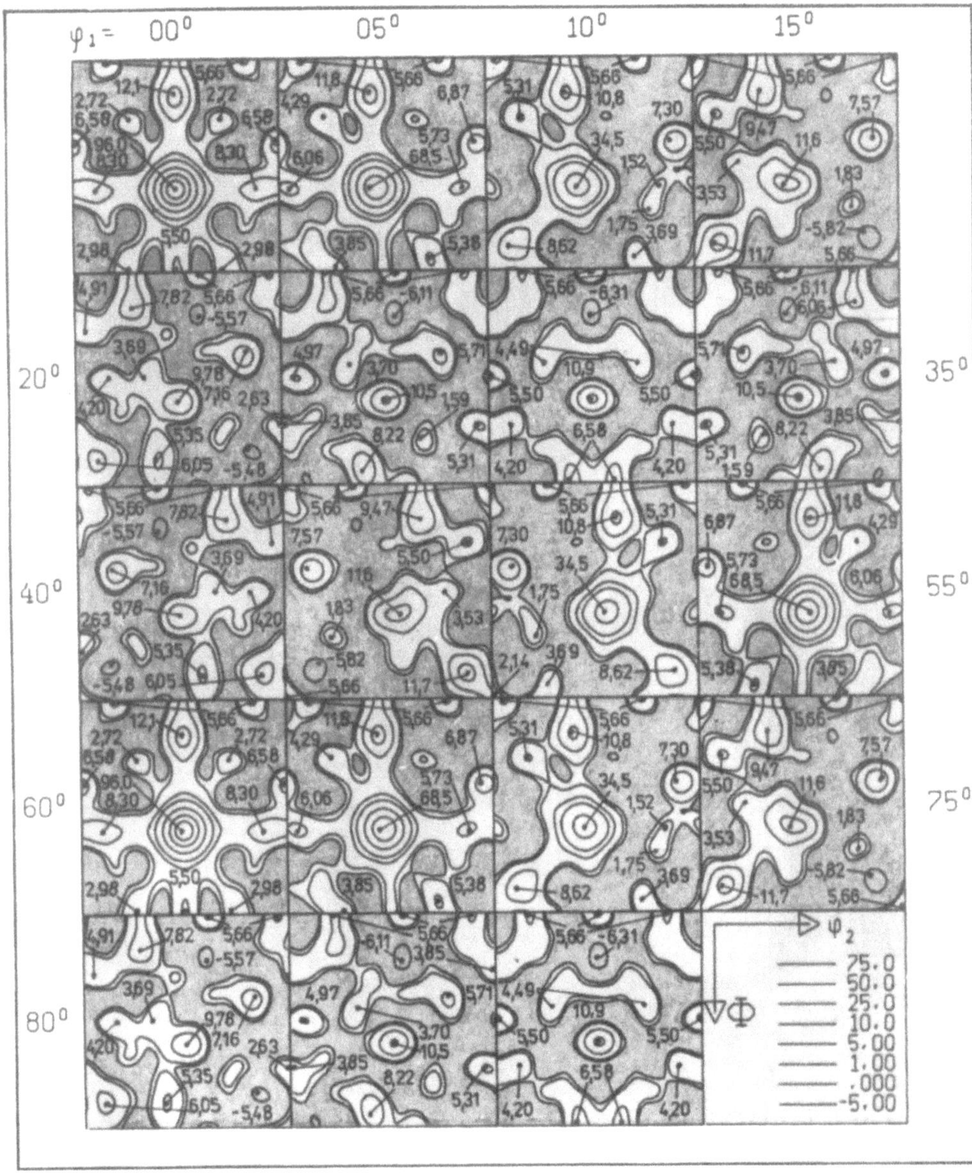

$\tilde{F}$, G, 12.5°, {111}<011>

$\tilde{F}_{MAX}$ = 96.04 (00°, 60°)

$\tilde{F}_{MIN}$ = −6.31 (30°, 90°)

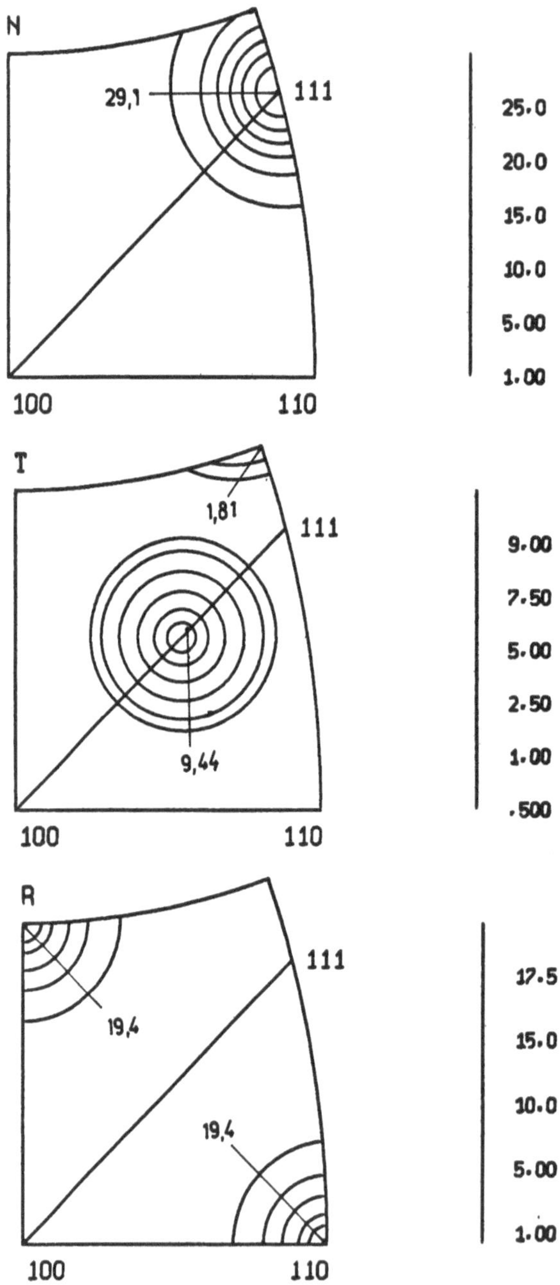

$\tilde{R}$, G, 12.5°, $\{111\}\langle 011\rangle$

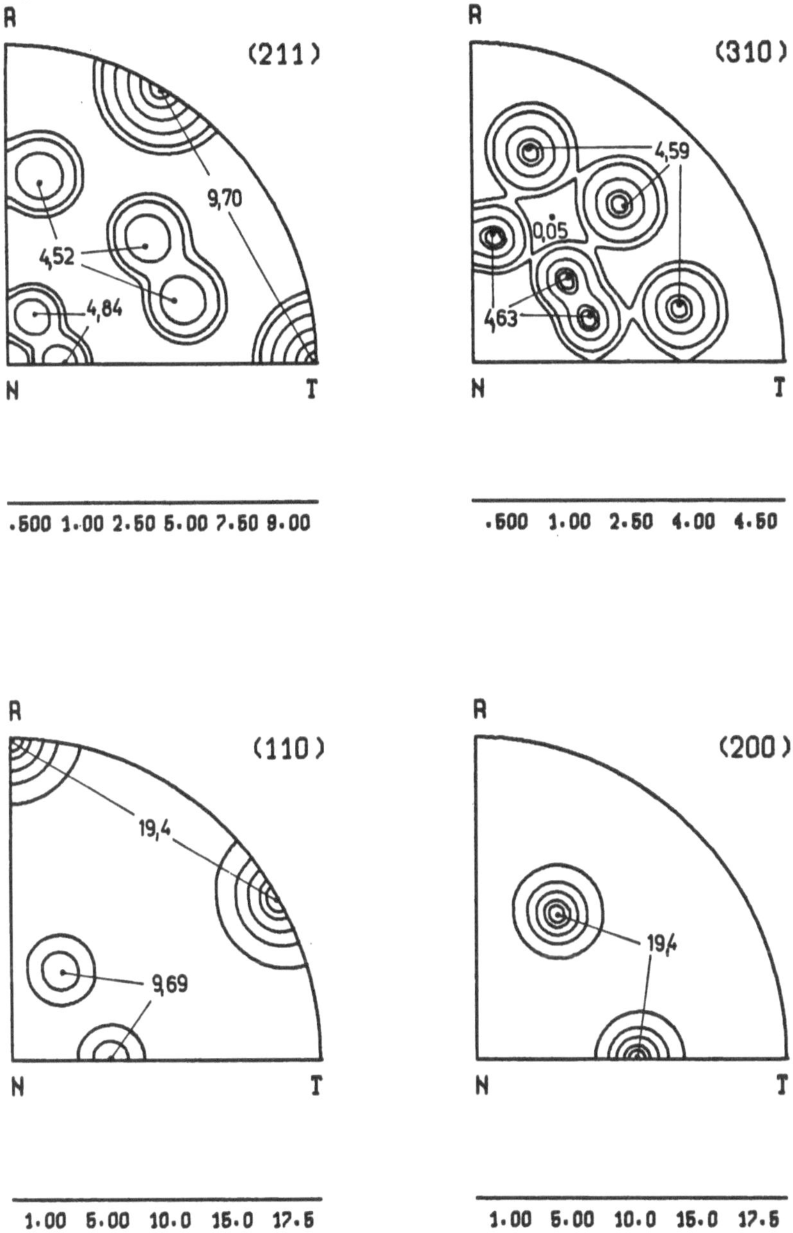

$\tilde{P}$, G, 12.5°, $\{111\}\langle 011\rangle$

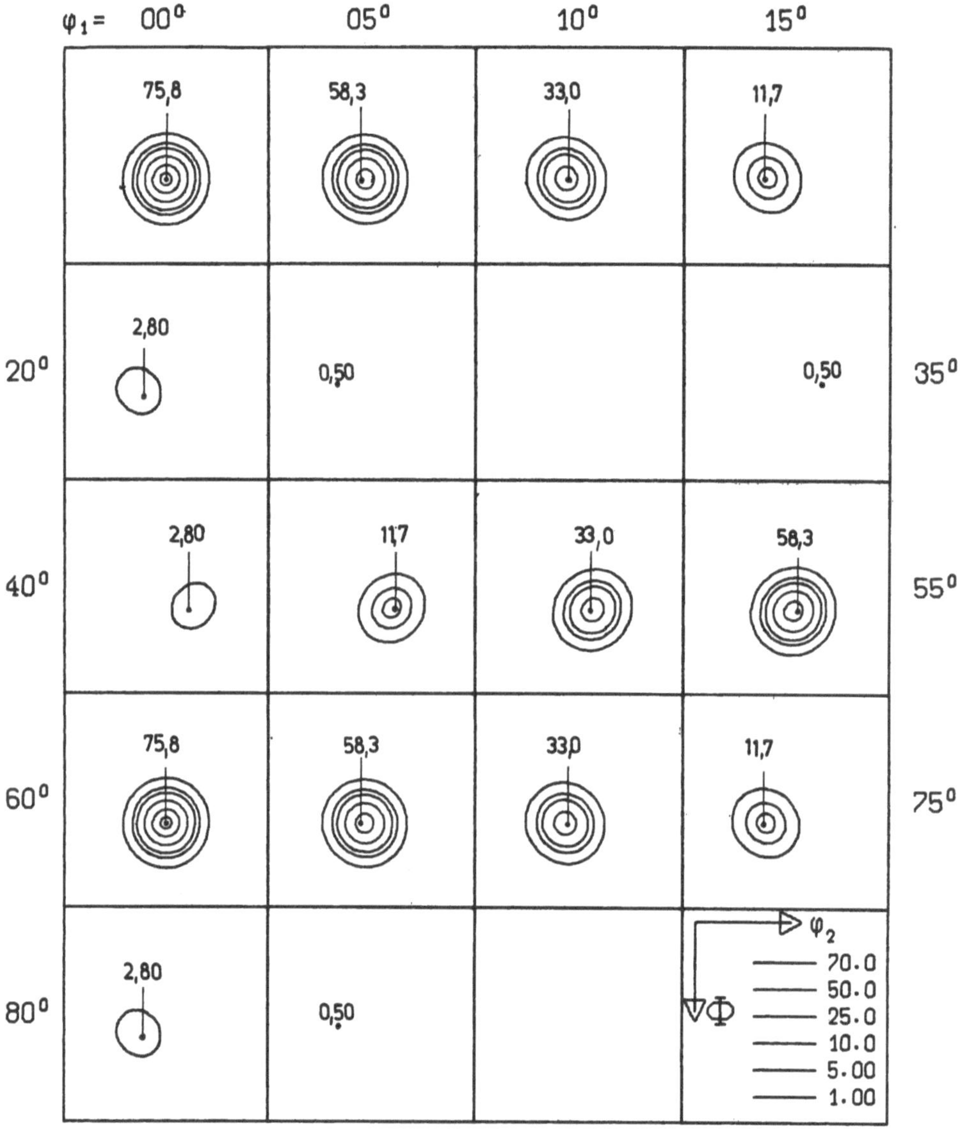

F, G, 15.0° , {111}<011>

F_{MAX} = 75.75 (00°, 60°)

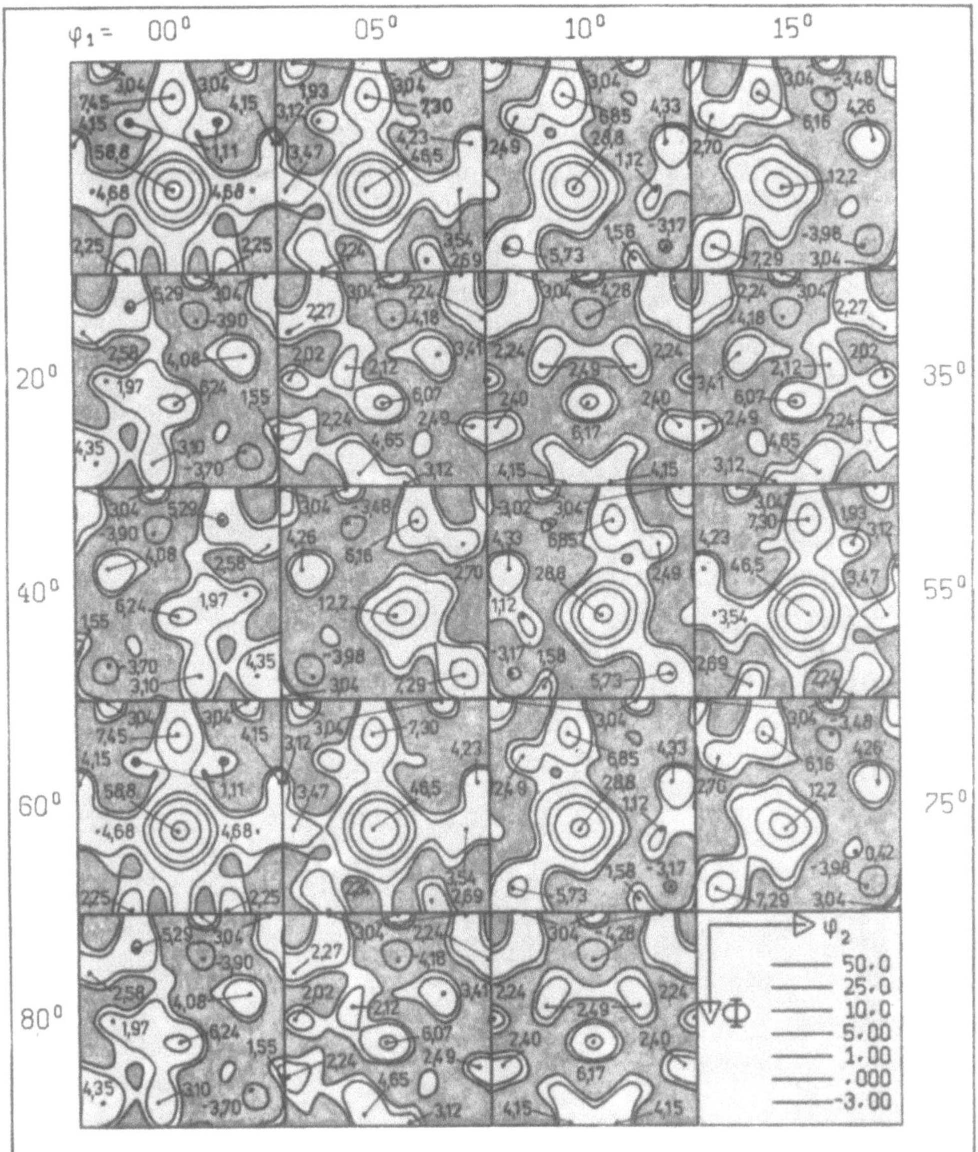

$\tilde{F}$, G, 15.0°, $\{111\}\langle 011\rangle$

$\tilde{F}_{MAX}$ = 58.78 (00°, 60°)

$\tilde{F}_{MIN}$ = -4.28 (30°, 90°)

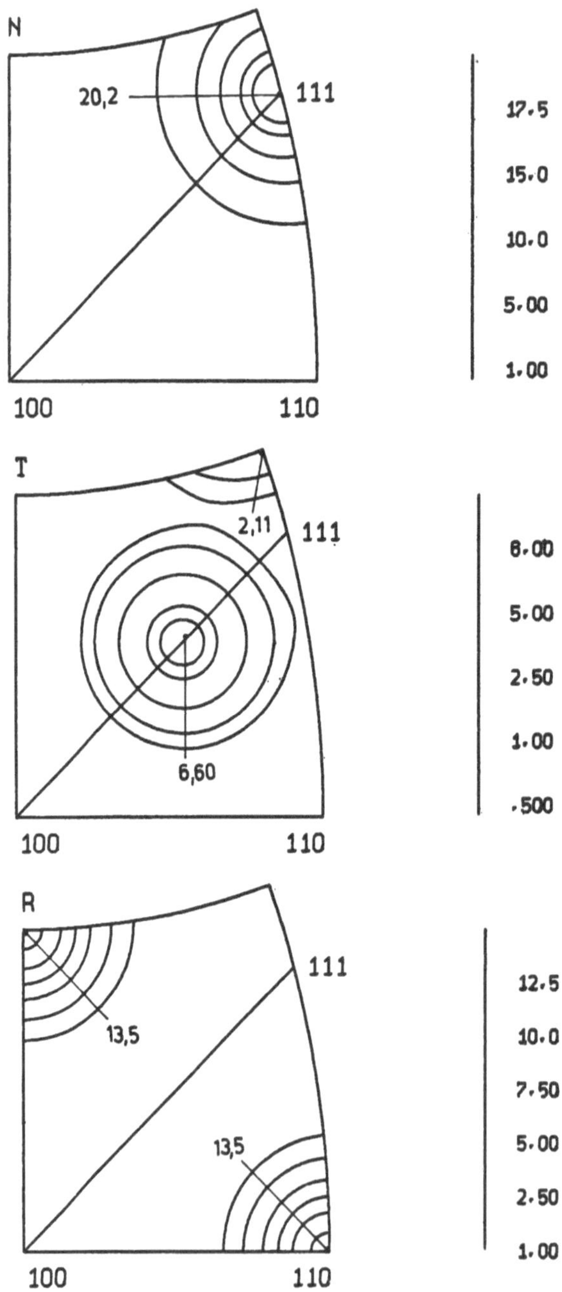

$\tilde{R}$, G, 15.0°, $\{111\}\langle 011\rangle$

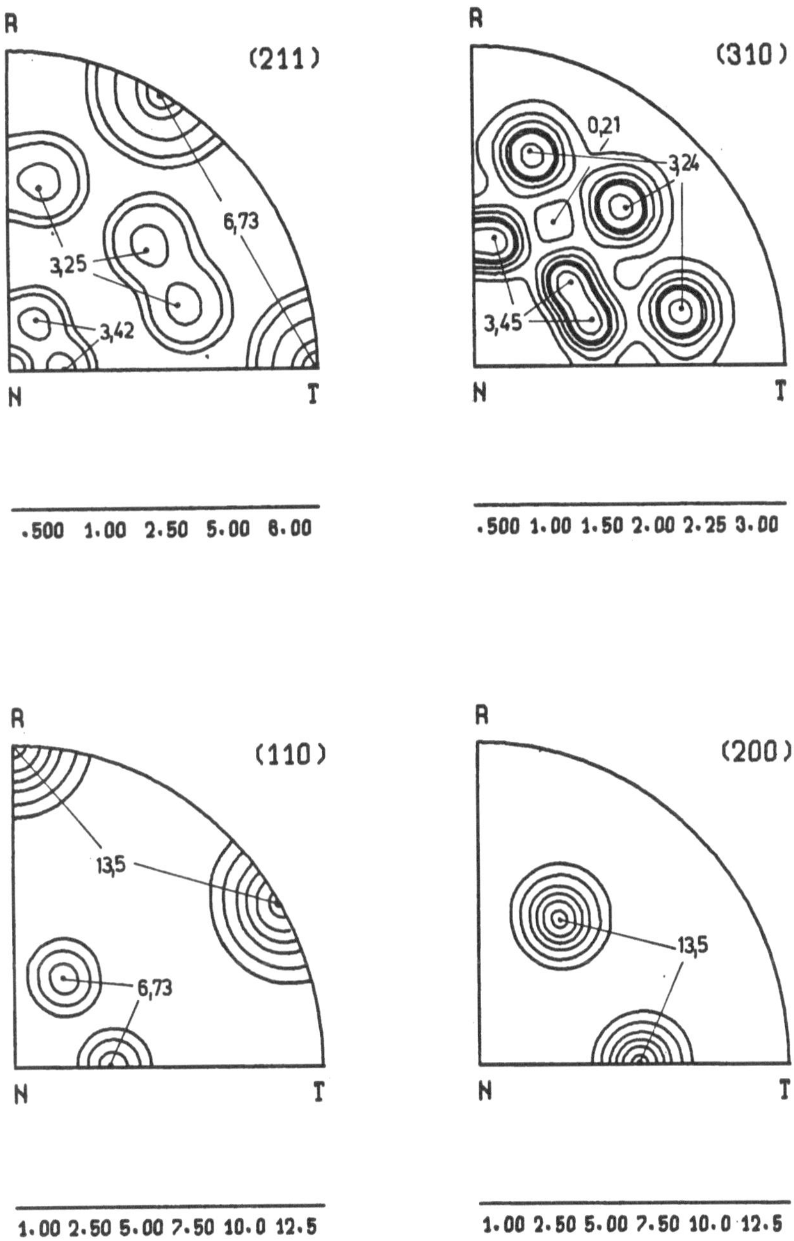

$\tilde{P}$, G, 15.0°, {111}⟨011⟩

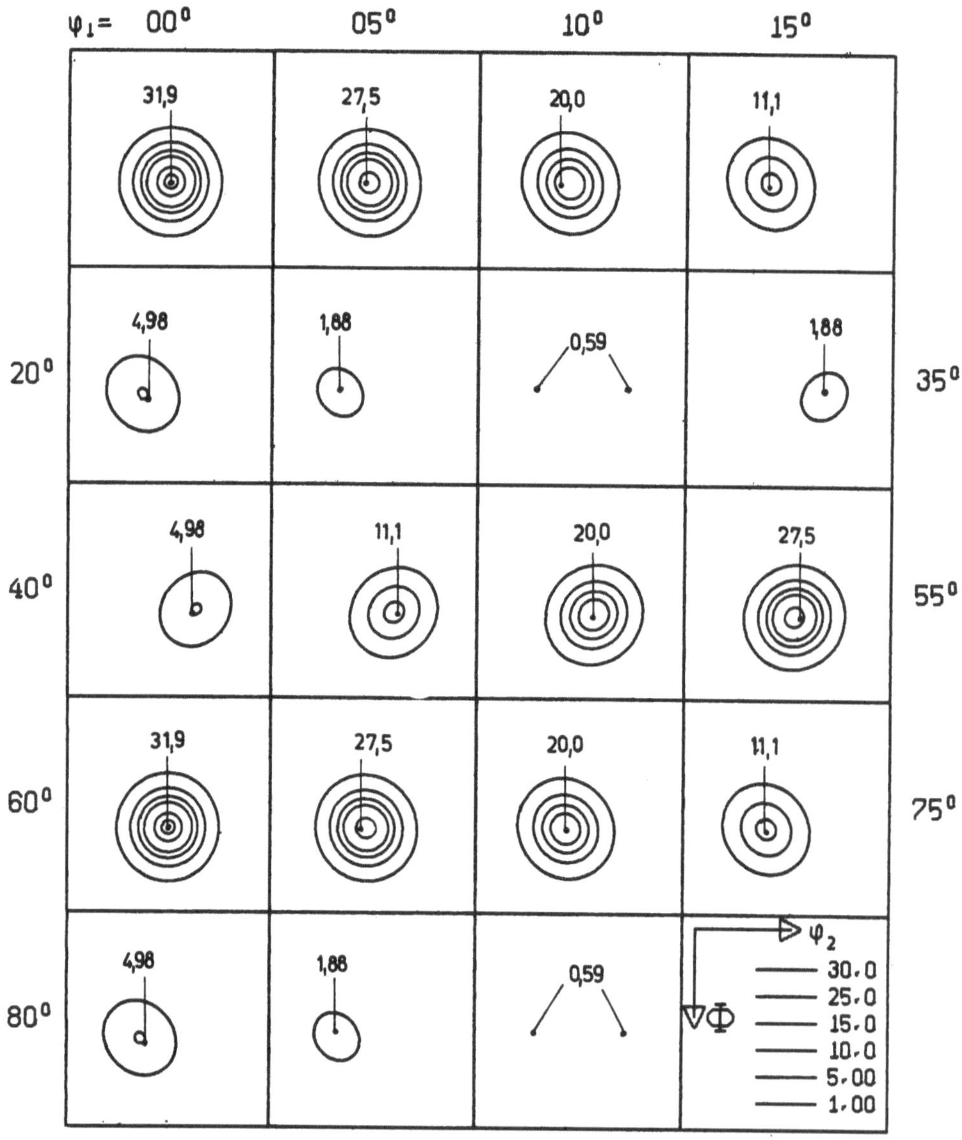

F, G, 20.0° , {111}<011>

F_{MAX} = 31.90 (00°, 60°)

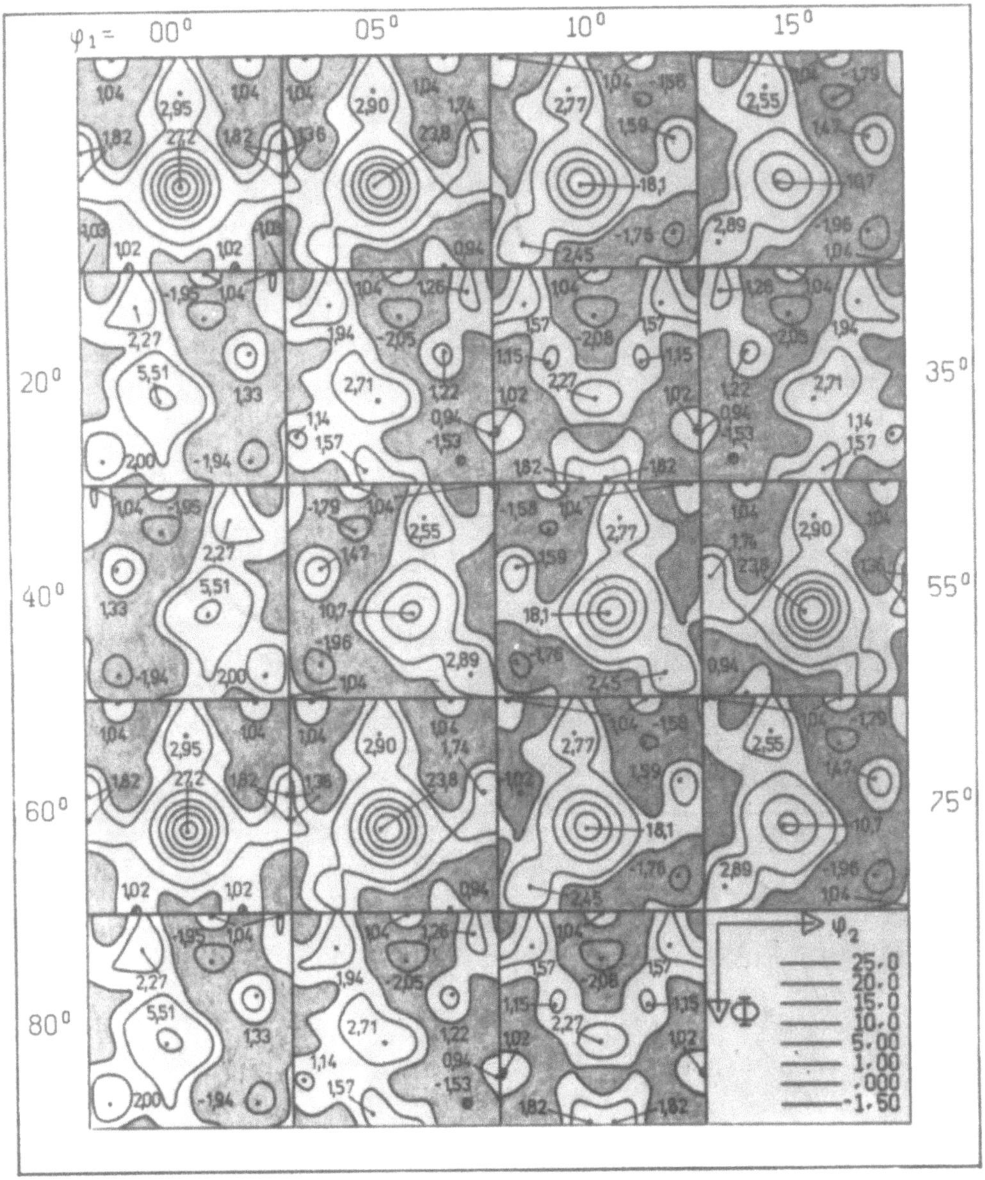

$\tilde{F}$, G, 20.0°, {111}<011>

$\tilde{F}_{MAX}$ = 27.19 (00°, 60°)

$\tilde{F}_{MIN}$ = −2.08 (30°, 90°)

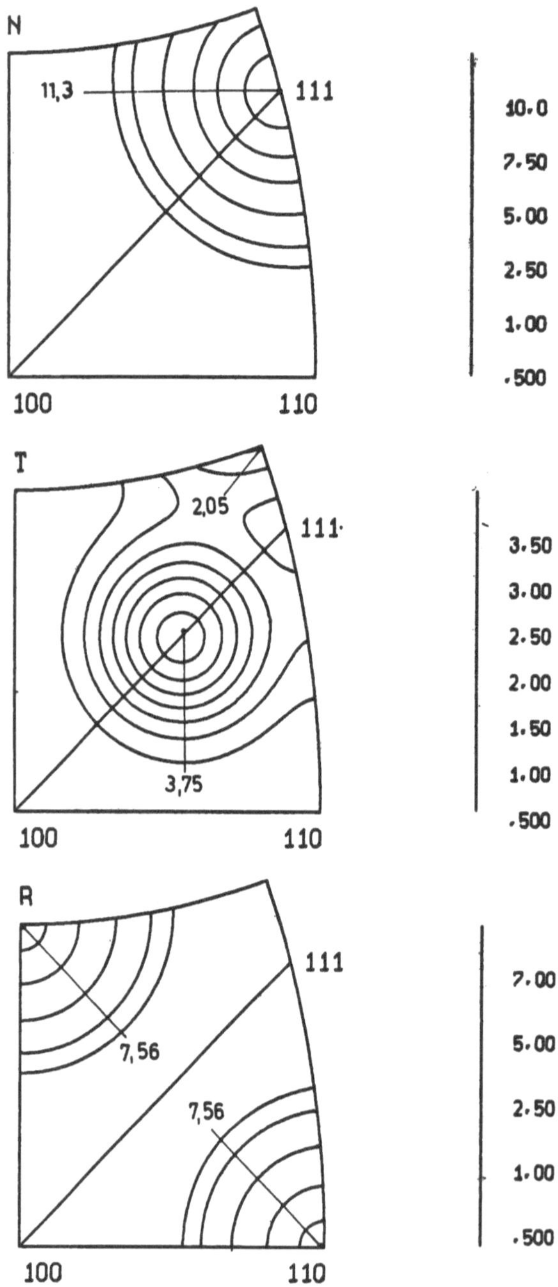

$\tilde{R}$, G, 20.0° , $\{111\}\langle 011\rangle$

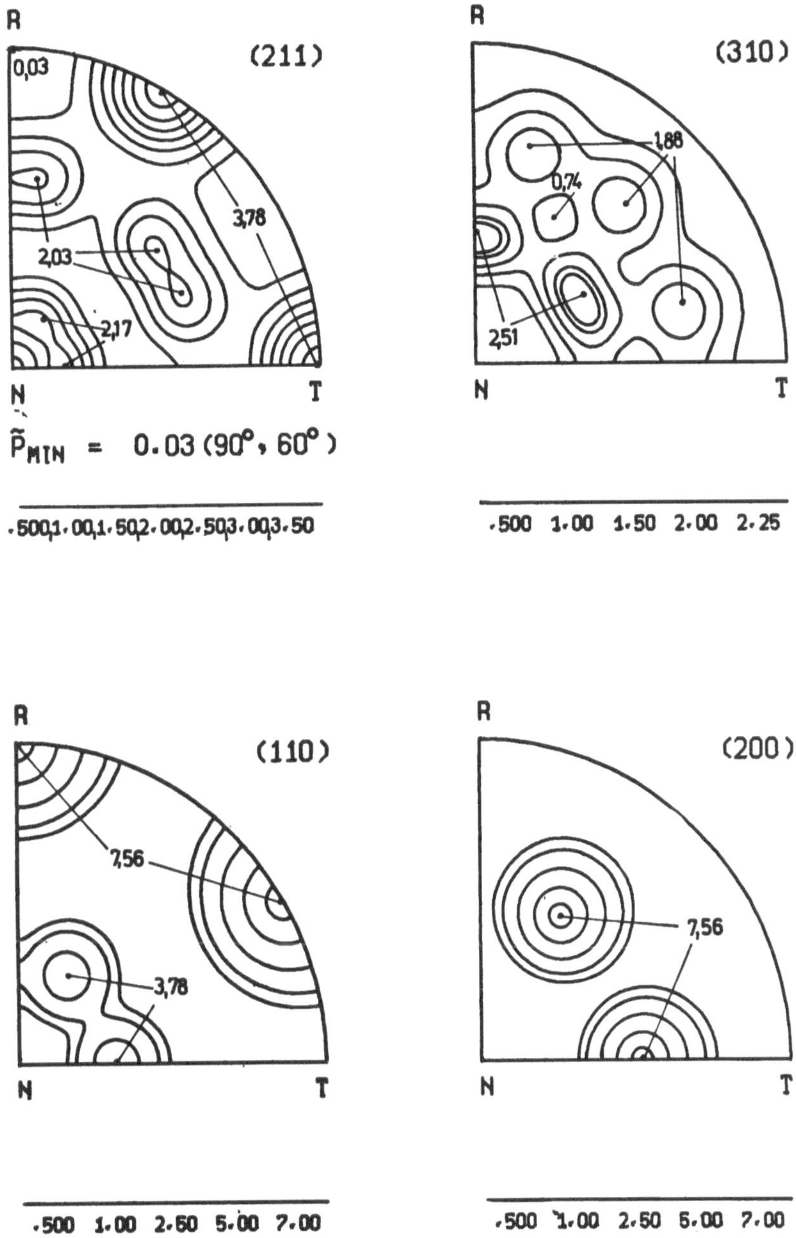

$\tilde{P}$, G, 20.0°, {111}⟨011⟩

15*

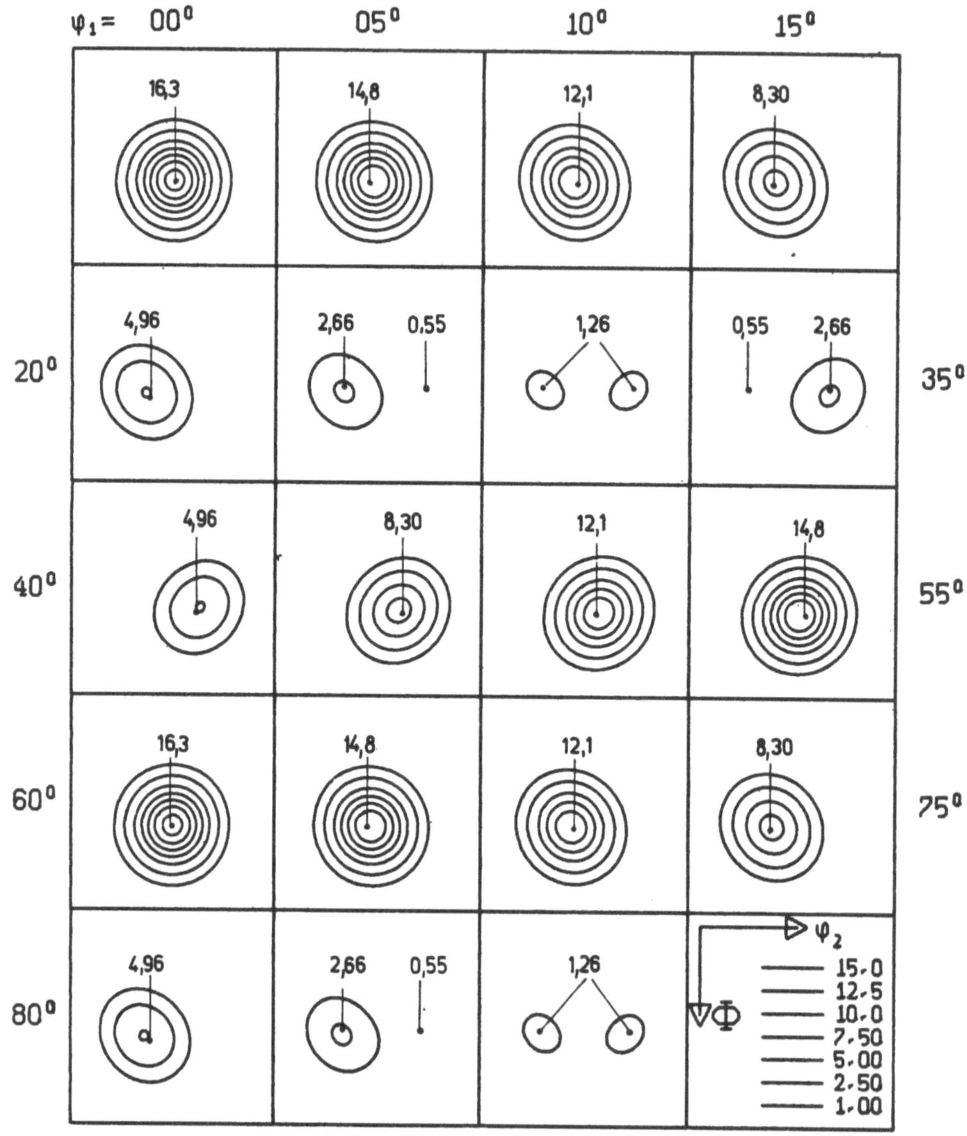

F, G, 25.0° , {111}<011>

F_{MAX} = 16.29 (00°, 60°)

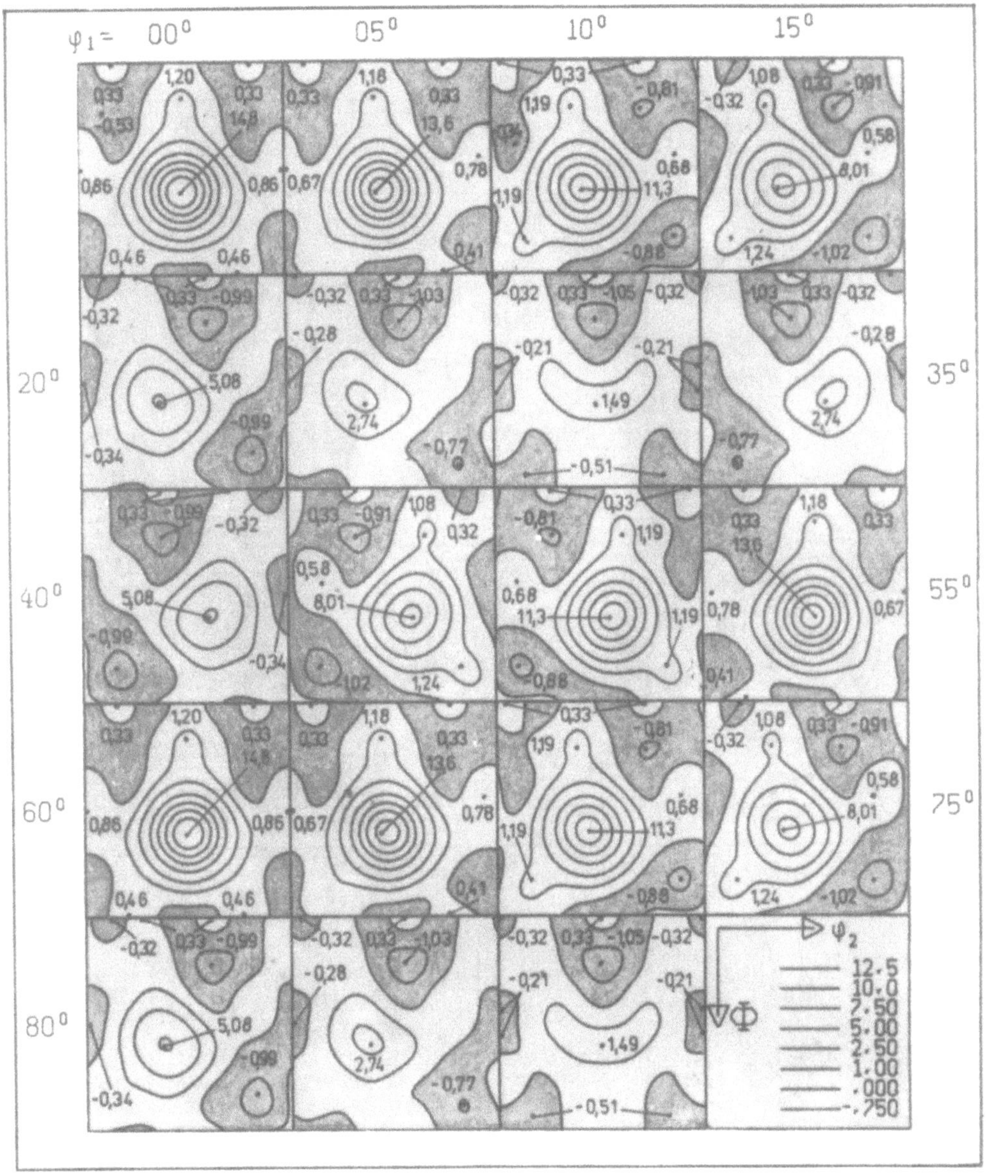

$\tilde{F}$, G, 25.0°, {111}<011>

$\tilde{F}_{MAX}$ = 14.81 (00°, 60°)

$\tilde{F}_{MIN}$ = -1.05 (30°, 90°)

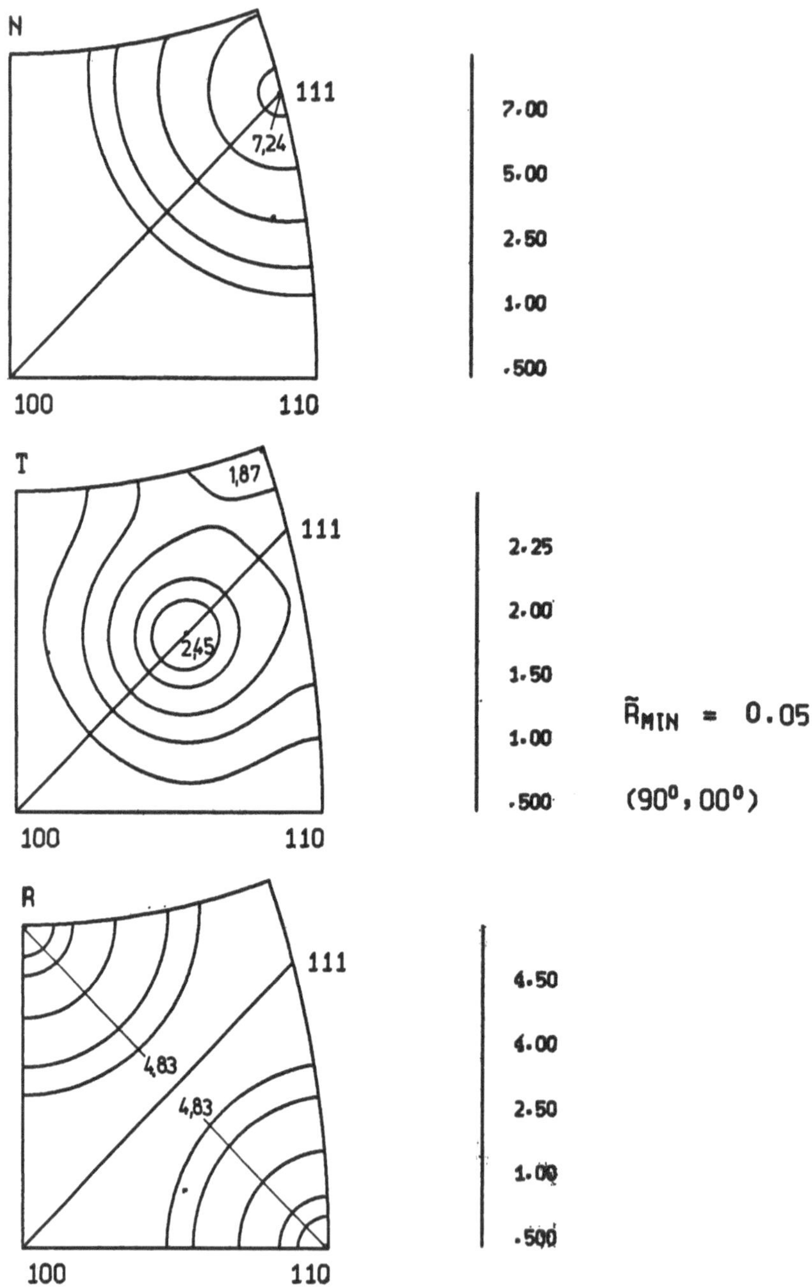

$\tilde{R}$, G, 25.0^{0}, $\{111\}\langle 011\rangle$

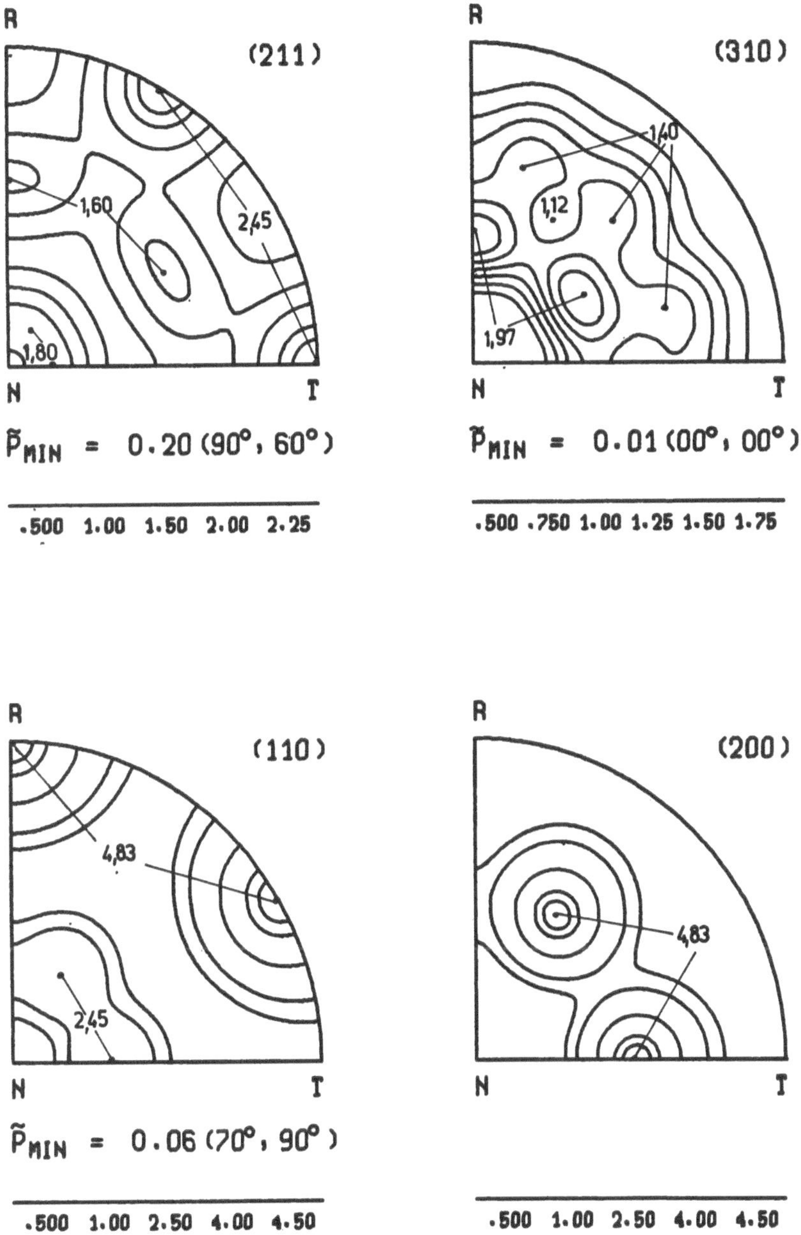

$\tilde{P}$, G, 25.0°, $\{111\}\langle 011\rangle$

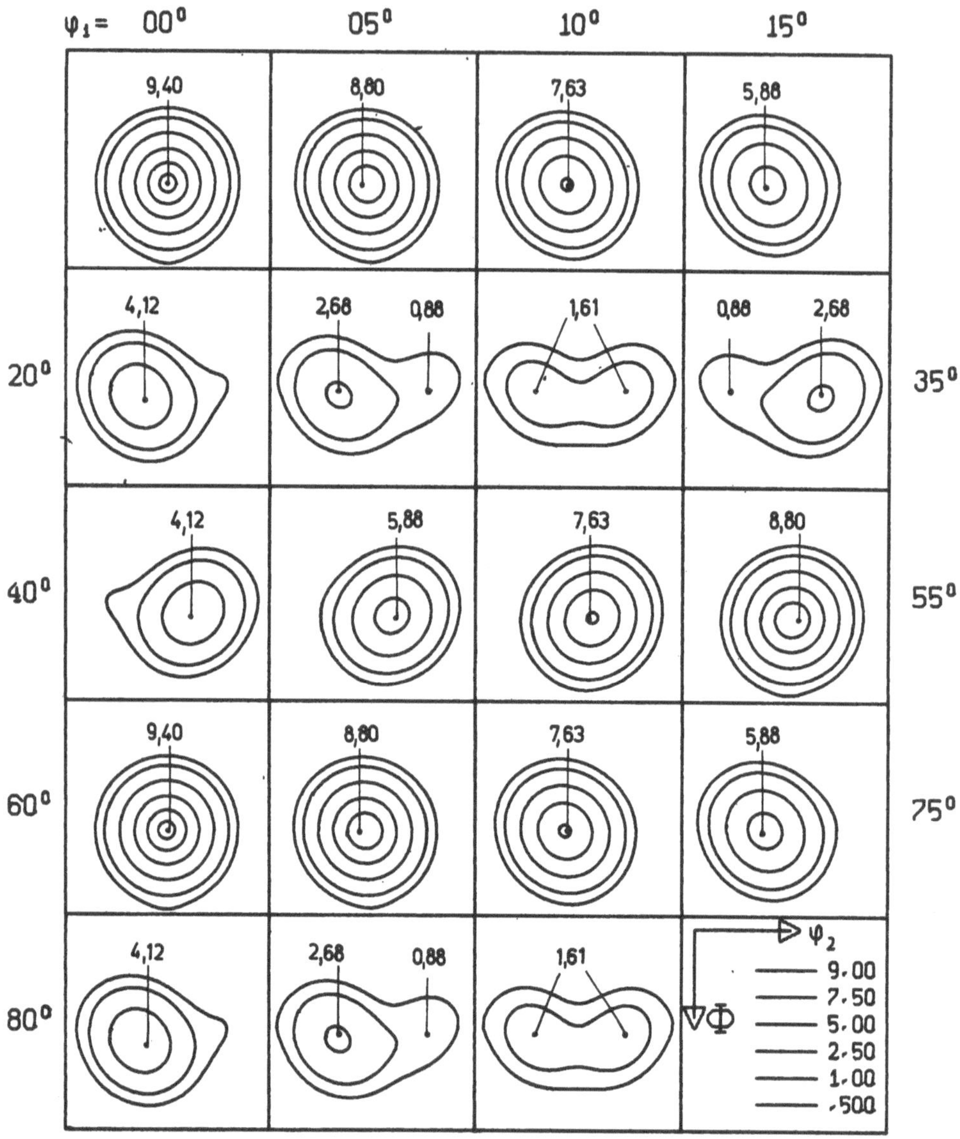

F, G, 30.0° , {111}<011>

F_{MAX} = 9.40 (00°, 60°)

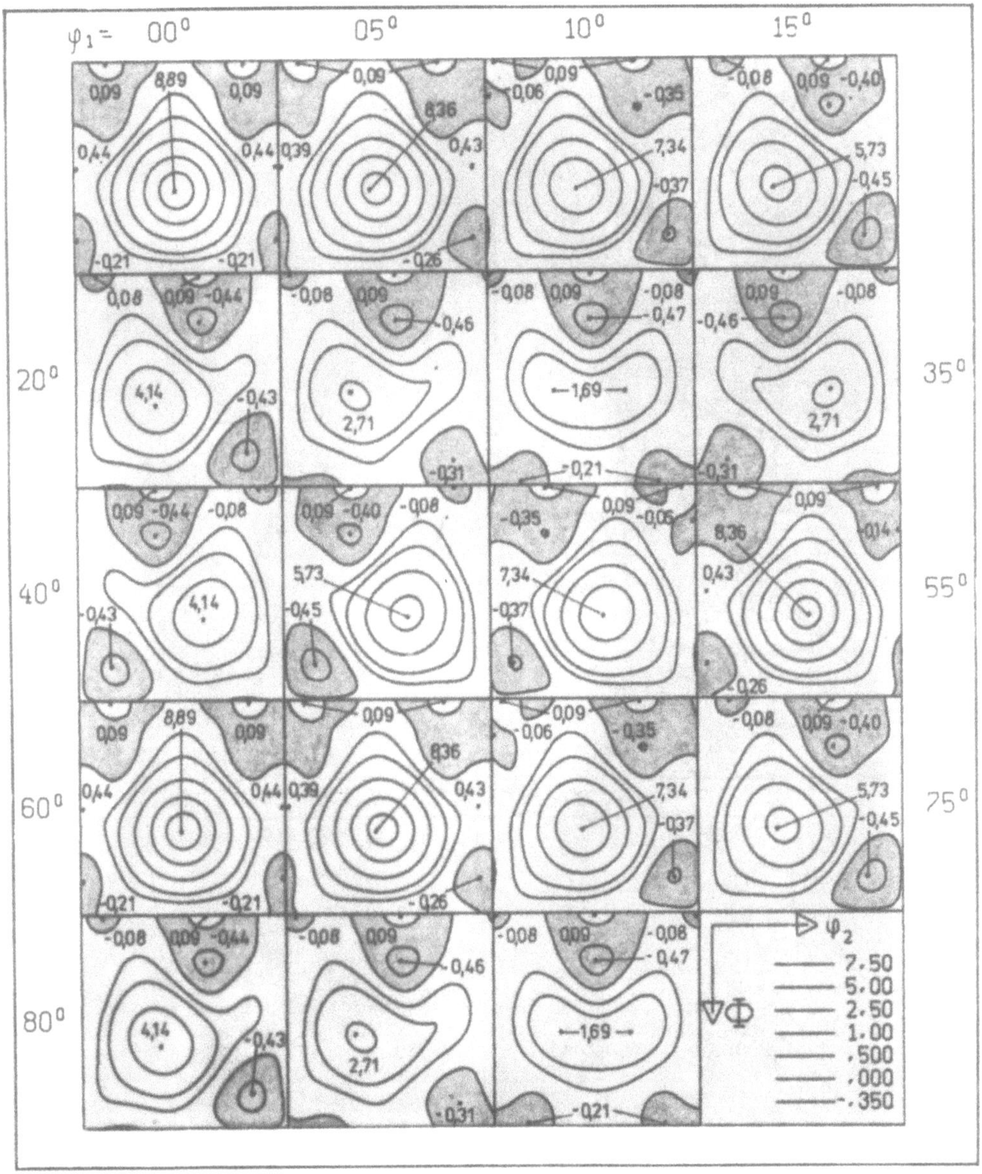

F̃, G, 30.0° , {111}<011>

$\tilde{F}_{MAX}$ = 8.89 (00°, 60°)

$\tilde{F}_{MIN}$ = -.47 (30°, 90°)

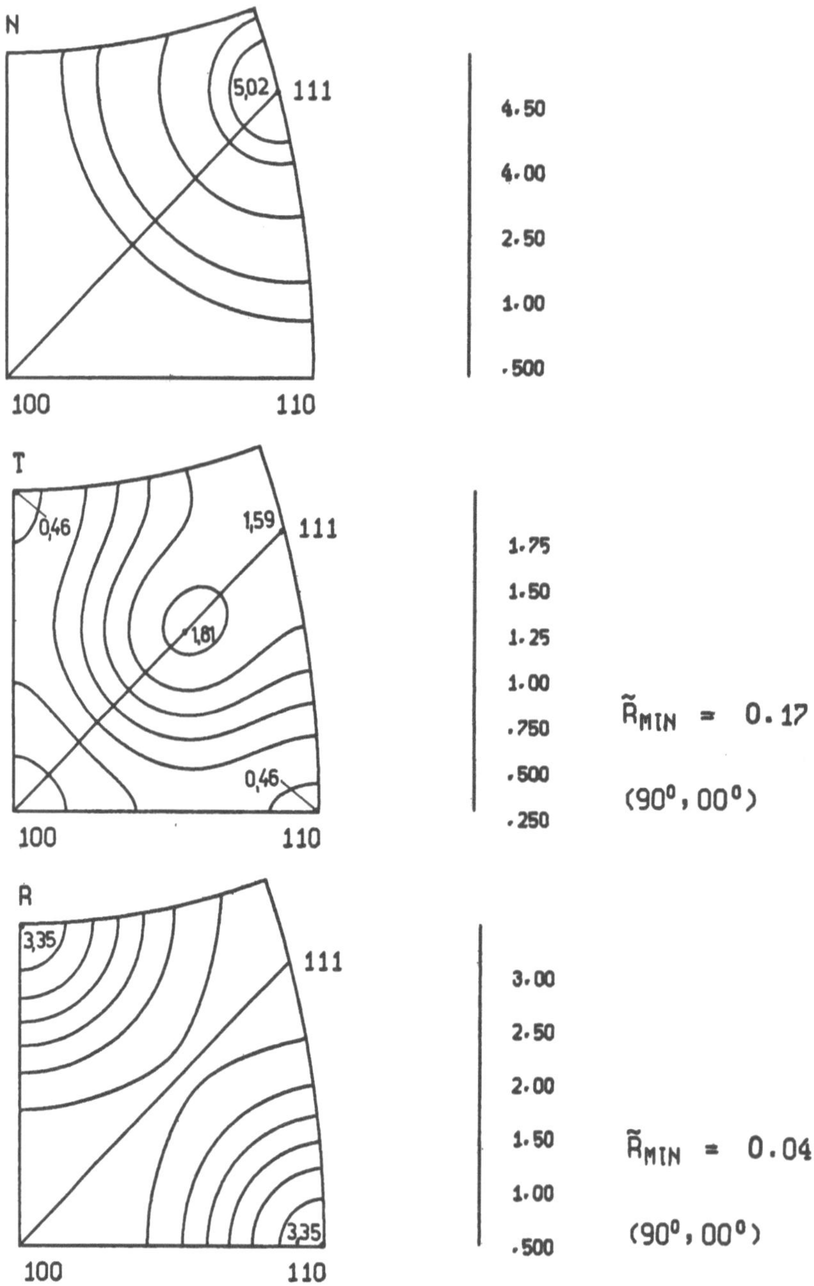

$\tilde{R}$, G, 30.0°, $\{111\}\langle 011\rangle$

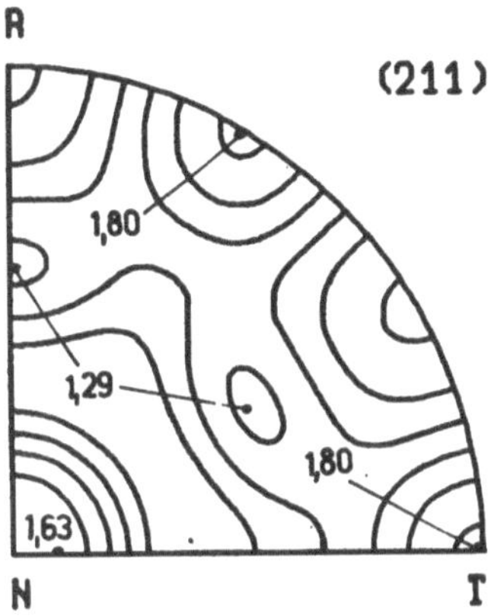

$\tilde{P}_{MIN}$ = 0.46 (90°, 60°)

.500 .750 1.00 1.25 1.50 1.75

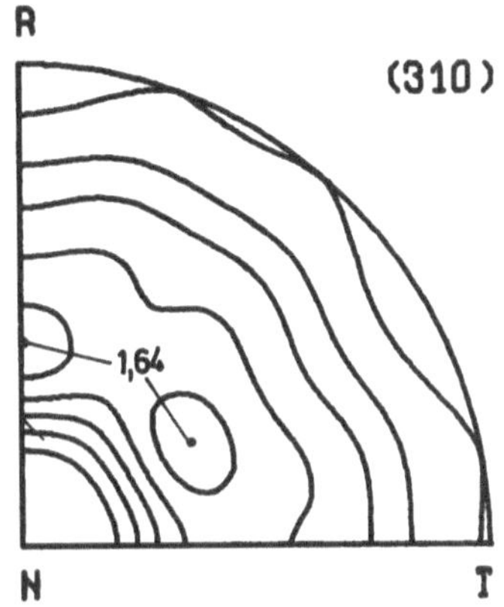

$\tilde{P}_{MIN}$ = 0.04 (00°, 00°)

.500 .750 1.00 1.25 1.50

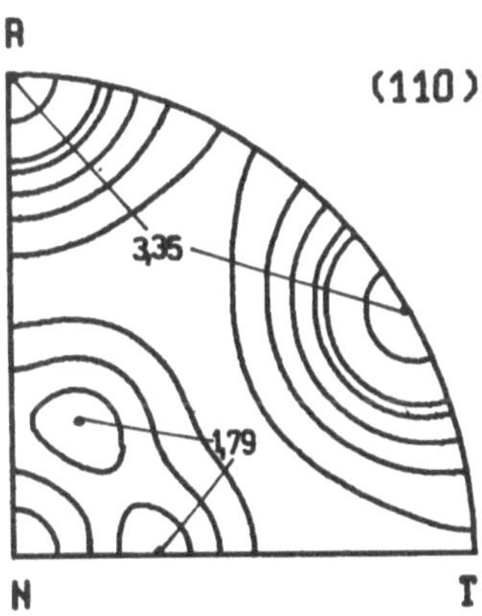

$\tilde{P}_{MIN}$ = 0.21 (70°, 90°)

.500 1.00 1.50 2.00 2.25 3.00

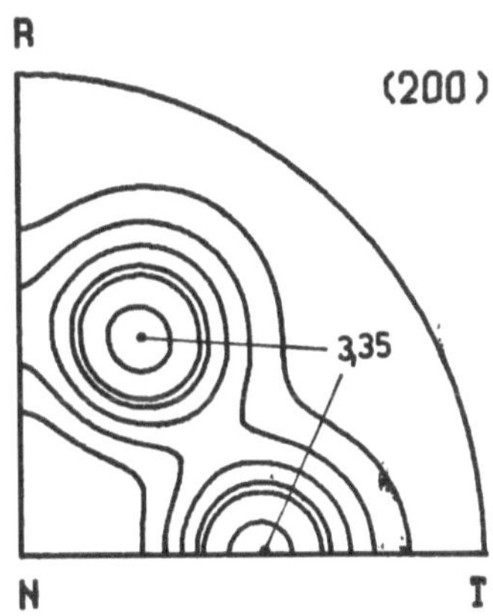

.500 1.00 1.50 2.00 2.25 3.00

$\tilde{P}$, 6, 30.0°, $\{111\}\langle 011\rangle$

Table III — $D^{l}_{\mu,\nu}(g_0^{-1})$, $G_A = D_2$, $G_B = O$ (For details see chapter 18 of volume 1.)

L	MU	NU	101 525	525 151	013 100	122 221	323 131	113 110	233 011	111 011
4	1	1	-1909407	-3166629	4200694	-3677376	-4434242	1641143	-4434242	-5091751
		2	7274070	-6149576	-3074085	0	-3175708	-2258281	3175708	0
		3	2184862	3672428	5874025	-3107950	2067192	-5121300	2067192	0
6	1	1	5745243	484108	-194454	-1498601	-4225840	-467509	-4225840	-6285394
		2	2727776	-427054	-1152782	0	1190890	6774843	-1190890	0
		3	-2638472	-4626993	3881970	3964925	-2657427	-1236912	-2657427	0
		4	-394050	-5073419	-1709852	0	-5427592	2854749	5427592	5629142
8	1	1	4039146	2044567	-671396	1664662	1601601	-4131565	1601601	2127616
		2	-2132401	4888951	-6596573	0	4131624	-2538645	-4131624	0
		3	2692879	618591	1017714	885294	-2086233	4023043	-2086233	0
		4	-462700	279633	-2925562	0	5385831	-487578	-5385831	-7554103
		5	-1939669	1883319	4818245	1348855	596731	3662501	596731	0
9	1	1	6045032	1409077	3985306	0	4384019	-2853853	-4384019	0
		2	474785	-4679135	1779196	5668561	-5252973	-2658067	-5252973	0
		3	-282825	-2509866	1914479	0	-3057388	-6534349	3057388	4040264
		4	3600766	-4431039	1891296	-3637453	-2237885	1805985	-2237885	0
10	1	1	128570	-2039362	2952594	-1033214	2234294	-1690551	2234294	6501537
		2	3657804	3710528	-252088	0	3479670	2738591	-3479670	0
		3	2563312	-398993	-2096909	1472383	-1628208	1749757	-1628208	0
		4	446066	2100674	-5929814	0	-2151470	-815302	2151470	4504058
		5	129242	1339927	1423242	1752486	1904685	-3247347	1904685	0
		6	-4178588	-3653554	-1969500	0	-2200136	-2866882	2200136	0
12	1	1	-3174023	-2087613	-723268	-1471238	-783153	-2782399	-783153	-862923
		2	3676603	-2579204	-5531401	0	-2473417	1536764	2473417	0
		3	-511199	-4072774	736659	3280035	-881470	4332772	-881470	0
		4	-351099	1752786	-2803672	0	-2084780	-1310451	2084780	7078815
		5	-2931756	-4933087	1148831	-6426645	-5752567	-2713867	-5752567	0
		6	-4602546	1255126	-2212578	0	3189859	2799658	-3189859	0
		7	-1699401	249311	4260364	214817	-742368	-3142611	-742368	-1002597
	2	1	5092695	-4786458	-2547256	-4491424	-792610	2665908	-792610	4062759
		2	2661799	2682991	375353	0	-913114	-1252306	913114	0
		3	-1457847	2424306	4408680	-4152071	4937067	4375102	4937067	0
		4	156420	46416	-2521563	0	1591131	-2551651	-1591131	-3999490
		5	-2637631	1856291	-3405654	812711	-485230	-1675225	-485230	0
		6	3937208	3754314	-4147861	0	2352691	-4076467	-2352691	0
		7	-3480458	4026670	457364	-4249927	4608493	1274913	4608493	4957115
13	1	1	-1810636	1099527	1960112	0	-3230459	3843064	3230459	0
		2	2994666	-1762379	2499294	1253399	1334840	-956322	1334840	0
		3	-145009	6534728	3742301	0	835465	1433777	-835465	4633058
		4	-2493735	237837	-556399	363725	1386132	2261389	1386132	0
		5	2493316	-97508	-1221668	0	-2134657	2382449	2134657	0
		6	4776098	-655911	1138146	-914751	3032081	240733	3032081	4534972
14	1	1	3060046	-1563689	3643262	-1100247	-1232991	-2719666	-1232991	-4636407
		2	726554	376832	-656587	0	-5451840	-3093018	5451840	0
		3	629342	-3409698	-2141184	1144211	2603339	-1409991	2603339	0
		4	-582133	2254736	-2529367	0	1582673	2022170	-1582673	-1238448
		5	2023846	-245264	460522	1227838	2475251	-4647261	2475251	0
		6	2478604	-2796598	-5351010	0	-3721867	2705299	3721867	0
		7	-1791986	-235615	287819	1490880	-3812769	4036070	-3812769	-6282519
		8	-3071422	-2505466	-2160286	0	-849278	2741635	849278	0
15	1	1	5375516	5575054	926870	0	-1894348	360775	1894348	0
		2	1310461	-2006182	-3653135	-1043643	5112956	-3338167	5112956	0
		3	125277	-551811	1262599	0	402421	-2179170	-402421	-5656104
		4	-150032	3198559	5323685	2820609	786598	-3856657	786598	0
		5	2715614	2308908	310324	0	2464038	397883	-2464038	0
		6	-4814245	2542101	-3540712	-1754466	921938	-1515755	921938	774154
		7	3105722	3662527	-2226089	0	2318926	3075467	-2318926	0
16	1	1	3078274	1691667	2603701	1213831	522580	1202545	522580	357535
		2	-3182376	2288703	-398442	0	1294411	2316386	-1294411	0
		3	1353498	2575270	3382409	-2785630	1734256	-1210299	1734256	0

L	MU	NU	101 525	525 151	013 100	122 221	323 131	113 110	233 011	111 011
16	1	4	26600	2421654	-1618474	0	687530	-4163080	-687530	-4306870
		5	-1865207	-602950	1944659	2215027	5816210	182745	5816210	0
		6	-3928321	5212229	-950910	0	-1396845	1435182	1396845	0
		7	-5078798	-4484973	880999	3916830	174384	1364829	174384	5283632
		8	-2635971	2210873	-2314969	0	2141551	-3084651	-2141551	0
		9	-272748	-182840	3816183	-393334	-446760	2635499	-446760	0
	2	1	688162	1171984	-2652893	3651501	2398217	2324783	2398217	-6060522
		2	3046853	1874896	248634	0	-2833822	-546068	2833822	0
		3	2046545	-3342205	3910428	2336110	-1138134	2961593	-1138134	0
		4	165769	-3452705	-1560127	0	-1826832	2930154	1826832	-2016543
		5	2511010	1357909	-637854	1112494	-699737	-287210	-699737	0
		6	-4398016	584195	-3336905	0	3473657	-925188	-3473657	0
		7	1286646	-1572497	-1628653	883069	1117779	3442259	1117779	3877533
		8	1455698	-90691	-3728871	0	-1536166	1189575	1536166	0
		9	-1200115	3491240	634275	3118429	2249158	-1541491	2249158	0
17	1	1	2461613	-35424	-1846691	0	1713511	5339137	-1713511	0
		2	-1220896	181800	-1045365	-2281085	1802550	281745	1802550	0
		3	-452084	-666603	-630582	0	-1710241	1010245	1710241	-5925783
		4	-1313815	-4757924	-2464431	-1084624	3345638	-53430	3345638	0
		5	-4099968	1251305	1387749	0	-2937969	-4272191	2937969	0
		6	138600	71889	-251832	-118499	-1466347	1677615	-1466347	-5510512
		7	3088155	-3424554	-2421276	0	-4491343	-1690149	4491343	0
		8	1086507	782143	409151	1786678	2197803	-1598762	2197803	0
18	1	1	-1846620	2261541	1386821	2623146	1444088	1821044	1444088	2646869
		2	1904789	798143	-2796719	0	3868299	-2258993	-3868299	0
		3	1528737	661030	680712	-2725664	1225241	-796525	1225241	0
		4	-3780	263385	2441277	0	-3708689	3572459	3708689	-4083617
		5	-3978296	-1525543	1152341	-108479	197288	573998	197288	0
		6	1147891	1011363	-913754	0	1202803	1617500	-1202803	0
		7	2655666	5089886	3551385	-4995496	1959701	2922590	1959701	-1919377
		8	1250991	615282	-3798008	0	2786367	-2981663	-2786367	0
		9	-1163841	-855602	-1076704	-2320191	-3320062	-2509563	-3320062	0
		10	706244	-604188	-2420978	0	1108603	-2939872	-1108603	-1617407
	2	1	4794292	-1799154	975953	2136054	3193581	-1125750	3193581	-1915385
		2	2606887	96299	299788	0	-294196	2572996	294196	0
		3	-1225371	3501087	-2004152	-1396535	-3987055	-2075649	-3987055	0
		4	192551	-1485534	-696413	0	443135	2479149	-443135	4620853
		5	-1332585	-3240895	4542755	-3617371	-1464004	-3524739	-1464004	0
		6	-1006562	-908089	-1665976	0	-3099475	-2791744	3099475	0
		7	3506363	-467397	-4325685	-65193	-404644	-3031333	-404644	-2525005
		8	-3047445	-2169770	-2159267	0	203616	-198910	-203616	0
		9	1011773	-3349028	2097804	-3100911	-2285429	-3662439	-2285429	0
		10	701639	-3467556	-132742	0	-4245759	617785	4245759	4736533
19	1	1	-1200714	-3834566	3759156	0	640720	328766	-640720	0
		2	2167362	-1522388	-2048357	-615475	-1523013	2491144	-1623013	0
		3	-408776	394556	254881	0	-3514548	-2509958	3514548	269427
		4	904285	486095	-228576	1029886	-1323019	-17699	-1323019	0
		5	-503104	-3212957	-2310768	0	3389331	-660372	-3389331	0
		6	3922940	-446605	33493	509775	329976	1866074	329976	4196391
		7	-2459075	725498	-663523	0	1125836	3831856	-1125885	0
		8	-395066	-827126	-3384919	-895235	-285696	-737321	-285696	0
		9	-1097767	1014019	-2688444	0	-2915559	-2539376	2915559	4940439
20	1	1	-2885376	-1336317	3865804	-906287	-367869	2203585	-367869	-150404
		2	3177157	-2019146	2085123	0	-720592	53751	720592	0
		3	-1204570	-2015752	4642352	1832168	-1399435	-3978975	-1399435	0
		4	-166090	-2616713	-468829	0	-924262	-663240	924262	2269131
		5	-61929	-923947	2794438	-717613	-3270234	3727429	-3270234	0
		6	-2248732	-1828231	-1163770	0	-2452309	972814	2452309	0
		7	-3550897	-1806998	966828	-1769230	2029105	-1524547	2029105	-6787487
		8	-3643638	3256651	-469900	0	-5307690	196853	5307690	0

L	MU	NU	101 525	525 151	013 100	122 221	323 131	113 110	233 011	111 011
20	1	9	-1287139	-3857637	832402	-2149813	1459888	-1500318	1459888	0
		10	574973	1782063	-2543963	0	199199	3060806	-199199	1123628
		11	349144	-236006	3434274	289149	-190932	-2172182	-190932	0
	2	1	2837956	-79370	-452902	-28066	-1419652	-1181121	-1419652	5959145
		2	1426191	-2974626	773581	0	3494232	-2674208	-3494232	0
		3	486011	3159938	747777	-4533754	146627	-1858759	146627	0
		4	-365868	2873296	-3311929	0	737537	-560735	-737537	3147300
		5	-195493	1760352	1501962	759846	-1223587	1962293	-1223587	0
		6	5395242	-2960940	1513670	0	584488	-4790773	-584488	0
		7	-3316204	-1698973	2641528	2904363	-1701506	1265995	-1701506	2643257
		8	-951057	2604544	-1937138	0	-538257	-1055497	538257	0
		9	664147	2155534	-440273	3589949	4270987	-953165	4270987	0
		10	-47989	258860	-3127262	0	2648746	744701	-2648746	-5183336
		11	2925304	2676233	777687	-2023023	970492	1647830	970492	0
21	1	1	-1867055	-651640	-3125563	0	-951228	-670711	951228	0
		2	1687081	61434	-2357041	1299599	-2299246	-1750055	-2299246	0
		3	189940	-778914	-3426246	0	336867	107112	-336867	4415349
		4	-2528762	3249037	-3079939	3316020	-2723312	-2155081	-2723312	0
		5	-2251389	913869	629725	0	265268	-1164288	-265268	0
		6	-4284712	500684	-2090955	-3791705	3633210	2648443	3633210	-313613
		7	-1167126	1258856	689599	0	2796126	2157769	-2796126	0
		8	690397	3379114	822063	2456662	-1075473	-3001181	-1075473	0
		9	-1073121	-3860265	-2745670	0	-339463	1639292	339463	-3908359
		10	-1798309	1353778	-284714	-1747119	1284133	2200570	1284133	0
	2	1	4988749	236696	-2035520	0	-1491667	-1103196	1491667	0
		2	1503371	1885931	75565	-3218355	-2238006	389172	-2238006	0
		3	144594	-2601365	2826991	0	2325852	-3053844	-2325852	5506877
		4	726746	-711753	-1939614	-3147753	-2633080	-1096966	-2633080	0
		5	-374839	-131840	-1085347	0	-3322634	-1532590	3322634	0
		6	397258	-2097714	2568752	1357009	-497580	2024185	-497580	-2840503
		7	-1825568	-2029470	-2138403	0	-1067413	1901045	1067413	0
		8	1239812	-1600252	-4407524	-1113201	-887935	2873710	-887935	0
		9	1042424	-2568406	-596242	0	-544678	-1755751	544678	-197301
		10	-2109304	-3133731	1024337	2999420	-2365554	2320655	-2365554	0
22	1	1	2099874	-2006808	327371	-2551321	-1609901	4476916	-1609901	-1400525
		2	-1211982	-2324595	-4139230	0	-2457408	670049	2457408	0
		3	-82985	705968	1563597	998904	-2941571	-953143	-2941571	0
		4	-386140	-1409130	3754226	0	2779613	-17585	-2779613	5284629
		5	31358	2906988	2108801	4525998	-1083108	-1804388	-1083108	0
		6	-5535843	-1541394	2190157	0	1137078	392875	-1137078	0
		7	-389998	-1742793	2628951	1393744	-1019024	-3256526	-1019024	4539735
		8	1341506	-3728079	-1808695	0	1870073	-117601	-1870073	0
		9	952571	1352306	3133974	-285683	-2153596	-570365	-2153596	0
		10	276154	1733502	-2853533	0	-438111	503958	438111	5732491
		11	3032897	-2749207	-1891185	3853442	-3349764	1938624	-3349764	0
		12	1825132	276635	-2647889	0	913560	3021549	-913560	0
	2	1	952617	3428214	-931362	698065	-4743773	-204981	-4743773	4515003
		2	2800261	-2743109	224193	0	2098857	3363803	-2098857	0
		3	1777240	-493684	907361	-790374	1904218	480770	1904218	0
		4	94279	-722197	-133477	0	3036444	2595066	-3036444	-328979
		5	2337540	2392627	330972	374246	259916	2945866	259916	0
		6	-1456737	3594873	-3147262	0	-1347630	-673757	1347630	0
		7	-3122455	-437018	2765800	-745179	1231055	-715920	1231055	-3029235
		8	3294676	-2068214	2347747	0	-895250	3242283	895250	0
		9	-659442	119743	-138149	-1431021	-3127049	1290427	-3127049	0
		10	146310	1217131	-1633457	0	-346696	3661629	346696	3288667
		11	-1747163	-497646	2438470	-342100	1348314	2599348	1348314	0
		12	3536500	-3349721	-205099	0	-2308636	-832218	2308636	0
23	1	1	2411565	1788402	4345585	0	194386	-687791	-194386	0
		2	-382417	4616279	-569381	-2288310	-1366079	5458707	-1366079	0
23	1	3	-202546	-1831704	1399047	0	4924551	1005607	-4924551	3748348
		4	-3626026	1711931	-2213175	2677144	-239079	938776	-239079	0
		5	871738	-1057489	-4357270	0	-260789	955793	260789	0
		6	-868230	1117254	-1758197	2377393	-3809777	-1087347	-3809777	2427853
		7	3126377	-182612	-779409	0	47788	3358483	-47788	0
		8	-275535	-239624	155913	405216	2819320	-4240632	2819320	0
		9	770996	3372733	-446972	0	1966806	-2817368	-1965806	-1986698
		10	-799325	1723095	-2788874	-3007720	3812136	868890	3812136	0
		11	-4039572	-685875	-2774730	0	-2739346	1539215	2739346	0
24	1	1	2765000	1094438	1144193	673068	248954	231744	248954	53901
		2	-3063645	1666929	-769351	0	447248	-1465446	-447248	0
		3	1281237	1881343	1951093	-1400226	909064	-998475	909064	0
		4	146920	1993756	-1666297	0	1088919	3392297	-1088919	-1118672
		5	-785067	2278151	2150480	1660061	1693076	2008665	1693076	0
		6	-284426	468745	-1723679	0	3382640	-2753227	-3382640	0
		7	-1893893	3112948	1329846	-2774714	-953551	-1612840	-953551	5674783
		8	-2297717	-1740939	-765727	0	3821549	884371	-3821549	0
		9	-1297287	983453	386597	4724376	1723146	716344	1723146	0
		10	1126117	1587997	-321167	0	-2669120	-894014	2669120	-3914917
		11	2406707	-2185765	976430	13067	2157245	1934201	2157245	0
		12	1452443	1120322	-2740800	0	-344068	-3002842	344068	0
		13	244109	-163715	3094176	-139878	-24772	1785418	-24772	58092
	2	1	-1269541	1607466	1124622	-793931	-816773	-1767949	-816773	-4392079
		2	1550362	-51295	1150772	0	-1939831	481400	1939831	0
		3	1802138	1035333	-964298	1060700	-2285872	-2063697	-2285872	0
		4	-82665	-5902481	-4362653	0	3157466	-1479749	-3157466	660374
		5	-1654284	-280047	1901894	-724095	-621480	3183122	-621480	0
		6	-2122242	787665	2325858	0	-994225	537077	994225	0
		7	5782921	1709662	2050146	335480	-1103765	859645	-1103765	-2394025
		8	-998689	222776	1373462	0	-1040011	2258027	1040011	0
		9	-559656	-4146665	4379364	-2241330	1385357	1383381	1385357	0
		10	87723	-2687150	-1711813	0	-1721758	278582	1721758	-3786254
		11	-2251268	922299	-808779	-804075	-878952	-2260908	-878952	0
		12	2058793	388783	-2421925	0	2736926	-918573	-2736926	0
		13	3136625	910824	966250	12947	-1142498	-1934082	-1142498	-1820744
	3	1	4608688	3173299	1251633	2626606	-2224672	1194748	-2224672	157763
		2	2546264	-2408778	-306840	0	1520768	-2039326	-1520768	0
		3	-1149118	-521041	-1814876	3966786	274857	1710407	274857	0
		4	210679	1048686	1173600	0	-1595332	-2774176	1595332	-4858812
		5	-886359	-1312468	1549512	1628502	3344357	1145285	3344357	0
		6	-1569554	444652	-2489513	0	2270315	-3802634	-2270315	0
		7	1839340	2904433	892943	-1970408	-97977	-2727467	-97977	2939809
		8	375587	1939887	-164917	0	1691674	-1650467	-1691674	0
		9	-837586	353902	58766	715175	1956567	1007713	1956567	0
		10	-929126	804899	2497968	0	-71161	-271129	71161	-1850460
		11	2534376	2300616	3001838	-1447868	-6261	1979468	-6261	0
		12	-2743765	3079879	-892847	0	2284880	-2664855	-2284880	0
		13	2231107	3072723	39642	3422902	4024846	308030	4024846	-4656820
25	1	1	1742204	704145	-1155234	0	657283	-4886464	-657283	0
		2	-1400920	762654	849479	-1184013	1754658	-1077460	1754658	0
		3	-292306	48322	-1306221	0	1116136	1897457	-1116135	-2717786
		4	954594	134579	-427344	-750612	1187147	-241604	1187147	0
		5	-3059457	-3866126	963185	0	2857940	2037369	-2857940	0
		6	-2421161	1618014	-1799322	-367992	-4503127	2329993	-4503127	4408111
		7	-3106461	-3673021	1541061	0	-82962	-2163247	82962	0
		8	-767477	-498271	-978904	-116790	-1714979	-1006284	-1714979	0
		9	-142213	-934285	44350	0	1316128	-1016519	-1316128	5633128
		10	-2610084	2973113	1472335	126757	-4344167	2669960	-4344167	0
		11	-3700661	-3308208	-2733461	0	1145506	-1106100	-1145506	0
		12	-1543351	1143179	-879379	1022918	189190	-2481386	189190	-555724

L	MU	NU	101 525	525 151	013 100	122 221	323 131	113 110	233 011	111 011
25	2	1	-807926	-2737427	-1880516	0	3299594	287375	-3299594	0
		2	1801181	2435989	-1359406	-339853	76050	-409286	76050	0
		3	-428933	-1635093	2284347	0	1694101	1129484	-1694101	-3189030
		4	601943	2392124	615554	278473	563867	-3795015	563867	0
		5	2219771	2371576	1608188	0	359065	-974313	-359065	0
		6	-473893	-224529	-2327296	-482856	2530501	-1925274	2530501	-3845790
		7	802955	991834	-5750544	0	-1921076	717184	1921076	0
		8	-1091202	214865	798092	-334644	-2418351	627110	-2418351	0
		9	-883875	-1129651	1067674	0	-822429	-3451570	822429	2164339
		10	326354	258497	-2778965	474219	-1097094	186467	-1097094	0
		11	2686317	900228	-357801	0	1490263	-577533	-1490263	0
		12	-3565976	-1252833	1525457	132667	2562596	-2654606	2562596	4961993
26	1	1	-1911349	2085718	1985514	2206096	1443665	589875	1443665	715670
		2	1558001	2440191	-2841552	0	1817050	422314	-1817050	0
		3	321367	674278	1243541	-844958	2650038	22633	2650038	0
		4	143645	-979419	727942	0	-101464	-2688915	101464	-4301945
		5	-2834742	662241	-832219	-2821391	-549049	-1514087	-549049	0
		6	-226581	-3405717	1202524	0	1440704	1251479	-1440704	0
		7	-5153378	4097506	573371	-1737241	-3412659	-678510	-3412659	-525433
		8	-1144986	882662	-1320618	0	-546188	1721151	546188	0
		9	201412	1088423	1828958	-771797	643828	3452130	643828	0
		10	-822362	-223077	-1928631	0	3324584	-3036924	-3324584	-838706
		11	-917238	381173	2684614	-629056	2925994	1030025	2925994	0
		12	2817348	3551179	-2077724	0	-1359473	1009763	1359473	0
		13	3539788	-3024838	-2271860	-2881965	-540557	-1465409	-540557	2245856
		14	745682	525983	-2818542	0	478051	-2954931	-478051	0
	2	1	2754291	473480	-2466035	-1007017	2969066	-1452134	2969066	-5952370
		2	1729183	-1577805	154531	0	-566620	-620048	566620	0
		3	469438	2903267	2919948	1817654	-2407884	-1219708	-2407884	0
		4	-262084	-602447	153993	0	-3147532	-591265	3147532	-2796532
		5	-556466	-2072262	-1293897	-2227776	514895	268965	514895	0
		6	4001044	-1586600	-3066783	0	718399	2388954	-718399	0
		7	384498	-1820412	2532414	150879	2049499	-4219595	2049499	-476233
		8	-3631809	1671981	809672	0	-638692	1349246	638692	0
		9	1050444	2880109	3104340	2375105	-1389828	-650300	-1389828	0
		10	-48200	-817178	2768699	0	1498772	-389286	-1498772	3231484
		11	1428149	-3005959	1844303	3077264	-691235	-3166795	-691235	0
		12	-1007480	-1452856	-1119725	0	-4009025	-3587743	4009025	0
		13	-1151440	-320023	2478896	-559983	-1920956	-1291612	-1920956	-4523883
		14	2482917	-2744788	-268811	0	-1064837	950965	1064837	0
27	1	1	-1694763	-1822166	1705868	0	-38439	-2716364	38439	0
		2	1279851	-2941140	-1975770	2940344	1827061	568955	1827061	0
		3	-76262	-2397382	2049751	0	-2395733	-274425	2395733	-4795494
		4	-364235	2206735	-846985	-2877231	-1731912	282856	-1731912	0
		5	-5925917	-2160535	-1276001	0	922728	-2236857	-922728	0
		6	113348	1979502	822299	-1685807	1139199	-1380921	1139199	-3950360
		7	-933903	500073	-386871	0	-265765	-631611	265765	0
		8	1102223	-1967467	-969890	-3333451	289847	-753231	289847	0
		9	-241559	-1381857	415018	0	-2653303	-504039	2653303	-4226661
		10	1817499	-3225260	1172865	1334254	803194	2735503	803194	0
		11	1824938	281873	-192548	0	-607670	1541012	607670	0
		12	-2709091	3129400	-2307727	3331354	507304	264923	507304	-4731910
		13	-2154652	-1749117	-2658254	0	-1938043	-730715	1938043	0
	2	1	4735850	-4386066	83478	0	2755207	308216	-2755207	0
		2	1564553	2805133	1318216	1303745	-953996	-1492107	-953996	0
		3	139351	944789	-771750	0	-2064832	652614	2064832	-4727848
		4	1131524	-2279366	-2617689	-767459	3810434	-2274402	3810434	0
		5	-604977	1014974	2617510	0	1168157	192154	-1168157	0
		6	-448843	1859754	1972733	-2660086	150146	371280	150146	3827502
		7	-2441	962625	-1985572	0	2676609	3177429	-2676609	0
27	2	8	-86772	1551365	-1624108	1113666	1660755	3020123	1660755	0
		9	-479341	1762273	-2464573	0	515365	2478517	-515365	-1388078
		10	2574175	1198687	-548477	-985058	712472	-25062	712472	0
		11	-3992223	1510654	2787704	0	190868	1952439	-190868	0
		12	3244091	2561516	1393969	1865472	555041	-2457853	555041	-579111
		13	-1381442	2752225	-393995	0	2405691	1479817	-2405691	0
28	1	1	-2659837	-905977	-1824979	-510116	-162702	-1281654	-162702	-27337
		2	2988460	-1382676	-4188699	0	-295069	-695089	295069	0
		3	-1278472	-1647345	-1306095	1147521	-566894	2328538	-566894	0
		4	-167190	-1823556	-3477937	0	-937036	2217826	937036	532004
		5	664221	-2033151	800626	-1973009	-1134206	-2647361	-1134206	0
		6	-819350	-1687694	-2471064	0	-2561861	-2942602	2561861	0
		7	-381302	-980261	1362197	2812584	-1057527	1611053	-1057527	-3854167
		8	-1167151	-2400466	-1255964	0	-1377023	1915788	1377023	0
		9	-767787	2618414	664444	-724483	-4516849	-443484	-4516849	0
		10	950315	-4002979	-351021	0	3299840	-472611	-3299840	5857861
		11	3211570	2477749	178600	-3918239	-2474912	-316351	-2474912	0
		12	3850606	-349780	-328084	0	-847717	1113996	847717	0
		13	2311542	-819251	1179605	874015	1089496	-2234594	1089496	-977954
		14	585492	541299	-2882557	0	-372208	2885947	372208	0
		15	18581	-87951	2788446	47262	19456	-1467875	19456	0
	2	1	1811319	-1292812	272626	546030	2082945	-84189	2082945	2820720
		2	-503441	-245938	56420	0	1363989	4111562	-1363989	0
		3	-243589	563914	201994	1331294	2702729	790129	2702729	0
		4	-367704	1446228	-1595995	0	-2816497	-1884433	2816497	-3698271
		5	-1392033	4553313	1753134	-410684	-769862	791573	-769862	0
		6	-1201207	-1432482	-881596	0	799034	-163028	-799034	0
		7	-3328029	-1862564	-105863	1135013	3653337	1492118	3653337	-2822179
		8	3813210	947762	1469178	0	-1029052	-2432567	1029052	0
		9	88827	362712	350000	-315238	-928839	1545248	-928839	0
		10	287062	2380064	-2459975	0	-2679734	-3095734	2679734	574527
		11	1660489	803170	3831929	-1563861	-466072	-3127177	-466072	0
		12	-2217514	-2047700	-651139	0	2937230	2252554	-2937230	0
		13	-1591938	655291	-794844	281615	741679	2404278	741679	4744144
		14	2150051	2312460	-1729604	0	3603539	1220368	-3603539	0
		15	331030	-229223	1177940	872779	-1187420	2220013	-1187420	0
	3	1	1101180	-53418	2225919	-4164255	2981637	2264762	2981637	-2427716
		2	2660195	-1295424	-175747	0	-1601947	-121576	1601947	0
		3	1606518	1280979	-3204961	-1361109	460719	2958671	460719	0
		4	67953	1885649	675789	0	-2069655	744845	2069655	2503262
		5	2179271	-1683660	2893796	-2059249	-764004	1628994	-764004	0
		6	-349462	-445223	-980148	0	-1483513	2195323	1483513	0
		7	-3213848	-813894	-768740	-281430	-1744993	-1545142	-1744993	2311116
		8	1182633	-2824965	-3285149	0	1916317	-1212319	-1916317	0
		9	686069	-897096	2812463	-1465837	1130229	2419098	1130229	0
		10	987529	2017718	4079448	0	-774025	373727	774025	-2730220
		11	-2019365	1504663	1707314	-2623086	1540052	1359722	1540052	0
		12	427388	-628423	1440360	0	2557920	-1218167	-2557920	0
		13	1436425	-917744	3122406	-1211565	-181306	1292413	-181306	2891823
		14	-1619017	853751	-1211194	0	-1223349	2539330	1223349	0
		15	442699	3225069	66551	-3040400	2377893	-450853	2377893	0
29	1	1	-1554220	-711891	836960	0	-507786	-1925275	507786	0
		2	1358499	-1069356	4062271	1331545	-1196779	1936708	-1196779	0
		3	256039	-512955	1666487	0	-1579271	1662663	1579271	1519098
		4	-1718759	-153231	2943560	-1144453	-906850	-408635	-906850	0
		5	916225	1210527	2040668	0	-2993440	1028436	2993440	0
		6	-2533033	2407358	-439427	1173748	1516220	-1510636	1516220	-5227798
		7	-1781334	-992759	2061939	0	1512299	-2979362	-1512299	0
		8	-1141160	4812403	-1328404	1633039	-860508	909811	-860508	0
		9	777154	-1474932	1011142	0	2426297	1961511	-2426297	-2444624

L	MU	NU	101 525	525 151	013 100	122 221	323 131	113 110	233 011	111 011
29	1	10	592923	73914	-357197	384513	2273190	-915605	2273190	0
		11	-2300516	408809	-443817	0	1579334	1460155	-1579334	0
		12	-3745416	1641458	1855893	-1845630	-2628681	-2317217	-2628681	3291399
		13	-1890604	-1991325	-2550973	0	1655845	407407	-1655845	0
		14	-139246	727397	-1362140	-410263	-181115	2596252	-181115	0
	2	1	2334217	928786	874081	0	-3426518	1980737	3426518	0
		2	70216	-79912	-1195457	3836875	574953	-419243	574953	0
		3	-130290	-1369946	469270	0	-3346025	4926206	3346025	-702184
		4	-3272481	230329	-270057	-1521674	232676	912362	232676	0
		5	-616828	-2098940	1585970	0	-597019	201067	597019	0
		6	3179174	-3127449	-1441495	2806481	1991821	1123221	1991821	1054977
		7	-269956	1776914	-816160	0	-698005	-690	698005	0
		8	538874	1234656	1555304	3505082	208416	3868303	208416	0
		9	989046	141460	-2346375	0	1726919	-1386864	-1726919	3796682
		10	-1189626	325399	724123	816333	-1675189	992687	-1675189	0
		11	-2030648	-2324785	2811917	0	-1528457	-337152	1528457	0
		12	2203083	-3374120	-1068724	-3899041	-2260016	-49217	-2260016	-66342
		13	560517	-483517	-11451	0	-2896832	1971271	2896832	0
		14	-540496	437292	1866797	-1856956	2898106	2413177	2898106	0
30	1	1	1871214	-2145190	3796158	-1968666	-1132433	-3920364	-1132433	-357706
		2	-1524642	-2454481	-923269	0	-1496969	-591598	1496969	0
		3	-25943	-1300950	1412882	1514567	-1959947	2566618	-1959947	0
		4	-189868	713266	-2015885	0	-1538566	-667919	1538566	2898797
		5	1365747	411465	-3704333	106465	781541	1339063	781541	0
		6	-3996317	1107100	-1317042	0	-2287213	1921480	2287213	0
		7	-622072	1001041	-2397524	2295058	3294623	-325862	3294623	-3288992
		8	-3443688	-3797290	-1621046	0	1548309	1461670	-1548309	0
		9	-670732	155117	960347	-1270887	209326	-1169612	209326	0
		10	85126	-245362	-1767717	0	-3693774	-2417477	3693774	-3991611
		11	-1954244	-2626802	1347674	4185782	-281904	-949726	-281904	0
		12	-2557314	-215958	-1640063	0	-1399524	3122819	1399524	0
		13	715501	-941951	2517391	1001056	2011716	-1307684	2011716	-5220390
		14	2327736	3062703	-1406769	0	-3486098	-1589423	3486098	0
		15	402834	-2407523	-2396828	1450160	690119	877247	690119	0
		16	-290825	446199	-2933232	0	87949	2807648	-87949	157595
	2	1	-869215	-1579622	-1657467	-1413478	-16464	-323369	-16464	5520563
		2	1471981	1092329	725290	0	-1403990	-2697208	1403990	0
		3	1830242	-285175	1575436	1023854	3288030	-699114	3288030	0
		4	-128338	-650482	-1486925	0	593668	-1754809	-593668	1541690
		5	-771235	1115342	375014	490479	1809325	-1710129	1809325	0
		6	-1725900	3001469	-473352	0	-1742871	2743011	1742871	0
		7	3178170	-190098	1056340	230364	-800622	-22029	-800622	3404791
		8	1862037	169019	-1211754	0	1220759	-624391	-1220759	0
		9	-1524215	-459128	1017945	1810609	1183203	838409	1183203	0
		10	-427254	-1235823	-490276	0	2327248	732199	-2327248	727207
		11	-928463	2024949	1197125	507302	-913273	-1605618	-913273	0
		12	367427	3511921	620335	0	-1812268	390862	1812268	0
		13	1974423	607818	2332510	1615507	1476857	3383563	1476857	-3905301
		14	-1744985	-1196140	-2304	0	-81471	1105677	81471	0
		15	100808	-110054	2470551	979947	-2206998	946775	-2206998	0
		16	-1410653	-1175383	-353017	0	1055183	-1166252	-1055183	-1864813
	3	1	4471227	2340056	-1107098	-2020038	45703	-1494967	45703	980462
		2	2480700	-295762	-72028	0	-1833251	1180831	1833251	0
		3	-1126904	-3715672	1831548	419024	3024434	-2384136	3024434	0
		4	224368	2096538	89170	0	869612	1156159	-869612	4493123
		5	-653374	1845015	-2693353	2527520	-3393729	-3086690	-3393729	0
		6	-1757589	-1300245	525544	0	-59541	505260	59541	0
		7	1047229	-435488	3864807	2707812	-647011	-3311516	-647011	-3531133
		8	933771	-152099	-2592873	0	-2978559	-1821695	2978559	0
		9	-487569	-1996448	-2346867	-740167	-1080439	32621	-1080439	0

L	MU	NU	101 525	525 151	013 100	122 221	323 131	113 110	233 011	111 011
30	3	10	12109	-2419700	459245	0	-131660	2355259	131660	1987382
		11	-1549280	-988304	3277569	1696962	-1541679	1320165	-1541679	0
		12	3325882	-224382	3846931	0	-1240548	2352523	1240548	0
		13	-3374826	-1085109	957678	-133713	292141	184312	292141	-1467862
		14	1936475	-2363488	-2056502	0	-159554	2970425	159554	0
		15	-319446	-2867885	350509	2857715	-2309615	-1768611	-2309615	0
		16	-799974	-2757349	-11989	0	-3863884	155535	3863884	4636597
31	1	1	1733860	1729649	-905607	0	-415679	-1199195	415679	0
		2	-970563	2141182	-3829297	-1580893	-1373110	-3678862	-1373110	0
		3	-115269	2952499	1150137	0	-318499	-1454925	318499	4119290
		4	-1517115	-402996	-46675	188061	2923766	1748508	2923766	0
		5	331744	-267724	2358361	0	-1864928	-790362	1864928	0
		6	-5987247	106596	3727997	3861088	1938768	1177073	1938768	673233
		7	-525813	-1785990	915285	0	-726844	1563245	726844	0
		8	-474790	-245955	1025344	-254963	799425	-5835	799425	0
		9	-722552	4066335	1574315	0	-2603990	3320940	2603990	1148553
		10	-1534583	724438	-905939	-1170675	233064	-2131352	233064	0
		11	998118	641627	-233674	0	831399	-185231	-831399	0
		12	2803949	-614871	1721991	1655149	1919692	-18780	1919692	2966311
		13	-82145	-1071513	215246	0	3425407	-1501442	-3425407	0
		14	-490592	3704938	-1836803	-2492527	-1262034	-1162549	-1262034	0
		15	1038018	-1808019	-2421485	0	-406995	60049	406995	-934646
	2	1	-545673	2705980	-1943512	0	-4435240	-105584	4435240	0
		2	1603592	252739	1415210	1783899	1934313	-79258	1934313	0
		3	-414085	-1433752	1128750	0	-376371	-1344718	376371	4650366
		4	298740	-1340031	-2426339	-1561092	-605588	164301	-605588	0
		5	3051471	2254745	881064	0	-2771792	-4396106	2771792	0
		6	-229868	-1629598	449102	-546606	-2395672	-1082800	-2395672	2289724
		7	-758642	-3450821	672740	0	1971896	-1902249	-1971896	0
		8	15569	-618500	-291688	-1794417	-89855	575155	-89855	0
		9	258002	98404	-2919945	0	-256581	-397176	256581	-3273932
		10	-2376379	195354	1601503	-1219846	2148332	-3666121	2148332	0
		11	3641111	1261689	1751410	0	1423589	-1507804	-1423589	0
		12	-1508165	709197	195259	1362480	1022819	-3312422	1022819	947720
		13	-832858	-959608	3052376	0	626649	541564	-626649	0
		14	422668	-683059	1812326	1750314	-2098043	1054963	-2098043	0
		15	1270999	1416336	-670635	0	-2196575	-2015659	2196575	4911084
32	1	1	2573620	751420	-1180166	390650	104920	-721244	104920	11754
		2	-2914942	1158182	-2978543	0	196928	637105	-196928	0
		3	1284025	1404212	-783609	-921143	362879	1768317	362879	0
		4	172476	1687891	-2747728	0	682776	-1521457	-682776	-247618
		5	-811750	1814604	854693	1708150	912036	-3154489	912036	0
		6	633757	1967223	-2359490	0	1659610	1341267	-1659610	0
		7	-593554	1223964	1533318	-1821309	1911613	3305808	1911613	2323659
		8	-302293	1660145	-1568071	0	731961	-463170	-731961	0
		9	-376945	638423	999693	-689824	4114124	-1873567	4114124	0
		10	538627	-803205	-637453	0	-474589	-39820	474589	-5965343
		11	2417238	3344008	313717	1661381	-86039	565121	-86039	0
		12	4108199	-4178841	-143420	0	3933432	-99727	-3933432	0
		13	3965101	3405244	123185	2478356	-2782445	442467	-2782445	2982119
		14	2018521	-1373858	-408144	0	919046	-1323208	-919046	0
		15	231425	30416	1391057	-969933	259857	2419877	259857	0
		16	-226127	182598	-2971617	0	-176439	-2716415	176439	-104616
		17	-59872	-37878	2513052	-5758	18804	1207024	18804	0
	2	1	-1550258	510620	-875000	-847078	-2285441	-382519	-2285441	-1689264
		2	1054178	649051	-1569183	0	-1722985	1550188	1722985	0
		3	719987	-1168383	1317446	-374641	-1869155	912725	-1869155	0
		4	112440	-212058	1622281	0	264043	-681305	-264043	4550549
		5	-1954177	-3706592	2500625	-2420779	3441687	-2700950	3441687	0
		6	-3554440	-854528	-2261200	0	-2139361	-1783372	2139361	0

L	MU	NU	101 525	525 151	013 100	122 221	323 131	113 110	233 011	111 011
32	2	7	-465305	1032417	-1783449	2239360	-833075	390211	-833075	3512937
		8	-2880247	1515298	-1744578	0	-1464588	-1718929	1464588	0
		9	1180310	-1957414	-3037622	1161460	1829521	277063	1829521	0
		10	-323230	683523	-1043603	0	2054507	969026	-2054507	3766282
		11	10796	-285176	1264051	-1470270	-523647	-1534533	-523647	0
		12	2807220	-1566238	-3438946	0	-605889	4271523	605889	0
		13	-118940	-174153	3061409	-2366111	-3884723	1226894	-3884723	2464707
		14	-1846946	-2374676	540506	0	-513129	-1909772	513129	0
		15	36121	-1659697	-386426	1645860	678052	-1868529	678052	0
		16	-1513140	3227245	-1095137	0	847138	-1657083	-847138	2844236
		17	-1404640	-694918	1390820	-969770	-716842	-2415799	-716842	0
	3	1	2720118	-915521	1244308	1085664	-1268227	333352	-1268227	4763585
		2	1893718	2692791	-266565	0	-1448628	-962888	1448628	0
		3	464676	-2244889	-1769773	2657881	1748620	348889	1748620	0
		4	-202534	-1062774	1036176	0	2654463	152971	-2654463	1139771
		5	-583791	-441252	1310920	2398974	479763	559194	479763	0
		6	3092173	2542679	-1833701	0	710138	864556	-710138	0
		7	1494449	1483221	561440	-1855266	-775905	2799438	-775905	-1069854
		8	-2909536	-223732	-452394	0	194860	-3586915	-194860	0
		9	-11081	1193345	2017021	-1493889	-1207454	1769281	-1207454	0
		10	-986666	41042	-2437861	0	-1345501	382841	1345501	-2048437
		11	2629710	-2511304	-219728	200006	2005684	567365	2005684	0
		12	-675746	-1103543	2558909	0	1084671	-1965030	-1084671	0
		13	-1419538	2200019	1867738	739799	-1213721	-150072	-1213721	3103112
		14	963991	2693657	365620	0	1383256	-1128035	-1383256	0
		15	-5605	926963	2766211	-2125293	3631597	-2827115	3631597	0
		16	710771	399709	-1374347	0	1429694	-1900934	-1429694	-4119582
		17	-3051288	2777683	91681	2216129	1152825	541509	1152825	0
33	1	1	1428364	721278	319834	0	387769	2847133	-387769	0
		2	-1260309	1122497	3096334	-1303504	833594	2171601	833594	0
		3	-260142	1015490	593456	0	1408537	-1812647	-1408537	-802142
		4	1552797	217835	2753945	1438165	1165160	-1513068	1165160	0
		5	-2058329	-40904	1063574	0	2088457	19682	-2088457	0
		6	508446	-2197443	30724	508000	1252070	-1778373	1252070	4297933
		7	-1526683	-483434	1801317	0	-2228212	502909	2228212	0
		8	-657053	-1693125	-1442471	-4706518	2425307	3172275	2425307	0
		9	868745	-2665927	1441100	0	-3226692	55013	3226692	-1830239
		10	2450652	1737046	-901820	2300831	-1949154	-1532377	-1949154	0
		11	1804848	-935083	461212	0	-2245703	-575749	2245703	0
		12	-940662	-1976142	2989	-1982251	2360326	1378133	2360326	-5251745
		13	-2134332	1907071	-770059	0	-1966247	-1966290	1966247	0
		14	-498444	-82709	2105046	2700121	-875445	2043784	-875445	0
		15	883913	-808690	-2274373	0	911547	237503	-911547	671641
		16	518822	361553	-1742863	57430	-205647	-2595373	-205647	0
	2	1	-1474063	724657	3374310	0	2157798	975898	-2157798	0
		2	1045951	-950009	-215707	-3047976	469111	-2366278	469111	0
		3	-185086	2282140	22243	0	1524920	1555016	-1524920	3350789
		4	-240090	-960471	-2042130	-1876190	2667700	1076825	2667700	0
		5	-4240841	2105641	-775828	0	-1553389	611512	1553389	0
		6	-2411347	1589689	-706748	-1580688	-1954186	-1890485	-1954186	3048538
		7	2616225	1850589	3017090	0	-24524	-686181	24524	0
		8	-40411	-2954396	3126016	-278522	883173	-1127266	883173	0
		9	-604766	-1865112	419458	0	2633815	-673942	-2633815	669575
		10	2538620	1862358	2232592	-1179936	-1292147	-1871914	-1292147	0
		11	301414	1471361	-606784	0	-270789	-1889009	270789	0
		12	-2293612	2325434	-14471	476795	37825	1482819	37825	-3327523
		13	-149730	1863743	2818848	0	-1017251	2183882	1017251	0
		14	390104	-2028134	185154	647218	1486215	-902965	1486215	0
		15	425964	-1930029	461313	0	-570123	-1891996	570123	-4854688
		16	3028388	1785959	2106843	2702439	2332030	-2076200	2332030	0

L	MU	NU	101 525	525 151	013 100	122 221	323 131	113 110	233 011	111 011
33	3	1	4553311	-1704587	1242824	0	-1479048	-540417	1479048	0
		2	1582157	-714346	-417171	2278022	2435268	643224	2435268	0
		3	133225	3149508	-1488081	0	-416333	-1456862	416333	3641470
		4	1352199	-1129530	1378984	2729851	-2760120	1103244	-2760120	0
		5	-478261	-1477143	1453203	0	1599510	-1336837	-1599510	0
		6	-989523	1285494	-3176591	1497511	-1201520	1278151	-1201520	-4386724
		7	229268	-186186	411008	0	-3262412	1554897	3262412	0
		8	33766	-1932651	3237080	-1516734	-755821	3383614	-755821	0
		9	-49635	-1590656	-1421667	0	-962992	2632130	962992	2236466
		10	-87696	-1425154	-2604811	1424813	-1792926	1087693	-1792926	0
		11	1467307	-1557145	-186314	0	-863744	-895076	863744	0
		12	-2891880	-1105996	3254584	-965940	-471678	-5536	-471678	-682291
		13	2440641	-868545	3426578	0	-364105	-1589434	364105	0
		14	-492325	-1602807	-206675	720421	108842	1751760	108842	0
		15	-1110364	-2525439	-963076	0	-673899	-2484713	673899	-751364
		16	1362227	-2455943	140881	-2631507	-2439894	880132	-2439894	0
34	1	1	-1804138	2093811	3070261	1762341	835414	-2576601	835414	175963
		2	1575114	2528790	-1270745	0	1224716	218675	-1224716	0
		3	-43166	1449458	1816037	-1840405	1475720	2187363	1475720	0
		4	133398	166416	-1727753	0	1879350	581397	-1879350	-1760849
		5	-1787303	-1275552	-2296253	299405	232880	1426699	232880	0
		6	2069397	-102100	-628925	0	1377257	-1072743	-1377257	0
		7	-3580400	-2266882	-2564365	1285460	-309764	-1853634	-309764	4674503
		8	-718587	2141908	-662162	0	-3986933	17144	3986933	0
		9	-1196125	1049289	284026	-2507015	1406417	-1926053	1406417	0
		10	666557	545590	-1650281	0	-181961	-148059	181961	3330661
		11	856833	955507	1416600	-2067516	1574179	3037771	1574179	0
		12	-1758467	3434472	-1194029	0	-896265	-260370	896265	0
		13	-2862813	-1867684	993488	-687644	2270826	594478	2270826	2604791
		14	-689712	-13045	-1551046	0	1793503	-2253207	-1793503	0
		15	317204	109181	2437920	-3098143	1471173	768392	1471173	0
		16	-1486214	1647099	-795628	0	-2278817	1846908	2278817	-2251030
		17	-1810032	-1429380	-2356519	-239265	967166	-250708	967166	0
		18	-433441	281580	-2998682	0	-53764	-2618723	53764	0
	2	1	1684281	836484	-251512	2138612	-1546201	2728375	-1546201	-4223695
		2	-91959	1265022	1628794	0	1059072	-363898	-1059072	0
		3	-204058	-2441703	-255253	-116684	-1845300	1963716	-1845300	0
		4	-328290	1579249	-3824553	0	-893987	765603	893987	1408871
		5	-1995048	-2174087	1534672	-2868397	-252687	-2092650	-252687	0
		6	-260093	-340852	2038598	0	363	1475838	-363	0
		7	-1470176	-1941757	1491550	-2287123	-1131246	1047715	-1131246	-31387
		8	1247917	392785	-1739719	0	952741	2284565	-952741	0
		9	1155657	7950	-1203430	-1058861	-1770954	-1499653	-1770954	0
		10	1086649	-1181475	-2370728	0	-1927	3039109	1927	-3008341
		11	-104292	803695	-1645253	-384815	662190	-1881845	662190	0
		12	-883611	-304110	-2661605	0	1285229	-447993	-1285229	0
		13	-1547658	-1560019	1293272	-175311	2825202	1539992	2825202	-1804846
		14	1620123	701154	280860	0	-1232894	-1546389	1232894	0
		15	-13460	931919	2396197	-361643	-2709023	-276300	-2709023	0
		16	1077810	-1796039	982532	0	-1018330	-27600	1018330	3840321
		17	-1918338	-1734926	2429493	-3087258	-3536696	-612209	-3536696	0
		18	-2786986	105670	-459594	0	1341626	1430165	-1341626	0
	3	1	1189979	-3773289	-124480	613924	680867	-349860	680867	363441
		2	2561605	2435105	-162201	0	966781	2694991	-966781	0
		3	1483117	1055077	394940	-668178	-3311237	-279559	-3311237	0
		4	57803	620726	314205	0	790310	2114139	-790310	-4096768
		5	2084905	-2108935	-1016212	493728	1021327	431080	1021327	0
		6	201004	-1731547	276451	0	2764902	293315	-2764902	0
		7	-2994190	2438732	1344243	-945722	1282500	1102793	1282500	-1269298
		8	172535	1821679	-2020685	0	-959081	-2455080	959081	0

L	MU	NU	101 525	525 151	013 100	122 221	323 131	113 110	233 011	111 011
34	3	9	806015	55057	1475707	720720	1163935	-1757310	1163935	0
		10	410360	1366128	-763630	0	77991	1712869	-77991	2588936
		11	1126004	1538355	64023	-440089	-2348061	-396537	-2348061	0
		12	-3501585	-944233	255085	0	-591365	-243073	591365	0
		13	3006198	-2227104	184433	-1922191	400007	-2653314	400007	-2325129
		14	-814808	-756382	1466130	0	-1785550	-831623	1785550	0
		15	-94105	924341	1034659	-92167	-2022794	-2870699	-2022794	0
		16	-795480	646930	-2561954	0	564305	-863801	-564305	2620539
		17	2066692	-1099578	533027	-229568	1124800	2009125	1124800	0
		18	-2943277	-3109287	-21624	0	-2452565	-244582	2452565	0
35	1	1	-1553982	-1294283	-700066	0	687346	3219799	-687346	0
		2	1080184	-2099468	-2593974	533556	1097642	-1616360	1097642	0
		3	80612	-1984823	835504	0	1467010	-131357	-1467010	-2955174
		4	149670	-1982797	-985076	-370334	-1765015	2135055	-1765015	0
		5	-3270949	1850939	2112387	0	566402	196719	-566402	0
		6	642242	-1451810	2397696	-224516	-704297	1626151	-704297	2698268
		7	-4119003	2756369	337474	0	-2273535	-458907	2273535	0
		8	-409298	-73067	1825742	-390033	865154	-1156816	865154	0
		9	475399	-768547	794102	0	2440254	-83744	-2440254	3230982
		10	-1457160	-3598624	-946939	-394112	1157829	-2214473	1157829	0
		11	-2551582	671668	1402558	0	-580726	-1744010	580726	0
		12	-477732	108832	-485028	-109459	-3912839	3867005	-3912839	2956825
		13	1630207	-1887174	-1064680	0	-540514	-1082892	540514	0
		14	263791	-121413	1872701	365261	-1300642	-1122608	-1300642	0
		15	744411	-1393138	710682	0	2716676	1450867	-2716676	4381393
		16	2985273	2844731	-1333311	507185	-2472488	1637389	-2472488	0
		17	1841497	-1350714	-2113980	0	297898	524903	-297898	0
	2	1	2279495	-705190	-3535976	0	4118026	-197211	-4118026	0
		2	339261	-3660535	522209	-580575	-194732	2652382	-194732	0
		3	-105682	3495572	2117354	0	427051	-499392	-427051	-2036084
		4	-2764835	249137	-664134	1546940	-312642	3767407	-312642	0
		5	-1355702	598405	1236694	0	2981107	185088	-2981107	0
		6	3724457	-630644	-1876896	-2295170	413091	-965251	413091	-2834097
		7	647817	1837104	-1469960	0	373002	719434	-373002	0
		8	-434233	3417868	11868	601067	-2557463	-74238	-2557463	0
		9	-44101	-942009	2701375	0	-1514048	3165544	1514048	-2414426
		10	1432299	-2224424	4286402	2301088	1984271	-863331	1984271	0
		11	-3804418	-607448	-1569552	0	-3179	951325	3179	0
		12	2160144	-335780	695777	726992	100861	752639	100861	2904514
		13	680269	1102635	2931161	0	1438742	4087883	-1438742	0
		14	-335253	3364890	437648	-2590154	777531	1808219	777531	0
		15	-347428	2478333	2663936	0	2411585	-659987	-2411585	923661
		16	-1621724	-223671	1895274	369956	2120861	589992	2120861	0
		17	3641673	-164881	-912517	0	-2906163	2163350	2906163	0
36	1	1	-2499390	-625445	1760412	-300050	-67736	498304	-67736	-5074
		2	2850486	-971549	1240710	0	-130491	741297	130491	0
		3	-1280534	-1199930	2419416	725475	-239626	-773189	-239626	0
		4	-178830	-1493447	18134	0	-464542	-2365946	464542	113676
		5	861788	-1716879	2322456	-1407385	-724641	606222	-724641	0
		6	-838980	-1810724	-1264062	0	-1114439	3549244	1114439	0
		7	397385	-1757057	2072264	1638451	-1775501	46467	-1775501	-1299314
		8	-317155	-1109461	-1528402	0	-1096884	-3133885	1096884	0
		9	-113946	-1780274	1380045	-956750	-2583397	-520684	-2583397	0
		10	258177	614698	-912525	0	-2168510	1584591	2168510	4875672
		11	1327470	-1573804	571174	2465229	1392761	391198	1392761	0
		12	2854638	-175175	-291856	0	-4618486	-413938	4618486	0
		13	3649302	1997412	131264	-3831901	1414989	-181357	1414989	-4880347
		14	2667356	-3511150	-66945	0	794933	284553	-794933	0
		15	496297	3127217	132406	-469102	-2155965	-670892	-2155965	0
		16	-983609	-1599442	-519911	0	1103055	1559919	-1103055	808995

L	MU	NU	101 525	525 151	013 100	122 221	323 131	113 110	233 011	111 011
36	1	17	-948876	372575	1593556	656129	-183981	-2530064	-183981	0
		18	-334499	10287	-3015429	0	-38771	2515353	38771	0
		19	-33920	-12008	2264881	-6280	8379	-992552	8379	-3364
	2	1	1568530	-79255	15893	1330947	2020768	-848563	2020768	967439
		2	-966532	-165223	-1793861	0	2098346	-2735653	-2098346	0
		3	-350901	304947	869934	-602086	1329091	-469562	1329091	0
		4	-219033	1318615	1412353	0	1223322	2913886	-1223322	-4013660
		5	415440	487297	1653113	1858303	-3335530	-900248	-3335530	0
		6	-1557631	4114499	-1387290	0	820063	44605	-820063	0
		7	-4765143	-2195988	-164896	-1148713	362151	1601493	362151	-644949
		8	-183882	588444	-1823019	0	776576	210191	-776576	0
		9	-1163135	-1105068	-2560045	18352	-1029550	2306721	-1029550	0
		10	-698135	625933	-9135	0	1037372	-170711	-1037372	-904672
		11	-1288848	-950078	-546164	-327181	-1194259	1081842	-1194259	0
		12	-1044501	449144	-1525247	0	1248427	-894502	-1248427	0
		13	2270724	3583021	2308125	2988450	-794636	-816894	-794636	-2735046
		14	1026471	776894	-3166713	0	460756	-1492670	-460756	0
		15	-266636	318281	2145491	1703498	706384	-631491	706384	0
		16	873154	-328697	1320332	0	-173462	440614	173462	-4494250
		17	-1586402	-2429417	162719	-459111	3465374	1523142	3465374	0
		18	-3502933	3066477	-507143	0	-808591	1897853	808591	0
		19	-1012751	-692258	1593526	656117	-170109	2529854	-170109	244993
	3	1	-553406	-1818580	-509913	1412657	-465541	-1893401	-465541	-5659564
		2	1484429	822538	-573462	0	3478643	-1033146	-3478643	0
		3	1799966	-892376	587811	-2204570	-2665005	-2556549	-2665005	0
		4	-150551	3750181	2061237	0	-2448766	-1114674	2443766	-2190579
		5	-372725	-964091	-744568	-220943	-2330965	-1164168	-2330965	0
		6	-1094733	-1998832	-3638309	0	2234874	-1647947	-2234874	0
		7	1824661	-1501001	2047128	705925	167679	2346601	167579	-2816103
		8	2143707	-918402	1896700	0	-703179	-566422	703179	0
		9	-919982	1118413	889418	651637	-160855	-1864817	-160855	0
		10	504198	-431415	-2521225	0	-1098379	-176630	1098379	1202548
		11	-3277542	-1176024	216714	2119244	-170	-70501	-170	0
		12	2105134	868226	-3266358	0	-1479539	-2900224	1479539	0
		13	701198	71925	-3173309	1171683	-1545505	-208271	-1545505	2108255
		14	-492235	-2647552	236325	0	2143447	451826	-2143447	0
		15	-155743	-2108294	2574044	2083674	1505027	792521	1505027	0
		16	-1002137	527907	387485	0	-1256128	3553116	1256128	-3661508
		17	1579840	1062961	2073907	1649273	581725	1952621	581725	0
		18	210840	-27810	-1526867	0	1795496	1728634	-1795496	0
		19	-3109208	1403926	124636	-455305	-917556	-680487	-917556	-1836290
	4	1	4357451	-1640345	-474140	-1328890	919196	650888	919196	-1449737
		2	2411788	1945067	227622	0	1133672	-2139271	-1133672	0
		3	-1128208	-922649	603981	-3817418	-3357503	960190	-3357503	0
		4	235757	-797421	-755067	0	1025329	-2493770	-1025329	-3591871
		5	-507457	2244482	-268679	-2077703	1138637	964198	1138637	0
		6	-1863921	-846735	1400006	0	-1846897	-2920591	1846897	0
		7	578840	-2031233	-794312	203023	2060192	511629	2060192	4010647
		8	1079212	806898	-1581479	0	2627312	-2251401	-2627312	0
		9	-261190	1510051	2865331	2154256	144500	-518877	144500	0
		10	219154	569631	-809931	0	1364301	1572584	-1364301	-2412738
		11	-1044805	1180854	-1849272	-676035	2131600	3226003	2131600	0
		12	282266	2197222	592585	0	461496	1774763	-461496	0
		13	1485914	1652773	2074496	1840886	281451	1782640	281451	1427230
		14	-1893361	432218	302073	0	1323503	-1994	-1323503	0
		15	473132	286014	-2490086	103140	762362	1355092	762362	0
		16	1308281	1318517	-2111352	0	-393952	-804464	393952	-1221638
		17	-2161705	2387863	1108414	1770564	309158	2982013	309158	0
		18	1985868	2684457	-131116	0	2343865	-1113152	-2343865	0
		19	-1471851	2489180	3648	-2926596	3731599	79006	3731599	4644140

L	MU	NU	101 525	525 151	013 100	122 221	323 131	113 110	233 011	111 011
37	1	1	-1318018	-698211	-1528826	0	-283855	2857451	283855	0
		2	1190779	-1144346	-259429	1165295	-603720	-745173	-603720	0
		3	250269	-1198280	-3120308	0	-1077628	-3051966	1077628	408241
		4	-1654175	-717305	-251683	-1409116	-1273443	356474	-1273443	0
		5	1880553	-5799	-1874310	0	-1507812	1001548	1507812	0
		6	-1610371	599853	-905553	-416195	-2143487	710	-2143487	-2969437
		7	143676	2196686	513988	0	868237	2222734	-868237	0
		8	-483700	-224147	-1675721	2431350	-1328263	644980	-1328263	0
		9	498691	3767543	1460759	0	253407	-2864002	-253407	4332417
		10	2301060	-747106	-1320118	915061	4250439	-965137	4250439	0
		11	3391742	573716	855612	0	-211271	1376612	211271	0
		12	2399809	1019356	-470124	-169293	1046220	288995	1046220	3906222
		13	140406	1047064	150914	0	-11011	294611	11011	0
		14	-322044	-3089925	222637	473623	3540438	-1411150	3540438	0
		15	1489010	3051278	-1019514	0	-2680885	2157133	2680885	-2756996
		16	2547735	-1168504	2268424	-2209510	723220	-1702554	723220	0
		17	1534684	-53022	-1943506	0	237386	-784097	-237386	0
		18	333668	129988	-2035528	71139	-103110	2513334	-103110	49247
	2	1	1660450	-911872	2929185	0	-783199	-881079	783199	0
		2	-642985	-766272	-1022341	1955692	-1175744	-2082467	-1175744	0
		3	-41633	121558	959330	0	109640	-2996557	-109640	-4188593
		4	-2094408	-2158779	-1223927	2394521	-4017259	-1268596	-4017259	0
		5	-606157	1827749	-1349575	0	1553709	1646641	-1553709	0
		6	-3070772	-3846788	-786808	324297	1119577	-1428109	1119577	-3164053
		7	-2864344	-616313	2354693	0	2081990	32852	-2081990	0
		8	950938	525747	1269102	1481029	-2800512	317364	-2800512	0
		9	-18834	2093097	766638	0	-1007296	-377019	1007296	-3433819
		10	-2077333	894399	2204289	-523935	-755624	2889367	-755624	0
		11	2503448	-3019273	-111928	0	2085227	-1728271	-2085227	0
		12	1540260	-950672	482207	-984184	2723258	3696117	2723258	-2582362
		13	-862151	-26538	-583184	0	-1108541	1566172	1108541	0
		14	-284152	-817354	-402178	1117677	-838945	-3277291	-838945	0
		15	-706020	921964	2423222	0	-3392633	-1580712	3392633	652673
		16	-1652824	-708825	1024411	-244901	-2019951	606487	-2019951	0
		17	2467007	-3182278	950134	0	1071269	1325212	-1071269	0
		18	2719588	2172366	2268670	-2209748	634412	1704311	634412	-1199009
	3	1	-360539	4014326	1945891	0	1837122	-230630	-1837122	0
		2	1480388	-2416384	373919	-1460653	-2613539	-432917	-2613539	0
		3	-394173	10485	-2247549	0	1276124	-429345	-1276124	-4954922
		4	112616	-1098043	-137635	968406	379882	-2006448	379882	0
		5	3303747	441929	1921298	0	2252725	-159112	-2252725	0
		6	355461	1977011	-649438	-1173402	957821	-4164350	957821	-362261
		7	-1423895	-883892	1026008	0	-8066	-368836	8066	0
		8	32042	611439	-1643380	94337	2741643	-981941	2741643	0
		9	-72860	3047986	-2218428	0	-352545	1180218	352545	3320248
		10	-158712	1389123	2631241	-1620304	-2227152	-139550	-2227152	0
		11	-810783	-312202	2062350	0	-188918	-2650362	188918	0
		12	2752446	-543127	1464705	-1502630	-724677	-825752	-724677	-2211207
		13	-2365905	-1200449	288299	0	-1551221	-1323561	1551221	0
		14	321780	-1382821	1207129	1491635	-902642	1542604	-902642	0
		15	-50420	64392	3012940	0	-1061817	-1355006	1061817	266242
		16	1825958	1279691	-422578	1219627	-130638	701866	-130638	0
		17	-3052898	331136	-1495008	0	2407831	2100901	-2407831	0
		18	2307434	-1527749	264981	497116	1856008	-1352731	1856008	4853776
38	1	1	1755856	-2000465	739674	-1546583	-604274	2036161	-604274	-85518
		2	-1583503	-2519689	-3311870	0	-957183	1067936	957183	0
		3	146745	-1630153	1644104	1843358	-1174269	-1748172	-1174269	0
		4	-117347	-527929	-241785	0	-1646156	-586238	1646156	1002129
		5	1459328	700342	1396994	-261632	-1138263	105616	-1138263	0
		6	-2856537	1134058	2483431	0	-781126	-2260730	781126	0

L	MU	NU	101 525	525 151	013 100	122 221	323 131	113 110	233 011	111 011
38	1	7	1826706	502909	93353	-2422670	-1455227	-74413	-1455227	-4301414
		8	-2221211	1722035	1833065	0	3504198	1355760	-3504198	0
		9	-348306	-3486317	560138	1845955	-425672	-108403	-425672	0
		10	878292	1457099	-644047	0	355585	2097994	-355535	135179
		11	2113369	-2714617	1553568	2581611	603786	1160558	603786	0
		12	1806719	-1158303	-1378127	0	536227	-2233310	-536227	0
		13	-774449	-1762189	1081383	1052739	-2869635	-1444215	-2869635	2210467
		14	-1774531	2145410	-730165	0	-1923458	1739655	1923453	0
		15	-308342	-1229508	820870	405533	-1752742	-1479792	-1752742	0
		16	-254073	-1654085	-1633968	0	2429361	1793010	-2429361	4741402
		17	-2648466	1604578	2342761	3404209	-1455185	-40319	-1455185	0
		18	-3255222	131677	-230587	0	-751924	-1925136	751924	0
		19	-1362068	-598149	-2202017	-345875	553516	-330500	553516	-324914
		20	-123300	140697	-3022306	0	-65065	2403533	65065	0
	2	1	-1318362	-1090035	-557729	-1433612	1872999	1970856	1872999	2915552
		2	830900	-1198395	1592845	0	466375	172176	-466375	0
		3	880868	932004	41862	-1496955	94308	1281247	94308	0
		4	57594	2262339	-3503494	0	1942200	1051277	-1942200	-3480696
		5	-1369391	-1313135	1696540	4705611	-2160076	-1184915	-2160075	0
		6	-4347306	2942345	875694	0	1980352	-2611085	-1980352	0
		7	-534912	-547509	780977	624621	533121	-1435462	533121	-3124168
		8	-428505	584222	-103388	0	1360332	453696	-1360332	0
		9	90792	1227563	-35152	2877095	-1731935	-1893486	-1731935	0
		10	-1132294	-14158	-2386650	0	-917577	-630037	917577	-1578085
		11	2334275	736705	-1947568	1462148	676777	-456938	675777	0
		12	781615	-1743714	-424842	0	-766638	-2243281	766638	0
		13	156676	-1198122	776676	-2120798	931946	925195	931946	2053935
		14	-1633034	1954525	-3086158	0	-379448	209720	379443	0
		15	139089	1300234	1220096	-3560868	919855	1549644	919855	0
		16	-848691	1098952	510903	0	2764957	-399411	-2764957	3472251
		17	1572857	2550350	2224202	1050591	-606848	-1508270	-606343	0
		18	1455077	40378	1556123	0	-109630	-326129	109630	0
		19	-2825370	-2987939	2341538	3402450	-1102116	31111	-1102116	3154647
		20	-1045493	764502	-581748	0	907235	-1673393	-907235	0
	3	1	2708328	-62967	1554898	1655556	-2220661	-248823	-2220661	-2804572
		2	1994192	1799999	-104557	0	2085143	1286603	-2085143	0
		3	456065	-2847558	-1967007	-1983981	557187	105717	557187	0
		4	-163029	-520666	82224	0	-101091	1107781	101091	1084457
		5	-530276	2349239	1309001	503427	-1420527	1150398	-1420627	0
		6	2546391	955779	818786	0	-2590490	1326325	2590490	0
		7	1859241	-310993	-871474	1889665	-367486	1000723	-367486	1972725
		8	-2209386	-3001451	-2784569	0	61186	2890275	-61186	0
		9	-437930	-1863816	2498366	-1509224	1648466	-3213245	1648466	0
		10	-857275	1169982	921870	0	369323	2001658	-369323	963087
		11	287549	220326	1614470	-2388682	-889273	1103379	-889273	0
		12	3193365	-916248	-2906456	0	1281870	1003824	-1281370	0
		13	-3501412	1042842	-2919114	-1409556	172420	-1160213	172420	-2439332
		14	913907	1938464	-1212651	0	-2428303	1301926	2428303	0
		15	120731	-476231	-1211587	-1036050	-582371	508456	-582371	0
		16	653016	-2725416	-422925	0	915981	2176413	-915981	2847441
		17	-654739	-2188681	984880	-3114215	-1791842	1795725	-1791842	0
		18	-675461	-558124	-2609486	0	-3269481	-970134	3269431	0
		19	1799920	-489212	654422	269790	-1073578	-1790347	-1073578	-3866759
		20	-1738260	-2793909	-31079	0	-1240508	306480	1240508	0
39	1	1	1469167	925991	1109924	0	-728487	3653071	728487	0
		2	-1027829	1742905	713070	-48625	-1058009	1391478	-1058009	0
		3	-121727	1835777	1902639	0	-1582235	731917	1582235	1908943
		4	-329767	1753094	-1629645	1258622	11047	-1021618	11047	0
		5	1337430	440982	-9787	0	629427	-1331780	-629427	0
		6	-3778121	-1427663	-1615625	-2378491	-970863	128465	-970863	-4231968

L	MU	NU	101 525	525 151	013 100	122 221	323 131	113 110	233 011	111 011
39	1	7	410638	1085667	-2287073	0	4026637	-2095636	-4026637	0
		8	-1424818	-3827801	126874	361162	-1096406	-482564	-1096406	0
		9	464299	2212181	-1232433	0	-936967	675303	936967	-3378702
		10	1591843	988961	-736258	-519224	-2816762	-593007	-2816762	0
		11	-1103425	1428170	1087276	0	1872602	2530370	-1872602	0
		12	-2440367	-4364	-1429181	3247709	207688	978555	207688	-3197447
		13	-1052264	906676	875345	0	1946612	-169027	-1946612	0
		14	193236	2861835	189063	-1243354	-812784	-2759439	-812784	0
		15	-1115434	-1590822	-1618990	0	1125168	1283781	-1125168	-3618929
		16	-279492	-465305	1732214	-1592751	1555973	1423791	1555973	0
		17	2917858	-154616	1169028	0	1380749	-1023795	-1380749	0
		18	2817686	1462506	-810201	908217	-1649255	-1834183	-1649255	1255323
		19	632180	-778891	-1765657	0	422396	-1018847	-422396	0
	2	1	-1273600	1513282	-2377975	0	-2651041	-1009464	2651041	0
		2	919001	1717087	436763	-1721671	-2480696	2005086	-2480696	0
		3	-234596	523910	987544	0	979484	-1148388	-979484	-1008795
		4	-427514	-4130560	-703303	940354	-1596835	2267257	-1596835	0
		5	-2873414	562556	2290189	0	47699	1991642	-47699	0
		6	-2928866	185607	-1722026	868950	-1073250	841520	-1073250	-723342
		7	2410035	-1529782	-1767401	0	174557	-1477877	-174557	0
		8	648334	-991750	-22504	882925	1405799	346018	1405799	0
		9	402289	-1779296	2073999	0	-56580	-486081	56580	1977481
		10	-269670	1636289	1159124	1526380	342434	593577	342434	0
		11	2760685	2298742	118447	0	-2819010	-1335963	2819010	0
		12	-3375098	-1013650	3684700	351332	-1139042	-1664310	-1139042	2873004
		13	238359	-1426557	-1473010	0	1834613	1547450	-1834613	0
		14	286954	-1314565	-1741405	216622	596530	-1903550	596530	0
		15	323847	-2230323	2368595	0	1301402	-2801183	-1301402	-1902893
		16	1600718	-242651	700430	-1153407	270807	-230443	270807	0
		17	-2351205	2453769	2213092	0	-1782755	-781476	1782755	0
		18	-298489	904601	1735958	-1596005	569909	-1388684	569909	-4760591
		19	1824830	-1651906	-1133208	0	-2574132	-2181040	2574132	0
	3	1	4412036	2939530	-475896	0	-463332	338868	463332	0
		2	1581401	-2660893	-546435	-1665898	-1803037	-761409	-1803037	0
		3	128757	79455	861898	0	2471621	1005114	-2471621	-2487606
		4	1491725	2038613	1001865	330833	63511	-1215981	63511	0
		5	-309744	-1801269	-1769798	0	-2416768	1549998	2416768	0
		6	-1296227	-504578	-883473	1683197	2642477	-557650	2642477	4543809
		7	146807	1297684	2890466	0	1719864	1865600	-1719864	0
		8	154637	-65045	-669502	2068527	-169126	1884160	-169126	0
		9	37119	64650	-1816586	0	2204772	2677370	-2204772	-2951464
		10	-23530	1572095	1091707	-953121	2090989	1321741	2090989	0
		11	295416	1849372	-431864	0	610687	-694500	-610687	0
		12	-39572	1498221	-366861	1655111	976714	-2189872	976714	1288405
		13	-702632	1430811	2150703	0	1080103	-1429172	-1080103	0
		14	347540	1137509	2978376	-917683	510091	-1811338	510091	0
		15	1426527	654110	133912	0	395626	132329	-395626	-319504
		16	-3018252	821829	-2476975	191[illegible]65	100877	-1744189	100877	0
		17	3098664	1733278	-770266	0	-217033	2070295	217033	0
		18	-1937690	2466932	499860	-2080282	822366	-2076005	822366	-833728
		19	637828	2213104	-48462	0	2467473	504305	-2467473	0
40	1	1	2434861	522377	2619486	230936	43996	690736	43996	2197
		2	-2791873	815713	2640489	0	85840	-80709	-85840	0
		3	1275113	1025140	3378798	-569333	160432	-1556251	160432	0
		4	182843	1306340	1128396	0	311108	-22095	-311108	-51705
		5	-922295	1578392	2787727	1176572	539747	2786949	539747	0
		6	910809	1721749	-647590	0	808401	651728	-808401	0
		7	-579641	1776153	2293480	-1683506	1344106	-3371221	1344106	690542
		8	171600	1495167	-1455813	0	1368991	-1307217	-1368991	0
		9	-90346	1241823	1660622	1899881	1631309	2538910	1631309	0

L	MU	NU	101 525	525 151	013 100	122 221	323 131	113 110	233 011	111 011
40	1	10	86299	1247146	-1153610	0	2839590	1238281	-2839590	-3463046
		11	625577	-562320	857339	-2317168	-344623	-1134361	-344623	0
		12	1530193	2426586	-505658	0	2708732	-627306	-2708732	0
		13	2390583	-2411188	273036	-229269	1917084	285007	1917084	5678738
		14	2209998	1746076	-123835	0	-2983320	141146	2983320	0
		15	550187	318602	52888	3814881	3632805	66976	3632805	0
		16	-1577706	-1976917	-48282	0	-1022393	-352560	1022393	-2306899
		17	-2488697	2206977	170999	-819780	-557022	878778	-557022	0
		18	-1792078	-1294772	-646954	0	703314	-1780882	-703314	0
		19	-666524	401356	1780313	-307541	-225392	2579007	-225392	117527
		20	-98426	-46518	-3021707	0	17466	-2299825	-17466	0
		21	618	-1320	2041221	6452	1806	816186	1805	0
	2	1	-1505190	-265014	2169025	-1631242	-1675899	1131322	-1675899	-535348
		2	1069419	-315819	-748155	0	-2138728	-2279388	2138728	0
		3	334947	-94947	84433	817210	-1323477	-1130281	-1323477	0
		4	159904	-834476	-950461	0	-1443110	3308846	1443110	3000598
		5	-1361685	-774920	-1078349	•442903	1416827	987270	1416827	0
		6	-566138	-1632626	-904389	0	1441347	1073715	-1441347	0
		7	-300061	-2235243	2023616	-1527467	-1566568	-271437	-1566568	-2347979
		8	-3939940	2535389	627185	0	2061124	-904945	-2061124	0
		9	-116687	-1418767	1139571	891651	-1304302	289703	-1304302	0
		10	942502	1315576	2177061	0	-447530	-2148085	447530	-2892020
		11	-1267909	1157314	-239136	-2655135	-1785474	-669168	-1785474	0
		12	-1838077	-831440	241560	0	1551176	-247087	-1551176	0
		13	-1777659	-1379252	1269739	-1544300	1865508	-2310652	1865508	-2299339
		14	890175	-3334341	-1757633	0	355045	3783669	-355045	0
		15	329793	613329	2354194	1157721	-438954	-127697	-438954	0
		16	95938	1073224	-2751738	0	-3877513	-826119	3877513	-1090692
		17	2237640	-1248566	1291746	-2248678	-744095	1236669	-744095	0
		18	658922	677	1710748	0	-1415132	561520	1415132	0
		19	-2587990	-1837043	701355	-1269119	2781517	-1126220	2781517	-3060150
		20	-1478248	2133242	32791	0	-1425747	-1902132	1425747	0
		21	22866	-495100	1780310	-307541	79585	-2579155	79585	0
	3	1	1629680	1900926	-692422	-1043717	659552	-783045	659552	5172349
		2	197867	-238321	-354947	0	-2484966	2422174	2484966	0
		3	-121242	-1136345	668095	-1353957	677222	-655970	677222	0
		4	-296260	-645212	1498340	0	3934395	284312	-3934395	528877
		5	-2200648	-1811460	-536527	1935580	1304762	714237	1304762	0
		6	-121635	2389694	-2725838	0	-892024	-1988833	892024	0
		7	-45850	3224378	1835898	-1904582	-943649	1893463	-943649	2085622
		8	399033	-854341	276089	0	-127892	1647421	127892	0
		9	912840	-20915	613575	-1812271	3088518	2377208	3088518	0
		10	386064	-49552	170723	0	9312	-1359499	-9312	2951038
		11	2560288	934210	-50002	-1105971	-464043	3482945	-464043	0
		12	-3934286	2002158	-3378981	0	-546232	-1090378	546232	0
		13	570993	-678623	-13787	687769	-1080308	1004948	-1080308	-870752
		14	464953	-1570326	-887153	0	389601	2095453	-389601	0
		15	144493	708156	-1761526	2121399	-1564062	1298116	-1564062	0
		16	986420	678662	-1068502	0	-1861642	1068943	1861642	-2738642
		17	-980335	-879037	2393550	977273	2149694	-3083900	2149694	0
		18	-1382298	249942	553175	0	2288615	-2518995	-2288615	0
		19	2371039	2177461	1281548	-2232737	1244816	-1345092	1244816	3171910
		20	-684069	1220300	-1692470	0	3357035	-1643165	-3357035	0
		21	90488	58934	169272	-814014	-1417801	869614	-1417801	0
	4	1	1242664	-1086512	-1695671	3655660	-2691260	1538744	-2691260	1218655
		2	2481057	1043348	188254	0	101757	-916577	-101757	0
		3	1385429	545895	2391649	2012848	3303970	1946964	3303970	0
		4	54990	-1675592	-613486	0	-524731	-681656	524731	4799013
		5	2033256	714327	-2225442	1080243	63940	1019816	63940	0
		6	525117	-255982	1009704	0	-1875894	-150769	1875894	0

L	MU	NU	101 525	525 151	013 100	122 221	323 131	113 110	233 011	111 011
40	4	7	-2796283	859129	1494420	1619431	-702885	-1039988	-702885	-83197
		8	-380551	1524256	-494256	0	-1081433	127729	1081433	0
		9	750351	-1927313	-428829	-43231	-2379901	-2978129	-2379901	0
		10	71380	-2777067	-2779771	0	772520	-1907978	-772520	-2348531
		11	1615895	-357977	3294011	1794356	1171659	1481818	1171659	0
		12	-1712663	-36873	2159296	0	-761505	-646243	761505	0
		13	-872786	-1145408	-1659694	1084032	904107	-916524	904107	2313179
		14	1976368	-173857	-3380867	0	2095373	-2739972	-2095373	0
		15	-454412	1820054	-2113616	-466851	167530	-879912	167530	0
		16	-794627	1859925	-615542	0	-91894	-2272618	91894	-1982225
		17	75442	93652	-1759491	1494763	1848276	-162908	1848276	0
		18	1387832	-1064456	-2517997	0	1551386	-2420309	-1551386	0
		19	-1904578	-395424	1576417	1171733	-856534	-2028814	-856534	2427776
		20	1193448	1281641	-218995	0	-1037567	1437496	1037567	0
		21	80140	2996880	7024	2981924	2528923	-132648	2528923	0
41	1	1	1227257	655429	-1958490	0	201279	-742015	-201279	0
		2	-1124714	1130310	-1293628	-1011943	442186	-2292677	442186	0
		3	-243661	1273804	-4198694	0	789480	126650	-789480	-202551
		4	1644802	1041960	-1246449	1441537	1147002	2639983	1147002	0
		5	-2100184	358763	-3191367	0	1285974	322038	-1285974	0
		6	1457755	-196311	-1104905	-528039	1959314	-273073	1959314	1850193
		7	-884795	-1238847	-488493	0	749425	502796	-749425	0
		8	-4738	-1467725	-1596319	-157259	292541	-2202509	292541	0
		9	327223	-635841	1253836	0	1869421	-1705986	-1869421	-4798419
		10	1311096	-3489535	-1578014	-978096	-4086064	2179683	-4086064	0
		11	2829020	2362372	1168212	0	83995	1566520	-83995	0
		12	3217824	-3225586	-820950	-1446048	-907962	-862291	-907962	-505280
		13	1878950	644875	451694	0	-1461283	-723380	1461283	0
		14	163810	-119119	-198072	-504185	-2608237	431848	-2608237	0
		15	512423	1305078	-12188	0	948588	-636150	-948588	4701711
		16	2629069	-3188083	378854	1316610	1023700	1556223	1023700	0
		17	3525637	3102154	-1236459	0	-2178293	-2168823	2178293	0
		18	2142695	-1491981	2363624	1223583	1004382	1284672	1004382	-664606
		19	518367	274725	-1582699	0	-121142	1229193	121142	0
		20	-6799	15979	-2253486	-81733	-24943	-2378450	-24943	0
	2	1	-1466202	1054064	747326	0	-59730	-806074	59730	0
		2	857224	1592553	-3328483	-2055704	878668	2411162	878668	0
		3	-17689	160245	1518820	0	-343910	-1575691	343910	3822114
		4	569303	868248	724829	446288	2652101	-1359379	2652101	0
		5	-3283093	340936	644049	0	1132632	2398162	-1132632	0
		6	-1668801	-185745	438543	-2322123	-2381747	624236	-2381747	570054
		7	-1336895	3445483	224843	0	-326753	1786693	326753	0
		8	-1367210	-359650	-2368458	1060964	303026	232459	303026	0
		9	-635691	-2075317	-1273341	0	1152145	399857	-1152145	562718
		10	-147700	120944	-197205	-707692	536192	665311	536192	0
		11	-3043175	-388040	-1710170	0	-1628660	-945437	1628660	0
		12	1332334	1764921	-29336	-2567708	-69408	-1069100	-69408	2212069
		13	1371206	19494	220084	0	-1305450	129390	1305450	0
		14	16728	-337044	59841	-980027	2123630	-3042787	2123630	0
		15	998763	2520604	-859377	0	1326817	237107	-1326817	3656903
		16	303947	979417	-583809	2691036	392576	2014546	392576	0
		17	-2634425	248495	1988547	0	688764	1247539	-688764	0
		18	-424606	582083	1514867	543986	-2024010	242951	-2024010	4[illegible]3777
		19	1597543	-3026511	1361585	0	2793783	-713811	-2793783	0
		20	-73508	1840427	2363653	1223598	-350552	-1283034	-350552	0
	3	1	2244230	-1886667	446794	0	-995974	907409	995974	0
		2	514029	-522134	878706	-2592817	-34381	-485095	-34381	0
		3	-96311	2132016	-904515	0	543537	2496619	-543537	3938944
		4	-2346320	471149	-861206	-207758	-376179	-1048144	-376179	0
		5	-1614239	-983456	687226	0	-3234859	2221380	3234859	0

L	MU	NU	101 525	525 151	013 100	122 221	323 131	113 110	233 011	111 011
41	3	6	3491540	142031	893	703373	-675283	-793126	-675283	3051250
		7	1433227	-2100961	2092087	0	-837967	-2156752	837967	0
		8	-677010	-394366	-2059362	-3237949	1353189	199749	1353189	0
		9	125529	-366757	-1785384	0	-82511	-528382	82511	538325
		10	-340704	-2398619	984872	-1805388	-4248	2043365	-4248	0
		11	-12245	-122488	999548	0	2464859	-1416532	-2464859	0
		12	-1763327	2063519	2886467	454942	-478256	-345916	-478256	-3081930
		13	2373322	1053081	-54341	0	-1946687	82149	1946687	0
		14	-377966	306350	43403	326756	-347770	2837632	-347770	0
		15	51650	-246594	-235263	0	-849585	34367	849585	1870946
		16	-1764808	-2292681	-844732	-1110394	-776004	1588363	-776004	0
		17	1730117	-3380785	1925933	0	-488454	797637	488454	0
		18	337671	-1519333	-589014	2747864	-2469542	-1770053	-2469542	1450042
		19	-1241983	576279	-1832261	0	-1499313	-966379	1499313	0
		20	-98375	-93221	390067	1345761	2847175	1614239	2847175	0
42	1	1	-1711041	1889584	-114206	1335155	435615	3177406	435615	41168
		2	1592456	2441872	-3860038	0	719684	97501	-719684	0
		3	-214475	1774292	1356624	-1750329	945476	-3521056	945476	0
		4	93132	782956	-183676	0	1325091	-312915	-1325091	-545558
		5	-1392623	-189947	2649604	605966	1467381	324479	1467381	0
		6	2497046	-1174298	3125435	0	884178	-212523	-884178	0
		7	-2731352	-781765	1313426	1261395	1643290	2293624	1643290	3252242
		8	1044113	-1149298	3020149	0	-1183555	821998	1183555	0
		9	-700440	90496	538821	457011	-1525807	-691948	-1525807	0
		10	317345	2304034	409302	0	1332959	562078	-1332959	-3060695
		11	2278683	-1387226	1348216	-3591602	-3425562	-1825405	-3425562	0
		12	2966991	4091271	-1297400	0	620965	-2078090	-620965	0
		13	2201532	228655	1402940	1378816	669048	1635471	669048	-4022102
		14	59307	81421	-992648	0	3814727	1313104	-3814727	0
		15	-297612	139709	636086	-3489401	-764592	82376	-764592	0
		16	1128843	1298304	-480234	0	1030249	-1652955	-1030249	-3624822
		17	735336	553310	826119	-334524	-308869	1977064	-308869	0
		18	-2018867	-2868741	-1779893	0	3274475	-1496832	-3274475	0
		19	-3046315	2665197	2190709	-2416989	-2301951	-580841	-2301951	2088252
		20	-1324057	-816564	281582	0	444127	1831738	-444127	0
		21	31780	-83795	-1968188	452857	153394	831641	153394	0
		22	83083	52541	-3012967	0	-33824	-2190428	33824	-12809
	2	1	1400382	1463481	-1968313	762543	-1811944	-1566391	-1811944	-1886099
		2	-650341	967[illegible]66	541229	0	-1676867	-986272	1676867	0
		3	-443019	-271277	1293708	1101497	330025	-949201	330025	0
		4	-207238	-2753928	-955652	0	-1540165	-279225	1540165	4130720
		5	-362528	-400348	2441639	-2041741	1904839	2370261	1904839	0
		6	-653435	-458543	-1655811	0	-256396	-1509200	256396	0
		7	-4805777	-1271991	-1550908	-2549303	-2044857	-1137790	-2044857	2867573
		8	-1204250	461116	-12404	0	-1437352	1092993	1437352	0
		9	90455	-203707	1008708	-917249	2019434	-34504	2019434	0
		10	158756	-2733819	235574	0	1117416	1925945	-1117416	3088656
		11	-3417793	978952	1836062	712435	1144110	-250835	1144110	0
		12	1957191	1068780	1739761	0	-2900640	2409883	2900640	0
		13	1070251	1404065	-187197	129583	-782985	-433862	-782985	2842112
		14	800545	360393	-273186	0	120452	1764482	-120452	0
		15	-318940	-3363679	2722090	866995	918615	1321564	918615	0
		16	322924	-2046983	-3023598	0	2160380	-3119526	-2160380	-35416
		17	-1876624	229391	359647	394582	-1205095	-1631155	-1205095	0
		18	-508138	-398912	539312	0	-436493	1819080	436493	0
		19	2325042	1140252	1959144	962196	-1289021	1684710	-1289021	-3431015
		20	-74560	1384893	1794338	0	-2957954	787868	2957954	0
		21	104499	-3286920	2190560	-2416825	779359	569777	779359	0
		22	835096	879182	-713816	0	262206	1879247	-262206	314001
	3	1	-290868	1159518	1773718	-88970	2030949	-806453	2030949	4737090

L	MU	NU	101 525	525 151	013 100	122 221	323 131	113 110	233 011	111 011
42	3	2	1531199	-1819730	-240355	0	-3096960	-2304160	3096960	0
		3	1753486	1029832	-2159593	328853	530119	-1022577	530119	0
		4	-159507	1272022	463515	0	837235	-1980218	-837235	1407965
		5	-155860	-721058	1176448	-255629	2138496	-963067	2138496	0
		6	-589173	-3141727	266620	0	-33010	-327556	33010	0
		7	1176167	1399813	-370872	-539060	1694177	-1355038	1694177	1460229
		8	1906274	2387294	-1008198	0	-697099	2081398	697099	0
		9	-494372	1540583	1735781	170497	-1224518	-825868	-1224518	0
		10	728221	512119	199319	0	625868	-2510220	-625868	-2258315
		11	-2149699	-1646428	823148	-160066	641321	-415197	641321	0
		12	-1430832	-338770	-1449920	0	1742328	-71806	-1742328	0
		13	3866255	2013914	1158489	838851	404112	-2985935	404112	-641953
		14	-1605152	570490	-2063138	0	-695333	-162158	695333	0
		15	-24703	-975654	-3213578	-293978	1544121	-391140	1544121	0
		16	-373934	816782	-759344	0	464032	361422	-464032	2563949
		17	-313654	2370069	-237266	390303	-2630841	-430236	-2630841	0
		18	1915320	884500	-1512239	0	-1040235	-1885135	1040235	0
		19	-1945650	-1044634	316153	371557	1065296	1063781	1065296	-3379785
		20	539266	-823562	-2453582	0	-855908	1086431	855908	0
		21	-26181	75652	776617	-307043	-1482328	1771269	-1482328	0
		22	1927360	-1601512	-43309	0	759176	-391291	-759176	-1772828
	4	1	4256563	-2279282	966211	1379459	-267466	-1356949	-267466	1362768
		2	2341062	501832	-34384	0	-127898	879352	127898	0
		3	-1140442	3281446	-1486311	639777	1162304	-2045340	1162304	0
		4	245431	-2469983	184866	0	-2266202	992292	2266202	2376740
		5	-407007	-786115	1835295	-2111625	1777493	-2336633	1777493	0
		6	-1943508	1642568	-637454	0	1781641	1099625	-1781641	0
		7	258319	-697419	-2267904	-2537847	-2758565	-2364678	-2758565	-4218725
		8	1122009	-206130	1680738	0	-566218	932846	566218	0
		9	-117327	1394269	2096875	-1466636	3583	-996677	3583	0
		10	270809	-181506	-2932504	0	-2634289	682799	2634289	2923071
		11	-562560	-1791951	-127913	1119916	-1618569	2531248	-1618569	0
		12	-592004	-1266560	885430	0	-290174	3283242	290174	0
		13	1210602	-870692	906098	-1343587	-1429541	1227915	-1429541	-1677267
		14	-337143	-1603861	725041	0	-1412768	518504	1412768	0
		15	-143103	-1876498	-1006814	1234616	-161416	-1025360	-161416	0
		16	-1018881	-992150	-3319733	0	-375265	-194712	375265	1074229
		17	2717502	-154593	-3158093	-463999	-1107003	-1470317	-1107003	0
		18	-3331285	-434777	-37164	0	-427532	507883	427532	0
		19	2532619	-1510655	1804121	512553	430234	-1897466	430234	-1049459
		20	-1122319	-2385144	-526179	0	-448228	2510566	448228	0
		21	-50733	-2517304	47467	-2691205	-2380286	-676364	-2380286	0
		22	779921	-2253316	-1113	0	-3613827	40243	3613827	4664582
43	1	1	-1374928	-645150	1454301	0	647521	-1408585	-647521	0
		2	1018750	-1271770	2029981	-274634	1046403	763998	1046403	0
		3	127900	-1716333	2133592	0	1420812	654152	-1420812	-1151121
		4	-41696	-1471080	-1167669	-1093427	1066460	-2593690	1066460	0
		5	-1658512	-1331247	-267739	0	-507011	-628132	507011	0
		6	2013299	871983	-3095112	1519845	1050532	770243	1050532	4185603
		7	-2763858	158813	-2789620	0	-2576059	-405457	2576059	0
		8	78818	1020307	-998084	2679164	-1528430	1986272	-1528430	0
		9	1022551	2083841	-2433437	0	1999850	1048536	-1999850	630490
		10	1597997	-2631542	-366996	-2461012	282853	-178214	282853	0
		11	2396889	-487865	195648	0	422572	1119210	-422572	0
		12	-282791	-36110	-1392825	-716025	-167824	-1561879	-167824	-790028
		13	-1406255	-2320166	1322517	0	706967	-2588774	-706967	0
		14	-316835	-849575	-1037361	925887	-134120	1768159	-134120	0
		15	-45992	-1325438	319243	0	-2524587	-550994	2524587	-1353604
		16	-2077906	2220249	749841	-1306848	-1553378	1678501	-1553378	0
		17	-1927974	-628056	-1922573	0	-1989314	-558519	1989314	0

L	MU	NU	101 525	525 151	013 100	122 221	323 131	113 110	233 011	111 011
43	1	18	1069762	-1939724	1413829	2210279	2665814	-1590808	2665814	-4016957
		19	1667337	1310594	1524157	0	-978872	429123	978872	0
		20	-78836	241825	-294261	-1403295	-543664	1831031	-543664	0
		21	-465736	-329772	-1395530	0	246468	1414136	-246468	113555
	2	1	1593207	-1993592	357668	0	1405855	-1262428	-1405855	0
		2	-405627	-881550	1441551	1067845	3598821	-1080760	3598821	0
		3	-13624	-1291886	-389204	0	-804959	-2059656	804959	3039758
		4	-2164607	3105482	-2407591	983395	1849189	-2163923	1849189	0
		5	-1601421	1752841	1592900	0	-451841	-761077	451841	0
		6	-1510598	-229681	-665049	-2594498	179218	1679633	179218	3134343
		7	-2613063	-414290	986585	0	-1296451	-1930639	1296451	0
		8	570748	2457805	1234334	-1998891	1640046	-871659	1640046	0
		9	-814911	-295289	-414361	0	-559019	-580426	559019	2172419
		10	1071362	257171	-2253614	399404	801258	-1163072	801258	0
		11	-616513	-378067	-888076	0	-36772	1489054	36772	0
		12	3161264	-1234050	-55690	854196	-58179	-2658103	-58179	-787786
		13	-1642678	1390834	-2663419	0	491923	2709303	-491923	0
		14	-149467	865514	1843224	363686	-2622609	457046	-2622609	0
		15	-631660	-571016	-383299	0	-729635	-15242	729635	-3283676
		16	-1021371	888833	-2721975	-122278	974168	1397452	974168	0
		17	2248308	596191	1325736	0	1234065	-231913	-1234065	0
		18	204962	-500369	769004	-1415953	3653380	582034	3653380	-808303
		19	-1308727	1778630	1765161	0	896480	1585287	-896480	0
		20	-35710	2390455	1414277	2210963	-800270	1643910	-800270	0
		21	-1832332	-2324004	-1337910	0	-855220	2133445	855220	-1376099
	3	1	-224222	-1014646	745964	0	1702735	-105708	-1702735	0
		2	1394940	-87084	-997353	-1022480	1337750	-473299	1337750	0
		3	-374957	427257	-341771	0	-2562327	-707109	2562327	4416195
		4	5325	1006809	1860839	-257659	764440	-480146	764440	0
		5	3369008	-1813169	-581541	0	-688849	-2180724	688849	0
		6	832841	1279538	-1906043	1799734	-97184	177867	-97184	-1515370
		7	-1650817	1075525	1311897	0	-1966688	-3243075	1956688	0
		8	-117346	-2152661	359312	116226	-3039849	843070	-3039849	0
		9	-262731	-908250	1258973	0	942636	291178	-942636	-2752023
		10	63087	-291489	-1451057	1582696	-4757	1949382	-4757	0
		11	-68236	-1995669	-3373946	0	-1106248	430166	1106248	0
		12	398114	-1621190	2866088	-422115	1634688	-1510285	1634688	2777579
		13	347176	88629	3337530	0	1693607	300945	-1693607	0
		14	-336242	707426	-136254	-1214183	411626	737033	411626	0
		15	-1453279	1064606	-1662425	0	918437	2825979	-918437	-1396835
		16	2380461	1572823	-28551	1245386	953542	610337	953542	0
		17	-852263	916614	-89229	0	685148	2519588	-685148	0
		18	-1131508	-723114	-2992969	-163776	1006899	-808009	1006899	-123112
		19	1293725	-1338891	-1073481	0	-307368	-116738	307368	0
		20	85196	-70962	874514	-1434693	-2556012	2332711	-2556012	0
		21	-1205238	1600724	-98831	0	-1545337	-851146	1545337	4805557
44	1	1	-2377862	-437338	186950	-178168	-28733	-11500	-28733	-953
		2	2738684	-685965	-450794	0	-56316	-523109	56316	0
		3	-1267620	-873358	494022	447063	-107462	-193336	-107462	0
		4	-185960	-1139024	-847144	0	-209150	1671189	209150	23366
		5	966916	-1417621	1076746	-980772	-382962	891441	-382962	0
		6	-1005106	-1631024	-1432687	0	-603305	-2643748	603305	0
		7	638532	-1707302	1624863	1584063	-966335	-1843512	-966336	-354038
		8	-284454	-1682688	-1733634	0	-1299263	2663644	1299263	0
		9	36039	-1303374	1643946	-1852909	-1312597	2231358	-1312597	0
		10	55781	-1341154	-1419419	0	-2351877	-1678303	2351877	2234369
		11	223753	-532309	1095194	1093547	-1165160	-1641926	-1165160	0
		12	712421	-378332	-756839	0	-1052134	619818	1052134	0
		13	1257058	-1373008	463750	1579117	-3604576	724354	-3604576	-5326771
		14	1383637	2392906	-250469	0	2406106	-114357	-2406106	0

L	MU	NU	101 525	525 151	013 100	122 221	323 131	113 110	233 011	111 011
44	1	15	421370	-3571796	118100	-1269899	-2182808	-193472	-2182808	0
		16	-1540799	3093190	-49151	0	-1553957	49248	1553957	4005148
		17	-3273072	-1391433	25253	-2725756	2613549	-128166	2613549	0
		18	-3431780	-421310	-54195	0	-1897302	451974	1897302	0
		19	-2099508	1130958	225381	1263711	377651	-1075679	377651	-658137
		20	-636882	-814671	-782286	0	190938	1967697	-190938	0
		21	14737	296034	1948182	73529	-129387	-2575093	-129387	0
		22	63430	-48881	-2997360	0	22176	2081470	-22176	8349
		23	9852	1802	1839650	3786	-518	-671157	-518	0
	2	1	1474567	606177	2954818	1761287	1371917	2472808	1371917	290014
		2	-1090041	662752	-525376	0	1929107	953100	-1929107	0
		3	-216666	275839	246832	-938129	1471530	-790881	1471530	0
		4	-164058	151748	-1620823	0	1301415	-1081241	-1301415	-2026859
		5	1089611	965170	-2344018	-1158147	226371	-535711	226371	0
		6	-1071423	465723	-836731	0	-2057379	545758	2057379	0
		7	-1854773	2582395	1827822	381538	1261834	-2022394	1261834	3888644
		8	427926	-513385	1043785	0	-2177313	-837230	2177313	0
		9	-1533130	-515963	2939965	2681853	-35532	243390	-35532	0
		10	176613	238055	2687664	0	1580877	-902313	-1580877	3267718
		11	2632607	-1486474	341643	1102970	2226036	1692631	2226036	0
		12	-805272	-1479745	1581179	0	-1497128	687757	1497128	0
		13	-1601329	2980451	588672	223856	-1372446	773507	-1372446	3114828
		14	-1497795	969144	-931191	0	-2259528	1474846	2259528	0
		15	37208	1349523	1571938	869120	2278895	-18996	2278895	0
		16	-965949	-434880	-1681155	0	1021200	-3741358	-1021200	3555717
		17	-1058737	61703	2126643	1302233	2247498	1570910	2247498	0
		18	1845792	2726030	-2387956	0	-594457	1284352	594457	0
		19	2017486	-845380	570313	127142	-368923	-1425610	-368923	4383153
		20	-453134	-855465	1819486	0	1290470	-1110314	-1290470	0
		21	100351	-390402	1153687	2523677	1190264	596287	1190264	0
		22	1289706	1057375	514479	0	-949698	1730645	949698	-553692
		23	442884	-278201	1948181	73529	120016	2575131	120016	0
	3	1	-1138364	-845606	326983	623151	-251568	131273	-251568	-4100708
		2	729656	-1038556	566071	0	538784	2880439	-538784	0
		3	963122	2224014	-697190	1966248	1129093	832364	1129093	0
		4	10585	-231892	-883705	0	-4141594	650940	4141594	1762832
		5	-1052976	1797610	311394	-357148	-551210	894299	-551210	0
		6	-4274973	-1664575	226338	0	-892510	-1299681	892510	0
		7	-1096819	-2321219	2259793	1599785	1908591	-2139573	1908591	1229581
		8	884343	-2316572	-2117939	0	-1205909	-581262	1205909	0
		9	17534	2275198	-1018906	-1185256	-534693	1133613	-534693	0
		10	-624403	90390	266652	0	-1404575	-1409518	1404575	-934259
		11	-22101	-2016537	531711	847331	549896	-631278	549896	0
		12	4271165	-825676	250983	0	2745892	-413676	-2745892	0
		13	-2785005	-672416	2431688	977352	-159740	-2014176	-159740	-3002048
		14	-221012	1645485	274373	0	-340341	-528830	340341	0
		15	-24904	2506029	1372203	-1406598	-1414553	-192122	-1414553	0
		16	-922637	-914844	-205722	0	-1164681	-939039	1164681	-68512
		17	1333082	-2316846	-545601	-2612012	1173048	-3266171	1173048	0
		18	1146116	-1082942	-1855338	0	-1051399	709206	1051399	0
		19	-2019633	-1684439	1433132	561496	-1547588	2159730	-1547588	3549480
		20	205830	-1926128	446315	0	945040	1009720	-945040	0
		21	-69138	1053657	569530	126891	-255430	1233640	-255430	0
		22	1385182	2586280	-1852308	0	1308781	1336547	-1308781	3306484
		23	2161862	-760115	225032	1262167	-1056896	-1071506	-1056896	0
	4	1	2707665	1822261	-1647414	-2567397	4053303	1328678	4053303	627718
		2	2059243	-2446805	152664	0	-1957884	224216	1957884	0
		3	441517	1137857	2320485	-1067252	-1302426	1747305	-1302426	0
		4	-133849	134442	-529685	0	-1921196	856804	1921196	-3167068
		5	-455644	1027195	-2122468	-2750982	1360729	1465653	1360729	0

L	MU	NU	101 525	525 151	013 100	122 221	323 131	113 110	233 011	111 011
44	4	6	2205687	-1174435	930674	0	2430482	1564430	-2430482	0
		7	1977580	-1157390	1323978	-591992	320514	1539859	820514	-2112709
		8	-1719419	321574	-568381	0	910275	583021	-910275	0
		9	-612331	282378	-290440	2124619	-411776	2558590	-411776	0
		10	-639060	2208765	-1618528	0	213550	-3187251	-213550	105203
		11	-869140	2344249	2437230	-114218	-745017	1836727	-745017	0
		12	3079669	-888705	-853027	0	-1763790	1315237	1763790	0
		13	-780305	-1552140	690382	-1572054	856982	810445	856982	1872375
		14	-1640606	527013	108637	0	901373	-1157193	-901373	0
		15	492554	414032	-1204254	-1134749	-1082381	1363736	-1082381	0
		16	829093	-1388941	-2452553	0	729039	639785	-729039	-2393727
		17	182471	-943133	-2558100	-825329	2341651	2517953	2341651	0
		18	-1458320	1553158	-993157	0	134222	1194428	-134222	0
		19	1085666	2768191	-653139	-2236808	-626780	2198789	-626780	2600140
		20	-53020	1671686	-2411668	0	2046639	3003875	-2046639	0
		21	35404	307336	1772675	1095205	2944220	574193	2944220	0
		22	-1201752	584002	-286527	0	800584	-1430588	-800584	-3709667
		23	2966048	2799769	10496	-2357600	1329890	172814	1329890	0
45	1	1	-1149409	-605498	-475192	0	-140428	-2468196	140428	0
		2	1067289	-1081332	1007209	868428	-320617	-513328	-320617	0
		3	235960	-1304014	-1247739	0	-575878	2907247	575878	93655
		4	-1649720	-1201427	1491893	-1434057	-921318	1095673	-921318	0
		5	2150174	-757066	-1225025	0	-1150839	-2053245	1150839	0
		6	-1708424	-45736	824515	1085553	-1576418	-635397	-1576418	-1076666
		7	775326	487845	-64609	0	-1541487	-251291	1541487	0
		8	-248999	1587339	-641623	-91360	-384851	-1216532	-384851	0
		9	33903	798871	1229155	0	-1959922	1701293	1959922	4078892
		10	789209	2030052	-1476732	-1731362	1518320	2471444	1518320	0
		11	1595951	1374939	1414073	0	1869508	-1255608	-1869508	0
		12	2463325	-1013122	-1122601	4424197	-1344887	-1875251	-1344887	-2614913
		13	2063036	3468320	757145	0	3835431	379703	-3835431	0
		14	431325	-2224075	-434245	-1295940	885098	673783	885098	0
		15	-788470	646824	207642	0	1271265	99033	-1271265	-4527735
		16	175790	609093	-59186	1728826	-2159634	-530057	-2159634	0
		17	2394432	465913	-107947	0	3305970	963141	-3305970	0
		18	3066514	-2124252	516163	-2657860	-907805	-1754117	-907805	2304000
		19	1540523	2353978	-1434075	0	-677445	2083299	677445	0
		20	-55167	-1270836	2398536	-336211	666385	-829989	666385	0
		21	-377074	324874	-1208939	0	-170884	-1575231	170884	-78097
		22	-120003	-24118	-2408566	52998	7900	2212114	7900	0
	2	1	1423705	-1310238	-1541	0	426377	-309939	-426377	0
		2	-807013	-1729400	-4078061	2217512	-129759	4239973	-129759	0
		3	-41024	-1236339	1532867	0	118845	1391496	-118845	-2970539
		4	-1029521	332390	710139	-1736278	-829996	-452190	-829996	0
		5	1245332	-1281441	1538017	0	-2891183	-465089	2891183	0
		6	-2586084	1258943	1694929	453936	2337572	-699924	2337572	2118442
		7	-2154088	-2494305	-309267	0	-697003	586239	697003	0
		8	-252732	-1046100	-2894812	684371	864926	-1842267	864926	0
		9	1209442	527201	-1596013	0	-801642	-710286	801642	2731391
		10	-1289797	1977795	-2037289	1934968	1522174	-641990	1522174	0
		11	-218398	-1387962	-2464151	0	-1486953	-1623864	1486953	0
		12	-2967340	1057772	103592	1089535	258703	1227771	258703	2165485
		13	186966	-71341	-495044	0	-984364	-1215776	984364	0
		14	276984	-1144860	-838006	2152600	908317	2500160	908317	0
		15	-551572	-956710	516168	0	1047039	794423	-1047039	589934
		16	1422826	-2967164	522524	-424723	-604628	-165884	-604628	0
		17	1903833	-27654	-1088083	0	334788	232538	-334788	0
		18	-1203727	1785384	-828934	-1562512	-2964284	-407169	-2964284	-1305604
		19	-1174081	-533778	1533366	0	-906271	-1357289	906271	0
		20	-31744	267017	1734284	-2253738	-1566826	-932939	-1566826	0

L	MU	NU	101 525	525 151	013 100	122 221	323 131	113 110	233 011	111 011
45	2	21	-1848797	-1894453	1655263	0	2181334	116989	-2181334	1721439
		22	-1657889	1194279	2398540	-336212	-618279	829520	-618279	0
	3	1	-1098798	-134547	-2189893	0	151982	1130288	-151982	0
		2	850350	2212986	477606	3372815	2802626	-960893	2802626	0
		3	-259133	-2756978	955366	0	-2093791	2776363	2093791	-1457419
		4	-621338	179983	125569	1455742	1183564	3183	1183564	0
		5	-1989091	-518869	180909	0	1218588	2491589	-1218588	0
		6	-2685182	1768365	-1514420	1322373	3004256	2283925	3004256	-1381805
		7	1764329	241797	868368	0	-598131	771076	598131	0
		8	985807	1846643	-856938	1476045	-1799902	-1273744	-1799902	0
		9	469734	1209043	1324936	0	-299132	1236991	299132	-2878857
		10	958373	-837120	1235288	1079383	-175389	241121	-175389	0
		11	-561336	877554	-1060637	0	1764765	1729062	-1764765	0
		12	391986	15868	-1563001	1236812	-327522	-450359	-327522	-923514
		13	-1806705	-1619615	-2159139	0	82085	-378923	-82085	0
		14	494679	225369	1535525	214021	2207084	2636369	2207084	0
		15	420003	1235394	-1383047	0	-486284	-1016782	486284	3021558
		16	1362637	614237	-1682678	206334	-1569650	-755863	-1569650	0
		17	-1408698	1420406	-143335	0	-1021378	-2209446	1021378	0
		18	-795431	1576626	-1678999	-668940	-1654292	-2700581	-1654292	-785221
		19	1181186	-894573	784059	0	541780	573699	-541780	0
		20	41493	-2249156	-831799	-1569416	1775571	949510	1775571	0
		21	707619	-146173	-2011599	0	-533982	64295	533982	-4610817
		22	-3174874	1439444	518763	-2668924	2724452	-1784527	2724452	0
	4	1	4297016	2482477	-680444	0	1193959	-299691	-1193959	0
		2	1571739	-212615	413284	-1298749	206808	665252	206808	0
		3	125871	-3083305	709200	0	-2326904	-820959	2326904	1446332
		4	1589453	2123886	-1044370	-2792002	2241439	1321522	2241439	0
		5	-154851	1067403	-571261	0	732239	-960966	-732239	0
		6	-1482421	-1986726	2025486	-1679404	-2779513	1811363	-2779513	-4318980
		7	4610	514297	-228769	0	911300	-137194	-911300	0
		8	224857	1166669	-2919903	-188290	-143024	1859891	-143024	0
		9	24418	-708565	2017145	0	-2950943	1472006	2950943	3536101
		10	185166	-762662	2077354	1483718	-1106241	1393013	-1106241	0
		11	-60144	-412038	-2174025	0	-726254	-274910	726254	0
		12	79031	-1235571	-1305496	-1122610	-1947086	-2201141	-1947086	-1846834
		13	-219810	-1797585	322878	0	-1247048	-2946932	1247048	0
		14	24099	-1583533	1820883	1566074	-523057	-1783594	-523057	0
		15	-307087	-1368106	1995309	0	-766047	-1321130	766047	750555
		16	1727015	-1173727	-482275	-859040	-628993	106124	-628993	0
		17	-3174232	-707535	-3252104	0	-354014	-819992	354014	0
		18	3149057	-431793	-2445828	204118	-306689	981301	-306689	-122628
		19	-1647547	-912577	698532	0	84677	-1685369	-84677	0
		20	-78521	-1853391	760992	-1003184	226090	2292907	226090	0
		21	973816	-2391859	-226263	0	-973851	-1549157	973851	-872620
		22	-909591	-2006554	16279	2359375	-2488171	282372	-2488171	0
46	1	1	1672071	-1765675	1366924	-1141456	-313603	-59324	-313603	-19666
		2	-1593810	-2330594	-1826270	0	-528837	-1157681	528837	0
		3	273644	-1836467	1753783	1629378	-744893	-291159	-744893	0
		4	-75397	-1039886	-1423894	0	-1056312	1595745	1056312	287655
		5	1246217	-117914	745945	-995799	-1400310	237049	-1400310	0
		6	-2507077	718299	-23965	0	-1171469	693786	1171469	0
		7	2484452	1252072	-845622	-351859	-1391922	1113217	-1391922	-2189393
		8	-1734171	640202	1153179	0	-630265	-1886773	630265	0
		9	283045	1278824	-1069089	161027	1817730	-1227751	1817730	0
		10	461927	-1709207	377163	0	-1338938	159143	1338938	4289828
		11	949704	-75291	438145	-324029	2735998	-1152406	2735998	0
		12	2776248	-1089485	-1127832	0	1488055	1179234	-1488055	0
		13	2866003	-2987053	1406409	1103496	-1359606	2598164	-1359606	2316784
		14	1682379	396476	-1298332	0	-1565797	-665457	1565797	0
46	1	15	118871	17317	956924	1609743	-396391	-1735771	-396391	0
		16	574356	-2274328	-539429	0	-492332	363276	492332	-324970
		17	2297666	809796	353378	1286605	-1906691	-271057	-1906691	0
		18	1970701	41019	-397860	0	-1925589	1434386	1925589	0
		19	-518658	1183210	935617	2041050	804883	-2009093	804383	-4270124
		20	-1440040	-3065467	-1923576	0	1185309	1106719	-1185309	0
		21	93845	2770816	1974717	797713	-1857407	1053769	-1857407	0
		22	1124882	-1116996	730393	0	703322	-1596725	-703322	404463
		23	631754	142025	-1681346	-329108	-54307	-1241758	-54307	0
		24	87426	9091	-2975602	0	-8820	1973789	8820	0
	2	1	-1326506	-1480676	-2146203	-345394	1753351	-2264918	1753351	1164439
		2	797700	-1183465	-82952	0	2198223	344813	-2198223	0
		3	498091	566050	1335795	-265321	249632	-725460	249632	0
		4	139601	1663961	229979	0	476688	-1373388	-476688	-3785461
		5	-886628	2762788	2969637	494294	-455777	3740855	-455777	0
		6	-2001084	-1129712	-2320710	0	-2257066	1431610	2257066	0
		7	-35	2079050	-1881171	1076144	3224948	632977	3224948	-435040
		8	-3108694	-1261872	-603221	0	337133	191825	-337133	0
		9	-848493	775354	-39799	-243959	325045	-16987	325045	0
		10	-208652	685315	1107871	0	-2762287	1051651	2762287	-224460
		11	878165	2332938	3370320	1013504	391175	-1232348	391175	0
		12	-4458390	-2098399	1935192	0	874790	26456	-874790	0
		13	803469	-2001469	669869	-835135	1615044	-750053	1615044	-1547461
		14	636555	592677	1722509	0	449784	-2489902	-449784	0
		15	276634	663592	541750	-515906	-2692499	1565797	-2692499	0
		16	569736	2526380	-1735138	0	-699431	-3249136	699431	-3180197
		17	1598392	790051	3232036	1080444	-901840	238412	-901840	0
		18	-1048627	-1405398	-2419857	0	2264999	3441135	-2264999	0
		19	-1855700	979256	-553784	-687775	2905163	553876	2905163	-2840070
		20	618024	1072908	297546	0	365167	-1379560	-365167	0
		21	-67533	158512	1625030	-87330	1036585	-1520184	1036585	0
		22	867099	1601075	1795093	0	-2836051	-1246361	2836051	-3518270
		23	2970467	-2603845	1974701	797706	1724322	-1060244	1724322	0
		24	1062186	697341	-851766	0	-90959	-2046949	90959	0
	3	1	1615328	264410	590504	-1945591	-139033	1135416	-139033	-5329079
		2	425078	-1127306	-773394	0	1534866	-1665636	-1534866	0
		3	-32867	2083723	-474848	833343	731419	914848	731419	0
		4	-271726	-2380239	2007771	0	-3218786	-903909	3218786	-1484325
		5	-2231040	1287192	-435995	-77376	-1030146	-894432	-1030146	0
		6	-149594	776955	-2037867	0	-457066	710963	457066	0
		7	813820	1261243	931125	3315910	338905	-1778762	338905	-2883955
		8	254902	-2531227	536633	0	-187597	1953442	187597	0
		9	576706	-2854310	1481593	382998	-1303821	1603179	-1303821	0
		10	40228	656307	-2112487	0	892169	1795774	-892169	-1717114
		11	2516503	441213	-692054	-172877	-1399723	-1964587	-1399723	0
		12	-1570610	170659	253533	0	-1099459	3045983	1099459	0
		13	-2865752	-666256	1392394	-542357	584217	-1197607	584217	2236344
		14	2400797	-2383548	-1162807	0	678352	876465	-673352	0
		15	-140207	-475647	3221179	1098767	1898801	1525581	1898801	0
		16	224081	2240173	2095619	0	322579	1829685	-322579	758520
		17	482011	1005115	-1702564	3024678	-912695	569621	-912695	0
		18	-2121582	-920454	-1492336	0	1619527	-871330	-1519527	0
		19	1568121	-156054	175995	1605910	830280	1241067	930280	-2997048
		20	111701	476213	-2017336	0	-2513217	-1311651	2513217	0
		21	62821	-1104976	-549548	-679583	-1905580	-1736396	-1905580	0
		22	-1264684	-2165266	-2202705	0	-1420271	-932717	1420271	2700407
		23	525943	-809790	922948	2016266	-3142006	-1870524	-3142006	0
		24	3106251	-244657	-60511	0	1440440	513245	-1440440	0
	4	1	1271148	3371549	746336	-1576490	1791609	-995498	1791609	-2059375
		2	2408375	-2167025	83774	0	-1229433	1565085	1229433	0

L	MU	NU	101 525	525 151	013 100	122 221	323 131	113 110	233 011	111 011
46	4	3	1302934	-842861	-1197825	1219219	-166374	-1354998	-166374	0
		4	55954	-490479	-162579	0	807041	1119344	-807041	-4532289
		5	2007688	1552087	1589736	27593	-1867540	-1126463	-1867540	0
		6	737106	1157407	-73450	0	320096	-46540	-320096	0
		7	-2650076	-2089028	-1987030	70832	308024	-648845	308024	1556781
		8	-728029	-358857	813793	0	2316032	-1998970	-2316032	0
		9	672944	638277	1551699	1051362	2018451	-365811	2018451	0
		10	-124138	-703676	-1224534	0	-598010	-2854352	598010	1848326
		11	1532026	961616	434929	-521362	1056771	-1482902	1056771	0
		12	-406690	2830539	-2113811	0	935141	1783684	-935141	0
		13	-1746461	1203821	1795647	1625305	-1755592	-386632	-1755592	-2370354
		14	1144411	-505604	2002878	0	-848011	-885264	848011	0
		15	48891	149164	-1084735	1635731	359179	-2059126	359179	0
		16	1049004	580684	-2204315	0	-1354079	27825	1354079	1959393
		17	-2760523	-830858	-1133269	200964	-1650639	-610006	-1650639	0
		18	2491088	-2053314	-1035313	0	103281	1421514	-103281	0
		19	-725548	-1291990	-1919997	2047529	-162165	-373565	-162165	-1711040
		20	-381205	427291	-273219	0	-1817617	1426071	1817617	0
		21	-54138	1095024	2460803	933140	-1136965	-891233	-1136965	0
		22	1218051	159918	-833125	0	1087110	-2347074	-1087110	2285480
		23	-2034834	-1420999	86016	618892	954341	968672	954341	0
		24	2381061	-2884494	-2279	0	-2604007	-71840	2604007	0
47	1	1	1299158	402408	-290527	0	-533304	-4649206	533304	0
		2	-991352	873942	183121	548381	-967587	-612866	-967587	0
		3	-140019	1361692	158914	0	-1269380	847189	1269380	661267
		4	160316	1498013	-801738	468280	-1418045	-369540	-1418045	0
		5	1093980	1184730	1210542	0	-289411	1750678	289411	0
		6	-2469264	603448	-979685	-754361	-553149	803995	-553149	-3373069
		7	1625837	-1312644	360451	0	489178	57064	-489178	0
		8	-968985	461500	628331	-1935728	3218315	1174109	3218315	0
		9	11853	-2883219	-1074760	0	-2024958	-1441854	2024958	2216340
		10	2571634	987956	963196	597972	1110163	-1242259	1110163	0
		11	2374389	886891	-187935	0	-710327	-81663	710327	0
		12	2491163	563500	-677478	694478	-95608	-1686533	-95608	3455310
		13	272375	358478	1259216	0	-2866542	805073	2866542	0
		14	-225343	3585617	-1344004	-410336	1212315	2366433	1212315	0
		15	1041219	-698000	1047165	0	1037791	325954	-1037791	3699414
		16	843754	149585	-546717	-283034	3578506	-2249506	3578506	0
		17	-1652681	-197992	-136528	0	-747624	1709203	747624	0
		18	-2295161	1184726	1145471	749128	580053	-1343081	580053	3994618
		19	-285374	909009	-2047850	0	-784947	-205208	784947	0
		20	-71199	-2996334	1004058	-992335	3026877	1648755	3026877	0
		21	-1804727	2202975	1754658	0	-1757942	164315	1757942	-1349478
		22	-1824423	-472734	189756	1169703	219162	-1670257	219162	0
		23	-549357	-63777	-1021389	0	71907	-1712931	-71907	0
	2	1	-1365730	1508101	1538741	0	-787957	747403	787957	0
		2	705029	1582012	1475275	622935	-3002751	-1475229	-3002751	0
		3	-73951	-197609	-411700	0	-701750	881609	701750	-3774203
		4	527935	-160395	-2523300	-2293644	-462121	-1617774	-462121	0
		5	-2714391	-4503135	482016	0	-1617006	-2001844	1617006	0
		6	-3127624	1095216	-1018040	2828310	2290334	2503729	2290334	-2622702
		7	-565161	-869364	2405606	0	274009	709178	-274009	0
		8	-918806	299931	2042907	-276209	-466541	1396783	-466541	0
		9	-105505	-1535790	-802081	0	-1978134	243841	1978134	-2728503
		10	-2881636	549398	-2069990	878067	-253873	1072769	-253873	0
		11	1097064	34250	-1379404	0	1975067	1090097	-1975067	0
		12	-877871	-1213402	-2463459	-1050270	197427	604556	197427	-2941500
		13	2212130	1240770	-2249490	0	766708	189925	-766708	0
		14	-181224	257801	751958	-3131510	-1662409	870438	-1662409	0
		15	719463	-115649	-1844725	0	-127379	-564747	127379	-882114

L	MU	NU	101 525	525 151	013 100	122 221	323 131	113 110	233 011	111 011
47	2	16	-201427	487771	941759	-1369774	556607	-1670116	556607	0
		17	-2201573	-2148460	630811	0	-1260819	-1718447	1260819	0
		18	635076	-2431217	-2685024	2965803	462904	1429939	462904	2640506
		19	1050131	-44740	267255	0	-791986	1169079	791986	0
		20	43446	-403207	544535	1715915	-171339	-915277	-171339	0
		21	1037222	263984	1294274	0	1169236	-1554599	-1169235	4459839
		22	-2139786	2815734	1004099	-992377	-2814869	-1667787	-2814859	0
		23	-2808578	-2187536	-1525143	0	346346	-2009097	-346346	0
	3	1	2222452	-701754	2633469	0	-3069670	-275369	3069670	0
		2	635193	3099233	-665590	1980802	686373	1124724	686373	0
		3	-92291	-2704583	-2064831	0	155806	-1008968	-155806	-4815532
		4	-2017451	138549	1163090	-1679416	955855	1844995	955855	0
		5	-1652375	-69513	688589	0	1133402	-1814136	-1133402	0
		6	3145193	632275	-683789	-176351	-21877	679479	-21877	-2085121
		7	1878522	-456731	790230	0	2204557	-1575016	-2204557	0
		8	-555289	-811596	-1295274	1296224	737319	-2952658	737319	0
		9	369904	2859701	497390	0	908021	-13784	-908021	1123520
		10	-972532	1910291	-431711	-2441538	-1477052	-801165	-1477052	0
		11	-194450	-407595	921379	0	-2117153	1138954	2117153	0
		12	-88415	751252	1954138	-2430678	1096446	-1955721	1096446	2369240
		13	149611	525383	-2955426	0	-240845	-1375916	240845	0
		14	214525	-1334870	-1131629	-421505	-1120500	-550252	-1120500	0
		15	1417934	-1188401	403545	0	1437170	1298723	-1437170	-2655820
		16	-2596618	-266505	-463156	76791	1505020	-1508736	1505020	0
		17	729768	-68781	-2594255	0	651638	-426953	-651638	0
		18	1382320	1047397	-2004831	-495229	944303	-2653699	944303	1080513
		19	-1024600	2931986	-103755	0	180725	-640912	-180726	0
		20	-21799	2913851	-2766084	3066792	465436	571578	465435	0
		21	-694491	722472	-1160580	0	2465353	-1538572	-2465353	1739010
		22	2435686	-708923	1185572	770182	1000424	-1822222	1000424	0
		23	-2874277	325702	-155045	0	-2755527	1099486	2755527	0

Appendix

A1. Some Numerical Aspects Concerning the Calculation of Harmonic Quantities with Standard Precision

With the help of the programs FFSGL33 and POLSGL33 having been given in volume 1 it is possible to construct model distributions in the G-space as well as in the space of pole figures with precision of standard character for all cases of crystal and sample symmetry of practical interest. Such distributions can be used for instance for tests of ODF reproduction programs. If for the solution of the reproduction problem the harmonic apparatus is used (cf. (11.45), (11.52), (12.10), (13.1), (13.2)) the attainable precision of the result will (among other things) depend on termination effects of the series about l, on the precision of the numerical procedures for the calculation of the (F-coefficient) integral in (13.2) as well as on the precision of the applied harmonic functions $D^{l}_{\mu,\nu}(g)$, $Y_{l,\mu}(\boldsymbol{r})$. If the reproduced ODF is determined by other reproduction methods (cf. e.g. the WIMV-method shortly referred in § 14.6, and working without any harmonic functions and series) harmonic expressions may also be of interest. So the determination of macroscopic properties of a polycristalline sample can elegantly be described by the harmonic apparatus.

Indeed, from (6.5)

$$\bar{E}(\boldsymbol{y}) = \int_G E(g \cdot \boldsymbol{y})\, f(g)\, \mathrm{d}g/8\pi^2 \,, \tag{1}$$

and

$$E(\boldsymbol{h}) = \sum_{l=0}^{\lambda} \sum_{\mu'=1}^{\mathscr{L}(\mathscr{G}_B, l)} e_{l,\mu'} Y_{l,\mu'}(\boldsymbol{h}) \,, \tag{2}$$

$$f(g) = \sum_{l=0}^{\infty} \sum_{\mu=1}^{\mathscr{L}(G_B, l)} \sum_{\nu=1}^{\mathscr{L}(G_A, l)} C_l^{\mu,\nu} D^{l}_{\mu,\nu}(g^{-1}) \tag{3}$$

the simple expressions

$$\bar{E}(\boldsymbol{y}) = \sum_{l=0}^{\lambda} \sum_{\nu=1}^{\mathscr{L}(G_A, l)} \bar{e}_{l,\nu} Y_{l,\nu}(\boldsymbol{y}) \,,$$

$$\bar{e}_{l,\nu} = \frac{1}{2l+1} \sum_{\mu=1}^{\mathscr{L}(G_B, l)} C_l^{\mu,\nu} w(G_B, \mathscr{G}_B, l, \mu)\, e_{l,\mu} \tag{4}$$

follow. For the $e_{l,\mu}$ and $C_l^{\mu,\nu}$ we have respectively

$$C_l^{\mu,\nu} = \frac{2l+1}{8\pi^2} \int_G f(g)\, D^{l*}_{\mu,\nu}(g^{-1})\, \mathrm{d}g \,, \tag{5}$$

$$e_{l,\mu} = \int_H E(\boldsymbol{h})\, Y^{*}_{l,\mu}(\boldsymbol{h})\, \mathrm{d}\boldsymbol{h} \,. \tag{6}$$

The advantage of the calculation of $\bar{E}(y)$ by harmonic expressions consists in the circumstance that we need in (4) the $C_l^{\mu,\nu}$-coefficients for l up to λ only if the microscopic property $E(\boldsymbol{h})$ can be described by finite series (2) about l.

In order to test the precision of such procedures it is necessary that the incoming key quantities $D_{\mu,\nu}^l(g)$, $Y_{l,\mu}(\boldsymbol{h})$ respectively $C_l^{\mu,\nu}$ or $\tilde{F}_l^\nu(\boldsymbol{h}_i)$ can be calculated or modelled with standard precision.

For a mixture of standard components (14.24)

$$f^M(g) = F + \sum_{n=1}^{N} I_n f^s(b_n, g_0^n, g)\,; \qquad F + \sum_{n=1}^{N} I_n = 1 \tag{7}$$

with GAUSSian or LORENTZian shape the C-coefficients are given by (cf. (18.5))

$$^M C_l^{\mu,\nu} = \sum_{n=1}^{N} I_n C_l(b_n)\, D_{\mu,\nu}^{l*}((g_0^n)^{-1}) + F\delta_{l,0}\,. \tag{8}$$

At this $C_l(b_n)$ corresponds to $C_l(S_n)$ or $C_l(t_n)$ depending on the form of the n-th component (cf. (16.6), (17.12)). Then the F-coefficients (13.1) are given by

$$^M\tilde{F}_l^\nu(\boldsymbol{h}_i) = \frac{4\pi}{2l+1} \sum_{\mu=1}^{\mathscr{L}(G_B,l)} {}^M C_l^{\mu,\nu} w(G_B, \tilde{\mathscr{G}}_B, l, \mu)\, Y_{l,\mu}^*(\boldsymbol{h}_i)\,. \tag{9}$$

Since the Y-functions are due to (11.24) a special case of the D-functions we focus our attention on the last ones only. As it was already explained in §§ 11.2—11.5 all expressions of interest can be represented by real (not complex) quantities if we are working with the real tesseral functions $\bar{D}_{\bar{m},\bar{n}}^l(g)$ (18.4) and using the $A_l^{\mu,\bar{m}}$-coefficients given by (11.35) or in tables II.1 and II.2 for the symmetrization (18.2).

A typical moment of the harmonic apparatus is that for numerical calculations (especially for large l) always a lot of positive and negative values of various magnitude has to be added. If the used computer possesses a small accuracy only (e.g. 6 significant digits) and if in the programs no special arrangements are realized for the organization of addition procedures then a great probability will exist for results of low quality.

In order to demonstrate this well known effect in numerical mathematics let us consider a simple example assuming that our computer is working with a precision of four digits in the mantissa only. I.e. a real number is given by $\pm 0.N_1N_2N_3N_4\ 10^{\pm M} \equiv \pm 0.N_1N_2N_3N_4\ E \pm M$ (N_1 ($\neq 0$), N_2, N_3, $N_4 = 0, 1, 2, \ldots, 9$; M — a positive integer). Now for this precision 1000 + 0.1 will be considered as 1000 and leads to an error of 0.01% only. But if there is a large number of small terms in a sum the deviation from the exact result may be more heavy.

So the exact result of 2000 — 1000 + 0.1 + 0.1 + ... + 0.1 (4440 terms) — 0.2 — 0.2 — ... — 0.2 (1110 terms) equals 1222. Depending on the order how these terms are by accident arranged in the sum being to be calculated by our computer the results may be quite different. For the given order we will get 1000. For 0.1 + 0.1 + ... + 0.1 (1110 terms) + 2000 — 1000 — 0.2 — 0.2 — ... — 0.2 (1110 terms) + 0.1 + 0.1 + ... + 0.1 (3330 terms) the result will be 1111. The arrangement 0.1 + 0.1 + ... + 0.1 (4440 terms) + 2000 — 1000 — 0.2 — ... — 0.2 (1110 terms) leads to 1444 and so on.

The smallest error will appear for a sum with a large number of terms (in our example we get the exact result) if the sum is devided into two sums (S_+, S_-) for the positive and negative terms respectively. At this in S_+ and S_- the terms are arranged in the order of increasing modulus. So we get $S_+ = 0.1 + 0.1 + \dots + 0.1$ (4440 terms) + 2000, $S_- = -(0.2 + 0.2 + \dots + 0.2$ (1110 terms) + 1000), $S = S_+ + S_- = 2444 - 1222 = 1222$.

Of course, for the realization of such an arrangement of terms in sums much computer time is necessary. For this reason and in order to minimize the roundoff errors it is desirable to avoid (if possible) sums with great numbers of terms especially if those may be of very different magnitude. In our problem such a situation arises for large l in the calculation of D-functions. At this the most critical moments are connected with the calculation of the $d^l_{m,n}(\beta)$-values (cf. (11.18)).

Usually the $d^l_{m,n}(\beta)$ are calculated by the expression (11.19)

$$d^l_{m,n}(\beta) = \sum_{s=0}^{l} (2 - \delta_{s,0})\, \Delta^l_{s,m}\, \Delta^l_{s,n} \cos(s\beta - [m - n]\,\pi/2)$$

$$\equiv \sum_{s=0}^{l} (a_l^{mns} \cos(s\beta) + b_l^{mns} \sin(s\beta))\,, \tag{10}$$

with

$$\Delta^l_{m,n} \equiv d^l_{m,n}(\pi/2)$$

$$= (-1)^{m+n}\, 2^{-l} \left(\frac{(l+m)!\,(l-m)!}{(l+n)!\,(l-n)!}\right)^{1/2} \sum_k \binom{l+n}{k} \binom{l-n}{k+m-n} (-1)^k\,. \tag{11}$$

The $\Delta^l_{m,n}$ or a_l^{mns}, b_l^{mns} have to be calculated once only and can be stored in a library then.

From a first sight there are no problems for this end using the simple expression (11), but remembering the above discussion complications may appear realizing the sum by a computer with limited precision. Analysing for instance the sum (11) for $\Delta^{46}_{0,0}$ we see that ($k = 0, 1, 2, \dots, 46$) the terms for small and large k are of the order of 1, whereas for $k = 23$ we get a number of the order of 10^{25}.

In order to avoid such difficulties ESLING and co-authors [13, 16]*) suggested to calculate the $\Delta^l_{m,n}$ ($m \geqq n \geqq 0$) by recurrence using an expression combining $\Delta^l_{m-1,n-1}$, $\Delta^l_{m+1,n+1}$, $\Delta^l_{m+1,n}$ and $\Delta^l_{m,n}$. The calculation of the starting values $\Delta^l_{l,n}$, $\Delta^l_{l-1,n}$ can be realized without problems (cf. (14)). Moreover, the $\Delta^l_{m,n}$ with $m, n < 0$ or $m < n$ follow immediately from the calculated $\Delta^l_{m,n}$ ($m \geqq n \geqq 0$) using the relation

$$d^l_{m,n}(\beta) = (-1)^{m+n}\, d^l_{n,m}(\beta) = (-1)^{m+n}\, d^l_{-m,-n}(\beta) = (-1)^{l+m}\, d^l_{m,-n}(\pi - \beta)\,. \tag{12}$$

for $\beta = \pi/2$.

Our more detailed analysis of the problem has shown that this scheme can additionally be simplified. At first, for a recurrence the connection

$$\Delta^l_{m-2,n} = [2n\, \Delta^l_{m-1,n} - \sqrt{(l-m+1)\,(l+m)}\, \Delta^l_{m,n}] / \sqrt{(l+m-1)\,(l-m+2)} \tag{13}$$

can be used combining three Δ only. The starting values are given by

$$\Delta^l_{l,n} = (-1)^{l+n}\, ((2l)!/[(l+n)!\,(l-n)!])^{1/2}/2^l\,; \qquad \Delta^l_{l-1,n} = n(2/l)^{1/2}\, \Delta^l_{l,n}\,. \tag{14}$$

Secondly, for even l the values of $\Delta^l_{0,0}$ and $\Delta^l_{1,1}$ connected with the largest number of recurrence steps can be used to test the accuracy of the results. For this end we can compare them

*) See in this connection Z. D. Liang, J. Z. Xu and F. Wang (1980), Texture, 4, 93, and the corresponding discussions at ICOTOM-6 ([16], page 1239) also.

with their exact values

$$\Delta^l_{1,1} = \Delta^l_{0,0} = 2^{-l} \sum_{k=0}^{l} \binom{l}{k}^2 (-1)^k = (-1)^{l/2} \binom{l}{l/2} 2^{-l} \quad (l - \text{even}) . \tag{15}$$

At the end we can avoid the calculation of the $\Delta^l_{m,n}$ and the organization of a library for their use in (10) at all. Indeed, the recurrence (13) is a special case of the common connection [44]

$$d^l_{m-2,n}(\beta) = \frac{2[n - (m-1)\cos\beta]\, d^l_{m-1,n}(\beta)/\sin\beta - \sqrt{(l-m+1)(l+m)}\, d^l_{m,n}(\beta)}{\sqrt{(l+m-1)(l-m+2)}} \tag{16}$$

only. Now with the help of

$$d^l_{l,n}(\beta) = \sqrt{\frac{(2l)!}{(l+n)!\,(l-n)!}}\,(-1)^{l+n} (\cos(\beta/2))^{l+n} (\sin(\beta/2))^{l-n} , \tag{17}$$

$$d^l_{l-1,n}(\beta) = \sqrt{2/l}\,(n - l\cos\beta)\, d^l_{l,n}(\beta)/\sin\beta , \tag{18}$$

$$d^l_{m,n}(0) = \delta_{m,n} , \qquad d^l_{m,n}(\pi) = (-1)^{l+m}\, \delta_{m,-n} , \tag{19}$$

and using (12) all necessary $d^l_{m,n}(\beta)$ can be calculated by an expense comparable with (10), but with much higher precision. This scheme was realized in the program CDFGL33 described below.

A2. The Program CDFGL33

Using (8) the program (page 246) calculates the $C_l^{\mu,\nu}$-coefficients ($l = 1, 2, \ldots$, LEND $\leqq 47$) with precision of standard character for a mixture (7) of $N \leqq 20$ components (GAUSSian or LORENTZian shape, any halfwidths), any crystal symmetry G_B and $G_A = D_2$, C_2 or C_1. The input parameters are sufficiently explained in the text part of the program. For ICD = 1 and IZPOL $\neq 0$ the $\tilde{F}_l^\nu(\boldsymbol{h}_i)$-coefficients (9) ($i = 1, 2, \ldots$, IZPOL $\leqq 12$) will be calculated also. For ICD = 0 the $D^l_{\mu,\nu}(g_0^{-1})$ of the first component will be given only.

The program is written in terms of the real tesseral functions $\bar{Y}_{l,\bar{m}}(\boldsymbol{r})$ (cf. (11.15), (18.3)), and $\bar{D}^l_{\bar{m},\bar{n}}(g)$ (18.4). The symmetric functions are defined by (18.1) and (18.2). For point groups of the type C_n, D_n the $A_l^{\mu,\bar{m}}$-coefficients are determined by (11.35) and for $G_B = O$ or T they have been given in tables II.1 and II.2. For the prescription how the corresponding crystal coordinate system K_B is defined see tables 5.1, 14.1 and figures 5.1—5.6 and 5.9—5.12. If $G_B = O$ or T the A-coefficients will be calculated in the given variant of the program by the subroutine SACOEF.

Like the programs FFSGL33 and POLSGL33 of volume 1 the program CDFGL33 need special attention in case of crystal symmetry $\mathcal{G}_B$ of type III (cf. table 14.1). Due to (13.16) the case of cyclic (fibre) textures is described by the $\nu = 1$ terms for $G_A = C_1$ or C_2 (fir-tree case) and $G_A = D_2$ (double fir-tree).

In order to test the attainable precision by the given computer beside tables II.4 or III (the last is given in this volume) the relation $D^l_{\mu,\nu}(g^{-1}) = A_l^{\mu,\bar{m}}$ for $g = g_{B_j}(G_A = C_1$, $g_{B_j} \in G_B)$ can be used (cf. tables 5.2, 5.4, 5.5, 5.7). At this $\bar{m}$ is connected with ν by the relation $\bar{m} = (-1)^{\nu+1}$ int $(\nu/2)$; $\nu = 1, 2, \ldots, 2l+1$. For $G_B = O$ or T all ten digits of the $A_l^{\mu,\bar{m}}$ in tables II.1 and II.2 are exact numbers independent of the order of the exponent.

For other tests (e.g. component mixing, *F*-coefficients) the exact values given in tables II.3 and II.5 can be used.

In order to reduce a possible bad precision depending on the computer the program CDFGL33 is written in double precision right from the beginning unlike the programs FFSGL33 and POLSGL33.

A3. Text of the Program CDFGL33

```
      *----------------------------------*
C     PROGRAM  CDFGL33       ZFK-ROSSENDORF 1986
C      CALCULATES FOR
C      ICD = 1 AND IZPOL = 0 THE C-COEFFICIENTS CLMUENUE
C      (L = 1,2.3,...,LEND.LE.47) OF A MIXTURE OF NC STANDARD
C      DISTRIBUTIONS (GAUSS OR LORENTZ SHAPE) AND POSSIBLE
C    - SAMPLE SYMMETRY  :
C                          ROTATION GROUP GA   CODE NUMBER IGA
C          ORTHORHOMBIC            D2                3
C          MONOCLINIC              C2                2
C          TRICLINIC               C1                1
C    - CRYSTAL SYMMETRY :
C                          ROTATION GROUP GB   CODE NUMBER IGB
C                                  O                 7
C                                  T                 6
C                                  D4                5
C                                  C4                4
C                                  D2                3
C                                  C2                2
C                                  C1                1
C                                  D6               11
C                                  C6               10
C                                  D3                9
C                                  C3                8
C      FOR ICD = 1 AND IZPOL.NE.0 THE (L-EVEN)
C      REDUCED POLFIGURE F-COEFFICIENTS FLNUE(HI) OF THE IZPOL
C      PROJECTION DIRECTIONS HI WILL ADDITIONALLY BE GIVEN
C      FOR ICD = 0 THE DLMUENUE (GO**-1) VALUES OF THE
C      FIRST TEXTURE COMPONENT ARE CALCULATED ONLY
C      ITITLE -TEXT ARRAY FOR FREE USE
C      IZPOL - NUMBER OF PROJECTION DIRECTIONS HI (O.LE.IZPOL.LE.12)
C      NC - NUMBER OF COMPONENTS TO BE MIXED (1.LE.NC.LE.20)
C      FON - BACKGROUND (0.LE.FON.LT.1) - NOT EXPLICITLY USED,
C      BUT SEE BELOW
C      EVERY PROJECTION DIRECTION HI IS CHARACTERIZED BY
C      THE VECTOR HI (TETAH,FIH) - SPHERICAL ANGLES (IN DEGREES)
C      IN REGARD TO THE CRYSTAL COORDINATE SYSTEM KB AND BY ITS
C      NAME (MILLER INDEXES MILH,MILK,MILL) TO BE USED FOR PRINT ONLY
C      EVERY COMPONENT IS DESCRIBED BY
C      ITS ORIENTATION (POSITION) GO (ALPHAO,BETAO,GAMMAO) IN DEGREES
C      AND THE PARAMETERS:
C      IBST,BST(B,S OR T),HIN(TOTAL INTENSITY, O.LT.HIN.LE.1) AND IGL
C          IBST = 0 HALFWIDTH GIVEN BY S (0.LE.S.LT.INFINITE)
C          IBST = 1 HALFWIDTH GIVEN BY B IN DEGREES (0.LT.B.LE.360)
C          IBST =-1 HALFWIDTH GIVEN BY T (0.LE.T.LT.1)
C          IGL  = 1 GAUSS-SHAPED CURVE (B OR S INPUT IS POSSIBLE)
C          IGL  = 2 LORENTZ-SHAPED CURVE (B OR T INPUT IS POSSIBLE)
C          ***********
C          INPUT DATA
C          ITITLE                          FORMAT(20A4)
C          IGA,IGB                         FORMAT(2I10)
C          LEND                            FORMAT(I10)
C          ICD                             FORMAT(I10)
C          NC                              FORMAT(I10)
C          COMPONENT DATA - NC TIMES TWO SETS :
C          ALPHAO,BETAO,GAMMAO             FORMAT(3F10.5)
C          IBST,BST,HIN,IGL                FORMAT(I10,2F10.5,I10)
C          IZPOL                           FORMAT(I10)
C          PROJECTION DATA - IZPOL SETS :
C          TETAH,FIH,MILH,MILK,MILL        FORMAT(2F10.5,3I10)
C          ***********
C      FOR THE PRESCRIPTION HOW THE CRYSTAL COORDINATE
C      SYSTEM KB IS DEFINED SEE TABLE  5.1, 14.1
C      AND FIG. 5.1-5.6,5.9-5.12 OF VOLUME 1
C      ATTENTION. IN ORDER TO GET RIGHT NORMALIZED C- AND
C      F-COEFFICIENTS FON + SUM OF THE NC HIN = 1 MUST BE VALID
C          ***********
C      ATTENTION: FOR THE TYPE 3 OF CRYSTAL SYMMETRY
C      GBS INSTEAD OF GB HAS TO BE USED (CF.TABLE 14.1) IN ORDER
C      TO GET THE RIGHT F-COEFFICIENTS OF REDUCED POLE FIGURES
C      FOR ECONOMICAL REASONS IN CASE OF CUBIC CRYSTAL
C      SUMMETRY IT IS RECOMMENDED TO CALCULATE THE
C      SYMMETRY COEFFICIENTS 'A' BY THE SUBROUTINE SACOEF
C      ONCE ONLY AND TO STORE THEM ON TAPE OR DISK.
C      THEN SACOEF CAN BE CHANGED FOR A READ INSTRUCTION
      REAL*8 PI,PIFAK,ACOEF,ALPHAO,BETAO,GAMMAO,BST,HIN,B,S,T
      REAL*8 C,TETAH,FIH,SGRENZ,PIFAK4,DMUNU,CL,CLH,SF,YMUE
      REAL*8 W2,PI4,HLFAK,F,YFAK,HBETA,HSIB,HCOB,HSIBHL,HCOBHL
      REAL*8 SIB,COB,SIBHL,COBHL,SIT,COT,SITHL,COTHL
      DIMENSION IGNAME(11)
      DIMENSION MUEZT(47),MUEZO(47)
      DIMENSION MILH(12),MILK(12),MILL(12)
      DIMENSION F(95)
      COMMON /CBST/ BST,B,S,T,IBST,IGL
      COMMON /CHIN/ HIN(20)
      COMMON /CG/ ALPHAO,BETAO(20,2),GAMMAO
      COMMON /SCB/ SIB(20,2),COB(20,2),SIBHL(20,2),COBHL(20,2)
      COMMON /CC/ C(95,95)
      COMMON /CACO/ ACOEF(8,45,12)
      COMMON /CYFAK/ YFAK,W2
      COMMON /TIT/ ITITLE(20)
      COMMON /CNMUEZ/ NUEZM(47),MUEZM(47)
      COMMON /CLTERM/ LTERM,LVORZ,ILVORZ,LL,MSSLEO,MSSLET
      COMMON /CHI/ TETAH(12),FIH(12)
      COMMON /CPI/ PI,PIFAK,PIFAK4,SGRENZ
      COMMON /CCL/ CL(47,20)
      COMMON /CMUMS/ MUMSA(2,95),MUMSB(2,95)
      COMMON /SCT/ SIT(12),COT(12),SITHL(12),COTHL(12)
```

```
      DATA MUEZT /0,0,1,1,0,2,1,1,2,2,1,3,
     1            2,2,3,3,2,4,3,3,4,4,3,5,
     2            4,4,5,5,4,6,5,5,6,6,5,7,
     3            6,6,7,7,6,8,7,7,8,8,7/
      DATA MUEZO /0,0,0,1,0,1,0,1,1,1,0,2,
     1            1,1,1,2,1,2,1,2,2,2,1,3,
     2            2,2,2,3,2,3,2,3,3,3,2,4,
     3            3,3,3,4,3,4,3,4,4,4,3/
      DATA IGNAME /
     1 '(C1)','(C2)','(D2)','(C4)','(D4)','( T)','( 0)',
     2 '(C3)','(D3)','(C6)','(D6)'/
      INP = 5
      IOUT = 6
      PI = DARCOS(-1.D0)
      PIFAK = PI/180.D0
      PIFAK4 = PI/720.D0
      PI4 = 4.D0*PI
      W2 = DSQRT(2.D0)
      SGRENZ = DLOG(2.D0)/2.D0

C     READ AND WRITE OF THE INPUT DATA

      READ (INP,240) ITITLE
      WRITE (IOUT,250) ITITLE
      READ (INP,260) IGA,IGB
      WRITE (IOUT,270) IGA,IGNAME(IGA),IGB,IGNAME(IGB)
      READ (INP,260) LEND
      WRITE (IOUT,280) LEND
      IF (LEND.LT.1.OR.LEND.GT.47) GOTO 888

C     CONSTRUCTION OF THE NUEZM,MUEZM,
C     OTHER BASIC ARRAYS AND PARAMETERS

      CALL SMNUEZ (MUEZT,MUEZO,IGA,IGB,LEND)
      WRITE (IOUT,290) (NUEZM(L),L = 1,LEND)
      WRITE (IOUT,300) (MUEZM(L),L = 1,LEND)
      IGAB = 1
      CALL SMUMS (IGA,LEND,IGAB)
      IGAB = 2
      IF (IGB.NE.6.AND.IGB.NE.7) CALL SMUMS(IGB,LEND,IGAB)
      CALL FAKLOG (LEND)
      CALL WURZEL (LEND)
      CALL C1234
      IF (IGB.EQ.6.OR.IGB.EQ.7) CALL SACOEF (IGB,LEND,MUEZT,MUEZO)
      READ (INP,260) ICD
      WRITE (IOUT,310) ICD
      READ (INP,260) NC
      IF (ICD.EQ.0) NC = 1
      WRITE (IOUT,320) NC
      DO 10 IK = 1,NC
      READ (INP,330) ALPHAO,BETAO(IK,1),GAMMAO
      IF (ICD.EQ.0) GOTO 20
      READ (INP,340) IBST,BST,HIN(IK),IGL
   20 CALL PARGLC (IK,LEND,ICD)
      WRITE (IOUT,350) IK,IGL,B,S,T,HIN(IK)
      WRITE (IOUT,360) IBST,BST
      FI1 = 90.D0 + ALPHAO
      IF (FI1.GE.360.D0) FI1 = FI1-360.D0
      FI = BETAO(IK,1)
      FI2 = 270.D0+GAMMAO
      IF (FI2.GE.360.D0) FI2 = FI2-360.D0
      WRITE (IOUT,370) ALPHAO,BETAO(IK,1),GAMMAO,FI1,FI,FI2
   10 CONTINUE
      IF (ICD.EQ.0) GOTO 30
      READ (INP,260) IZPOL
      WRITE (IOUT,380) IZPOL
      IF (IZPOL.EQ.0) GOTO 30
      READ (INP,450) ((TETAH(IP),FIH(IP),MILH(IP),MILK(IP),
     1                MILL(IP)),IP = 1,IZPOL)
      WRITE (IOUT,470)((TETAH(IP),FIH(IP),MILH(IP),MILK(IP),
     1                MILL(IP)),IP = 1,IZPOL)
   30 CONTINUE

C     L-LOOP

      ILS = 0
      DO 40 L = 1,LEND
      MUEZ = MUEZM(L)
      IF (IGB.EQ.6) MUEZOH = MUEZO(L)
      IF (MUEZ.EQ.0) GOTO 40
      NUEZ = NUEZM(L)
      IF (NUEZ.EQ.0) GOTO 40
      LVORZ = (-1)**L
      LTERM = (1+LVORZ)/2
      ILVORZ = 1
      IF (LVORZ.LT.0) ILVORZ = 2
      LL = L-2
      MSSLEO = (L/4)+1
      MSSLET = (L+2)/4
      DO 50 MUE = 1,MUEZ
      DO 50 NUE = 1,NUEZ
   50 C(MUE,NUE) = 0.D0

C     COMPONENT - LOOP

      DO 60 IK = 1,NC
      CLH = CL(L,IK)

C     DLMN(BETA) - CALCULATION

      INUL = 0
      IPI = 1
      CALL DKLR (L,IK,IPI,INUL)
      IPI = 2
      CALL DKLR (L,IK,IPI,INUL)

C     MUE - LOOP

      DO 70 MUE = 1,MUEZ

C     NUE -LOOP

      DO 80 NUE = 1,NUEZ

C     DLMUENUE(*G(IK)*) CALCULATION
C     IN SUBROUTINE PARGLC G(IK) HAS BEEN TRANSLATED TO
C     *G(IK)* = G(IK)**-1

      CALL SDMUNU (IGB,MUE,NUE,IK,DMUNU,MUEZOH)
      C(MUE,NUE) = C(MUE,NUE) + CLH*DMUNU
```

```
   80 CONTINUE
   70 CONTINUE
   60 CONTINUE
      WRITE (IOUT,390) L,MUEZ,NUEZ
      IF (IGB.NE.6.AND.IGB.NE.7) WRITE(IOUT,400)
     1 (MUMSB(ILVORZ,MUE),MUE = 1,MUEZ)
      WRITE (IOUT,410) (MUMSA(ILVORZ,NUE),NUE = 1,NUEZ)
      DO 90 MUE = 1,MUEZ
      IF (ICD.EQ.0) WRITE (IOUT,420) MUE
      IF (ICD.EQ.1) WRITE (IOUT,430) MUE
      WRITE (IOUT,440) (C(MUE,NUE),NUE = 1,NUEZ)
   90 CONTINUE

C     DETERMINATION OF F - COEFFICIENTS, L - EVEN

      IF (LVORZ.LT.0) GOTO 40
      IF (ICD.EQ.0) GOTO 40
      IF (IZPOL.EQ.0) GOTO 40
      HLFAK = PI4/(2.DO*L+1.DO)
      YFAK = 1.DO/HLFAK
      YFAK = DSQRT(YFAK)

C     PROJECTION DIRECTION LOOP

      DO 100 IP = 1,IZPOL
      IF (ILS.EQ.0) CALL FHM(LEND,IP)
      INUL = 1
      IPI = 1
      HBETA = BETAO(IP,1)
      BETAO(IP,1) = TETAH(IP)
      HSIB = SIB(IP,1)
      HCOB = COB(IP,1)
      HSIBHL = SIBHL(IP,1)
      HCOBHL = COBHL(IP,1)
      SIB(IP,1) = SIT(IP)
      COB(IP,1) = COT(IP)
      SIBHL(IP,1) = SITHL(IP)
      COBHL(IP,1) = COTHL(IP)
      CALL DKLR(L,IP,IPI,INUL)
      BETAO(IP,1) = HBETA
      SIB(IP,1) = HSIB
      COB(IP,1) = HCOB
      SIBHL(IP,1) = HSIBHL
      COBHL(IP,1) = HCOBHL
      DO 110 NUE = 1,NUEZ
      SF = 0.DO
      DO 120 MUE = 1,MUEZ

C     CALCULATION OF YLMUE (HI)

      CALL SYMU (IGB,MUE,IP,YMUE,MUEZOH)
  120 SF = SF+YMUE*C(MUE,NUE)*HLFAK
  110 F(NUE) = SF
      WRITE (IOUT,460) IP,MILH(IP),MILK(IP),MILL(IP),
     1            (F(NUE),NUE = 1,NUEZ)
  100 CONTINUE
      ILS = ILS+1

C     END OF L -LOOP

   40 CONTINUE
  888 CONTINUE
      STOP
  240 FORMAT (20A4)
  250 FORMAT (1H1/5X,'PROGRAM CDF33  ZFK-ROSSENDORF 1986'/
     1 5X,37(1H-)//5X,
     2 'COMPUTES C COEFFICIENTS (F-COEFFICIENTS) FOR A MIXTURE',
     3 ' OF STANDARD COMPONENTS'/
     4 5X,'OR D-FUNCTIONS FOR A SINGLE COMPONENT'/
     5 5X,'FOR ALL POSSIBLE POINT SYMMETRIES'//
     6 5X,'INPUT DATA AS THEY ARE READ'//5X,20A4//)
  260 FORMAT (2I10)
  270 FORMAT (//
     1 5X,'SAMPLE  SYMMETRY  IGA = ',I2,2X,A4,
     2 5X,'CRYSTAL SYMMETRY  IGB = ',I2,2X,A4/)
  280 FORMAT (5X,'LEND = ',I3/)
  290 FORMAT (5X,'NUEZ = ',30I3/12X,17I3/)
  300 FORMAT (5X,'MUEZ = ',30I3/12X,17I3/)
  310 FORMAT (/5X,'ICD = ',I3/)
  320 FORMAT (5X,'NUMBER OF COMPONENTS NC TO BE MIXED = ',I3/)
  330 FORMAT (3F10.5)
  340 FORMAT (I10,2F10.5,I10)
  350 FORMAT (15X,'COMP. NR. = ',I2,'  IGL = ',I3,
     1 '  B = ',F7.2,'  S = ',D15.5,'  T = ',D15.5,
     2 '  HIN = ',F10.5/15X,98(1H-))
  360 FORMAT (15X,'IBST = ',I3,'   BST = ',F10.5/)
  370 FORMAT (15X,'POSITION GO  :    ALPHAO = ',F7.3,
     1 3X,'BETAO = ',F7.3,3X,'GAMMAO = ',F7.3/
     2 34X,'  FI1 = ',F7.3,2X,'   FI = ',F7.3,
     3 4X,'  FI2 = ',F7.3/)
  380 FORMAT (5X,'IZPOL = ',I3/)
  390 FORMAT (/1X,119(1H*)/
     1           30X,'L = ',I3,5X,'MUEZ = ',I3,2X,'NUEZ = ',I3/)
  400 FORMAT (5X,'MUE CORRESPONDS TO MS = ',30I3,3(/29X,30I3))
  410 FORMAT (5X,'NUE CORRESPONDS TO NS = ',30I3,3(/29X,30I3))
  420 FORMAT (5X,'MUE = ',I3,5X,'D - FUNCTIONS')
  430 FORMAT (5X,'MUE = ',I3,5X,'C - COEFFICIENTS')
  440 FORMAT ((8X,10F11.7))
  450 FORMAT (2F10.5,3I10)
  460 FORMAT (5X,'PROJECTION DIRECTION NR. ',I3,'   ( ',
     1          3I4,' ) , F-COEFFICIENTS'/10(8X,10F11.7/))
  470 FORMAT (5X,' PROJECTION DIRECTIONS, THETA, PHI'/
     1           12(15X,2F10.5,' ( ',3I4,' )'/))
      END


*-----------------------------------*

      SUBROUTINE C1234

C     CONSTRUCTION OF THE C1M(IVORZMT,IVORZNT),C2M,C3M,C4M ARRAYS
C     FOR THE CALCULATION OF TESSERAL D-FUNCTIONS

C     IVORZMT = 1 CORRESPONDS TO MT.GT.0
C     IVORZMT = 2 CORRESPONDS TO MT.LT.0
C     IVORZMT = 3 CORRESPONDS TO MT = 0, ANALOGICALLY FOR NT

      REAL*8 W2,C1M,C2M,C3M,C4M
```

```
      COMMON /CC1234/ C1M(3,3),C2M(3,3),C3M(3,3),C4M(3,3)
      W2 = DSQRT(2.DO)
      DO 10 IVORMT = 1,3
      DO 20 IVORNT = 1,3
      C1M(IVORMT,IVORNT) = 0.DO
      C2M(IVORMT,IVORNT) = 0.DO
      C3M(IVORMT,IVORNT) = 0.DO
   20 C4M(IVORMT,IVORNT) = 0.DO
   10 CONTINUE
      C1M(1,1) = 1.DO
      C1M(2,2) =1.DO
      C1M(1,3) = W2
      C1M(3,1) = W2
      C1M(3,3) = 1.DO
      C2M(1,2) =-1.DO
      C2M(2,1) = 1.DO
      C2M(2,3) = W2
      C2M(3,2) = -W2
      C3M(1,1) = 1.DO
      C3M(2,2) = -1.DO
      C4M(1,2) = 1.DO
      C4M(2,1) = 1.DO
      RETURN
      END


     *------------------------------------*

      SUBROUTINE SMNUEZ (MUEZT,MUEZO,IGA,IGB,LEND)

C     DETERMINATION OF THE NUMBERS OF NUE AND MUE
C     IN DEPENDENCE OF L, GA AND GB

      DIMENSION MUEZT(47),MUEZO(47)
      COMMON /CNMUEZ/ NUEZM(47),MUEZM(47)
      IA = IGA
      IB = IGB
      DO 20 L = 1,LEND
      LFAK = (1+(-1)**L)/2
      I = 0
      GOTO (1,2,3,4,5,6,7,8,9,10,11),IA
   30 I = I+1
      IF (I.GT.1) GOTO 20
      GOTO (1,2,3,4,5,6,7,8,9,10,11),IB
    1 IH = 2*L+1
      GOTO 40
    2 IH = 2*(L/2) + 1
      GOTO 40
    3 IH = (L/2) + LFAK
      GOTO 40
    4 IH = 2*(L/4) + 1
      GOTO 40
    5 IH = (L/4) + LFAK
      GOTO 40
    6 IH = MUEZT(L)
      GOTO 40
    7 IH = MUEZO(L)
      GOTO 40
    8 IH = 2*(L/3) + 1
      GOTO 40
    9 IH = (L/3) + LFAK
      GOTO 40
   10 IH = 2*(L/6) + 1
      GOTO 40
   11 IH = (L/6) + LFAK
   40 IF (I.EQ.0) NUEZM(L) = IH
      IF (I.EQ.1) MUEZM(L) = IH
      GOTO 30
   20 CONTINUE
      RETURN
      END


     *------------------------------------*

      SUBROUTINE PARGLC (IK,LEND,ICD)

C     CALCULATES B,S, OR T, THE CL(IK) FACTORS
C     AND WORKING ARRAYS FOR THE DETERMINATION
C     OF THE DLMN(G(IK)**-1) - TESSERAL

      REAL*8 CL,SIB,COB,SIBHL,COBHL,SIA,COA,SIG,COG,HN2,HN3
      REAL*8 ALPHAO,BETAO,GAMHAO,ALPHA,BETA,GAMMA,BST,B,S,T
      REAL*8 PI,PIFAK,SGRENZ,ARGH,BR4,EMAS,HN,TAUG,TGRENZ
      REAL*8 TAU,TAU2,TAU3,TAU4,AC,HG,AC3,PIFAK4,HIN
      DIMENSION EMAS(101)
      COMMON /CHIN/ HIN(20)
      COMMON /CBST/ BST,B,S,T,IBST,IGL
      COMMON /CG/ ALPHAO,BETAO(20,2),GAMMAO
      COMMON /CPI/ PI,PIFAK,PIFAK4,SGRENZ
      COMMON /CCL/ CL(47,20)
      COMMON /SCB/ SIB(20,2),COB(20,2),SIBHL(20,2),COBHL(20,2)
      COMMON /SCAG/ SIA(48,20),COA(48,20),SIG(48,20),COG(48,20)
      NN = LEND +.1
      IDEZ = 10
      IF (ICD.EQ.1) GOTO 10
      IGL = 888
      B = 8888.88DO
      S = 0.88888D8
      T = 0.88888D8
      HIN (IK) = 1.DO
      IBST = 888
      BST = 8888.88888DO
      GOTO 200

C     CALCULATION OF B,S,T

   10 IF (IGL.EQ.2) GOTO 70
      T = 0.88888D8
      IF (IBST) 50,20,50
   20 S = BST
      B = 8888.88DO
      IF (S-SGRENZ) 60,30,40
   30 B = 360.DO
      GOTO 60
   40 ARGH = DSQRT (SGRENZ/S)
```

```
      B = DARSIN (ARGH)/PIFAK4
      GOTO 60
   50 B = BST
      BR4 = B*PIFAK4
      S = SGRENZ / (DSIN(BR4)**2)

C     CL -FACTORS GAUSS

   60 CALL DBSINE (S,NN,IDEZ,EMAS)

C     FOR DBSINE USE SUBROUTINE BESIN GIVEN IN VOLUME 1.
C     BEGINNING FROM LABEL 70  IT MUST (IF NECESSARY FOR THE
C     GIVEN COMPUTER)
C     BE REWRITTEN IN DOUBLE PRECISION IN ORDER TO OBTAIN
C     A PRECISION OF 10 DIGITS

      HN = EMAS(1) - EMAS(2)
      DO 130 L = 1,LEND
      LP = L + 1
  130 CL(L,IK) = ((EMAS(LP)-EMAS(LP+1))/HN)*HIN(IK)
      GOTO 210
   70 S = 0.88888D8
      IF (IBST) 80,110,110
   80 B = 8888.88D0
      T = BST
      TAUG = (5.DO + DSQRT(17.DO))/2.DO
      TGRENZ = DSQRT(TAUG) - DSQRT(TAUG-1.DO)
      IF (T - TGRENZ) 120,90,100
   90 B = 360.DO
      GOTO 120
  100 TAU = ((1.DO + T*T)**2)/(4.DO*T*T)
      TAU2 = TAU*TAU
      TAU3 = TAU*TAU2
      TAU4 = TAU*TAU3
      ARGH = 5.DO *TAU4 - 8.DO *TAU3 +2.DO *TAU2 + 1.DO
      HN = ((2.DO *TAU2 -TAU + 1.DO) - DSQRT(ARGH))/(1.DO + TAU)
      HN = DSQRT (HN)
      B = DARCOS(HN) / PIFAK4
      GOTO 120
  110 B = BST
      BR4 = B*PIFAK4
      HN = DCOS(BR4)**2
      HN2 = HN*HN
      HN3 = HN*HN2
      AC = (19.DO*HN2 - 34.DO*HN + 19.DO)
      AC3 = AC**3
      HG = (-82.DO*HN3 + 240.DO*HN2 - 246.DO*HN + 80.DO)
     1      /DSQRT (AC3)
      HG = DARCOS(HG) /3.DO
      TAU = (2.DO*DSQRT(AC)*DCOS(HG) + (5.DO - 4.DO*HN))/3.DO
      AC = TAU -1.DO
      T = DSQRT(TAU)-DSQRT(AC)

C     CL - FACTORS LORENTZ

  120 DO 140 L = 1,LEND
  140 CL(L,IK) = (2.DO*L + 1.DO)*(T**(2*L))*HIN(IK)
      GOTO 210
  200 DO 150 L = 1,LEND
  150 CL(L,IK) = 1.DO

C     ARRAYS DEPENDING ON BETAO(IK)

  210 BETAO(IK,2) = 180.DO - BETAO(IK,1)
      DO 230 IPI = 1,2
      BETA = BETAO(IK,IPI)
      IF (BETA.EQ.0.DO.OR.BETA.EQ.180.DO) GOTO 220
      BETA = BETA*PIFAK
      SIB(IK,IPI) = DSIN(BETA)
      COB(IK,IPI) = DCOS(BETA)
      BETA = BETA/2.DO
      HN = DSIN(BETA)
      SIBHL(IK,IPI) = DLOG(HN)
      HN = DCOS(BETA)
      COBHL(IK,IPI) = DLOG(HN)
      GOTO 230

C     DUMMY VALUES

  220 SIB(IK,IPI) = 1.DO
      COB (IK,IPI) = 1.DO
      SIBHL(IK,IPI) = 1.DO
      COBHL(IK,IPI) = 1.DO
  230 CONTINUE

C     ARRAYS DEPENDING ON ALPHAO(IK),GAMMAO(IK)
C     G TO G**-1 TRANSFORMATION

      ALPHA = (180.DO -GAMMAO)*PIFAK
      GAMMA = (180.DO - ALPHAO)*PIFAK
      DO 240 MNL = 1,NN
      HG = MNL - 1.DO
      ARGH = ALPHA*HG
      SIA(MNL,IK) = DSIN(ARGH)
      COA(MNL,IK) = DCOS(ARGH)
      ARGH = GAMMA*HG
      SIG(MNL,IK) = DSIN(ARGH)
  240 COG(MNL,IK) = DCOS(ARGH)
      RETURN
      END


      *-----------------------------------*

      SUBROUTINE FAKLOG (LEND)

C     CALCULATES LOG (L - FACTORIAL), L=LL-1=0,1,...2*LEND

      REAL*8 FAL,LOG2
      COMMON /CLOG/ FAL(95),LOG2
      FAL(1) = 0.DO
      LOG2 = DLOG(2.DO)
      LLEND = 2*LEND + 1
      DO 10 LL = 2,LLEND
      LLM1 = LL - 1
   10 FAL(LL) = FAL(LLM1) + DLOG(LLM1 + 0.DO)
      RETURN
      END
```

```
      *---------------------------------*

      SUBROUTINE WURZEL (LEND)

C     DETERMINES SQRT(L)  L=LL-1=0,1,2,...,2*LEND+2

      REAL*8 WU,HL
      COMMON /CWU/ WU(97)
      WU(1) = 0.D0
      LLEND = 2*LEND + 3
      DO 10 LL = 2,LLEND
      HL = LL - 1.D0
   10 WU(LL) = DSQRT(HL)
      RETURN
      END


      *---------------------------------*

      SUBROUTINE DKLR (L,IK,IPI,INUL)

C     CALCULETES DLMN(BETA) , 1.LE.L.LE.47 BY RECURRENCE
C     M,N = 0,1,2,...,L.  ML=M+1, NL=N+1. RESULT IN DKL(ML,NL,IPI)

C     IPI = 1 BETA = BETA0(IK), IPI = 2 BETA = 180.- BETA0(IK)
C     INUL=0  N = 0,1,2,...L
C     INUL=1  N = 0 IS ONLY PERFORMED

      REAL*8 F,HLVORZ,FL2,ALPHA0,BETA0,GAMMA0,BETA,DKL,WU,FAL
      REAL*8 LOG2,HLP,HLM,HNVORZ,DL,D,DE,COBHL,SIBHL,COB,SIB
      COMMON /CLOG/ FAL(95),LOG2
      COMMON /CWU/ WU(97)
      COMMON /CG/ ALPHA0,BETA0(20,2),GAMMA0
      COMMON /CDKL/ DKL(48,48,2)
      COMMON /SCB/ SIB(20,2),COB(20,2),SIBHL(20,2),COBHL(20,2)
      F = FAL(2*L + 1)
      LM1 = L - 1
      HLVORZ = (-1)**L + 0.D0
      L1 = L + 1
      LN = L1
      IF (INUL.EQ.1) LN = 1
      FL2 = WU(3) / WU(L1)
      BETA = BETA0(IK,IPI)

C     BETA = 0.OR.180 DEGREES

      IF (BETA.EQ.0.D0) GOTO 10
      IF (BETA.NE.180.D0) GOTO 20
   10 DO 30 ML = 1,L1
      DO 30 NL = 1,LN
      DKL(ML,NL,IPI) = 0.D0
      IF (ML.EQ.NL.AND.BETA.EQ.0.D0) DKL(ML,NL,IPI) = 1.D0
      IF (ML.EQ.1.AND.NL.EQ.1.AND.BETA.EQ.180.D0)
     1    DKL(ML,NL,IPI) = HLVORZ
   30 CONTINUE
      RETURN

C     BETA.NE.0.OR.180 DEGREES

   20 DO 40 NL = 1,LN

C     M = L LINE, N.LE.M
       N = NL - 1
       HLP = L + N + 0.D0
       HLM = L - N + 0.D0
       HNVORZ = (-1)**N + 0.D0
       DL = 0.5D0 * (F - FAL(L+NL) - FAL(L1-N))
       D = DL + HLP*COBHL(IK,IPI) + HLM*SIBHL(IK,IPI)
       DE = 0.D0
       IF (D.GT.-175.D0) DE = DEXP(D)

C     175 PROTECTION AGAINST UNDERFLOW

       DKL(L1,NL,IPI) = HLVORZ*HNVORZ*DE
   40 CONTINUE

C     M = L-1 LINE, N.LE.M

       LE = L
       IF (INUL.EQ.1) LE = 1
       DO 50 NL = 1,LE
       N = NL - 1
       DKL(L,NL,IPI) = FL2*(N-L*COB(IK,IPI))*DKL(L1,NL,IPI)
     1                /SIB(IK,IPI)
   50 CONTINUE

C     M - RECURRENCE

       IF (LM1.EQ.0) GOTO 70
       LN1 = LM1
       IF (INUL.EQ.1) LN1 = 1
       DO 80 NL = 1,LN1
       N = NL - 1
       DO 90 MLH = 1,LM1
       ML = L - MLH
       M = ML - 1
       ML1 = ML + 1
       ML2 = ML + 2
       HLP = WU(L-M) * WU(L+ML+2)
       HLM = WU(L+ML+1) * WU(L-M+1)
       F = 2.D0*(N-ML*COB(IK,IPI)) / SIB(IK,IPI)
       DKL(ML,NL,IPI) = (F*DKL(ML1,NL,IPI) - HLP*DKL(ML2,NL,IPI))
     1                 /HLM
   90 CONTINUE
   80 CONTINUE

C     COMPLETION OF THE DKL-ARRAY FOR N.GT.M

       IF (INUL.EQ.1) GOTO 120
   70  DO 100 ML = 2,L1
       M = ML - 1
       DO 110 NL = 1,M
       HLVORZ = (-1)**(ML+NL)+0.D0
       DKL(NL,ML,IPI) =HLVORZ*DKL(ML,NL,IPI)
  110  CONTINUE
  100  CONTINUE
  120  CONTINUE
       RETURN
       END
```

```
*-----------------------------------*

      SUBROUTINE SDMUNU (IGB,MUE,NUE,IK,DMUNU,MUEZOH)

C     CALCULATES DLMUENUE(*G(IK)*) FOR GIVEN L,MUE,NUE
C     CRYSTAL AND SAMPLE SYMMETRIES

      REAL*8 DMUNU,DT,DSS,S,ACOEF
      DIMENSION DSS(12)
      COMMON /CMUMS/ MUMSA(2,95),MUMSB(2,95)
      COMMON /CLTERM/ LTERM,LVORZ,ILVORZ,LL,MSSLEO,MSSLET
      COMMON /CACO/ ACOEF(8,45,12)
      NS = MUMSA(ILVORZ,NUE)
      IF (IGB.EQ.6.OR.IGB.EQ.7) GOTO 10

C     CRYSTAL SYMMETRY  NOT CUBIC (GB.NE.(O.OR.T))

      MS = MUMSB(ILVORZ,MUE)
      CALL SDTES (MS,NS,IK,DT)
      DMUNU = DT
      RETURN

C     CUBIC CRYSTAL SYMMETRY

   10 IF (IGB.EQ.6.AND.MUE.GT.MUEZOH) GOTO 20

C     GB = O .OR. GB = T O-PART

      DSS(1) = 0.DO
      DO 30 MSSL = 1,MSSLEO
      IF (MSSL.EQ.1.AND.LVORZ.LT.0) GOTO 30
      MS = LVORZ*(MSSL-1)*4
      CALL SDTES (MS,NS,IK,DT)
      DSS(MSSL) = DT
   30 CONTINUE
      MSSLE = MSSLEO
   60 S = 0.DO
      DO 40 MSSL = 1,MSSLE
   40 S = S + ACOEF(MUE,LL,MSSL) * DSS(MSSL)
      DMUNU = S
      RETURN

C     GB = T  SPECIFIC T-PART

   20 DO 50 MSSL = 1,MSSLET
      MS = LVORZ * ((MSSL-1)*4+2)
      CALL SDTES (MS,NS,IK,DT)
      DSS(MSSL) = DT
   50 CONTINUE
      MSSLE = MSSLET
      GOTO 60
      END
```

```
*-----------------------------------*

      SUBROUTINE SMUMS (IG,LEND,IGAB)

C     DETERMINES FOR A POINT GROUP IG OF TYPE CN OR DN
C     THE CORRESPONDENCE OF MU AND MT
C     INDICES OF SYMMETRIZED OR TESSERAL HARMONICS
C     MT = MUMSA(ILVORZ,MU) OR MUMSB(ILVORZ,MU)
C     ILVORZ = 1 L-EVEN, = 2 L-ODD
C     IGAB = 1 SAMPLE, = 2 CRYSTAL SYMMETRY

      COMMON /CMUMS/ MUMSA(2,95),MUMSB(2,95)
      I = IG
      MUEND = 2*LEND + 1
      DO 20 ILVORZ = 1,2
      LVORZ = 1
      LTERM = 1
      IF (ILVORZ.EQ.2) LVORZ = -1
      IF (ILVORZ.EQ.2) LTERM = 0
      DO 30 MU = 1,MUEND
      MUFAK = -(-1)**MU
      MU2 = MU/2
      GOTO (1,2,3,4,5,6,7,8,9,10,11),I
    1 N = 1
      GOTO 50
    2 N = 2
      GOTO 50
    3 N = 2
      GOTO 60
    4 N = 4
      GOTO 50
    5 N = 4
      GOTO 60
    6 CONTINUE
    7 M = 888

C     DUMMY VALUE

      GOTO 40
    8 N = 3
      GOTO 50
    9 N = 3
      GOTO 60
   10 N = 6
      GOTO 50
   11 N = 6
   60 M = LVORZ * N *(MU-LTERM)
      GOTO 40
   50 M = MUFAK*N*MU2
   40 IF (IGAB.EQ.1) MUMSA(ILVORZ,MU) = M
      IF (IGAB.EQ.2) MUMSB(ILVORZ,MU) = M
   30 CONTINUE
   20 CONTINUE
      RETURN
      END
```

```
*--------------------------------*

      SUBROUTINE SDTES (MT,NT,IK,DT)

C     CALCULATES TESSERAL HARMONIC DLMN(*G(IK)*) = DT

      REAL*8 DT,C1M,C2M,C3M,C4M,HCOA,HCOG,HSIA,HSIG,COA,COG
      REAL*8 SIA,SIG,CC,SS,SC,CS,S,DK,C1,C2,S1,S2,DKL
      COMMON /CLTERM/ LTERM,LVORZ,ILVORZ,LL,MSSLEO,MSSLET
      COMMON /CC1234/ C1M(3,3),C2M(3,3),C3M(3,3),C4M(3,3)
      COMMON /SCAG/ SIA(48,20),COA(48,20),SIG(48,20),COG(48,20)
      COMMON /CDKL/ DKL(48,48,2)
      MTABS = MT
      IF (MTABS.LT.0) MTABS = -MTABS
      NTABS = NT
      IF (NTABS.LT.0) NTABS = -NTABS
      ML = MTABS + 1
      NL = NTABS + 1
      HCOA = COA(ML,IK)
      HCOG = COG(NL,IK)
      HSIA = SIA(ML,IK)
      HSIG = SIG(NL,IK)
      CC = HCOA * HCOG
      SS = HSIA * HSIG
      SC = HSIA * HCOG
      CS = HCOA * HSIG
      IMT = 1
      IF (MT.LT.0) IMT = 2
      IF (MT.EQ.0) IMT = 3
      INT = 1
      IF (NT.LT.0) INT = 2
      IF (NT.EQ.0) INT = 3
      S = 0.D0
      DK = DKL(ML,NL,1)
      IF (DK.EQ.0.D0) GOTO 20
      C1 = C1M(IMT,INT)
      S1 = 0.D0
      IF (C1.EQ.0.D0) GOTO 30
      S1 = C1 * (CC-SS)
   30 S2 = 0.D0
      C2 = C2M(IMT,INT)
      IF (C2.EQ.0.D0) GOTO 40
      S2 = C2*(SC+CS)
   40 S = ((-1)**(MT+NT))*DK*(S1+S2)
   20 IF (MT.EQ.0.OR.NT.EQ.0) GOTO 10
      DK = DKL(ML,NL,2)
      IF (DK.EQ.0.D0) GOTO 10
      C1 = C3M(IMT,INT)
      S1 = 0.D0
      IF (C1.EQ.0.D0) GOTO 50
      S1 = C1*(CC+SS)
   50 S2 = 0.D0
      C2 = C4M(IMT,INT)
      IF (C2.EQ.0.D0) GOTO 60
      S2 = C2 *(SC-CS)
   60 S = S + LVORZ*DK*(S1+S2)
   10 DT = S
      RETURN
      END
```

```
*--------------------------------*

      SUBROUTINE FHM (LEND,IP)

C     CALCULATES WORKING ARRAYS FOR THE DETERMINATION
C     OF TESSERAL YLM(TETAH(IP),FIH(IP))

      REAL*8 TETAH,FIH,SIT,COT,SITHL,COTHL,SIF,COF
      REAL*8 FI,TETA,PI,PIFAK,PIFAK4,SGRENZ,HN
      COMMON /CHI/ TETAH(12),FIH(12)
      COMMON /SCT/ SIT(12),COT(12),SITHL(12),COTHL(12)
      COMMON /SCF/ SIF(48,12),COF(48,12)
      COMMON /CPI/ PI,PIFAK,PIFAK4,SGRENZ
      NN = LEND+1
      TETA = TETAH(IP)
      IF (TETA.EQ.0.D0.OR.TETA.EQ.180.D0) GOTO 20
      TETA = TETA*PIFAK
      SIT(IP) = DSIN(TETA)
      COT(IP) = DCOS(TETA)
      TETA = TETA/2.D0
      HN = DSIN(TETA)
      SITHL(IP) = DLOG(HN)
      HN = DCOS(TETA)
      COTHL(IP) = DLOG(HN)
      GOTO 30

C     DUMMY VALUES

   20 SIT(IP) = 1.D0
      COT(IP) = 1.D0
      SITHL(IP) = 1.D0
      COTHL(IP) = 1.D0
      FIH(IP) = 0.D0
   30 CONTINUE
      FI = FIH(IP)*PIFAK
      DO 40 ML = 1,NN
      HN = ML-1.D0
      HN = FI*HN
      SIF(ML,IP) = DSIN(HN)
      COF(ML,IP) = DCOS(HN)
   40 CONTINUE
      RETURN
      END
```

```
*--------------------------------*

      SUBROUTINE SYMU(IGB,MUE,IP,YMUE,MUEZOH)

C     CALCULATES YLMUE(TETA(IP),FI(IP)) FOR GIVEN L,MUE, AND
C     CRYSTAL SYMMETRY

      REAL*8 YFAK,W2,YMUE,ACOEF,HMVORZ,Y,DKL,YSS,S,SIF,COF
      DIMENSION YSS(12)
      COMMON /CDKL/ DKL(48,48,2)
      COMMON /CACO/ ACOEF(8,45,12)
      COMMON /CYFAK/ YFAK,W2
      COMMON /CMUMS/ MUMSA(2,95),MUMSB(2,95)
```

```
      COMMON /CLTERM/ LTERM,LVORZ,ILVORZ,LL,MSSLEO,MSSLET
      COMMON /SCF/ SIF(48,12),COF(48,12)
      IF (IGB.EQ.6.OR.IGB.EQ.7) GOTO 10

C     CRYSTAL SYMMETRY NOT CUBIC (GB.NE.(O.OR.T))

      MS = MUMSB(ILVORZ,MUE)
      MSA = MS
      IF (MSA.LT.0) MSA = -MSA
      HMVORZ = (-1)**MSA+0.DO
      MSAL = MSA+1
      Y = YFAK*HMVORZ*DKL(MSAL,1,1)
      IF (MS.GT.0) Y = Y*W2*COF(MSAL,IP)
      IF (MS.LT.0) Y = Y*W2*SIF(MSAL,IP)
      YMUE = Y
      RETURN

C     CUBIC CRYSTAL SYMMETRY

   10 IF (IGB.EQ.6.AND.MUE.GT.MUEZOH) GOTO 20

C     GB = O. OR. GB = T   O-PART

      YSS(1) = 0.DO
      DO 30 MSSL = 1,MSSLEO
      IF (MSSL.EQ.1.AND.LVORZ.LT.0) GOTO 30
      MS = LVORZ*(MSSL-1)*4
      MSA = MS
      IF (MSA.LT.0) MSA = -MSA
      MSAL = MSA+1
      Y = YFAK*DKL(MSAL,1,1)
      IF (MS.GT.0) Y = Y*W2*COF(MSAL,IP)
      IF (MS.LT.0) Y = Y*W2*SIF(MSAL,IP)
      YSS(MSSL) = Y
   30 CONTINUE
      MSSLE = MSSLEO
   60 S = 0.DO
      DO 40 MSSL = 1,MSSLE
   40 S = S + ACOEF(MUE,LL,MSSL)*YSS(MSSL)
      YMUE = S
      RETURN

C     GB = T SPECIFIC T-PART

   20 DO 50 MSSL = 1,MSSLET
      MS = LVORZ*((MSSL-1)*4+2)
      MSA = MS
      IF (MSA.LT.0) MSA = -MSA
      MSAL = MSA+1
      Y = YFAK*DKL(MSAL,1,1)
      IF (MS.GT.0) Y = Y*W2*COF(MSAL,IP)
      IF (MS.LT.0) Y = Y*W2*SIF(MSAL,IP)
      YSS(MSSL) = Y
   50 CONTINUE
      MSSLE = MSSLET
      GOTO 60
      END
```

```
*-----------------------------------*

      SUBROUTINE SACOEF (IGB,LEND,MUEZT,MUEZO)

C     CALCULATES FOR LL+2=L=3,4,...LEND.LE.47 THE A COEFFICIENTS
C     (ACOEF(MUE,LL,MSL)  FOR GB = O (IGB=7) OR GB = T (IGB=6)

C     IN ORDER TO TEST THE PRECISION OF THE VALUES COMPARE
C     THEM WITH THE EXACT NUMBERS GIVEN IN TABLE II OF VOLUME 1.
C     IF NECESSARY DOUBLE THE COMPUTER PRECISION FOR THIS AND
C     CALLED SUBROUTINES

      REAL*8 ACOEF,W2,AH,DREIEK
      DIMENSION MUEZT(47),MUEZO(47),AH(4,12)
      COMMON /CACO/ ACOEF(8,45,12)
      COMMON /CDREIK/ DREIEK(48,48)
      W2  = DSQRT(2.DO)
      DO 10 N1 = 1,8
      DO 10 N2 = 1,45
      DO 10 N3 = 1,12
   10 ACOEF(N1,N2,N3) = 0.DO

C     L - LOOP

      DO 20 L = 3,LEND
      MUEZOH = MUEZO(L)
      MUEZ = MUEZOH
      IF (IGB.EQ.6) MUEZ = MUEZT(L)
      IF (MUEZ.EQ.0) GOTO 20
      LL = L-2
      LKLAM = 2
      IF ((-1)**L.LT.0) LKLAM= 0
      CALL DREIK(L)
      IF (MUEZOH.EQ.0) GOTO 70

C     O - PART

      MSLE = L/4+1
      DO 30 MUE = 1,MUEZOH
      MSLO = MSLE - MUE+1
      MOL = 4*(MSLO-1)+1
      DO 40 MSL = 1,MSLE
      IF (MSL.NE.1) GOTO 50

C     MS.EQ.0

      IF (LKLAM.NE.0) GOTO 60
      GOTO 40
   60 KRON = 0
      IF (MSLO.EQ.MSL) KRON = 1
      ACOEF(MUE,LL,1) = 2.DO*(2.DO*DREIEK(1,MOL)+KRON)
      GOTO 40

C     MS.NE.0

   50 KRON = 0
      IF (MSLO.EQ.MSL) KRON = 1
      ML = 4*(MSL-1)+1
      ACOEF(MUE,LL,MSL) = W2*(4.DO*DREIEK(ML,MOL)+KRON)
```

```
   40 CONTINUE
   30 CONTINUE

C     CONSTRUCTION OF ORTHONORMALIZED SETS WITH CONDITIONAL
C     END ZEROS AND COMMON SIGN

      MUEA = 1
      MUEB = MUEZOH
      CALL ORTNON(MUEA,MUEB,MSLE,LL)

C     CHANGE OF THE MUE ORDER

      DO 80 MUE = 1,MUEZOH
      DO 80 MSL = 1,MSLE
   80 AH(MUE,MSL) = ACOEF(MUE,LL,MSL)
      DO 90 MUE = 1,MUEZOH
      MUES = MUEZOH-MUE+1
      DO 90 MSL = 1,MSLE
   90 ACOEF(MUES,LL,MSL) = AH(MUE,MSL)
      IF (IGE.EQ.7) GOTO 20

C     SPECIFIC T - PART

   70 MUEZR = MUEZ-MUEZOH
      IF (MUEZR.EQ.0) GOTO 20
      MUEA = MUEZOH+1
      MSLE = (L+2)/4
      DO 100 MUE = MUEA,MUEZ
      MUEH = MUE-MUEZOH
      MSLO = MSLE-MUEH+1
      MOL = 4*(MSLO-1)+3
      DO 110 MSL = 1,MSLE
      KRON = 0
      IF (MSLO.EQ.MSL) KRON = 1
      ML = 4*(MSL-1)+3
      ACOEF(MUE,LL,MSL) = 4.DO*DREIEK(ML,MOL)-KRON
  110 CONTINUE
  100 CONTINUE
      CALL ORTNON (MUEA,MUEZ,MSLE,LL)
      DO 120 MUE = MUEA,MUEZ
      MUEH = MUE-MUEZOH
      DO 120 MSL = 1,MSLE
  120 AH(MUEH,MSL) = ACOEF(MUE,LL,MSL)
      DO 130 MUEH = 1,MUEZR
      MUES = MUEZ-MUEH+1
      DO 130 MSL = 1,MSLE
  130 ACOEF(MUES,LL,MSL) = AH(MUEH,MSL)
   20 CONTINUE

C     END OF L - LOOP
C     HERE THE A-COEFFICIENTS CAN BE WRITTEN ON TAPE OR DISK

      RETURN
      END
```

```
*-----------------------------------*

      SUBROUTINE ORTNON (MUEA,MUEB,MSLE,LL)

C     NECESSARY FOR THE CALCULATION OF THE CUBIC A-COEFFICIENTS ONLY
C     ORTHONORMALIZATION OF (MUEB-MUEA+1) VECTORS
C     OF DIMENSION MSLE. CONDITIONAL ZEROS AND COMMON SIGN

      REAL*8 GAMMA,ACOEF
      DIMENSION GAMMA(4,12)
      COMMON /CACO/ ACOEF(8,45,12)
      MUEZZ = MUEB-MUEA+1
      MUEZZ1 = MUEZZ-1
      DO 10 MUE = MUEA,MUEB
      MUEH = MUE-MUEA+1
      DO 10 MSL = 1,MSLE
   10 GAMMA(MUEH,MSL) = ACOEF(MUE,LL,MSL)
      IF (MUEZZ.EQ.1) GOTO 40
      DO 20 MUEH = 1,MUEZZ1
      JSPALZ = MSLE-MUEH+1
      IZEILZ = MUEZZ-MUEH+1
   20 CALL ENDNUL(GAMMA,IZEILZ,JSPALZ)
   40 CALL ORTNO(GAMMA,MUEZZ,MSLE)
      DO 30 MUEH = 1,MUEZZ
      MUE = MUEA+MUEH-1
      DO 30 MSL = 1,MSLE
   30 ACOEF(MUE,LL,MSL) = GAMMA(MUEH,MSL)
      RETURN
      END
```

```
*-----------------------------------*

      SUBROUTINE DREIK(L)

C     NECESSARY FOR THE CALCULATION OF THE CUBIC A-COEFFICIENTS ONLY
C     CALCULETES FOR 1.LE.L.LE.47 THE DLMN(PI/2)
C     IN ARRAY DREIEK(ML,NL) BY RECURRENCE
C     ML-1=M, NL-1=N=0,1,2,...,L
C     FOR A TEST OF PRECISION COMPARE FOR EVEN L
C     THE CALCULATED VALUE OF
C     DL11(PI/2) WITH ITS EXACT VALUE = DL00(PI/2)=
C     ((-1)**L/2)*(2**-L)*BINOMIAL COEFFICIENT(L,L/2)

      REAL*8 FAL,LOG2,DREIL,F,FAK,FAKL,DREIEK
      COMMON /CDREIK/DREIEK(48,48)
      COMMON /CLOG/ FAL(95),LOG2
      L1 = L+1
      LM1 = L-1
      F = FAL(2*L+1)
      FAKL = DSQRT(2.DO/L)

C     M = L LINE, N.LE.M

      DO 10 NL = 1,L1
      N = NL-1
      DREIL = -(L+0.DO)*LOG2+0.5DO*(F-FAL(L1+N)-FAL(L1-N))
   10 DREIEK(L1,NL) = ((-1)**(L+N))*DEXP(DREIL)
```

```
C     M = L-1 LINE, N.LE.M

      DO 20 NL = 1,L
      FAK = 0.DO
      IF (NL.NE.1) FAK = (NL-1.DO)*FAKL
   20 DREIEK(L,NL) = FAK*DREIEK(L1,NL)

C     M - RECURRENCE

      IF(LM1.EQ.0) GOTO 70
      DO 30 NL = 1,LM1
      N = NL-1
      DO 40 MLH = 1,LM1
      ML = L-MLH
      M = ML-1
      ML1 = ML+1
      ML2 = ML+2
      F = 0.DO
      IF (N.NE.0) F = 2.DO*N*DREIEK(ML1,NL)
      FAK = (L-M-1.DO)*(L+M+2.DO)
      FAK = -DSQRT(FAK)*DREIEK(ML2,NL)
      FAKL = (L+M+1.DO)*(L-M+0.DO)
      FAKL = DSQRT(FAKL)
   40 DREIEK(ML,NL) = (F+FAK)/FAKL
   30 CONTINUE

C     COMPLETITION OF THE DREIEK ARRAY FOR N.GT.M

   70 DO 50 ML = 2,L1
      M = ML-1
      DO 60 NL = 1,M
   60 DREIEK(NL,ML)= ((-1)**(ML+NL))*DREIEK(ML,NL)
   50 CONTINUE
      RETURN
      END



      *-----------------------------------*

      SUBROUTINE ENDNUL (GAMMA,IZEILZ,JSPALZ)

C     NECESSARY FOR THE CALCULATION OF THE CUBIC A-COEFFICIENTS ONLY
C     CREATES ZEROS IN THE LAST COLUMN OF AN IZEILZ*JSPALZ MATRIX,
C     EXCEPT THE FIRST STROKE

      REAL*8 GAMMA,HM1,HM2
      DIMENSION GAMMA(4,12),HM1(12),HM2(12)
      IF(IZEILZ.EQ.1) RETURN
      IEND=IZEILZ-1
      DO 10 I=1,IEND
      I1=I+1
      DO 20 J=1,JSPALZ
      HM1(J)=GAMMA(I1,JSPALZ)*GAMMA(I,J)
      HM2(J)=GAMMA(I,JSPALZ)*GAMMA(I1,J)
   20 CONTINUE
      DO 30 J=1,JSPALZ
   30 GAMMA(I,J)=HM1(J)-HM2(J)
   10 CONTINUE
      RETURN
      END


      *-----------------------------------*

      SUBROUTINE ORTNO(GAMMA,MUEZ,JEND)

C     NECESSARY FOR THE CALCULATION OF THE CUBIC A-COEFFICIENTS ONLY
C     ORTHONORMALIZATION OF MUEZ VECTORS OF DIMENSION JEND
C     THE FIRST FROM THE END COMPONENT OF EACH VECTOR
C     NOT EQUAL ZERO IS A POSITIVE NUMBER

      REAL*8 GAMMA,H,PSI,SN,SP,SKAPRO
      DIMENSION GAMMA(4,12),H(4,12),PSI(4,12),SKAPRO(4)

C     MUE=1

      SN=0.DO
      DO 10 J=1,JEND
   10 SN=SN+GAMMA(1,J)*GAMMA(1,J)
      DO 20 J=1,JEND
   20 PSI(1,J)=GAMMA(1,J)/DSQRT(SN)
      IF(MUEZ.EQ.1) GO TO 30
      DO 40  MUE=2,MUEZ
      MUE1 =MUE-1
      DO 50 MUES=1,MUE1
      SP=0.DO
      DO 60 J=1,JEND
   60 SP=SP+PSI(MUES,J)*GAMMA(MUE,J)
   50 SKAPRO(MUES)=SP
      DO 70 J=1,JEND
      SP=0.DO
      DO 80 MUES=1,MUE1
   80 SP=SP+SKAPRO(MUES)*PSI(MUES,J)
   70 H(MUE,J)=GAMMA(MUE,J)-SP
      SN=0.DO
      DO 90 J=1,JEND
   90 SN=SN+H(MUE,J)*H(MUE,J)
      DO 100 J=1,JEND
  100 PSI(MUE,J)=H(MUE,J)/DSQRT(SN)
   40 CONTINUE
   30 DO 110 MUE=1,MUEZ
      JLEZT=JEND-(MUEZ-MUE)
      SN=1.DO
      IF(PSI(MUE,JLEZT).LT.0.DO) SN=-1.DO
      DO 120 J=1,JEND
  120 GAMMA(MUE,J)=SN*PSI(MUE,J)
  110 CONTINUE
      RETURN
      END
```

Amendment

In connection with the program CDFGL33 (p. 246) the following is of importance. Although in the comment part of the program text the chosen K_B variants are specified, for the case $G_B = D_3$ the program (using the formula (11.35) of Volume 1) leads to results belonging to a K_B with $\vec{Y}_B \| \vec{a}_1'$ (cf. Figure 5.11). In order to realize the K_B variant of this figure in the formula (11.35) for $\mathcal{G} = D_n$ the number $\overline{m}'$ is to be changed for the given $\overline{m}'$ multiplied by the factor $(-1)^{l+\mu+1)n}$. Correspondingly in the subroutine SMUMS (p. 252) after the line with label 40 the new line

```
IF(I.EQ.9) M = M * (-1) ** (ILVORZ + MU)
```

is to be added.

Matthies et al., Standard Distributions 7637674
ISBN 3-05-500248-2

FSC
www.fsc.org
MIX
Papier | Fördert
gute Waldnutzung
FSC® C083411

Kolibri 360 GmbH
Ferdinand-Jühlke-Straße 7
99095 Erfurt, Deutschland
produktsicherheit@kolibri360.de